THREE FACES OF ANTISEMITISM

Three Faces of Antisemitism examines the three primary forms of antisemitism as they emerged in modern and contemporary Germany, and then in other countries.

The chapters draw on the author's historical scholarship over the years on the form antisemitism assumed on the far right in Weimar and Nazi Germany, in the Communist regime in East Germany, and in the West German radical left, and in Islamist organizations during World War II and the Holocaust, and afterward in the Middle East. The resurgence of antisemitism since the attacks of September 11, 2001, has origins in the ideas, events, and circumstances in Europe and the Middle East in the half century from the 1920s to the 1970s. This book covers the period since 1945 when neo-Nazism was on the fringes of Western and world politics, and the persistence of antisemitism took place primarily when its leftist and Islamist forms combined antisemitism with anti-Zionism in attacks on the state of Israel. The collection includes recent essays of commentary that draw attention to the simultaneous presence of antisemitism's three faces. While scholarship on the antisemitism of the Nazi regime and the Holocaust remains crucial, the scholarly, intellectual, and political effort to fight antisemitism in our times requires the examination of antisemitism's leftist and Islamist forms as well.

This book will be of interest to scholars researching antisemitism, racism, conspiracy theories, the far right, the far left, and Islamism.

Jeffrey Herf is a Distinguished University Professor Emeritus of History at the University of Maryland, College Park, USA. His previous publications include: *Reactionary Modernism: Technology, Culture and Politics in Weimar and the Third Reich* (1984), *Divided Memory: The Nazi Past in the Two Germanys* (1997), *The Jewish Enemy: Nazi Propaganda During World War II and the Holocaust* (2006), *Nazi Propaganda for the Arab World* (2009), *Undeclared Wars with Israel: East Germany and the West German Far Left, 1967–1989* (2016), and *Israel's Moment: International Support for and Opposition to Establishing the Jewish State* (2022).

Studies in Contemporary Antisemitism

Series editors

David Hirsch, *Senior Lecturer in Sociology, Goldsmiths, University of London and Academic Director of the London Centre for the Study of Contemporary Antisemitism and* **Rosa Freedman**, *Professor in the School of Law, University of Reading and Research Fellow at the London Centre for the Study of Contemporary Antisemitism*

Published in conjunction with the London Centre for the Study of Contemporary Antisemitism, *Studies in Contemporary Antisemitism* is a timely, multidisciplinary book series, drawing primarily, but not exclusively, on the social sciences and the humanities. The series encourages academically rigorous and critical publications across several disciplines and that are explicit in understanding and opposing the presence and ascendancy of contemporary antisemitism in both its theoretical and empirical manifestations. The series provides a unique opportunity to offer an intellectual home for a diversity of works that, taken together, crystallize around the study of contemporary antisemitism. The series consists of research monographs, edited collections and short form titles.

For more information about this series, please visit: www.routledge.com/studies-in-contemporary-antisemitism/book-series/SICA

THREE FACES OF ANTISEMITISM

Right, Left and Islamist

Jeffrey Herf

Routledge
Taylor & Francis Group

LONDON AND NEW YORK

Designed cover image: © Sonya Michel, March 2021. "Squares"

First published 2024
by Routledge
4 Park Square, Milton Park, Abingdon, Oxon OX14 4RN

and by Routledge
605 Third Avenue, New York, NY 10158

Routledge is an imprint of the Taylor & Francis Group, an informa business

British Library Cataloguing-in-Publication Data
A catalogue record for this book is available from the British Library

Library of Congress Cataloging-in-Publication Data
Names: Herf, Jeffrey, 1947– author.
Title: Three faces of antisemitism: right, left and Islamist / Jeffrey Herf.
Description: First. | New York, NY: Routledge, [2024] |
Series: Studies in contemporary antisemitism |
Includes bibliographical references and index.
Identifiers: LCCN 2023034116 (print) | LCCN 2023034117 (ebook) |
ISBN 9781032583372 (hardback) | ISBN 9781032583013 (paperback) |
ISBN 9781003449669 (ebook)
Subjects: LCSH: Antisemitism—History—21st century. |
Antisemitism—History—20th century. | Germany—Politics and
government—1945– | Europe—Politics and government—1945– | Nazi
propaganda—Arab countries—History—20th century. | Antisemitism—Arab
countries—History—20th century. | Left-wing extremists—History—21st
century. | Right-wing extremists—History—21st century. | Islamic
fundamentalism—History—21st century.
Classification: LCC DS145 .H4246 2024 (print) | LCC DS145 (ebook) |
DDC 323.1192/409—dc23/eng/20230809
LC record available at https://lccn.loc.gov/2023034116
LC ebook record available at https://lccn.loc.gov/2023034117

ISBN: 978-1-032-58337-2 (hbk)
ISBN: 978-1-032-58301-3 (pbk)
ISBN: 978-1-003-44966-9 (ebk)

DOI: 10.4324/9781003449669

Typeset in Sabon
by codeMantra

For Sonya Michel, yet again.

CONTENTS

FOREWORD FOR JEFFREY HERF'S
THREE FACES OF ANTISEMITISM

David Hirsh

This book looks at antisemitism in three distinct areas of social, and in particular political, life: left-wing antisemitism, right-wing antisemitism, and Islamist antisemitism. In its treatment of all three together and its analysis of what is common to them, it breaks new ground. Scholarship and other public debates about antisemitism have a tendency to focus on one of these types of antisemitism, and this is often related to a value judgment, explicit or implicit, about their relative importance.

People on the left sometimes see right-wing antisemitism as "the real threat" because, to their minds, antisemitism is implicit within the logic of right-wing politics and its traditions, whereas even if they recognize the existence of left antisemitism, they see it as something fundamentally contingent or alien to authentic left-wing thinking—an error in doctrine that can be put right. And there is a similar dynamic observable on the part of right-wing critics: that antisemitism is authentically left wing, even if it sometimes appears on the right. This right-wing view understands the left thought as something close to conspiracy fantasy, a framework that sees social life as being dominated by hidden privileged elites that exploit the majority by fooling them into consenting to their own subordination. The right is aware of the danger of what Bebel called "the socialism of fools" and its more recent antizionist variant, the anti-imperialism of idiots. The left worries about right-wing traditions of nationalism, family values, and racism in which Jews have been othered as unpatriotic, racially inferior, or corruptors of society's morality, traditional forms, and white purity. While the right worries about left-wing traditions of opposition to democratic structures and values as oppressive, and the designation of Jews as white, as privileged and as central to, and symbolic, of structures of domination.

People who focus on the threat of Islamist antisemitism are sometimes tempted down routes that essentialize antisemitism as being inherent to Islam itself, or to Muslims, rather than to specific political traditions within Islam.

Jeffrey Herf's approach frees the understanding of antisemitism from these preconceptions, which portray it as being naturally associated with layers of social life that the critic already believes to be key to all that is wrong with the world. His work shows how "the three faces" of antisemitism are related to each other not only in content but also in their lineage and development. There are historical threads that connect them together. None of the three forms, he says, contains ideas that were not already present in previous manifestations of antisemitism, in particular those of twentieth-century totalitarianism: Nazi and Soviet Communist—and in Islamist totalitarian movements that, themselves, inherited much from them.

Antisemitism is not inherent to the right or to the left, nor is it inherent to Muslims or to Islam; as it was not, in the past, inherent to Spain, England, France, Germany, or Russia, or to Christianity; nor was it inherent to liberalism, nor nationalism or anti-nationalism, nor modernity or anti-modernity, nor capitalism or socialism.

Recent survey research[1] has shown that antisemitism today in Britain appears equally on both the right and the left, but it is significantly stronger among people who embrace views of the world as being run by powerful conspiracies, and among people who feel that they would be justified in resorting to repressive measures against political opponents. Antisemitism is correlated with specific forms of political belief, which appear in right-wing, left-wing, and Islamist forms. They are beliefs which are characteristic of twentieth-century totalitarianism, also of Islamist movements, and which show themselves in embryonic forms in the new twenty-first-century populism.

Herf remembers twentieth-century totalitarianism, where it came from, how it was supported, and how it was defeated. He was born in the USA in 1947; his father was a refugee from Nazi Germany and his mother's family was a refugee from Ukraine, a generation earlier. Biography, of course, is not everything; it does not determine how a person thinks, but neither is it nothing; there may be significance in the memory, or in the family memory, of what happens when the guarantees of civilization collapse. Herf also remembers twentieth-century totalitarianism through his life's research and writing, particularly through his work to understand antisemitism.

There is a reluctance within contemporary scholarship to study Islamist antisemitism. The fear is that such scholarship would not always be distinguished from a significant contemporary thread of Islamophobic thinking, which portrays Muslims and Islam as being inherently prone to antisemitism. In a world in which Muslims are frequently thought of, in Islamophobic terms, as being uncivilized and backward, there is little appetite to risk feeding that fire by offering Muslim antisemitism as a case study. But it seems to me that this is a misplaced and counterproductive reluctance.

Antisemitism amongst Muslims ought to be studied, and it ought to be thought about with seriousness; an effort ought to be made to understand it. It is not more inherent in Islam than it is in Christianity, and it is no more inherent in Arabs than it is in Europeans. Islamist antisemitism must be studied precisely because it cannot be understood by racializing Muslims or by demonizing their religion. It is a phenomenon characteristic of particular kinds of political movements that define themselves around specific readings of Muslim holy texts, movements that Herf calls "Islamist." Sometimes antisemitism amongst Muslims is downplayed by the claim that it was imposed onto Muslims by European colonists, against their will and without their agency. Herf, and Matthias Küntzel too, show that there are relationships between Islamist antisemitism and older European antisemitisms, but they are more complex and more interesting than a simplistic re-telling of the evils of orientalism and imperialism.

Islamist antisemitism is often assumed to be nothing but an epiphenomenon of the conflict between Israel and the Palestinians. To the extent that Israel is thought of as a colonialist oppressor and the Palestinians as its victims, Islamist antisemitism is often felt to be an understandable, or even a rational response to the oppressors. The new populism sometimes portrays racism as the cry of the oppressed, albeit slightly mis-directed, and anti-racism is portrayed by populism as a discourse of power that serves to de-legitimize that authentic cry. In an analogous reversal, antisemitism is sometimes thought of as the cry of the Arab and Muslim oppressed, and opposition to antisemitism as an illegitimate rhetorical device, mobilized in bad faith by the powerful, for the covert purpose of silencing criticism of Israel.

In his work and in this book, Jeffrey Herf demonstrates that Islamist antisemitism, at least in significant part, is related, both ideationally and in its very lineage, to the antisemitism of both of the twentieth-century totalitarian movements. He also shows that contemporary left anti-Zionism, which is related to Islamist anti-Zionism, has ancestors not only in twentieth-century Communism but also in Nazism. Herf's work is complementary to that of Matthias Küntzel, whose book *Nazis, Islamic Antisemitism and the Middle East* was the first in this *Studies in Contemporary Antisemitism* series. Taken together, these two scholars have changed the way we think about these relationships.

Our account of Islamist antisemitism, and Arab Nationalist antisemitism too, is significant for how we understand Israel and the difficulties that it has encountered in normalizing its relationships with its neighbors. The hypothesis is that antisemitism in the Middle East is already embedded in the frameworks through which people in the region understand their own relationships with Israel. Perhaps antisemitism is not only an effect of the conflict but also a contributor to the enduring heat and apparent insolubility of the conflict. Herf and Küntzel show that antisemitism in the Middle East cannot be boiled down solely to a mystification of legitimate grievances against Israel or the Zionist movement and that there are other important, independent causes underlying antisemitism in the region. If that is so, antisemitism may be as much a cause as an effect.

Extremist Islamist movements have much in common with their Nazi and Communist ancestors, beyond their obsession with Jewish evil. They share a radical rejection of every institution and political structure that exists in favor of a fixation on an imagined, final, utopia. They completely devalue "the pursuit of happiness" or a politics of interest in the here and now, in favor of eventual total victory. They reject debate and concern with evidence in favor of the certainty of the leader principle and its reliance on violence and terror. Antisemitism, as a way of offering an image of the otherwise abstract enemy of the people is core to these movements.

This is the fourth book in the series, which is a collaboration between the *London Centre for the Study of Contemporary Antisemitism* and *Routledge*. The other two of the first four, are multi-authored collections. One, edited by Alan Johnson, is a compilation of some of the most significant work that appeared over a decade in hi *Fathom* journal, together with some new material: *Mapping the New Left Antisemitism*. The other multi-authored book, edited by me, David Hirsh, features eleven of the key scholars who were active in resisting the campaign to boycott Israeli universities, the anti-Zionism upon which it was based, and the antisemitism with which it was associated: *The Rebirth of Antisemitism in the 21st Century*.

The series is part of a wider project to challenge the intellectual underpinnings of contemporary antisemitism, to critique scholarly work that itself incorporates and repeats antisemitic themes, and to address the hostile environment for antisemitism scholarship, and for Jews in general, in universities. The book series is part of the *London Centre's* project to address the fact that to a significant extent, antisemitism scholarship has been closed out of the existing scholarly infrastructure of the universities, research funding, and publishing.

In this hostile environment and heading towards the middle of the twenty-first century, it is no longer to be assumed that a scholar has either a personal or an intellectual memory of twentieth-century totalitarianism, the fight against it, and the Cold War that was the long, drawn out end of it. Memory is not an archive of facts, it is a life's work of the curation of the facts into always provisional frameworks of understanding. And it is also a complex social process, which values some scholarly focuses and devalues others.

Twentieth-century totalitarianism is too often remembered in a simplified "good and evil" sense of a morality tale or a passion play. The detail is forgotten about how it worked and how people like us, in a world like ours, not least intellectuals in universities, were open to it. Some of that forgetting is not a gentle, organic fading from the memory, but a conscious and well-policed process. Some of the elements of totalitarian thinking, complete with their antisemitic potential, are returning, unnoticed, or angrily denied, into the discourse of the democratic states and even academic thought. A key characteristic of the new populism is the blurring of the distinction between democratic and totalitarian thinking.

Contemporary populism normalizes the idea that democratic structures are like theatre scenery erected by "elites," which function to disguise the realities of power, hiding them from "the people." Populism needs some of the lessons of the twentieth century to have faded. It needs us to forget that such political conspiracy fantasy requires an "enemy of the people" to endure, so that it can be blamed for the eventual failure of the promised Utopia. When today's populists invoke a metropolitan, educated, liberal, cosmopolitan class, only out for itself and only loyal to others of its own kind, they seem to have forgotten the destruction that, in the past, followed from such an invocation. It is inconvenient for the new populists to remember too clearly that the antisemitic notion of the Jew had evolved over centuries, in diverse times and places, as an emotionally satisfying way of visualizing the abstract conspiracies that cause human suffering; a way of giving chimeric and unseeable evil an ugly human face. In Nineteen Eighty-Four, Orwell dramatizes this in his depiction of the daily ceremony of "two minutes hate," in front of the huge face of "Emmanuel Goldstein," the enemy of the people.

Jeffrey Herf's memory is precious and fragile. This book is a distillation of some of the things that are important there, in his memory and in his understanding, always built on a foundation of the highest quality scholarly research. This book brings together writing that has been previously published over a career and it presents it within a clear framework.

Herf's scholarship is brilliant, careful, original, well researched, and courageous. He did not always benefit personally from taking his own path, and resisting some of the frameworks that were thought to be sophisticated at the time he was writing. But his reputation shines through.

ACKNOWLEDGMENTS

My deep debts to my fellow scholars are evident in this collection's text and footnotes.

As the essays in this volume draw on work of the past four decades, it is a pleasure to express appreciation to my editors, and for the literary erudition, and scholarly judgment they brought to bear on my work. They are Frank Smith, and Michael Watson at Cambridge University Press; Aida Donald, and Joyce Seltzer at Harvard University Press; and Jonathan Brent and Chris Rogers at Yale University Press. I express my appreciation to reviewers of those books, both in scholarly journals, and in periodicals aimed at more general readers. For their work on *Three Faces of Antisemitism,* thanks as well to Craig Fowlie, and Elizabeth Hart, my editors at Routledge/Taylor and Francis, to the anonymous reviewers of this essay collection, and to Rosa Freedman, of the Centre for the Study of Contemporary Antisemitism.

Thanks as well to editors and reviewers at the following scholarly journals: *Antisemitism Studies*; *Central European History*; *Holocaust and Genocide Studies*; *Jewish Political Studies Review*; *Journal of Cold War Studies*; and *Journal of Contemporary History*. My thanks as well to editors and staff at journals of opinion who agreed to publish my essays on history and current politics in *The American Interest, American Purpose, Dissent, Fathom Journal, Die Frankfurter Allgemeine Zeitung, History News Network, The Israel Journal of Foreign Affairs, The New Republic, Quillette, The Tablet Magazine, Telos, The Times of Israel, the Washington Post, Die Welt,* and *Die Zeit.*

Particular thanks are due, as well, to David Hirsh, for his bold work on contemporary left antisemitism, for his initiative in the launch of the London Centre for the Study of Contemporary Antisemitism, and the series of works on antisemitism in which this book appears. Special thanks, yet again, go to my wife, the fine historian and now fine artist, Sonya Michel. Over these many years, her editorial judgment and careful reading have been invaluable. The book is, again and with pleasure, dedicated to her.

Note

1 Daniel Allington, David Hirsh and Louise Katz, "Antisemitism Is Predicted by Anti-Hierarchical Aggression, Totalitarianism, and Belief in Malevolent Global Conspiracies," *Humanities and Social Sciences Communications* 10 (2023), 155. ISSN 2662-9992, https://doi.org/10.1057/s41599-023-01624-y.

INTRODUCTION

Three Faces of Antisemitism

The essays in this volume rest on my conviction that the more closely one looks at the radical antisemitism that accompanied the Holocaust, the more one should devote attention to the other two predominant forms of antisemitism, those of Communism and the radical left, and of Islamists. All three survived, and then thrived, in the decades following the Nazi extermination of 6 million Jews in Europe. The three faces emerged clearly from the 1930s to the 1970s around the globe. The antisemitism that exists in world politics in 2023 contains no ideas that were not expressed often in that crucial 40-year burst of totalitarianism and Jew-hatred, first in Nazi Germany, then in the Soviet Union and the Soviet bloc, and finally in the Islamist organizations and Arab states.[1]

For the historian of antisemitism, the twentieth century was not, as many thought following the collapse of the Communist regimes in Europe in 1989–1991, a short century. Rather, the hatreds and extremism of the anti-Jewish half-century have persisted into the twenty-first century. The defeats of Nazism and Communism in Europe did not bring an end to antisemitism. Rather, the hatreds and extremism of the anti-Jewish half-century have persisted into the twenty-first, giving antisemitism a vibrant afterlife.[2] The reckoning with the Jew-hatred of Nazi Germany during the Holocaust is extensive; Jew-hatred in the Soviet bloc during the Cold War or the Jew-hatred and resulting anti-Zionism and hatred of Israel of the Islamists before, during, and after World War II has not been nearly as widely acknowledged. One purpose of this collection is to present readers with equally unflinching gaze at Jew-hatred whether it comes from the Nazis and their successors or from the Communists, the radical left, and the Islamists. In doing so, these essays examine similarities as well as differences in these three predominant forms

DOI: 10.4324/9781003449669-1

of antagonism to Judaism, Jews, and then to the State of Israel. Of course, not all criticisms of Israel are forms of antisemitism, but the following essays examine those instances in which antisemitism convergences with the hatred of the Jewish state.

From the 1920s to the 1970s in Europe and the Middle East, antisemitism was not only a set of ideas that could draw on both old religious and modern secular traditions. It also benefitted from sponsorship by powerful states, most obviously Nazi Germany, but then the Soviet Union during the Cold War, Arab states in their conflict with Israel, and the Islamic Republic of Iran since 1979. Throughout that period, antisemitism was both a firm belief and served as a cynical tool of foreign policy and domestic repression. It should come as no surprise that the antisemitism of that era left residues that persist into our own time. During those decades and since, there were at most 20 million Jews in the world–that is, a tiny fraction of the globe's population. Yet in the twentieth century and now, antisemites of the right, the left, and among the Islamists shared a fantasy that the Jews possessed enormous power to shape world politics in ways that were damaging to the vast mass of humanity. The Nazis openly declared their intention to exterminate the Jews. While the antisemites of the left denied their Jew-hatred and largely refrained from openly calling for policies of extermination, Islamists' calls to wipe out the state of Israel could amount to the same thing. Some observers have referred to a "new antisemitism" of recent decades, but as this and other histories of the subject indicate, the faces of Jew-hatred in 2023 have origins in the distinctive half century examined in the following pages.

The following essays are revised and updated versions of articles, chapters in books, and lectures that I've written since 1984, and they reflect my preoccupation with these issues as a historian of modern German history. They draw on and update material in five books I've published since 1984: *Reactionary Modernism: Technology, Culture and Politics in Weimar and the Third Reich* (1984); *Divided Memory: The Nazi Past in the Two Germanys* (1997); *The Jewish Enemy: Nazi Propaganda During World War II and the Holocaust* (2006); *Nazi Propaganda for the Arab World* (2009); *Undeclared Wars with Israel: East Germany and the West German Far Left, 1967–1989* (2016). A distinctive aspect of these works is that, taken together, they address all three forms of antisemitism. By *addressing all three forms of antisemitism at the same time in the same volume*, I intend the present collection of essays to overcome an intellectually untenable and unjustifiable polarization of scholarly discussion and intellectual debate about these matters.

Antisemitism, as a result of Nazi, Communist, and Islamist propaganda, attained global reach in the middle of the twentieth century.[3] Antisemitism's three faces appeared in Germany in these crucial 40 years, first in Nazi Germany, then in the Communist regime in East Germany, and in the West German radical left.[4] Jew-hatred was embedded in the core of Nazism; it was its essence. There was no Nazism that was without hatred of Judaism, Jews, and the Zionist project.[5] Yet the enormity of Nazism's evil and the totality of its complete defeat raised hopes that antisemitism around the world as well as in Europe would be consigned to the past. Hitler and Nazism stood for a radical evil that was also a lost and defeated cause. Antisemitism associated with the far right survived only on the remote fringes of Western societies.[6] Yet in the decades following Nazism's defeat, antisemitism persisted because a mixture of Communists, radical leftists, some of the Arab states, the Islamic Republic of Iran, and Islamist organizations gave it renewed energy.

The Communists emerged victorious from the maelstrom of World War II buoyed by the role of the Red Army and Air Force in defeating Nazism. In the immediate postwar years, the Communists emerged as the fierce and victorious foe of Nazism *and therefore also* of antisemitism.[7] The Soviet bloc and leftist support for the establishment of the Jewish state in Palestine suggested that the anti-Jewish prejudices that lurked in traditions of Marxism would become things of the past.[8] The class struggle against a hatred of capitalism, not of the Jews, and then the battle against "fascism" had been the primary defining features of leftist ideologies. Yet hatred and disdain for Judaism and the Jews did not completely disappear from the tradition of the modern left. It had been prominent in Karl Marx's infamous essay *On the Jewish Question* of 1843[9] and reappeared in the early years of the Cold War, when antisemitism of a Nazi sort was in abeyance but Stalin's "anti-cosmopolitan" purges revived antisemitism and shifted it from the margins to the mainstream of Soviet policy and ideology.[10] In what became an era of a "second antifascism," Communists and then radical leftists in the Western democracies and third-world leftist movements redefined the meaning of antifascism to convey, of all things, attacks on the Jewish state as a bastion of racism and fascism. Denouncing people who had been the prime victims of Naziism as "Nazis" and fascists became a standard theme of Soviet-era propaganda.

As a result, the Communists and radical leftists gave antisemitism a second wind in the very decades when it had been discredited due to its association with Nazism. The Communists and then the global radical left applied old stereotypes of the powerful, evil, even murderous Jew of centuries past to the state of Israel, which they branded as a racist, colonialist aggressor in league with American imperialism. These sentiments of the era of a redefined second antifascism emerged in the governing ideas and policies of the Communist dictatorship in East Germany, oddly called the German Democratic Republic. They spread to the West German radical left of the 1960s–1980s and in more recent years to academic efforts, especially in Britain and the United States, to boycott and delegitimize the state of Israel.[11] Several of the essays in this volume examine episodes when parties and states of the left, which regarded themselves as opponents of something so retrograde as antisemitism, wrote important new chapters in the history of the longest hatred. In the history of antisemitism, a distinctive feature of the Communist variant was that its advocates indignantly rejected the suggestion that their attacks on Israel had anything at all to do with antisemitism.

Antisemitism after Nazism shifted its center of gravity from Europe to the Middle East. Nowhere else did public figures who praised Hitler and Nazism find as much respect and prominence in political life as they did there. Some of the enthusiasts, like Egyptian's President Gamal Abdel Nasser and an earlier Anwar Sadat, spoke the language of secular anti-colonialism and praised the Nazis for their fight against Zionism and British and French presence in the Middle East. But the core and driving force of antisemitism in that part of the world drew from a radical interpretation of the religion of Islam expressed by iconic figures of the Muslim Brotherhood: Hassan al-Banna, Haj Amin al-Husseini, and Sayyid Qutb. These and other Islamist writers and political figures interpreted Islam as a religion that was ineradicably hostile to Judaism and Jews and then to the Zionist project. They took the Koran's pejorative denunciations of "the people of the book," the Koranic phrase for the Jews, to be a core, not peripheral, element of the religion. Beginning in the 1930s, partly encouraged by the rise of Nazism in Germany, these and other Islamists made an independent contribution to the history of Jew-hatred. Their works were not primarily a transfer of ideas from Europe, though in wartime Berlin a fusion of perspectives became evident in the regime's Arabic-language propaganda. They argued that the religion of Islam was an inherently anti-Jewish tradition and that its ancient hatreds could be combined with the conspiracy theories of modern history. Today we call that doctrine "Islamism," even though its advocates insisted that they were keepers of the true and uncorrupted version of Islam.[12]

The Islamists benefitted enormously from the support they received from Nazi Germany, which amplified their hatreds in print and on radio air waves. As with Nazism, there was and is no "moderate Islamism," if by that one means a doctrine free of hatred of the Jews. Jew-hatred and the resulting wars against the Jewish state were and remain a part of Islamism's essence. Islamism became part of German history as the Nazi regime sought to rally Islamists to its cause in North Africa, the Arab Middle East, Iran, and southeastern Europe during World War II and the Holocaust. One of Nazism's most important aftereffects was the diffusion of Islamist Jew-hatred to the Middle East where it left disastrous residues in the post-1945 history of the Middle East. Like the Communists of the 1950s and 1960s but from very different cultural starting points, the Islamists made antisemitism a significant political force in the same decades in which it was declining, or at least losing respectability, in the Western democracies. Several essays in this volume examine the years in which Islamists contributed to recentering of antisemitism from Europe to the Middle East and Iran.

While scholarship on the antisemitism of Nazi Germany is vast, work on antisemitism's other two faces, those from the Communists and the radical left, and from the Islamists, is far less so and has remained more marginal in the historical profession. The West German, then the German and international tradition of what is called in German *Aufarbeitung der Vergangenheit*, or coming to terms with the past, stimulated a large scholarship on the Holocaust and other crimes of the Nazi regime.[13] Until recent years, Nazi antisemitism was safely contained on the margins of Western societies. The essays in this collection offer evidence that while Nazism has an afterlife, the most important contributors to antisemitism for much of the period since the Holocaust came from the far left, and from Islamists. The shadows of Nazism and the Holocaust will persist for centuries, but they should not prevent us from looking clearly at antisemitism when it takes other forms.

My debts to authors both in Germany and outside it, are evident in the footnotes. In the postwar decades when appeals to "draw a line under the past" became part of West German election campaigns, primarily liberal intellectuals and politicians such as Theodor Heuss, Kurt Schumacher, Theodor Adorno, Franz Bohm, and Fritz Bauer inaugurated the unique tradition of public reckoning with the crimes of the past. Chancellor Konrad Adenauer combined willingness to integrate former Nazi-era officials with a determination to offer practical support to the Jewish survivors of the Holocaust and to the state of Israel.[14] From its beginning until the present, there were conservatives who denounced judicial reckoning as a blow to the nation's good name, something that would be bad for German export markets, and constituted part of an effort to unfairly victimize the Germans. The Communists denounced West German reckoning as a cynical effort to purchase a good name, all the while rebuilding the real source of Nazism—the market economy.

In fact, as Freud's writing on resistance in psychoanalysis suggested, the tradition of honest reckoning with the Nazi past angered its critics precisely because it got to the truth of the matter and smashed efforts to repress realities with a blizzard of excuses, denial, and apologia, some coming with elaborate theoretical accompaniment. As Theodor Adorno famously observed, resistance to truthful discussion of the crimes of the Nazi regime was less the result of forgetting than of "an all too wide- awake consciousness."[15] Close examination of Nazi-era Jew-hatred contributes reveals similar themes of conspiracy, evil, and power attributed to Jews, whether it came from the Communists, radical leftists, or from Islamist organizations and states. Simply put, the defeat of Nazi Germany did not mean the definitive end of antisemitism. The following essays examine the dominant forms of antisemitism's post-Holocaust renewal, forms in which attacks on the state of Israel assumed a predominant role.

As antisemitism now arrives from all three directions, it comes as no surprise that even the old Nazi-era antisemitism has found new advocates in recent years. However, to fight and defeat antisemitism in the present and in years to come, recalling the history of the Holocaust is a necessary but not sufficient endeavor. The history of antisemitism's three faces of the crucial 40 years in the twentieth century resonates in the renewal of Jew-hatred in the twenty-first century. Holocaust denial, previously limited to small, isolated groups of cranks, now finds a larger audience via the social media.[16] In the United States, Trump and Trumpism created a link between the antisemitic conspiracy theories of the extremist right and parts of the Republican Party. Both before and since the attack on the U.S. Capitol on January 6, 2021, this right-wing form of antisemitism has justly received much attention. In political essays of the past two decades, I have addressed that current as well. My essays in journals of opinion have addressed the three faces of antisemitism as they have appeared since the Islamist terrorist attacks of 9/11, leftist academic efforts to boycott the state of Israel, and the return of a politically consequential right-wing antisemitism not seen in American national politics since the 1930s, when the United States' first "America First" movement tried and but failed to prevent the United States from entering the war against Nazi Germany. As each of these political essays expresses a particular moment, I have decided to publish them here without revisions.

Notes

1 Jeffrey Herf, "Die drei Gesichter des Antisemitismus," *Frankfurter Allgemeine Zeitung* (March 26, 2020): https://www.faz.net/aktuell/feuilleton/debatten/jeffrey-herf-der-heutige-antisemitismus-hat-drei-urspruenge-16696194.html?premium; "Three Faces of Antisemitism in 2020," unpublished lecture, Bahá'í Chair for World Peace series on Structural Racism and the Root Cause of Prejudice and Human Nature, University of Maryland, College Park, October 6, 2020.
2 On examination of antisemitism in the twenty-first century, see Murray Baumgarten, Peter Kenez, and Bruce Thompson, eds., *Varieties of Antisemitism: History, Ideology, Discourse* (Newark: University of Delaware Press, 2009); Doron Rabinovici, Ulrich Speck, and Natan Sznaider, eds., *Neuer Antisemitismus: Eine globale Debatte* (Frankfurt/Main: Suhrkamp Verlag, 2004); Alvin H. Rosenfeld, ed., *Resurgent Antisemitism: Global Perspectives* (Bloomington: Indiana University Press, 2013); Charles Asher Small, ed., *Global Antisemitism: A Crisis of Modernity*, 4 vols. (New York: Institute for the Study of Global Antisemitism and Policy, 2013).
3 On the leftist and Islamist aspects of antisemitism, especially since the Holocaust, see Robert Wistrich, *A Lethal Obsession: Antisemitism from Antiquity to the Global Jihad* (New York: Random House, 2010); and his *From Ambivalence to Betrayal: The Left, the Jews, and Israel* (Lincoln: University of Nebraska Press and Vidal Sassoon International Center for the Study of Antisemitism, Hebrew University of Jerusalem, 2012).
4 See Anthony McElligott and Jeffrey Herf, eds., *Antisemitism Before and Since the Holocaust* (London: Palgrave/Macmillan, 2017).
5 I have made these arguments in *The Jewish Enemy: Nazi Propaganda during World War II and the Holocaust* (Cambridge, MA: Harvard University Press, 2006); and *Nazi Propaganda for the Arab World* (New Haven, CT: Yale University Press, 2009).

6 On the end of Nazism as a major political force in postwar East and West Germany, see Jeffrey Herf, *Divided Memory: The Nazi Past in the Two Germanys* (Cambridge, MA: Harvard University Press, 1997).

7 On the importance of antifascism for the Soviet Union and the appeal of Communism in Europe, see Francois Furet, *The Passing of an Illusion: The Idea of Communism in the Twentieth Century* (Chicago, IL: University of Chicago, 1999); and Anson Rabinbach, "Part II, Antifascism," in Stefano Geroulanos and Dagmar Herzog, eds., *Staging the Third Reich: Essays in Cultural and Intellectual History* (New York and London: Routledge: 2020), 187–292.

8 On Soviet support for establishment of the Jewish state in Palestine, see Jeffrey Herf, *Israel's Moment: International Support for and Opposition to Establishing the Jewish State, 1945–1949* (Cambridge: Cambridge University Press, 2022).

9 Karl Marx, "On the Jewish Question," in Robert C. Tucker, ed., *The Marx-Engels Reader* (New York: W.W. Norton, 1978), 26–52. Also see Jerry Muller, "Karl Marx: From Jewish Usury to Universal Vampirism," in his *The Mind and the Market: Capitalism in Modern European Thought* (New York: Alfred A. Knopf, 2002); and David Nirenberg, "Modernity Thinks with Judaism," in his *Anti-Judaism: The Western Tradition* (New York: W.W. Norton, 2013), 423–460.

10 On the purges in East Germany, see Herf, *Divided Memory*, 106–161.

11 On the West German far left, see Jeffrey Herf, *Undeclared Wars with Israel: East Germany and the West German Far Left, 1967–1989* (Cambridge and New York: Cambridge University Press, 2016). On the boycott campaign and the presence of antisemitism in the British Labor Party, see David Hirsch, *Contemporary Left Antisemitism* (New York and Abingdon: Routledge, 2018).

12 See Herf, *Nazi Propaganda for the Arab World*, and Matthias Küntzel, *Aftershock: The Nazis, Islamic Antisemitism and the Middle East* (London: Routledge, 2023).

13 For a valuable collection of essays on the tradition, and on recent scholarship on continuities as well as breaks, see Magnus Bretchken, ed., *Aufarbeitung des Nationalsozialismus: Ein Kompendium* (Göttingen: Wallstein Verlag, 2021). On the origins of the tradition, see Herf, *Divided Memory*, 201–334. On resistance to reckoning, premature amnesty, and justice delayed, see Eckart Conze, Norbert Frei, Peter Hayes and Moshe Zimmerman, *Das Amt und die Vergangenheit: Deutsche Diplomaten im Dritten Reich und in der Bundesrepublik* (Munich: Karl Blessing Verlag, 2010); Norbert Frei, *Adenauer's Germany and the Nazi Past: The Politics of Amnesty and Integration* (New York: Columbia University Press, 2002); and Mary Fulbrook, *Reckonings: Legacies of Nazi Persecution and the Quest for Justice* (New York and Oxford: Oxford University Press, 2018).

14 On Adenauer, Adorno, Bauer, Bohm, Heuss, Schumacher and others in the 1940s and 1950s, see Herf, *Divided Memory*.

15 Theodor W. Adorno, "Was bedeutet Aufarbeitung der Vergangenheit," in his *Gesammelte Schriften 10: 1* (Frankfurt am Main: Suhrkamp Verlag, 1977), 555–572.

16 See Jeffrey Herf, "Postwar Antisemitism and Holocaust Denial," forthcoming in Laura Jockusch and Devon Pendas, eds., *Cambridge History of the Holocaust, Volume 4: Outcomes, Aftermath, Repercussions.*

1

REACTIONARY MODERNISM, THE JEWS, AND ANTICAPITALISM IN WEIMAR AND NAZI GERMANY

The pejorative association of Judaism and Jews with capitalism has firm roots in the traditions of Christianity and among prominent authors ranging from Voltaire to Marx who, from the eighteenth to the twentieth centuries, modernized the longest hatred and made it an element of leftist anticapitalism.[1] For the antisemites of that era, especially those drawn to fascism and Nazism, Jews personified a political, economic, and cultural modernity that they had come to detest.[2] As the historian George Mosse pointed out, because fascists and Nazis defended the established order against the presumed threat of Communist revolutions, the reality of what he provocatively called "the fascist revolution" was underestimated by contemporaries and historians.[3] In the course of attacking liberal democracy, the writers of Weimar's "conservative revolution," and the Nazis as well, redefined the meaning of capitalism and thus of anticapitalism. Associating the Jews with what they denounced as sinister "high finance" and "plutocracy," they equated an attack on capitalism so defined as a "revolution" whose target was Jews, not private ownership of the means of production. This right-wing anticapitalism still sounds anomalous in a world in which it is the left that most proudly announces its antagonism to the market economy.

This anomalous connection between a redefined meaning of anticapitalism and antagonism to Judaism and the Jews emerged clearly in what I have called the ideological and cultural tradition of "reactionary modernism," which emerged in Germany's Weimar Republic and persisted in Nazi Germany.[4] The now-familiar phrase reactionary modernism refers to a set of ideas first articulated in Germany in the anti-democratic right and its conservative revolution and continued into the Third Reich. The reactionary modernists made the case that liberal democracy and its divisions were a

DOI: 10.4324/9781003449669-2

relic of the nineteenth century and that authoritarian rule combined with technological advance was the true face of modernity. Within their vision of modernity, Jews did not have a place.

Instead, the reactionary modernists who wrote about capitalism saw in the Jews a destructive and sinister influence. The anti-capitalist conservative revolution of the antisemitic writers among the reactionary modernists left existing structures of economic and political power unscathed. Instead, they saw in "the Jews" the personification of what they despised about the modern economy and society. As the pejorative association of Jews with capitalism has reentered world politics in recent decades, especially on the far right, the essays and books published a century ago in Germany have a disturbing contemporary echo and thus merit renewed attention.[5] Those writings argued that modern technology was a product of distinctly German philosophical and cultural traditions and was thus separate from the liberal political modernity of the United States, France, and Britain—the victors of World War I. In books like Oswald Spengler's *Decline of the West* (1923); Ernst Jünger's *Battle as an Inner Experience* (1922), *Storm of Steel* (1920) and *Der Arbeiter* (The Worker, 1932); Hans Freyer's *Revolution von Rechts* (Revolution from the Right); and Carl Schmitt's *Political Romanticism* (1919) and *The Concept of the Political* (1932), authors produced a body of work that exempted modern technology from their assault on liberalism and incorporated instead it into their vision of a conservative revolution that would lead to what they extolled as an authoritarian national community.[6] As the cultural critic Walter Benjamin understood at the time, Jünger's postwar books and essays imagined the outlines of a future national community that would arise from an idealized version of the male community (*Gemeinschaft*) of the trenches. When others denounced technology as the handmaiden of slaughter and dehumanization, Jünger and the other leading reactionary modernists saw it as indispensable for a Germany that could emerge from defeat and from a despised liberal democracy to renewed power based on a "total mobilization" of state and society.[7]

The pejorative association of the Jews and capitalism, deeply rooted in European culture, entered into German conservative social theory most significantly in 1911 via Werner Sombart's *The Jews and Modern Capitalism*. Though his antipathy to capitalism was evident in works he had published in the previous decade, *The Jews and Modern Capitalism* brought an antisemitic argument into scholarly debate about the origins of capitalism in Europe.[8] In so doing, the book rejected Max Weber's thesis that it was the psychological stresses resulting from the elimination of priestly confession during the Reformation that had produced a "Protestant ethic" of hard work and delayed gratification crucial for capital accumulation.[9]

Sombart's riposte was a reactionary counterpart to Marx's "Essay on the Jewish Question" of 1843. Both secularized the Christian association of Jews with money and brought it into the concepts of anti-capitalist social theory, first within Marxist denunciation of capitalism and then through Sombart's contribution to conservative anticapitalism" in Germany before and after World War I. Where Marx introduced an element of antisemitism into the socialist and communist tradition, Sombart's professorial tome lent academic respectability to an antisemitic interpretation of the development of capitalism in Europe.[10] As the economic historian David Landes put it, *The Jews and Modern Capitalism* "should have been dismissed out of hand as a pseudo-scholarly hoax, [and as] a pedantic effort to confer, by the lavish use of polyglot footnote references, an academic respectability on errant nonsense already current in plane German terms."[11] What economic historians dismissed as a hoax served to lend respectability in the educated middle class to what social theorist Max Horkheimer would later call the "revolt of nature"—a form of antisemitism that denounced the Jews simultaneously as agents of capitalist rationality and as symbols of a backward religion.[12]

Sombart's antisemitic interpretation of the development of capitalism in Europe depicted the transition from feudalism to capitalism as one from a *Gemeinschaft* or community infused with Christianity to a society (*Gesellschaft*) penetrated by the spirit of Judaism. It was, he claimed, the Jews who introduced the spirit of acquisition and calculation to a medieval community organized around respect for honest labor and a just price. The "creation of useful goods" had not yet been displaced by "pure commodity production." But it was the Jews who "stormed" into the pre-modern idyll and brought about the regrettable domination of the economy over politics, culture, and religion. Moreover, the Jews were the bearers of a "capitalist world economy," one that was international and without roots in particular places.[13]

While Sombart examined the social and economic place of Jews as urban merchants in largely agrarian Europe, *The Jews and Modern Capitalism* repeated the very old and by-then familiar Christian denunciations of Judaism as a religion that, compared to Christianity, was a doctrine of reason and contracts rather than of emotion and feeling. Sombart postulated an elective affinity between the Jewish religion interpreted in that manner and the modern capitalism he despised. Judaism, he wrote, was "a work of reason" and thus lacked the feeling and emotion of the "natural" world. "The Jewish religion knows no mystery" and was the "only" religion about which that could be said.[14] It, not Weber's Protestant asceticism, had fostered modern capitalism and the rationalization of European society. Its affinity to modern capitalism arose from the fact that "the whole religion is basically nothing more than a contract between God and the chosen people."[15] Judaism replaced "natural instincts" with self-discipline and purpose, and the idea that "life is a great struggle against hostile powers of human nature."[16]

These aspects of Judaism were sources of the spirit of acquisition, calculation, and thus the development of modern capitalism. In response to Weber's argument about the Protestant ethic and the spirit of capitalism, Sombart asserted that "Puritanism is Judaism."[17] The abstract nature of capitalist society "represents the exact counterpart to the Jewish spirit." In both, "all qualities are dissolved through purely quantitative exchange value," merchants replace "multicolored technical activity.... Both capitalism and Judaism express their innermost essence in money."[18] The proximity of Sombart's "sociological "analysis" to traditional Christian anti-Judaism was evident in his assertion that "the Christian ascends to heaven as an engineer, while the Jew does so as a traveling salesman or clerk."[19]

Sombart's antisemitism was evident in his definition of capitalism and view of technology.

> In its essence, capitalism means nothing other than the dissolution of economic processes into two constituent elements: technology and commerce, and [consequently] the primacy of commerce over technology. From its beginnings, capitalist industry offered the Jews the opportunity for activity that was in keeping with their character.[20]

If capitalism stood for the primacy of commerce over technology, circulation over production, exchange value over use value, then anticapitalism meant reversing this relationship by making technology and production predominant over commerce. The ideological program called for incorporating technology into a German, and Christian world of use-value that did battle against an alien, international, Jewish universe of exchange value. Sombart's "anticapitalism" entailed incorporating modern technology into German *Kultur* and expelling the Jewish spirit from the German economy and society.

In his 1934 *Deutscher Sozialismus* (German Socialism), Sombart welcomed the "new spirit" of German socialism that had begun with Hitler's entry into power and would "lead Germany out of the desert of the economic age."[21] Sombart insisted that he did not accept a racism grounded in biology, but passages of *Deutscher Sozialismus* suggested otherwise. Some races were particularly "soulful." Science could "never rule out a particular correspondence between body and mind," but neither could it confirm a necessary correlation. The Jewish spirit had spread beyond the Jews into modern German society and would continue there "even if every last Jews and Jewish family were to be annihilated." It was "sedimented and objectified in a thousand organizations[,]...above all in our economy." In 1934, the primary task for Germans and for German socialism was liberating the nation from the Jewish *Geist* (spirit). German socialism combined nationalism with anticapitalism, and that, in turn, required a "struggle against the Jewish spirit."[22]

Though Sombart did not belong to the Nazi Party, his *Deutscher Sozialismus* reflected and lent scholarly prestige to the Nazi regime's by-then firmly established policies of anti-Jewish persecution and their association with nationalism. His contribution to reactionary modernism was to fuse the language of social theory with that of race and racism in a set of then compelling juxtapositions. On the one hand stood German technology—a phenomenon that he associated with the concrete authentic rather than the abstract—and universal. Germany stood for use value and production rather than exchange value and circulation, *Kultur* rather than *Zivilisation* and, after 1933, with National Socialism rather than international socialism (Marxism) and/or international capitalism.

While the reception of Sombart's work was most important in the universities, Oswald Spengler's *The Decline of the West* reached a broader readership. It became the bestseller of the conservative revolution of the 1920s in Germany.[23] It comprised the full panoply of reactionary discontent with liberal democracy and expressed a yearning for a future of technological advance and authoritarian politics. In 1918, Spengler wrote to his friend Hans Klores that "truly our future lies on the one hand in Prussian conservatism after it has been cleansed of all feudal-agrarian narrowness, and on the other hand, in the working people after they have freed themselves from the anarchist-radical masses."[24] Spengler became the most widely read of the reactionary modernist writers who managed to shift technology from the realm of allegedly superficial "Western" *Zivilisation* into the presumably deeper, more profound—and German—realms of *Kultur.* In the process of doing so, he offered reactionary redefinitions of capitalism and socialism.

In *Preussentum und Sozialismus*, a 1919 polemic against England and France, Spengler defined socialism not as an effort to replace private ownership of the means of production or reduce income inequality but rather as the expression of virtues he held to be distinctively German: loyalty, discipline, selflessness, sacrifice, and the well-being of the national community rather that of individualism. He denounced the actual leftist revolution of 1918–1919 in Germany as "the most senseless act in German history," led by "literary scum." Socialism, in his view, was one of the Prussian virtues which opposed the "inner England, against the worldview (Marxist and liberal rationalism) which permeates our whole life as a people, paralyzes it, and takes away its soul." Germany needed "men" and "hardness.... We need a class of socialist master characters [*Herrennaturen*]. Once again: socialism means power, power, and yet again power." The goal was a Prussian socialism that aimed at a "dictatorship of organization" to replace the "dictatorship of money" that he thought was leading Germany to ruin. This association of "socialism," Prussian authoritarianism, and nationalism was part of Spengler's attack on liberalism, Marxism, and what had been conventionally understood as socialism.[25]

In *The Decline of the West*, Spengler offered a redefinition of the meaning of the word "capitalism," one that contributed to what became known at the time as "German anticapitalism." At its core were a set of juxtapositions between abstraction and concreteness, production and parasitism, and the forces of "blood and tradition" to those of "thinking in terms of money" (*Gelddenken*). Spengler wrote that "the earth is something real and natural; money is something abstract and artificial."[26] The military and the family had been untouched by the cash nexus as was the generation of veterans who emerged from the trenches of World War I. Democracy, too, was implicated in "the triumph of money" over the allegedly deeper forces of blood and instinct. A primacy of politics should serve to end the era of elections and self-interested political parties. Indeed, the modern economy debased the soul and sapped the "energy of the race." Real culture was opposed to the comforts of bourgeois culture and found its true expression in war. Success in war required the most modern means—that is, modern technology.[27]

What Spengler called capitalism was the world of urban merchants and the circulation of commodities, all in contrast to the "firmly self-contained life of the countryside." It is here that Spengler's antisemitism appears, for the Jews were among those urban merchants who have no feeling for the beauty of rural landscapes and instead think only of "abstract money value." Money was "above all the form of spiritual energy" that expressed a "will to domination."[28] *The Decline of the West* brought centuries-old clichés about the Jews and money into the discourse of the cultural criticism common in Weimar's conservative revolution. The work is a document of reification, that is, the assertion that social and economic relations were actually the emanations of distinct stereotypical individuals. It was in this manner that Spengler's "anticapitalism" fueled racist antisemitism, for he included "the Jew" or "the Jews" as archetypical capitalists.

Spengler's revolt against abstraction made the case for technological advance. He looked to the German engineer, "erudite priest of the machine," to offer political leadership and grasp those romantic and irrational aspects of technology not yet corrupted by the power of money. He depicted a battle between industry and finance as a modern form of the "primordial struggle between productive and creative versus plundering" economics, one ultimately between "money and blood." He hoped for a new "Caesarism" in an authoritarian state that would "break the dictatorship of money and its political weapon, democracy." He described this "socialism" as a national political community that would replace "capitalism," understood as self-seeking liberal individualism: "money can be overcome and mastered only by blood."[29]

The Decline of the West became a canonical work of German right-wing "anticapitalism." Having redefined capitalism to refer to finance and money and socialism to be a national community devoted to technological progress, the work expressed hope amidst the right-wing anger over the lost war. It was one of a number of texts of Weimar's conservative revolution that fostered the equation of Jews with capitalism and Germany with a national and socialist revolt against both.

Reactionary Modernism and German Engineers

The effort to incorporate modern technology into the complex of German *Kultur* and separate it from association with Western *Zivilisation*—that is, Britain, France, the United States, and, sometimes, the Soviet Union as well— was an important preoccupation of the professors of engineering in Germany who wrote books and journal articles on the subject.[30] In 1934, the national association of German engineers (*Verein deutscher Ingenieure*) published *Die Sendung des Ingenieure im neuen Staat* (The Mission of the Engineers in the New State), a collection of essays that welcomed the Nazi regime for placing technology "in the service of the totality of the *Volk*.[31] In the course of making their distinctive contribution to the reactionary modernist tradition, these engineers wrote essays and books that echoed the right-wing anticapitalism of Spengler and Sombart, distinguished between the "technical" and the "capitalist" man, and presented technology as a distinctively German phenomenon. They brought the themes of reactionary modernism developed by literary, political, and social scientific intellectuals to the attention of their fellow engineers.

The Nazis were also aware of the enthusiasm for technology in the conservative revolution and made efforts to stimulate it. In 1919, Gottfried Feder, an engineer and early member of the Nazi Party, distinguished between "Jewish finance capital" and "national capital" in his book *Das Manifest zur Brechung der Zinsknechtschaft des Geldes* (The Manifesto on Breaking the Interest Slavery of Money).[32] "Breaking the bonds [or slavery] of interest" was a key theme of the Nazi Party's Twenty-five-point program of February 1920.[33] Three years later, in his "Manifesto for Breaking the Bondage of Interest," Feder denounced "Mammonism" as a "frame of mind" driven by unnamed "international financial superpowers" and a "golden international" that "rules over the rights of self-determination of individual peoples." It spread through "the broadest segments of the population," leading to a "frightening decline in moral values." It was "carried to its extreme in the international plutocracy" and gained its power by the "multiplication of wealth by interest," which was "the diabolical invention of big capital"; the only way to "cure suffering humanity" was to break "the bondage of interest."[34] In this manifesto, Feder insisted that "the Jew" was remote from productive labor and thus fostered a parasitic spirit. On the other hand, German big industry—the firms of Krupp, Mannesman, and Thyssen—were "not at all in conflict with the interest of the totality. The fundamental recognition of private property is deeply anchored in the clear awareness of the Aryan spiritual structure."[35] In 1933, in his *Kampf gegen Hochfinanz* (The Struggle against High Finance), Feder distinguished between "creative" (schaffendes) (i.e. German) and "parasitic" (raffendes) (i.e., Jewish) capital, connecting the latter to international financiers who drained the resources of the nation.[36]

Feder's anti-capitalist rhetoric eventually fell out of favor as Hitler developed close ties with some German industrialists, but Feder's distinction between creative and parasitic capital echoed the German engineers' "anti-capitalist" texts. The first of Nazism's statements about modern technology was published in 1930, in the "National Socialist Library," a series Feder directed. That text, Peter Schwerber's *Nationalsozialismus und Technik: Die Geistigkeit der nationalsozialistischen Bewegung* (National Socialism and Technology: The Spirituality of the National Socialist Movement), fused Nazi ideology with the traditions of the engineers.[37] It remains a classic statement of the synthesis of Jew-hatred and enthusiasm for technology in the Nazi party. Schwerber wrote that National Socialism, far from being hostile to technological advance, sought to liberate it from the "domination of money" and the "fetters" of Jewish materialism, which was alien to the "autonomous life element of the German *Volk*." The generation of the "front experience" in the Great War grasped the idea of freedom from physical labor and the opportunity for free time that was inherent in technology. Yet the goal of freedom was unrealized due to "domination of a power alien to the essence of technology, that is, the power of money...the Jewish materialist suffocating embrace [*Umklammerung*] of our life elements."[38] Nazism, Schwerber continued, went beyond complaint to "the act of liberation." Only "blood" and action could prevail against "the titanic power of money." Both technology and Nazism possessed a "primal life instinct," and both were arrayed against "Jewish materialist restrictions."[39] Where Jews destroyed technology, the Nordic race was ideally suited to it. The "liberation" of technology thus went hand in hand with an attack on the Jews who, Schwerber asserted, stood in the way of its full realization. His message to his fellow engineers was that antisemitism was key to technological advance.

In *Mein Kampf*, Hitler joined in the reactionary modernist determination to exempt modern technology from the general cultural anti-modernism of German right-wing nationalism and the Nazi Party. He praised Feder's work on interest as

> a theoretical truth which would inevitably be of immense importance for the future of the German people. The sharp separation of stock exchange capital from the national economy offered the possibility of opposing the internationalization of the German economy without at the same time menacing the foundations of an independent national self-maintenance by a struggle against capital.

Hitler stressed that "the fight against international finance and loan capital became the most important point in the program of the German nation's struggle for economic independence and freedom."[40] The pejorative association of the Jews with "international finance" was one of the sins that

Hitler assigned to the Jews as a "race." Also in *Mein Kampf*, he described the "Aryan" as a "founder of culture," one based on a synthesis of "Hellenic spirit and Germanic technology."[41] His enthusiasm for modern technology, apparent in his attraction to automobiles, the radio, and aviation, was also evident in the Nazi regime's rearmament programs.[42]

Nazi propaganda minister Joseph Goebbels cleverly incorporated themes of German romanticism with enthusiasm for technology. In a February 1939 speech at the Berlin Auto Show, he insisted that Nazism had "never rejected or struggled against technology. Rather, one of its main tasks was to consciously affirm it, to fill it inwardly with soul...." He referred to the "steely romanticism of our century[,]...a new romanticism in the results of modern inventions and technology." While "bourgeois reaction" was skeptical or hostile to technology, "National Socialism understood how to take the soulless framework of technology and fill it with the rhythm and hot impulses of our time."[43]

For most of the period since the Holocaust, the blend of the reactionary anticapitalism with antisemitism, first in Weimar's conservative revolution, then in Nazi Germany, ceased to play a significant role in politics in the liberal democracies. It reemerged in the Islamists' blend of cultural reaction and enthusiasm for modern technology, and in the attacks in recent decades by far-right political parties on sinister international financiers. Hence, examination of the century-old tradition of reactionary modernism remains relevant for understanding these faces of antisemitism in our own time.

Notes

Selections reprinted with permission from *Reactionary Modernism: Technology, Culture and Politics in Weimar and the Third Reich* by Jeffrey Herf, Cambridge University Press, Copyright 1984. 'Reproduced with permission of Cambridge University Press [the Licensor] through PLSclear.' All rights reserved.

1 On the antipathy to Judaism as materialistic as opposed to the soulful nature of Christianity, see David Nirenberg, *Anti-Judaism: The Western Tradition* (New York: W.W. Norton, 2013). On the secularizers of anti-Judaism, also see the chapter on Voltaire, and on Karl Marx in Jerry Z. Muller, *The Mind and the Market: Capitalism and Modern European Thought* (New York: Knopf, 2002).

2 On the association of antisemitism with the cultural and political revolt against liberal modernity, including modern capitalism, see George Mosse, *The Crisis of German Ideology: Intellectual Origins of the Third Reich* (New York: Gossett and Dunlop, 1964; Madison: University of Wisconsin Press, 2021); Fritz Stern, *The Politics of Cultural Despair* (Berkeley and Los Angeles: University of California Press, 1961, and 1974); and Shulamit Volkov, *Germans, Jews, and Antisemites: Trials in Emancipation* (New York and Cambridge: Cambridge University Press, 2006).

3 George Mosse, *The Fascist Revolution: Toward a General Theory of Fascism* (New York: Howard Fertig, 1999).

4 Jeffrey Herf, *Reactionary Modernism: Technology, Culture, and Politics in Weimar and the Third Reich* (New York: Cambridge University Press, 1984).

5 On Jews and capitalism, see Jerry Z. Muller, *Capitalism and the Jews* (Princeton, NJ: Princeton University Press, 2010).

6 On the idea of a "conservative revolution," see Herf, *Reactionary Modernism*, 18–48. For visions of national community, see Jerry Z. Muller, *The Other God that Failed: Hans Freyer and the Deradicalization of German Conservatism* (Princeton, NJ: Princeton University Press, 1987).

7 On Jünger's books and essays of the Weimar era, see Herf, *Reactionary Modernism*, 70–108; and Walter Benjamin, "Theories of German Fascism," in Michael Jennings, Howard Eiland and Gary Smith, eds., trans. Jerold Wikoff, *Walter Benjamin: Selected Writings, Volume 2, 1927–1934* (Cambridge, MA: Harvard University Press, 1999), 312–321. On Martin Heidegger's ambivalent view of technology and his enthusiasm for the Nazi regime, see Herf, *Reactionary Modernism*, 109–114. On the connection between his philosophy, his place in the conservative revolution, and his antisemitism, see most recently Richard Wolin, *Heidegger's Ruin: Between Ideology and Philosophy* (New Haven, CT: Yale University Press, 2022); and Jeffrey Herf, "Heidegger's Downfall," *Quillette* (February 22, 2023): https://quillette.com/2023/02/22/heideggers-downfall/

8 On Sombart's early antipathy to capitalism, see Werner Sombart, *Sozialismus und soziale Bewegungen im neunzehnten Jahrhundert* (Jena: Verlag Gustav Fischer, 1896); and *Der Moderne Kapitalismus* (Leipzig: Duncker & Humblot, 1902). On antisemitism of Sombart's analysis, see Jeffrey Herf, *Reactionary Modernism*, 130–151; and David Landes, "The Jewish Merchant-Typology and Stereotypology in Germany," *Leo Baeck Institute Yearbook*, 19 (1974), 11–23. On the comparison of Weber and Sombart, see Muller, *Capitalism and the Jews*, 52–61; Paul R. Mendes-Flohr, "Werner Sombart's 'The Jews and Modern Capitalism': An Analysis of Its Ideological Premises," *Leo Baeck Institute Yearbook* 20 (1975), 87–107; and Werner Mosse, "Judaism, Jews and Capitalism: Weber, Sombart, and Beyond," *Leo Baeck Institute Yearbook* 24 (1979), 3–15.

9 The literature on "the Weber thesis" is vast. See Max Weber, *The Protestant Ethic and the Spirit of Capitalism* trans. Talcott Parsons (New York: Charles Scribner, 1976 (1958)).

10 Landes, "The Jewish Merchant," 22. On Nazism and respectability, see George Mosse, "Nazi Aesthetics: Beauty without Sensuality," in *The Fascist Revolution: Toward a General Theory of Fascism*, (New York: Howard Fertig, 1999), 191–194.

11 Landes, "The Jewish Merchant," 22.

12 See Max Horkheimer, *The Eclipse of Reason* (New York: Oxford University Press, 1947; Seabury Press, 1974); and Max Horkheimer and Theodor Adorno, first published as *Dialektik der Aufklärung* (Amsterdam: Querido Verlag, 1947). The first English translation, as *Dialectic of Enlightenment*, was by John Cummings (New York: Seabury Press, 1972). Horkheimer and Adorno wrote: "Bourgeois anti-Semitism has a specific economic reason: the concealment of domination in production," p. 173. Also see Herbert Marcuse, "The Struggle Against Liberalism in the Totalitarian View of the State," in Herbert Marcuse, ed., *Negations*, trans. Jeremy Shapiro (Boston, MA: Beacon Press, 1968), 3–42; and the discussion of the critical theorists on antisemitism in Herf, *Reactionary Modernism*, 9, and 33–35.

13 Sombart, *Die Juden und das Wirtschaftsleben*, (Leipzig: Juncker & Humblot, 1911), 142–155, 199–223.

14 Ibid., 242–243.

15 Ibid., 244–245.

16 Ibid., 265.

17 Ibid., 293. Thirty years later, during the Third Reich, Wolf Meyer-Christian, in his *Die englisch-jüdische Allianz* (The English-Jewish Alliance) drew on Sombart's

arguments regarding the pejorative association between Puritanism and Judaism in his antisemitic propaganda aimed at Britain. On that, see the discussion in this volume, chapter two, "Nazi Anti-Zionism."

18 Ibid., 329.
19 Ibid., 134.
20 Ibid., 132.
21 Werner Sombart, *Deutscher Sozialismus* (Charlottenburg/Berlin: Buchholz & Weisswange, 1934), 160.
22 Ibid., 189–195.
23 Oswald Spengler, *Der Untergang des Abendlandes* (Munich: C.H. Beck'sche Verlagsbuchhandlung, 1923; reprint, 1972). See discussion of Spengler in Herf, *Reactionary Modernism*, 49–69.
24 Oswald Spengler to Hans Klores, in *Briefe 1913–1936*, ed. Anton M. Kotanek and Manfred Schroter (Munich 1936), 115, cited in Walter Struve, *Elites Against Democracy* (Princeton, NJ: Princeton University Press, 1973), 236–237.
25 Oswald Spengler, *Preussentum und Sozialismus* (Munich: Beck Verlag, 1922 [1919]), 10, 97–98, 65, 81.
26 Spengler, *Der Untergang des Abendlandes*, Band II, 660–661, and 669–671.
27 Ibid., 1148, 1118–1119.
28 Ibid., 1161–1167.
29 Spengler, *Der Untergang des Abendlandes*, Band II, 1, 190–191, 194.
30 On the German engineers and reactionary modernism, see Herf, *Reactionary Modernism*, 152–188. For a typical and synthetic work, see Heinrich Hardensett, *Der kapitalistische und der technische Mensch* (Munich: R. Oldenbourg, 1932) and discussion in *Reactionary Modernism*, 181–186.
31 Rudolf Heiss, ed., *Die Sendung des Ingenieure im neuen Staat* (Berlin: VDI [Verein Deutscher Ingenieure] Verlag, 1934), 152. See Heinrich Hardensett, "Vom technischen-schöpferischen Menschen," 12–18; and Rudolf Heiss, "Wird der Nationalsozialismus die technische Kulturkrise lösen?," 1–11.
32 Gottfried Feder, *Das Manifest zur Brechung der Zinsknechtschaft des Geldes* [Manifesto for Breaking the Bondage of Interest] (Munich: Franz Eher Verlag, 1919, 1932). On the engineers in Nazi Germany, see Herf, *Reactionary Modernism*, 189–216.
33 "The Program of the German Worker's Party: The Twenty-Five Points," in Anson Rabinbach and Sander L. Gilman, eds., *The Third Reich Sourcebook* (Berkeley and Los Angeles: University of California Press, 2013), 12–14.
34 Gottfried Feder, "Manifesto for Breaking the Bondage of Interest," *Third Reich Sourcebook*, 14–15.
35 Gottfried Feder, *Der deutsche Staat auf nationaler und sozialer Grundlage* (Munich: Deutschvölkische Verlagsbuchhandlung, 1923), 21.
36 Gottfried Feder, *Kampf gegen Hochfinanz* (Munich: Zentral Verlag der N.S.D.A.P, Franz Eher Verlag, 1933). On German engineers in Nazi Germany, the standard work is Karl-Heinz Ludwig, *Technik und Ingenieure im Dritten Reich* (Dusseldorf: Droste, 1974). More recently, John Guse addresses them in *Nazi Volksgemeinschaft Technology: Gottfried Feder, Fritz Todt and the Plassenburg Spirit*, forthcoming (New York and London: Palgrave Macmillan, 2023).
37 Peter Schwerber, *Nationalsozialismus und Technik: Die Geistigkeit der national-sozialistischen Bewegung* (Munich: Franz Eher Verlag, 1930).
38 Ibid., 6.
39 Ibid., 21, 23.
40 Adolf Hitler, *Mein Kampf* (Boston, MA: Houghton-Mifflin, 1943), 213. Also see Christian Hartmann, Thomas Vordermayer, Othmar Plöckinger and Roman Töppel, eds. *Hitler, Mein Kampf: Eine kritische Edition*, vol. 1 (Munich-Berlin: Institut für Zeitgeschichte, 2016), 573–575.

41 Ibid., 290; Hartmann, et al., Hitler, Mein Kampf: Eine kritische Edition, 755–756.

42 On the synthesis of Nazi antisemitism and cultural anti-modernism with enthu-
siasm for modern technology during World War II and the Holocaust, see Herf,
Reactionary Modernism, 212–216; Ludwig, *Technik und Ingenieure im Drit-
ten Reich*; the essays on research on armaments and in the wartime economy in
Doris Kaufman, ed., *Geschichte der Kaiser-Wilhelm-Gesellschaft im Nationalso-
zialismus* (Göttingen: Wallstein Verlag, 2000); and Adam Tooze, *The Wages of
Destruction: The Making and Breaking of the Nazi Economy* (New York and
London: Allan Lane/Penguin, 2006).

43 Joseph Goebbels, Speech at the Opening of the Berlin Auto Show, February 17,
1939, *Deutsche Technik* (March 1939), 105–106; cited in Herf, *Reactionary
Modernism*, 196.

2

THE JEWISH ENEMY

Nazi Germany's Core Antisemitic Conspiracy Theory

From January 30, 1939, to the early fall of 1941, Hitler publicly justified the murder of the Jews of Europe and then of Jews in the entire world. He made that case in a conspiracy theory that accused "world-" or "international Jewry" of launching World War II so that this evil bunch could "exterminate" the German people. In response to this attempted mass murder, he promised to turn the tables and kill the Jews before they could kill the Germans. Hitler and other Nazi leaders presented "the Final Solution of the Jewish Question in Europe," the Holocaust, as a massive act of national self-defense.

Joseph Goebbels, the Nazi "Minister of Propaganda and Public Enlightenment," amplified this basic accusation in numerous essays and radio broadcasts. Otto Dietrich, the head of the Nazi regime's Reich Press Office, communicated its core themes to German newspapers and magazines on a daily basis during World War II and the Holocaust. Nazi think tanks offered antisemitic "scholarship" in essays and books, while artists used modern techniques to present the vast conspiracy in multi-colored wall posters. The case was public, and blunt, but only in recent decades have historians presented its full dimensions. The result was and remains a significant advance in our understanding of the relationship between ideology and policy, belief, and mass murder during the Holocaust.

Throughout the war, E.H. Gombrich, who later gained renown as an art historian, worked at the British Broadcasting Corporation, the BBC, monitoring German radio broadcasts. In a 1969 lecture in London, Gombrich described the Nazi propaganda as the "imposition of a paranoiac pattern on world events" and a "gigantic persecution mania" focused on the Jews that held "the various strands of German propaganda together."[1] For the

DOI: 10.4324/9781003449669-3

Nazis, he wrote, "the war is only a war against the devil, the Jew," who, they claimed, was the real power behind the Allied leaders.[2] In 1975, Lucy Dawidowicz, in *The War Against the Jews, 1933–1945,* called for incorporating the history of murder of the Jews into general histories of the period.[3] In crucial histories of the timing and context of Holocaust decision-making, Christopher Browning, in *The Origins of the Final Solution* and other essays, and Richard Breitman, in *The Architect of Genocide: Himmler and the Final Solution,* documented and interpreted the connections between those decisions and the course of World War II in spring to fall 1941.[4] In his two-volume synthesis *Nazi Germany and the Jews* (1997 and 2007), Saul Friedlander documented the radicalization of a "redemptive antisemitism" and the importance of Nazism's antisemitic conspiracies from the "years of persecution" to the "years of extermination."[5]

In *The Jewish Enemy: Nazi Propaganda During World War II and the Holocaust,* published in 2006, I built on these and other works to offer a more comprehensive account of the Nazi regime's translation of conspiracy theory into an ongoing antisemitic narrative of the events of World War II. Hitler and other Nazi officials offered a persistent and very public rant justifying the murder of the Jews.[6] Some documents were famous, if underexamined; others became accessible only after Nazi Germany was defeated. A half century after the Holocaust, the translation of Nazism's antisemitic ideology into its narrative of World War II as "the Jewish war," and with it an expanded understanding of the meaning of the phrase "the war against the Jews," has begun to enter the historical scholarship on the Nazi era.[7]

In his work on the impact of the propaganda, David Bankier concluded that in the broad German population, it was effective in fostering indifference and hostility to the Jews "because large sectors of German society were predisposed to be antisemitic." Studying the myth surrounding Hitler, Ian Kershaw observed a similar indifference.[8] However skeptical, some Germans may have been about the messages emanating from the Propaganda Ministry and however embittered and disillusioned they became once the military tide in the war turned after the defeat in Stalingrad, the German armies kept fighting to the end of the war.[9] The regime had significant popular support, but as a dictatorship which had crushed opposition before the war began, popular sentiment was largely irrelevant to policymaking. It was the beliefs of Hitler and the Nazi leadership, and the willingness of assorted armed organizations to share them and to follow their orders, which were decisive.

Nazi propaganda did not consist primarily of endless repetitions of quotes from Hitler's *Mein Kampf.* In addition to the creation of a myth of infallibility surrounding Hitler, the regime's propagandists, beginning with Hitler himself, continuously translated antisemitic hatred into an interpretive framework that served to make sense (and nonsense) of ongoing events. The Nazi leadership believed that the conspiracy theory of radical antisemitism explained the central paradox of World War II, namely the emergence, deepening, and persistence of the alliance between the Soviet Union and the Western democracies. Both President Franklin Roosevelt and Prime Minister Winston Churchill had decided to make a pact with the lesser evil, Stalin's Soviet Union, in order to defeat what they viewed as the greater evil, Hitler's Germany. In the Allies' view, this represented a necessary blend of *Realpolitik* and moral clarity. For the Nazi leaders, however, the anti-Hitler coalition had been created by a political actor entitled "international Jewry," which had brought these strange bedfellows together into an unlikely alliance.

Nazi propaganda was simultaneously a cynical, utilitarian political instrument as well as a fanatical and deeply believed interpretive framework.[10] It projected Nazi Germany's aggression and mass murder onto an enemy and, in so doing, served as a justification of German responses in kind. It deepened loyalty to the regime within the Nazi party and regime by forging bonds of complicity in crime. It sought to undermine support for the war effort in Britain, the United States and the Soviet Union by presenting World War II as one waged by and for the Jews and thus presumably not in the national interests of the countries involved, and it attempted to split the anti-Nazi coalition with charges that its members were merely puppets of the Jews. The propaganda was not primarily a tool to pursue other purposes; rather, it expressed the actual intention of the Nazi regime, that is, to murder the Jews, as an end in itself.

The evil intent was public knowledge. The mixture of mendacity and evil in the Nazi regime's public statements have inclined some scholars, and some OSS analysts at the time, to view the Nazis as cynics for whom the antisemitic conspiracy was primarily a useful tool of domination.[11] George Orwell's influential essay "Politics and the English Language" and his novel *1984*, as well as Berel Lang's more recent examination of "language rules explicitly designed to conceal literal meaning," have contended that totalitarian regimes couched their lies in a fog of euphemisms and that the truth of what they were doing would be buried in secret office memoranda.[12] Yet, in fact, amidst the lies and famous euphemisms such as "the Final Solution" and "deportation to the East," the Nazis made strikingly blunt, forthright and perversely honest statements about their murderous intentions and actions. In her *Origins of Totalitarianism*, Hannah Arendt astutely noted that "in order not to overestimate the importance of the propaganda lies one should recall the much more numerous instances in which Hitler was completely sincere and brutally unequivocal in the definition of the movement's true aims," but, she continued, these assertions "were simply not acknowledged by a public unprepared for such consistency."[13] A similar point was made by the historian and journalist Caesar Aronsfeld in his 1985 work, *The Text of the Holocaust: A Study of the Nazis' Extermination Propaganda 1919–1945*, but Aronsfeld's work, published by a small press, did not lead a needed revision of conventional wisdom in the historical profession.[14]

Four words in the German language were at the core of this language of mass murder, and none of them, in any context was a euphemism. They were the verbs *vernichten* and *aussrotten*, which are synonyms for annihilate, exterminate, totally destroy, and kill; and the nouns, *Vernichtung* and *Ausrottung*, meaning annihilation, extermination, total destruction, and killing. Whether taken on their own from their dictionary definitions or placed within the context of the speeches, paragraphs, and sentences in which they were uttered, their meaning was unambiguous. Hitler and other Nazi leaders and propagandists often projected these intentions and plans onto the Jews who, they claimed, planned to "exterminate" or "annihilate" not only the Nazi regime or the Nazi party or the German armies, but the German people as a whole. When the Nazis imputed a policy of *Vernichtung* or *Ausrottung* to the collective singular noun "international Jewry," the meaning of the words in that context was clear: the Nazis accused the Jews of supporting a policy of mass murder of the entire German people. These were not euphemisms or totalitarian doubletalk; *for those who took them seriously*, their meanings were straightforward.

Hitler set the agenda, most famously in his speech to the Reichstag on January 30, 1939. It was then that he uttered his infamous prophecy:

> If international finance Jewry inside and outside Europe should succeed in plunging the nations once more into a world war, the result will not be the bolshevization of the earth and thereby the victory of Jewry, but the annihilation (*Vernichtung*) of the Jewish race in Europe![15]

Between 1939 and 1945, this reversed logic of aggression and self-righteous retaliation continued to form the core of Nazi antisemitic propaganda. Throughout, projection and paranoia were the handmaidens of aggression and mass murder.

On January 30, 1941, Hitler repeated this "prophecy" without using the word *Vernichtung* when he said that the Jews' role in Europe was finished.[16] In a speech in the Berlin Sportpalast on September 30, 1942, he said, to the accompaniment of applause, that it would be the Jews and not the "Aryan peoples" who would be "exterminated" (*ausgerottet*).[17] Two months later, on November 8, 1942, in a speech in Munich, he repeated that the results of World War II would not be the "extermination" (*Ausrottung*) of the "European races but rather the extermination (*Ausrottung*) of Jewry in Europe."[18] Each of these speeches was front-page news in the official government newspaper, the *Völkischer Beobachter* [People's Observer] and other major papers. They were broadcast on national radio and repeated in pamphlets. Some were excerpted in thousands of multi-colored posters placed each week in public places in German cities and posters. In a clear example of what Ian Kershaw called "working towards the Führer," it was not "polycratic" infighting but rather a stunning unity of purpose that was evident in the eagerness with which all of the regime's propaganda organs took their cues from Hitler's pronouncements about the Jews.[19]

Two, among hundreds of antisemitic public statements broadcast on German radio, convey this consensus. In December 1939, Robert Ley, the head of the Nazi labor front, spoke in German-occupied Lodz, Poland. At this early stage in the war, but twelve months after Hitler's prophecy speech, Ley warned that if England won the war,

> the German people, man, woman, and child would be exterminated *(aus-gerottet)*.... The Jew would be wading in blood. Funeral pyres would be built on which the Jews would burn us.... Hence it should rather be the Jews that fry, rather that they should burn, that they should starve, that they should be exterminated *(ausgerottet)*.[20]

Toward the end of a speech he delivered to German and Dutch workers in Amsterdam on May 10, 1942, Ley said,

> The Jew is the great danger to humanity. If we don't succeed in extermi-nating him *(ihn auszurotten)*, then we will lose the war. It's not enough to bring him someplace *(ihn irgend wohin zu bringen)*. That would be as if one wanted to lock up a louse somewhere in a cage. (Laughter.) They would find a way out and again they come out from under and itch you again. (Laughter.) You have to annihilate *(vernichten)* them, you have to exterminate *(ausrotten)*.... (Interrupted by ongoing applause).[21]

On October 4, 1942, Herman Göring, designated Hitler's successor in 1934, director of the Four-Year Plan, Chief of the Luftwaffe and generally regarded as the second most powerful figure in the Nazi regime, spoke in the Berlin Sportpalast. "If we lose the war," he asserted, "you (Germans) will be anni-hilated *(vernichtet)*.... This is not the Second World War. This is a great race war. It's about whether the German and Aryan will survive or if the Jew will rule the world and that is why we are fighting abroad. (Applause.)"[22] The Nazi leaders were as clear about general policy as they were vague about details regarding its implementation.

The German press, and above all the regime's official organ, *Der Völkis-cher Beobachter (VB)*, was central to a series of well-coordinated campaigns. Examination of the front-page stories and headlines containing antisemitic themes for the period of 1939–1945 indicates the timing of these episodic, at times long-running, barrages that came in response to particular develop-ments in the war. During these six years, only four percent (84 of 2,100) re-ferred to the extermination of the Jews, but they came in concentrated bursts. There were two such headlines in 1939; none in 1940; 17 in 1941; four in

1942; 50 in 1943; ten in 1944; and two in the spring of 1945. Four periods accounted for most of the front-page stories: July–August 1941 (seven); April-July 1943 (26); October–November 1943 (13); and May–June 1944 (nine). Twenty-six antisemitic headlines appeared during the war and the Holocaust at other times. The headlines were part of a coordinated barrage that could include a speech by Hitler or Goebbels, directives sent to hundreds of newspapers, articles in other leading newspapers and magazines, and posters pasted up in prominent public places such as train stations and post offices. None of these articles, speeches, and posters contained factual material about the Final Solution. A reader of the press or radio listener would know, however, that the Nazi regime had declared the Jews "guilty" for the war and all its suffering and that the regime was implementing Hitler's prophecy that it would exterminate the Jews.[23]

The campaigns against the Jews took place when the tide of war was flowing in the regime's favor, in July and August 1941, as well as when the tide turned against it, in the spring of 1943. Following the affirmation by Roosevelt and Churchill of the goal of unconditional surrender at their conference in Casablanca in January 1943 and the defeat of the German Sixth Army in Stalingrad at the end of that month, the Reich Press Office directives called for an intensified focus on antisemitism. Similarly, the Normandy invasion of June 1944 and the weeks of anticipation before it elicited ten antisemitic headlines. These presented the invasion as further proof that a world Jewish conspiracy was directing the war behind the scenes and that Roosevelt and Churchill had become Stalin's dupes in a "Jewish-Bolshevik plot" to dominate all of Europe.[24]

Usually, Goebbels held a morning conference in which he delivered a monologue about the events of the day and conveyed instructions regarding how the press and radio should present the day's news to domestic and foreign audiences.[25] Shortly thereafter, Otto Dietrich, Chief of the Reich Press Office, or one of his officials would hold a "press conference" at which Dietrich or more often one of his staff issued press directives or orders in oral and written form to several hundred journalists and editors.[26] Their orders were conveyed to editors and publishers working at the over 3,000 newspapers in Germany.[27] The press directives were regarded as top-secret material and were to be destroyed or sent back to the Ministry after they were used and digested. Revelation of their contents would lead to punishment extending from expulsion from the government-approved association of journalists to prison terms to, in one case of revelation of the directives to foreigners, an execution. The coordination of the German press was thus a secret daily— and for magazines, a weekly—detailed exercise of direct dictatorial control over the press.

A torrent of anti-Jewish propaganda took place in the aftermath of the defeat in Stalingrad and the beginning of a series of defeats on Germany's

Eastern Front.[28] The Periodical Service of February 5, 1943, directed magazine editors to

> Fight Bolshevism and Jewry!...If Bolshevism in the Soviet Union led by the Jewish power holders succeeded in breaking the protective barrier of the German Wehrmacht in the East and the iron wall of German determination on the home front, it would repeat in far greater measure the extermination, enslavement and immiseration of people that it has brought about in the Soviet Union. All articles that are written based on the material delivered by the *Wochendienst* must take up the theme of the threatening Jewish-Bolshevik danger.[29]

On May 5, 1943, the Nazi Party's Reich Propaganda Directorate sent a classified directive to regional and local party officials entitled "The Jewish Question as a Domestic and Foreign Policy Weapon."[30] The "Jewish question," it asserted, must not disappear from public consciousness because

> this is a war of Jews against Germany and its allies. Just as the domestic struggle ended with the antisemitic revolution in Germany, so this war must end with an antisemitic world revolution. In Germany we made the whole nation antisemitic. We did so by repeatedly pointing our finger at the Jews, even as they tried to camouflage themselves. Again and again, we tore the masks from their faces....
>
> In the wave of meetings [to be organized by the Nazi party] in the near future, the Jewish question must be the constant key point of all presentations. Every German must know that everything he or she must endure—the discomforts, restrictions, extra hours at work, bloody terror toward women and children, and the bloody losses on the field of battle—is to be traced back to the Jew. In every meeting, the following points must be treated
>
> That the international Jew wanted this war, occupies the most important economic positions among all the enemy peoples and countries, and ruthlessly uses his power to drive the peoples into war, forms public opinion, owns the press, radio and film[;]...that there is no crime in which the Jew is not involved[;]...that where the Jews do not themselves appear as power holders, they have bought personalities in public life who, as dependent and service tools, do the Jews' business; that the Jews profit from the war and thus have an interest in a long war. However, scarcely a single Jew carries a weapon or earns his income by the labor of his hands; as was the case here earlier in Germany, the Jews leave the fighting and labor to others; that the Jews unleashed this war as a final attempt to assert their power in the world and to strike down those who have recognized them and their intentions; that this war will end with an anti-Semitic world

revolution and with the extermination of Jewry throughout the world, both of which are a precondition for enduring peace. The core sentence of this statement: The Jews are guilty of everything![31]

The directive drew recipients' attention to Goebbel's essay "The War and the Jews," copies of which would be made available to all speakers of the Nazi Propaganda Directorate. The coordinated and unified message of the Nazi regime and Nazi party were evident in the May 6, 1943, headline of the *Völkischer Beobachter*, which read: "USA and England under the Command of World Jewry; Plutocrats Identify with Jewish-Bolshevik Murderers."[32]

On August 13, 1943, Otto Dietrich sent a press directive to editors expressing his lack of satisfaction at what he called insufficient enthusiasm in parts of the press for the intensified antisemitic campaign he was fostering that spring and summer: The word of the day from the Reich Press Chief of August 9, 1943 again clearly pointed out that Bolshevism and capitalism are components of the identical Jewish world swindle only operating under different names. Yet in the treatment of Bolshevik themes, the newspapers repeatedly succumb to the illusion that capitalism and Bolshevism are two different and antagonistic perspectives. In particular, communist agitation is repeatedly given a boost because the press takes Bolshevik statements seriously, as if Bolshevism really wanted to destroy capitalism. In reality, both of these Jewish systems are working hand in hand with one another. Now the German press must finally put an end to this false and dangerous tendency which sabotages the line of our policy. Editors who violate this word of the day will be held personally responsible for doing so.[33]

Throughout the Holocaust, Hitler remained its driving force, but as he retreated from public view when the tide of war turned against Germany, Goebbels became the public voice and scribe of Nazi propaganda. While Heinrich Himmler, as Richard Breitman put it, was "the architect of genocide" who transformed Hitler's orders into the actual decisions to carry out the murder of Europe's Jews, Goebbels turned Hitler's hatred into the Nazi regime's public justification and incitement for genocide.

Goebbels' output was enormous. Several texts were particularly important for the Holocaust, including "The Jews Are Guilty," an editorial in *Das Reich* of November 16, 1941; the "Iron Heart" speech to the *Deutschen Akademie* at the main lecture hall of Friedrich Wilhelm University in Berlin on December 1, 1941; and "The War and the Jews" of May 9, 1943, published in *Das Reich* and then read over German radio; as well as the less well-known but important radio address of February 28, 1945.[34] In these and other writings, Goebbels offered a narrative of the events of World War II that became the central, constantly repeated justification to "exterminate" the Jews. Given Goebbels famous close connection to Hitler, readers and listeners would be correct in assuming that he was speaking for Hitler, a fact that underscored the importance of his message.

Franklin Roosevelt viewed Nazi domination of the European continent, threats to invade Britain and block shipping in the Atlantic as direct threats to the national security of the United States. Should Britain and the British Navy fall into the hands of Hitler's Germany, the threat to the United States would, he believed, be direct and dire. Though Roosevelt was appalled by Nazi anti-Jewish persecution, he did not present American intervention in a European war as a means of opposing Hitler's attack on the Jews.[35] This, of course, contradicted Goebbels' articles of 1939 and 1940, which, following an antisemitic interpretation of American and British policy, asserted that it was only the Jews' sinister influence and vast power that were responsible for American and British opposition to Hitler's policies.[36]

In "*Was Will eigentlich Amerika?*" (What Does America Really Want?), an essay in the *Völkischer Beobachter* of January 21, 1939, Goebbels wrote that hatred and lies about Nazi Germany were being spread in "almost all the American press, above all in its Jewish-dominated parts."[37] The Jews were the "inspirers and beneficiaries of this witch-hunt *(Hetze)*." The Jews dominated "the New York press.... [A]lmost all of the press...radio...and film" in the United States served the anti-German witch-hunt. Indeed, non-Jewish America had become "the victim" of the Jews.[38] In this essay, Goebbels sought to exploit and deepen already existing antisemitism in the United States in the hope that the non-Jewish majority in the United States would hold Jews and their alleged influence on Roosevelt responsible for the war between Germany and America.[39] Given the extent of antisemitism in American life, such a policy fell on some sympathetic ears.[40] The Roosevelt administration's much-examined rhetorical reticence about Nazi persecution and then murder of the Jews did not prevent Nazi propagandists from asserting that it was the Jews and their alleged stooge Roosevelt who were driving the United States to war against Nazi Germany.[41]

Nazi antisemitic propaganda was an indictment of the Jews. In 1939, Goebbels asserted that "the Jews are guilty" of launching the war. In violation of the Munich agreements, Germany invaded and occupied the remainder of Czechoslovakia on March 14, 1939. Now that Hitler's broad plans for expansion were undeniable, Britain and France declared their willingness to defend Poland, should Nazi Germany invade it. Goebbels offered a contrasting explanation of the sources of a new war in his essay of April 1, 1939, "*Wer will den Krieg?*" (Who Wants War?).[42] The Jews were the

anonymous power that stands behind everything.... The Jews are guilty. If in a dark hour a war should break out again in Europe, the call must go out around the earth: the Jews are guilty! They want war and they are doing everything in their power to push the peoples into war. They believe they won't be victims but beneficiaries of such a war. That is why they fan this infernal witch-hunt against Germany and Italy and call for a fighting block of democratic against authoritarian states.[43]

As British resistance from summer 1940 to early 1941 frustrated Hitler's plans to win a quick victory, Goebbels escalated his attacks on Winston Churchill in *Das Reich*. In *"Im Gelächter der Welt"* (The Object of the World's Laughter), of February 16, 1941, he saw similarities between the English and the Jews. The English were "the Jews among the Aryans," a theme repeated in a series of essays and books by Nazi propagandists about the elective affinities between the Jews and Protestantism in Britain.[44] In *"Britannia rules the waves,"* of March 30, 1941, Goebbels, as he had before and would do again, imputed genocidal intentions to Nazi Germany's enemies. If Churchill could, he would "exterminate Germany *(Deutschland aussrotten)*, destroy our people *(unser Volk vernichten)* and leave our country in soot and ashes."[45]

For the Nazis, the emergence and persistence of the anti-Hitler coalition encompassing the Soviet Union with the Western democracies was one of the central riddles of the World War II. They took its existence to be proof of the existence of an international Jewish conspiracy. On June 22, 1941, following the German invasion of the Soviet Union, the British Prime Minister stated, "We have but one aim and one single, irrevocable purpose. We are resolved to destroy Hitler and every vestige of the Nazi regime."[46] As a result, Churchill offered an alliance with the Soviet Union in common cause against the Third Reich. The split between the Soviet Union and the West and the resulting absence of unified resistance had to give way to an alliance with the Soviet Union if Britain was to be defended, and Nazi Germany was to be defeated.

In *"Die alte Front,"* published in *Der Völkischer Beobachter* on June 26, 1941, Goebbels dismissed Churchill's rationale for the emergence of the anti-Hitler coalition with the by-then familiar conspiracy theory.[47] While political neophytes were stunned by the "Moscow-London conspiracy against the Reich caught between plutocracy and Bolshevism," it confirmed long-standing Nazi suspicions. Goebbels claimed that the same alliance between "plutocracy and Bolshevism" which opposed the Nazis during the Weimar era within Germany had reconstituted itself on the international level in June 1941 in the Soviet-British alliance. Just as the Nazis had triumphed over their domestic foes, so they would vanquish this new form of the "old front."[48]

Following the German invasion of the Soviet Union, Goebbels and his propagandists renewed their offensive against "Jewish-Bolshevism." In "Mimikry," an article in *Das Reich* of July 20, 1941, he wrote that the Jews were masters at adapting to surroundings "without losing their essence. They practice mimicry.... An experienced Jewish expert" was necessary to "unmask them." Soviet expansion would mean "the domination of Jewry over the world." The Nazi antisemitic conspiracy solved the apparent mystery of the emerging alliance between "the Jewish Bolsheviks in Moscow and the Jewish plutocrats in London and Washington" who had been "deep enemies." The conspiracy theory about the Jews solved the riddle.

> Above all it is the same Jews, on both sides, whether open or camouflaged, who establish the tone and establish the line. When they pray in Moscow and go to London to sing the International, they are doing what they have done for ages. They practice mimicry. They adapt to the respective conditions and situation and slowly, naturally, and step for step so that the peoples will not be suspicious and alert. They are naturally so furious with us because we unmask them.[49]

As the *Einsatzgruppen* were beginning the Holocaust with mass murders behind the lines of the German Army in Poland and the Soviet Union, Goebbels wrote that "the blow must be delivered without pity or grace. The world's enemy *(Weltfeind)* is collapsing, and Europe will have its peace."[50]

In meetings with Hitler on August 19 and with Reinhard Heydrich on September 24, 1941, Goebbels learned of Hitler's determination to realize the "prophecy" and Heydrich's intention to deport Jews to the East.[51] By then, according to the leading historians of Holocaust decision-making, Hitler had ordered Himmler to expand the mass shootings of Jews on the Eastern Front of summer and early fall 1941 into a program of genocide of all European Jews.[52] On November 16, 1941, Goebbels published *Die Juden sind Schuld*" (The Jews Are Guilty) in *Das Reich*.[53] "The Jews Are Guilty" marked the public acknowledgement by a leading Nazi official that the "extermination" *(Vernichtung)* of European Jewry was taking place. Goebbels dispensed with the "if-then," conditional tense of Hitler's famous prophecy, replacing it with the simple declarative verb tense referring to an ongoing action.[54]

Goebbels wrote that "international Jewry" was waging war against Germany. Now, Germany would wage war on the Jews in response to the war the Jews had launched against it. Though Goebbels never mentioned the Final Solution, he repeatedly used verbs meaning exterminate, annihilate, destroy and murder to refer ongoing government policy directed at Europe's Jews. Further, he defended this assault as one front in a war of national self-defense which of necessity grew in intensity and ruthlessness in response to the war which the Jews were presumably waging against Germany. He wrote:

> By unleashing this war, world Jewry completely misjudged the forces at its disposal. Now it is suffering a gradual process of annihilation which it had intended for us and which it would have unleashed against us without

hesitation if it had the power to do so. It is now perishing as a result of its [world Jewry's] own law: Eye for and eye, tooth for a tooth.... In this historical dispute every Jew is our enemy, whether he vegetates in a Polish ghetto or scrapes out his parasitic existence in Berlin or Hamburg or blows the trumpets of war in New York or Washington. Due to their birth and race, all Jews belong to an international conspiracy against National Socialist Germany. They wish for its defeat and annihilation and do everything in their power to help to bring it about.[55]

The Jews, who, he asserted, had started the war, were "now" suffering a "gradual process of extermination," one which they had originally intended to inflict on Germany. In place of the hypothetical, conditional tenses of Hitler's now famous prophecy, Goebbels used simple, declarative sentences of ongoing policy. The Jews had started the war and wanted to "exterminate" (*vernichten*) the German Reich and people. Hence, all Jews without exception were "sworn enemies" of the German people. The death of every German soldier "was listed in the guilt account (*Schuldkonto*) of the Jews. It is on their conscience, and they must therefore pay for it." Because the Jews bore the guilt for starting the war, the treatment the Germans were handing out to them was not an injustice. "They have more than deserved it." Thus, it was "the government's policy to finally be done with them."[56] According to Goebbels' logic, the more German soldiers who died or were wounded in the war, the more the government would fan the flames of hatred against the Jews.

Two weeks later, on December 1, 1941, Goebbels delivered a two-hour lecture to diplomats, government officials, members of the Nazi Party, senior Wehrmacht officers, journalists, industrialists, and members of the *Deutschen Akademie* assembled in the main lecture hall of the Friedrich Wilhelm University of Berlin. He called the invasion of the Soviet Union a necessary preemptive strike. The Red Army's "first task would have been to exterminate the national intelligentsia and the spiritual leadership of the nation."[57] The invasion was a defense of culture and civilization. Britain and the United States were betraying Europe by leaving it at the mercy of Bolshevism.[58] The Jews, he repeated, had launched, and expanded, World War II but had miscalculated the balance of forces. Before this distinguished audience, he asserted that the Jews were experiencing "now a gradual process of extermination" (*nun einen allmählichen Vernichtungsprozeß*).[59] Again, this was not a discourse of euphemism, bureaucratic indirection or banality. It was a blunt and forthright declaration that the Nazi regime was then engaged in a policy of mass murder of Jews. He claimed that "the historical guilt of world Jewry for the outbreak and expansion of this war has been so extensively demonstrated that there's no need to waste any more words about it. The Jews wanted their war, and now they have it."[60]

Goebbels repeated that "every Jew is our enemy" and that, "due to their birth and race, all Jews belong to an international conspiracy against National Socialist Germany. They seek its defeat and extermination and do everything in their power to help bring that about."[61] Now, he told the assembled in a lecture hall of Berlin's major university, "one of the first and most important tasks of the coming period was the definitive and final (endgültig) solution of the Jewish question."[62] As Germany's enemies were united "in the firm will that Germany must be subjugated, exterminated, killed and wiped out," the Germans had to unite behind Hitler and the Nazi regime to prevent their own annihilation and extermination.[63] The specter of the extermination of the Germans in the event of defeat remained a leitmotif of Nazi wartime propaganda. That evening, Goebbels wrote in his diary that he was "extraordinarily satisfied" with the reception of his talk by the "Berlin intelligentsia."[64]

In his diary of December 12, 1941, five days after the Japanese attack on Pearl Harbor and after the entry of the United States into the war in Europe, Goebbels described Hitler's speech to a meeting that day of Nazi Gauleiter in Berlin.[65] Hitler had already begun the Holocaust before America's entry, yet he lied to the assembled by asserting that as the world war was now here, "the extermination of Jewry must be the necessary consequence." In view of the "160,000" German deaths on the Eastern Front, "the originator of this bloody conflict must pay with his own life."[66] Hitler lent to the Final Solution a causal and inherent, not contingent or accidental connection, to World War II. As the number of German soldiers dying in battle and German civilians dying from allied bombing increased, the Nazi leadership focused on the supposed connection between an international Jewish conspiracy, the anti-Hitler coalition of the Soviet Union, Great Britain, and the United States, the death and suffering of the German people and the resulting necessity to realize Hitler's prophecy. By pointing their accusing fingers at the Jews, Hitler and Goebbels, offered every German family who lost a loved one during the war a personal, intimate reason to hate Jews. Therefore, in popular sentiment, the abstract slogan "the Jews are guilty" assumed direct emotional significance. Goebbels' narrative sought to foster deeper hatred of the Jews as the toll of death, injury, and devastation the Germans suffered at the hands of the Allies grew. As the Allies turned the tide against the German armed forces, Goebbels and the Ministry of Propaganda asserted that "the Jews are guilty."

"The War and the Jews," (Der Krieg und die Juden), published in Das Reich of May 9, 1943, was the third of Goebbels' wartime essays devoted exclusively to the Jews.[67] He expressed exasperation and surprise that there were people who were "still too naive" to understand what the war was about and what role the Jewish question played in it. The "Jewish race" and its "helpers" were waging war against "Aryan humanity as well as against Western culture and civilization." The Jews "form the glue that holds the enemy coalition together" (*Damit bilden sie überhaupt den Kitt, der die feindliche Koalition zusammenhält.*).[68] The Jews had started a "race war" which had "no other goal but the annihilation and extermination of our people. We stand now as the only barrier against Jewry on its path to world domination. If the Axis powers were to lose this struggle, then the damn which could rescue Europe from the Jewish-Bolshevik danger would no longer exist."[69] Either Germany and its allies would win the war or "countless millions of people in our own and other European countries…would be delivered without defense to the hatred and will for extermination (*Vernichtungswillen*) of this devilish race if we would become weak and fail in the end in this battle."[70] Hence in May 1943, he assured his thousands of readers and millions of listeners that

"we are moving ahead. The fulfillment of the Fuhrer's prophecy, about which world Jewry laughed in 1939 when he made it stands at the end of our course of action. Even in Germany, the Jews laughed when we stood up for the first time against them. Among them laughter is now a thing of the past. They chose to wage war against us. But Jewry now understands that the war has become a war against them. When Jewry conceived of the plan of the total extermination of the German people, it thereby wrote its own death sentence. In this instance as in others, world history will also be a world court."[71]

In "The War and the Jews," Goebbels repeated the essential projection mechanism of Nazi propaganda. The Jews launched a war to exterminate the Germans. Instead, the Germans turned the tables and were fulfilling Hitler's prophecies, that is, they were now exterminating the Jews. In these and many other texts, Goebbels combined the big lie or lies—that is, that there was something called international Jewry which was directing a conspiracy against Germany; that Germany had not started the war; and that the allies were lackeys of an unseen but all-powerful international conspiracy—with the blunt and truthful assertion that Nazi Germany was at that time murdering the Jews of Europe and did so as what the Nazi leaders called *a legitimate act of self-defense in wartime.*

This antisemitic conspiracy and its genocidal projections remained the core of Nazi propaganda until the end of the war. On February 28, 1945, with Allied armies closing the ring around Germany, Goebbels spoke to the nation over the radio to explain why Nazi Germany had suffered such serious defeats.[72] He claimed that Germany's setbacks

were possible only because the European West and the plutocratically led USA gave the Soviet military backing on the flanks and tied our hands with which we are still today trying to strike bolshevism to the ground. The plutocrats' plans for blood-soaked hatred and revenge against the Reich and against the German people are in no way inferior to those of the Soviets.... It will be the eternal shame and disgrace of this century that in the moment of its greatest threat from the East, Europe was shamefully left in the lurch and abandoned by the Western countries. Indeed, these nations sunk so low that they even encouraged the storm from inner Asia and at the same time tried to break apart the last protective dam on which it could have been broken. In any case, we expected nothing else. Through years of systematic labor of disintegration and subversion international Jewry so poisoned public opinion in these countries that they were no longer capable of thinking—not to mention acting—for themselves.[73]

Once again, as after World War I, the Jewish conspiracy was the cause for Nazi Germany's impending defeat: it had been betrayed and abandoned by the Western allies who had succumbed to Jewish domination. For the Nazi hard core, World War II ended as had World War I, with a noble Germany betrayed, this time not from within but from a stab in the back delivered from abroad at the hands of the Western, "Jewish plutocracies." It was, according to Goebbels, Jewish domination over policy in London and Washington that caused Nazi Germany to lose World War II. In the death marches of spring 1945, the murders of the Jews continued up to the very end of the war.

Social and intellectual historians have documented that after the defeat in Stalingrad in February 1943, disillusionment and deradicalization spread in the German public. For many Germans, the myth of Hitler's genius had collapsed.[74] Yet the armies, not only the hardcore of the SS, fought fiercely to the bitter end.[75] For Hitler, Goebbels and the Nazi true believers, impending defeat only served to reinforce the conviction that an international Jewish conspiracy in the form of the alliance between the Soviet Union, England, and the United States was going to be the victor of World War II. It is no wonder that Viktor Klemperer, among Goebbels' most acute and perceptive listeners within Germany, wrote in his diary soon after D-Day that "however much I resisted it, *the Jew* is in every respect the center of LTI [the language of the Third Reich], and *of its whole view of the epoch.*"[76] In the same four years in which the absolute powerlessness and defenselessness of Europe's Jews had become horrifyingly obvious, Nazi propaganda continued to spread the lie about vast Jewish power.

On April 29, 1945, Hitler wrote a "Political Testament." The following day he committed suicide by shooting himself in the head. The last days of Hitler soon entered popular imagination as evidence that the dictator had gone mad. Yet the remoteness from reality of his words was not due to a descent into madness that began in the spring of 1945. Rather, his "testament" repeated the core of the conspiracy theory he had first articulated more than six years earlier, on January 30, 1939. It was "not true that I or anyone else in Germany wanted war in 1939. It was desired exclusively by those international statesmen who either were of Jewish origin or worked for Jewish interests." Hatred against the Jews should be renewed, as they were "the people whom we have to thank for everything." The "truly guilty part of this murderous battle is Jewry."[77]

Hitler's testament offered nothing new. Hitler, along with Goebbels and other officials of the Nazi regime, had threatened to murder the Jews of Europe and the world during the entire period of World War II. Hitler first voiced the murderous prophecy on January 30, 1939, eight months before he invaded Poland. The Nazis made similar threats following the invasion of the Soviet Union in June 1941 when victory seemed imminent, and Hitler took the decision to launch or expand the Final Solution. They did so again when the extermination camps began full operation in the spring of 1942, and they intensified their claims of ongoing murder in winter, spring, and summer of 1943 as the tide of war turned against the Third Reich. The paranoid vision flowing from Hitler's pen on April 29, 1945, that of an international Jewish conspiracy waging an aggressive and genocidal war against an innocent Nazi Germany, had been the central element in the text and imagery of the Nazi regime's antisemitic propaganda from the beginning to the end of World War II and the Holocaust.

Notes

Selections taken from Jeffrey Herf, *The Jewish Enemy: Nazi Propaganda During World War II and the Holocaust* (Cambridge, MA: Harvard University Press, Copyright 2006 by the President and Fellows of Harvard College). Used by permission. All rights reserved. Jeffrey Herf, "The 'Jewish War'": Goebbels and the Antisemitic Campaigns of the Nazi Propaganda Ministry," *Holocaust and Genocide Studies* 19, 1 (Spring 2005), 51–80. Reproduced with permission of Oxford University Press [the Licensor] through PLSclear. All rights reserved. "'The War and the Jews': Nazi Propaganda in the Second World War," Jeffrey Herf in Jörg Echternkamp, ed. *Germany and the Second World War: Volume IX/II: German Wartime Society 1939–1945: Exploitation, Interpretations, Exclusion*, 163–204. Copyright 2014. Oxford University Press. Reproduced with permission of Oxford University Press [the Licensor] through PLSclear. All rights reserved.

1 E. H. Gombrich, Myth and *Reality in German War-Time Broadcasts* (London: Athlone, 1970), 18. Also see Jeffrey Herf, *The Jewish Enemy: Nazi Propaganda during World War II and the Holocaust* (Cambridge, MA: Harvard University Press, 2006).

2 Ibid., 22–23.

3 Lucy Dawidowicz, *The War Against the Jews: 1933–1945* (New York: Holt, Rinehart and Winston, 1975).

4 Christopher R. Browning with contributions by Jürgen Matthäus, *The Origins of the Final Solution: The Evolution of Nazi Jewish Policy, September 1939–March 1942* (Lincoln and Jerusalem: University of Nebraska Press and Yad Vashem,

2004); see also Browning's *The Path to Genocide* (New York: Cambridge University Press, 1992); and Richard Breitman, *Architect of Genocide: Himmler and the Final Solution* (New York: Alfred Knopf, 1991).

5 Saul Friedlander, *Nazi Germany and the Jews, vol. 1, The Years of Persecution, 1933–1939* (New York: HarperCollins, 1997); and *Nazi Germany and the Jews, vol. 2, The Years of Extermination* (New York: HarperCollins, 2007).

6 Herf, *The Jewish Enemy*. Also see Jeffrey Herf, "The "Jewish War": Goebbels and the Antisemitic Campaigns of the Nazi Propaganda Ministry," *Holocaust and Genocide Studies* 19, 1 (Spring 2005), 51–80, https://doi.org/10.1093/hgs/dci003; and "'The War and the Jews': Nazi Propaganda in the Second World War," in Jörg Echternkamp, ed., *Germany and the Second World War*, vol IX/2, *German Wartime Society 1939–1945: Exploitation, Interpretations, Exclusion* (Oxford: Oxford University Press, 2014), 163–204. For a work that brought the images of Nazi propaganda to a broader audience, see Susan Bachrach and Steven Luckert, eds., *State of Deception: The Power of Nazi Propaganda* (Washington, DC: United States Holocaust Memorial Museum, 2009).

7 On antisemitism in Nazi propaganda, see Caesar Aronsfeld, "Perish Judah! Extermination Propaganda," *Patterns of Prejudice* 12, 5 (September–October 1978), 17–26; and his *The Text of the Holocaust: A Study of the Nazis' Extermination Propaganda 1919–1945* (Marblehead, MA: Michah Publications, 1985); see also Gombrich, *Myth and Reality in German War-Time Broadcasts*. For scholarship in the postwar decades see Ernest Bramsted, *Goebbels and National Socialist Propaganda, 1925–1945* (East Lansing: Michigan State University, 1965); Jay Baird, *The Mythical World of Nazi War Propaganda, 1939–1945* (Minneapolis: University of Minnesota Press, 1974); Robert Herzstein, *The War that Hitler Won: The Most Infamous Propaganda Campaign in History* (New York: G.P. Putnam's Sons, 1978); Jürgen Hagemann, *Die Presselenkung im Dritten Reich* (Bonn: Bouvier, 1970); as well as Erich Goldhagen, "Obsession and Realpolitik in the Final Solution," *Patterns in Prejudice* 12 (January–February, 1978), 1–16; Derrick Sington and Arthur Weidenfeld, *The Goebbels Experiment: A Study of the Nazi Propaganda Machine* (New Haven, CT: Yale University Press, 1943).

8 Ian Kershaw, *Hitler 1889–1936 Hubris* (New York: W.W. Norton, 1998). On the impact of the propaganda, also see David Bankier, *The Germans and the Final Solution: Public Opinion under Nazism* (Oxford and Cambridge, MA: Blackwell, 1992); Ian Kershaw, *The Hitler Myth* (Oxford: Oxford University Press, 1987); Aristotle A. Kallis, *Nazi Propaganda and the Second World War* (London: Palgrave Macmillan, 2008); and David Welch, *The Third Reich: Politics and Propaganda*, 2nd ed. (London and New York; Routledge, 2002).

9 Robert M. Citino, *The Wehrmacht's Last Stand: The German Campaigns of 1944–1945* (Lawrence: University Press of Kansas, 2017).

10 The Nazi regime's antisemitic propaganda was, as Erich Goldhagen put it, "a complex and singular blend of rational calculation and unreasoning fanaticism"; Goldhagen "Obsession and Realpolitik in the Final Solution," 1. On the simultaneity of ideological and utilitarian motives in the Holocaust, see Ulrich Herbert, "Extermination Policy: New Answers and Questions about the History of the 'Holocaust' in German Historiography," in Herbert, ed. *National Socialist Extermination Policies: Contemporary German Perspectives and Controversies* (New York: Berghahn Books, 2000), 1–54.

11 The most consequential example of that misinterpretation came from Franz Neumann, the Director of the Office of Research and Analysis of the Office of Strategic Services (OSS) in his classic work of 1942 and 1944, *Behemoth: The Structure and Practice of National Socialism* (New York: Oxford University Press, 1944). He wrote that "the internal value of antisemitism will…never allow

a complete extermination of the Jews. The foe cannot and must not disappear; he must always be held in readiness as a scapegoat for all the evils originating in the socio-political system," 125. On the dispute within the OSS between Neumann and Charles Dwork, who took the Nazi threats of genocide more seriously, see Shlomo Aronson, *Hitler, the Allies and the Jews* (New York: Cambridge University Press, 2004). Later, as a professor at Columbia University, Neumann advised Raul Hilberg's doctoral dissertation which, when published as *The Destruction of the European Jews* (Chicago, IL: Quadrangle Books, 1961), became a seminal work on the extermination which Neumann, in 1944, thought the Nazis would not implement.

12 See George Orwell, "Politics and the English Language," in Sonia Orwell and Ian Angus, eds., *George Orwell: The Collected Essays, Journalism and Letters of George Orwell, Volume 4, In Front of Your Nose, 1945–1950* (New York: Harcourt, Brace and Janovich, 1968), 127–140; as well as George Orwell, *1984* (New York: Alfred Knopf, 1949); and Berel Lang, *Act and Idea in the Nazi Genocide* (Chicago, IL: University of Chicago, 1990).

13 Hannah Arendt, *The Origins of Totalitarianism* (Cleveland and New York: Meridian, 1958, 1951), 343.

14 See Caesar Aronsfeld, *The Text of the Holocaust;* and his "Perish Judah! Extermination Propaganda."

15 Max Domarus, ed., *Hitler: Reden und Proklamationen, 1932–1945,* 2 vols. (Neustadt: Schmidt, 1972), 1058.

16 30.1.1941 Adolf Hitler, "Kundgebung im Berliner Sportpalast zum 8. Jahrestag der nationalsozialistische," in Walter Roller and Susanne Höschel, eds., *Judenverfolgung und jüdisches Leben unter den Bedingung der nationalsozialistischen Gewaltherrschaft.* vol. 1, *Tondokumente und Rundfunksendungen, 1930–1946* (Potsdam: Verlag Berlin-Brandenburg, 1996), 165–166.

17 Adolf Hitler, "Ansprache auf einer Kundgebung im Berliner Sportpalast zur Eröffnung des Kriegswinterwerks," in Roller and Höschel, *Judenverfolgung und jüdisches Leben* (September 30, 1942), 216–217.

18 Adolf Hitler, "Ansprache im Münchener Löwenbräukeller anläßlich einer Gedenkfeier zum Marsch auf die Feldherrnhalle 1923," in Roller and Höschel, eds., *Judenverfolgung und jüdisches Leben* (November 11, 1942), 219.

19 Herman Göring, and Robert Ley were among other leaders who contributed to the propaganda assault against the Jews; see Herf, *The Jewish Enemy,* 154–155, and 168–169.

20 Robert Ley, "Ansprache vor deutschen Arbeitern in Lodz," in Roller and Höschel, eds., *Judenverfolgung und jüdisches Leben...* (ende 1939), 158.

21 Robert Ley, Ansprache auf einer gemeinsamen Kundgebung der NSDAP und der NSB in Heerlen, "in Roller and Höschel, *Judenverfolgung und jüdisches Leben* (May 10, 1942), 210.

22 Hermann Göring, "Ansprache auf einer Feier zum Erntedankfest im Berliner Sportpalast," in Roller and Höschel, eds., *Judenverfolgung und jüdisches Leben* (October 4, 1942), 217.

23 See Herf, *The Jewish Enemy,* 26-27, and "Appendix: The Anti-Semitic Campaigns of the Nazi Regime as Reflected in Lead Front-Page Stories in *Der Völkischer Beobachter*," 281–288.

24 For example, see, "Der große Entschluß des Führers: Wie die jüdische-bolschewistische Weltverschwörung vereitelt wurde: Invasion–der Weg zum Ziel Moskaus," *Völkischer Beobachter* (Münchener Ausgabe), June 22, 1944, 1. On the place of the idea of "Jewish-Bolshevism" in Europe see Paul Hannebrink, *A Specter Haunting Europe: The Myth of Judeo-Bolshevism* (Cambridge, MA: Harvard U.P., 2018).

25 Willi A. Boelcke, ed., *Kriegspropaganda, 1939–1941: Geheime Ministerkonferenzen im Reichspropagandaministerium* (Stuttgart: Deutsche Verlags-Anstalt, 1966); and Willi A. Boelcke, ed. *Wollt Ihr den totalen Krieg? Die geheimen Goebbels-Konferenzen, 1939–1945* (Stuttgart: Deutsche Verlags-Anstalt, 1967); also see the English translation, Willi A. Boelcke, ed., *The Secret Conferences of Dr. Goebbels: The Nazi Propaganda War, 1939–1943*, trans. Ewald Osers (New York: E. P. Dutton, 1970).

26 On the daily press conferences see Alexander Hardy, *Hitler's Secret Weapon: The 'Managed' Press and Propaganda Machine of Nazi Germany* (New York: Vintage, 1967); Ralf Reuth, *Goebbels: Eine Biographie* (Munich: Piper, 1995); and Bramsted, *Goebbels and National Socialist Propaganda 1925–1945*.

27 For the Nazi regime's orders to the press see the Sammlung Oberheitmann, "Vertrauliche Informationen" des Reichsministerium für Volksaufklärung und Propaganda für die Presse, Zeitgeschichtliche Sammlung, ZSg 109, July 1939–March 1945, Bundesarchiv Koblenz.

28 From the extensive recent scholarship, see Paul Hannebrink, *A Specter Haunting Europe: The Myth of Judeo-Bolshevism* (Cambridge: Harvard University Press, 2018).

29 "Die Kampfparole," *Zeitschriften Dienst* 195/65, no. 8312 (February 5, 1943). Documents were also used in preparation for the Ministries Trial after the war; See, for example, "Die Kampfparole" (February 5, 1943), *Deutscher Wochendienst* directive 8312, U.S. Nüremberg War Crimes Trials, *United States of America vs. Ernst von Weizäcker et al.,* case 11, November 4, 1947, in United States National Archives, College Park (NACP), RG 238, War Crimes Records Collection, M 897, roll 34, doc. 4714, prosecution exhibit, 1265.

30 "Die Judenfrage als innen- und außenpolitische Kampfmittel," Redner-Schnellinformation, NDSAP. Reichspropagandaleitung, Hauptamt Propaganda Amt: Rednerwesen, May 5, 1943, NACP, Captured German Records, T-81, roll 693, 4721685–4721686.

31 Ibid.

32 "USA und England under dem Befehl des Weltjudentums, Plutokraten identifizieren sich mit den jüdisch-bolschweistische Mördern," *Völkischer Beobachter* (May 6, 1943), 1.

33 Otto Dietrich, *Parole des Tages* (August 13, 1943), cited in Helmut Sündermann, *Tagesparolen: Deutsche Presseanweisungen 1939–1945: Hitler's Propaganda und Kriegführung* (Leoni Am Starnberger See: Druffel-Verlag, 1973), 255–256.

34 Joseph Goebbels, "Die Juden sind Schuld!" 16 November 1941, in Joseph Goebbels, ed., *Das Eherne Herz: Reden und Aufsätze aus den Jahren 1941/42* (Munich: Zentralverlag der NSDAP, 1943), 85–91; Joseph Goebbels, *Das Eherne Herz: Rede vor der Deutschen Akademie* (Munich: Zentralverlag der NSDAP, 1942); Joseph Goebbels, "Nr. 17. 18.2.43—Berlin, Sportpalast—Kundgebung des Gaues Berlin der NSDAP," 172–208; "Der Krieg und die Juden," 9. Mai. 1943, 263–270, in Joseph Goebbels, *Reden, 1939–1945*, Band 2 (Munich: Wilhelm Heyne Verlag, 1972); Joseph Goebbels, *Der Steile Aufstieg: Reden und Aufsätze aus den Jahren 1942/43* (Munich: Zentralverlag der NSDAP, Franz Eher, 1944); Joseph Goebbels, "Nr. 30, 28.2.45–Rundfunkansprache" in Helmut Heiber, ed. *Goebbels Reden Band 2*, 429–446.

35 On Roosevelt's perceptions of Nazi Germany's threat to the United States, see Richard Breitman and Allan J. Lichtman, *FDR and the Jews* (Cambridge, MA: Harvard University Press, 2014); Robert Dallek, *Franklin Delano Roosevelt and American Foreign Relations, 1932–1945* (New York: Oxford University Press, 1979); Saul Friedlander, *Prelude to Downfall: Hitler and the United States: 1939–1941* (New York: Knopf, 1967); Warren F. Kimball, *Forged in War: Roosevelt,*

Churchill and The Second World War (New York: William and Morrow, 1997); and Warren F. Kimball, ed., *Churchill and Roosevelt: The Complete Correspondence I: Alliance Emerging* (Princeton, NJ: Princeton University Press, 1984).

36 This mixture of antisemitism and anti-Americanism is evident in the flood of pamphlets and books published by the Nazis. See Hans Diebow, *Die Juden in den USA* (Berlin: Zentralverlag der NSDAP, 1941); Theodor Siebert, *Das amerikanische Rätsel: Die Kriegspolitik der USA in der Ära Roosevelt* (Berlin: Zentralverlag der NSDAP, 1941); Johann von Leers, *Kräfte hinter Roosevelt* (Berlin: Theodor Fritsch Verlag, 1941); Hans Schadewalt, *Was Will Roosevelt?* (Dusseldorf: Völkischer Verlag, 1941); P. Osthold and R. Wagenführ, *Roosevelt zwischen Spekulation und Wirklichkeit* (Berlin: Verlag E.S. Mittler & Son, 1943). For analysis of these and related texts, see Phillip Grassert, *Amerika im Dritten Reich: Ideologie, Propaganda und Volksmeinung, 1933–1945* (Stuttgart: Franz Steiner Verlag, 1997). On Hitler's views on the threat of the United States to Germany, see Adam Tooze, *The Wages of Destruction: The Making and Breaking of the Nazi Economy* (New York: Penguin, 2006); and Gerhard Weinberg, *Germany, Hitler and World War II: Essays in Modern German and World History* (New York: Cambridge University Press, 1995).

37 Joseph Goebbels, "Was Will eigentlich Amerika," in *Die Zeit ohne Beispiel: Reden und Aufsätze aus den Jahren 1941–42* (Munich: Zentralverlag der NSDAP, 1943), 24. On Goebbels's assertion that the United States caused World War II, see his "*Wer will den Krieg,*" April 1, 1939, in *Die Zeit ohne Beispiel*, 90–96.

38 Ibid., 26–27.

39 On the concerns of American government officials that World War II would be interpreted within the United States as a war to save the Jews and thus undermine public support for the war effort, see Peter Novick, *The Holocaust in American Life* (Boston, MA: Houghton-Mifflin, 1999); and Saul Friedlander, *Prelude to Downfall*.

40 Four surveys conducted by the Opinion Research Corporation from 1939 to 1941 found that about a third of the American population answered "yes" when asked whether "the Jews in this country would like to get the United States into the European war." On the extent of antisemitism in the United States in the 1930s and 1940s, and its increase during the war, see Charles Herbert Stember et al., *Jews in the Mind of America* (New York: Basic Books, 1966).

41 On what the United States and Britain did and did not do to save the Jews of Europe, see, most recently, Richard Breitman and Allan J. Lichtman, *FDR and the Jews* (Cambridge, MA: Harvard University Press, 2014); *The United States and the Holocaust* (United States Holocaust Memorial Museum: 2022): https://encyclopedia.ushmm.org/content/en/article/the-united-states-and-the-holocaust; and Bernard Wasserstein, *Britain and the Jews of Europe, 1939–1945*, 2nd ed. (London and New York: Leicester University Press, 1999).

42 Joseph Goebbels, "*Wer will den Krieg,*" April 1, 1939, in *Die Zeit ohne Beispiel*, 90–96.

43 Ibid., 94.

44 Joseph Goebbels, "Im Gelächter der Welt," (16. February 1941) in Goebbels, *Die Zeit ohne Beispiel*, 394–395. See, for example, Wolf Meyer-Christian, *Die englisch-jüdische Allianz: Werden und Wirken der kapitalistischen Weltherrschaft*, 3rd ed. (Berlin Leipzig: Nibelungen-Verlag, 1942).

45 Joseph Goebbels, "*Britannia Rules the Waves,*" March 30, 1941, in Goebbels, *Die Zeit ohne Beispiel*, 441–445.

46 Churchill, *The Second World War*, vol. 3, The Grand Alliance, 371–373.

47 Joseph Goebbels, "Die alte Front," 26. Juni 1941, in Goebbels, *Die Zeit ohne Beispiel*, 508–513.

48 Ibid., 512–513. The Nazis offered a visual depiction of the antisemitic dimensions of the Soviet-British alliance in "Jewish Conspiracy against Europe" (*Juden Komplott gegen Europa*), a poster of summer 1941 (Reich Ministry for Propaganda and Public Enlightenment, Imperial War Museum, London, PST, 8395). A disembodied and caricatured Jewish head peers over a handshake between figures representing Britain and the Soviet Union. The handshake looms over a map of Europe. See *"Juden Komplott gegen Europa"* and other antisemitic images of Nazi propaganda in Herf, *The Jewish Enemy.*

49 Joseph Goebbels, "Mimikry," July 20, 1941, in *Die Zeit ohne Beispiel.* 527–528.

50 Ibid., 530-531. Cited in Herf, *The Jewish Enemy,* 109-110.

51 See entries for August 19 and September 24, 1941, in Elke Fröhlich, ed., Joseph Goebbels, *Die Tagebücher von Joseph Goebbels, Teil II, Diktate 1941–1945, Band I, Juli-September 1941,* 268 and 480–481.

52 Richard Breitman, *Architect of Genocide: Himmler and the Final Solution* (New York: Alfred Knopf, 1991), argues that the crucial decisions had been taken by spring 1941, while Christopher Browning, in *The Origins of the Final Solution* (Lincoln: University of Nebraska Press; Jerusalem, Yad Vashem, 2004), concluded that a two-stage set of decisions leading to a continent-wide genocide was completed by early fall 1941.

53 Joseph Goebbels, "Die Juden Sind Schuld!" 16 November 1941, in Goebbels, *Das Eherne Herz,* 85–91.

54 Also see discussion in Herf, *The Jewish Enemy,* 120–126.

55 Goebbels, "Die Juden sind Schuld!", 88.

56 Ibid., 91.

57 Joseph Goebbels, *Das Eherne Herz*, "Rede vor der Deutschen Akademie," 23. On Goebbels' pleasure with the reception of the speech, see the diary entries for December 2 and 3, 1941 Joseph Goebbels, "December 3, 1941," Elke Fröhlich, ed., *Die Tagebücher von Joseph Goebbels, Teil II, Diktate 1941–1945, Band 2, Oktober-Dezember 1941 (Munich: K.G. Saur, 1996),* 416 and 420. The German reads as follows: *"erste Aufgabe darin bestanden hätte, die nationale Intelligenz und die geistige Führung der Nation auszurotten...."*

58 Ibid., 25.

59 Ibid., 34–35.

60 Ibid.

61 Ibid., 35–36.

62 Ibid., 37.

63 Ibid., 41.

64 Elke Fröhlich, ed., Joseph Goebbels, "2.12.1941," (December 2, 1941) *Die Tagebücher von Joseph Goebbels: Teil II, Diktate 1941–1945,* Band 2 (Oktober-Dezember 1941), 417.

65 See Ian Kershaw, *Hitler 1936–1945: Nemesis* (New York: Norton, 2000), 448–449.

66 Elke Fröhlich, ed., Joseph Goebbels, "13.12.1941" (December 13, 1941) *Die Tagebücher von Joseph Goebbels: Teil II, Diktate 1941–1945,* Band 2 (Oktober-Dezember 1941), 498–499. On this see Christian Gerlach, "Die Wannsee Konferenz, das Schicksal der Deutschen Juden und Hitlers Politische Grundsatzentscheidung, Alle Juden Europas zu Ermordern," *Werkstatt Geschichte* 18 (1997), 7–44; and his, "The Wannsee Conference, the Fate of German Jews and Hitler's Decision in Principle to Exterminate All European Jews," *Journal of Modern History* 70 (1998), 759–812.

67 Der Krieg und die Juden," 9 Mai. 1943, in, Joseph Goebbels, *Der Steile Aufstieg,* 263–270.

68 Ibid., 263–264.

69 Ibid., 264.
70 Ibid., 269–270.
71 Ibid., 270.
72 Joseph Goebbels, "Nr. 30, 28.2.45–Rundfunkansprache," in Helmut Heiber, ed. *Goebbels Reden* Band 2, 429–446.
73 Ibid., 433.
74 On disillusionment and deradicalization in popular and elite opinion, see Martin Broszat, Klaus Dietmar Henke and Hans Woller, eds., *Von Stalingrad zur Währungsreform: Sozialgeschichte des Umbruch in Deutschland* (Munich: R. Oldenbourg, 1988); Kallis, *Nazi Propaganda and the Second World War*; and his "The Decline of Interpretive Power: National Socialist Propaganda during the War," in Jörg Echternkamp, ed., *Germany and the Second World War: German Wartime Society 1939–1945, Exploitation, Interpretations, Exclusion* (Oxford: Oxford University Press, 2014), 205–252; Klaus Dietmar Henke, "Die Trennung vom Nationalsozialismus: Selbstzerstörung, politische Säuberung, 'Entnazifizierung,' Strafverfolgung," in Hans Woller, ed., *Politische Säuberung in Europa* (Munich: Deutscher Taschenbuch Verlag, 1991), 21–83; and Kershaw, *Hitler, 1936–1945: Nemesis*, chaps. 12–17; and Jerry Z. Muller, *The Other God that Failed: Hans Freyer and the Deradicalization of German Conservatism* (Princeton, NJ: Princeton University Press, 1987).
75 Citino, Wehrmacht's Last Stand.
76 Victor Klemperer, (July 20, 1944) *I Will Bear Witness, 1942–1945*, trans. Martin Chalmers (New York: Knopf, 2000), 335; and Victor Klemperer, *Tagebücher 1944* (20. Juli 1944) (Berlin: Aufbau Verlag, 1995), 85.
77 Max Domarus, ed., *Hitler: Reden und Proklamationen, 1932–1945*, vol. 2, 2236. Also see Herf, *The Jewish Enemy*, 261–263; Ian Kershaw, *Hitler: Nemesis 1936–1945* (New York: Norton, 2001).

3
NAZI ANTI-ZIONISM

In 1975, the United Nations (UN) General Assembly passed a resolution that denounced Zionism as a form of racism. Though the UN rescinded the resolution in 1991, the association of anti-Zionism with leftist sympathies has persisted in politics, journalism, and in the universities. Forgotten or, for many, never known, is Nazi Germany's unrelenting opposition to the Zionist project. Antagonism to Zionism was a continuing theme of Nazism from the publication of Hitler's *Mein Kampf* in 1924 to the last days of the Nazi regime in 1945. Hitler's enemies noticed. During crucial years when the state of Israel was established, leftists and liberals in the United States and Western Europe as well as East European Communists were well aware of the close connection between Nazism, fascism, and anti-Zionism and support for establishing the Jewish state in Palestine became a defining feature of their politics in those years.[1]

In recent decades, historians have offered abundant evidence of the Nazis' intense and persistent hatred of Zionist aspirations, both in the form of hostile propaganda, and in the course of a failed effort to extend the Final Solution of the Jewish Question in Europe outward to the Jews of North Africa, Palestine, and the Middle East during World War II.[2] Aware that the term "antisemitism" was raising concerns among Arab, Turkish, and Iranian diplomats that the Nazis were hostile to them as "semites," Nazi officials in preparing for the Berlin Olympics in 1936 clarified the identity of their government's policies toward the Jews. They asserted that the regime's policy was not one of "antisemitism." Rather, it was better defined as antagonism to Jews (*Judengegnershaft*).[3] That ideological clarification demonstrated the convergence of Nazi antagonism to Judaism and the Jews with opposition to the Zionist project as well as support for Arabs who opposed it.

DOI: 10.4324/9781003449669-4

In *Mein Kampf*, Hitler had expressed racist disdain for Arabs (something conveniently left out of Nazi Arabic translations of the work) and denounced the "lie" that Zionism was primarily a movement focused only on a homeland for the Jews in Palestine.

> For while the Zionists try to make the rest of the world believe that the national consciousness of the Jew finds its satisfaction in the creation of a Palestinian state, the Jews again slyly dupe the dumb *Goyim*. It doesn't even enter their heads to build up a Jewish state in Palestine for the purpose of living there; all they want is a central organization for their international world swindle, endowed with its sovereign right and removed from the intervention of other states: a haven for convicted scoundrels and a university for budding crooks.[4]

Alfred Rosenberg, a leading ideologist of the Nazi Party in the 1920s, exerted a significant impact on Hitler's and Nazism's views about Zionism.[5] In 1921, he published *Der Staatsfeindliche Zionismus* (Zionism Hostile to the State), a text that the Nazi Party reissued in 1938.[6] Rosenberg was influential and close to Hitler. He joined the Nazi Party in 1919, participated in the Beer Hall Putsch of 1923, and became editor of the party paper the *Völkischer Beobachter (VB)* the same year. From 1933 to 1945, he was the head of the Party's "Office of Foreign Affairs," the *Amt Rosenberg* (Rosenberg Office), handling "cultural policy" and "surveillance." In July 1941, Hitler appointed him Reich Minister for the Occupied Eastern Territories, where played a significant role in the Holocaust. A defendant in the Nuremberg trials, he was convicted of crimes against peace, planning, and waging a war of aggression, war crimes, and crimes against humanity, sentenced to death, and executed in 1946. Rosenberg's prominence before and after 1933 contributed to making *Staatsfeindliche Zionism* an agenda-setting text on anti-Zionism.

Rosenberg favored Zionist efforts as a means of removing Jews from Germany but worried that their gathering in Palestine could evolve into a "Jewish Vatican" that would become part of an international Jewish conspiracy.[7] With centuries of Jewish statelessness in mind, he was skeptical that the Jews were capable of forming a state at all. If the British empire crumbled, "the Jews would turn to a new patron," namely the United States, where, he claimed, the 3.5 million living there had control over the press, film, government, and business.[8] Yet Rosenberg was convinced that Zionism would fail because it represented "the powerless effort of an incapable people to engage in productive activity."[9] This contradictory and incoherent mixture of contempt for Jewish political ability with fear of potential Jewish power in Palestine remained an enduring feature of Nazi Germany's ideology and policy towards Zionism and the Zionist project.

Under the terms of the Haavarah (Transfer) Agreement concluded in 1933 between the German Ministry of the Economy and Zionist representatives, the Nazi regime allowed Jews to emigrate to Palestine with a small part of their assets. As a result, between 1933 and 1939, about one hundred million marks were transferred to Palestine and most of the 60,000 Jews who arrived there had some economic resources.[10] By 1937, Nazi officials in Palestine were well aware of Arab resistance to the influx. As Lukasz Hirszowicz put it in his 1966 classic study, *The Third Reich and the Arab East*, the "Palestine question was as if made to order for the needs and aims of Nazi Propaganda."[11] Persecution of the Jews in Germany stimulated German Jewish immigration to Palestine, while Nazi anti-Jewish propaganda coincided with the assertions of Arab nationalists that there was a "British-Jewish conspiracy to take over Palestine from its inhabitants." Nazi policy, Hirszowicz wrote, reflected "two tendencies of Nazi antisemitism…. One was the tendency to drive the Jews out of Germany."[12] The other was to exacerbate already existing antisemitism outside Germany as well. Neither had anything to do with seeking to establish Jewish sovereignty in Palestine.

The Nazi-controlled press opposed Zionism and offered support to its Arab opponents. Before and during World War II, the Nazi Propaganda Ministry controlled the press through secret daily and weekly directives sent to several thousand newspaper and magazine editors. They originated in the Reich Press Office directed by Otto Dietrich with occasional input from the Propaganda Minister, Joseph Goebbels. On June 13, 1939, the Press Office, reflecting the above-mentioned ideological clarifications of 1936, instructed editors not to use the term "antisemitism" because doing so undermined efforts to establish friendly relations with the Arab world. Instead, the appropriate terms to describe Nazi policy were "defense against the Jews" or "hostility to the Jews' *(Judengegnerschaft)*.[13] In 1944, Dietrich's staff again voiced concern that the term "antisemitism" was appearing with great frequency in the German press. This was to be avoided because its appearance there "could destroy our relationships with non-Jewish Semites, namely the pan-Arab world that is so important for us." Therefore, the Press Office ordered newspapers and magazines to replace the words "antisemitism," and "antisemitic" with expressions such as "opposition to Jews," "hostility to Jews," "anti-Judaism" and "antagonistic to Jews" or "anti-Jewish."[14] In 1936, the Nazi regime sought to reassure Arabs that Jews, not Arabs, were the intended targets of Nazi racism.

The Turning Point of 1937

In March 1937, Walter Doehle, the German Counsel General in Jerusalem, began the effort in the German Foreign Office to turn Nazi anti-Zionism from an ideological postulate into practical policy, and thus one that would oppose any Jewish emigration to Palestine facilitated by the Transfer Agreement.[15] In so doing, he drew out the logical implications of Nazism's ideological opposition to the Zionist project. In a March 22, 1937 memo to the Foreign Office in Berlin, he wrote that German policy since 1933 risked turning the Arabs into adversaries "as a result of our assistance to the construction of a Jewish national home and Jewish economy."[16] A Jewish-dominated Palestine would be a competitor to German industry, he argued, whereas an Arab-dominated Palestine would become "one of the few in which we could count on strong sympathy for the new Nazi Germany" and on export markets for German goods. The German Jews in Palestine would adapt to the anti-German mentality of their "Polish racial comrades." Conversely "among Palestinian Arabs sympathy for the new Germany and its Führer is widespread" because they saw themselves as "in a common front with the Germans" against the Jews. He urged that German policy should encourage "the existing Arab sympathy for the new Germany and its Führer" by "moving closer to Arab wishes."[17]

Several months later, Doehle's recommendations received support in the Foreign Office in Berlin. In June 1937, Foreign Minister Konstantin von Neurath sent guidelines to the German Embassies in London, Cairo, and Jerusalem which stressed that the creation of a Jewish state was "not in the German interest.... It would create an additional power for international Jewry, one recognized by international law as the Vatican State does for political Catholicism or Moscow for the Comintern."[18] A memo of June 22, 1937 by Vicco Bülow-Schwante, chief of protocol in von Neurath's office, offered further evidence of the convergence of anti-Jewish and anti-Zionist components of Nazi policy.[19] He sent it to every German embassy and many German general consulates including those in Beirut and Jerusalem. With the aid of "the Jewish friendly press abroad," he wrote, "World Jewry" had "banged the drum" for the formation of a Jewish state in Palestine. The Transfer Agreement led to the consolidation of Jewry in Palestine" and could foster the view that Nazi Germany favored the Zionist ambitions. Bülow-Schwante's memo made clear that was not the case: "In reality, however, the greater German interest lies in preserving Jewry's division and splintering." Germany's Jewish question would "not be solved when there are no more members of the Jewish race left on German soil." In fact, "international Jewry will always be the ideological and thus political adversary of National Socialist Germany. The Jewish question is thus one of the most important problems of German foreign policy." Just as the Vatican was a power base for Catholics, so a Jewish state in Palestine would "create an additional power basis" for Jews "which could have a fateful impact on German foreign policy."[20]

A month later, Ernst von Weizäcker, the State Secretary in the Foreign Office, told Doehle in Jerusalem that Germany should try to prevent the establishment of a Jewish state by "direct and indirect support of movements working against a Jewish state," including "direct support for the Arabs with weapons and money whether in Palestine itself or via other Arab countries such as Iraq."[21] By 1938, the Nazi regime's policy was shifting from initial reservations due to hopes of a German alliance or rapprochement with Britain to willingness to deliver weapons to the Palestine Arabs during the revolt of 1936–1939. Official contacts by German officials, including those in Adolf Eichmann's Jewish Affairs Department, with Haj Amin al-Husseini, the Mufti of Jerusalem, had begun at the latest by 1937.[22] In June 1939, Admiral Wilhelm Canaris, head of one of the Nazi regime's intelligence agencies, the *Abwehr*, which reported directly to the Supreme Command of the Army, wrote that "the Grand Mufti had his representative communicate to me his sincere thanks for the support provided thus far. It was only through the funds provided by us that he was able to carry out the revolt in Palestine."[23]

Klaus Michael Mallmann and Martin Cüppers conclude that "it is certain that German weapons were used in the Arab revolt in Palestine," and that in 1938 it was also "certain" that Canaris and Major Helmut Groscurth, head of the Abwehr's II office, "met with the Mufti in Baghdad and remained in friendly contact afterward."[24] As Matthias Küntzel points out in his 2019 study of Nazi policy in the Middle East, Husseini, especially in a text of 1937 on "Islam and the Jews" delivered at a conference in Bludan, Syria, gave the Nazis compelling evidence that his sympathies for the Third Reich rested on a rejection to Zionist ambitions that were deeply grounded in his interpretation of Islam. In Husseini, German ideology and policy found a willing counterpart to what Küntzel calls the "turning point of 1937."[25] The Nazis and Husseini and his followers met on the common ideological terrain of Jew-hatred and the anti-Zionism.[26] As Mallmann and Cüppers put it, the events of 1937–1938 displayed "a process of steadily growing consensus and a shared enmity [to the Jews and Zionists] that would lead to solidarity in the event of war."[27]

Anti-Zionist Texts from Nazi "Research" Institutes

After the turn of 1937, Nazi propagandists and antisemitic writers based in Nazi "research" institutions published books that combined antisemitism and anti-Zionism. A Propaganda Ministry directive in the Magazine Service of August 26, 1939, brought to editors' attention Heinrich Hest's *Palästina–Judenstaat?–Weltjuda ohne Maske* [Palestine: Jewish State? World Jewry Without a Mask] and strongly urged them to review it favorably. Hest was a pseudonym for Herman Erich Seifert, the author of several essays published by the NSDAP including *Der Aufbruch in der Arabischen Welt* [Revolt in the Arab World] in 1941.[28] The magazine service praised the "excellent mastery" of material which allowed Hest to "clearly analyze the striving for a new, perhaps decisive base for Jewish world power" in Israel, accomplished with the use of terror against the Arab population. Hest offered new material about the "community of interests between England and Jewry."[29] In a related book, *Palästina: Judenstaat? England als Handlanger des Weltjudentums* [Palestine: Jewish State? England as the Agent of World Jewry], Hest asserted that "English colonial policy" had become a "tool of world Jewry," and the Arabs had responded with a "heroic war of defense."[30] Nazi Germany, then waging a war of colonial conquest in Eastern Europe, was thus, in Hest's view, an opponent of a colonialism associated with England and the Jews.[31]

Hest's books offered emphatic support for Arab opposition to Jewish migration. He favorably cited Husseini's opposition to a Jewish state, asserted that English policy was dominated by the Jews, and rejected any possible compromise between Palestine Arabs and Zionists.[32] England tolerated Jewish emigration to Palestine because the Jews would be "the best guarantee against a successful Arab freedom struggle" and because England was

> now under the pressure of the financial power of world Jewry and had long ago ceased to be free in its decisions. As a result of its policy in Palestine, it had become an instrument of world Jewry, the previously proud Albion![33]

On March 28, 1941, Rosenberg, then the publisher of the regime's official newspaper, the *VB*, spoke at the Institute for Research on the Jewish Question *(Institut zur Erforschung der Judenfrage)* in Frankfurt/Main, in a conference to mark the opening of this government-financed antisemitic think tank, which he directed. The speech was broadcast on national radio and published the following day on the front page of the *VB*.[34] He presented the Zionist project as an "encirclement policy of Jewish-British high-finance" that had emerged in World War I. "The Jewish world press" and "British-Jewish high-finance" from the Rothschild house had worked together with "[J.P] Morgan" and a group of Jews around Woodrow Wilson led by Bernard Baruch, who "controlled all of industry in the United States," to support the Allies during that war. He presented support for Zionism in Britain and the United States as evidence of extensive Jewish political power, adding that fortunately, the Nazi regime and its Nuremberg race laws completed the destruction of "Jewish rule in Germany" and thus prevented a repetition of Germany's defeat in 1918.[35] The "solution" to "the Jewish question" was a "Jewish reservation," presumably in Europe under police observation, but not in Palestine.[36]

In 1941, the Nazi Party also published Seifert's *Der Aufbruch in der Arabischen Welt* [Revolt in the Arab World], in which he claimed that Nazi Germany and Fascist Italy were partisans for the Arabs in their struggle against British and French colonialism.[37] Mohammed and Islam were inherently antagonistic to the Jews. It was no accident that the Arab-Jewish conflict was sharpest where the Arabs "are dominated by the democratic, liberal states where the Jews are the unchecked beneficiaries of the plutocracies to which they closely linked."[38] While Seifert insisted that there were no racial affinities between Arabs and Jews, he claimed to observe an

> inner bond between Jews and the French since the beginning of the conquest of Algeria...because France's victory did not only rest on its weapons but even more on the secret but therefore all the more effective support of its campaign from the Jews.[39]

Yet as serious as France's "guilt" was for supporting "exploitation of the Arabs by the Jews," England's guilt was far greater, for it had broken promises to the Arabs, imposed its rule with violence and "unleashed world Jewry" on the Palestinian Arabs. "The last mask fell" in England's policy toward the Palestinians when the war in Europe began and Chaim Weizmann wrote to Neville Chamberlain that the Jews in Britain "stand and fight on the side of the democracies" and Chamberlain replied to affirm shared goals. For Seifert, Weizmann's statement was evidence of "the clear bond between the English government and Zionists."[40] The Arabs, however, were prepared "for a decisive struggle for freedom" and had learned that "English order is nothing but slavery. The Arabs want to be free!"[41]

Giselher Wirsing was another Nazi propagandist who examined Zionism through the lens of Nazi ideology. He did so on the eve of World War II in his 1939 work *Engländer, Juden, Araber in Palästina* [The English, Jews, and Arabs in Palestine].[42] Wirsing wrote that the Zionist goal in Palestine was the "establishment of a Vatican of world Jewry. A firm base is to be built on which in later years Jewish world policy can rest." Prevention of formation of Jewish state in Palestine was, from the Nazi perspective, an act of national security against a spreading international foe.

Throughout the war, Nazi propaganda associated Britain with the Jews in a persistently pejorative manner. Britain's declaration of strict limits on Jewish emigration to Palestine in the White Paper of 1938 and its insistence on those limits during World War II did not deter the Nazis from insisting on the close link between Britain, the Jews, and Zionism.[43] Along these lines, on November 8, 1940, the Press Office Magazine Service directed "all magazines that reviewed political books" to review Wolf Meyer-Christian's *Die englisch-jüdische Allianz* (The English-Jewish Alliance). By 1942, the book had sold 20,000 copies. The officials wrote that "the book shows the wide-ranging identification between the English and the Jews and presents the essential presuppositions for understanding the deeper reasons for the current war, one that is simultaneously an English and a Jewish war." It offered an "intellectual framework for the definitive confrontation with the English-Jewish world power."[44] The Jewish question in Europe and in Germany would only be solved if it is first solved in England, that is "if the alliance between the traditional English upper class and the leadership of world Jewry is broken once and for all. For this alliance is Europe's deadly enemy."[45] The "degeneration of the English upper stratum" culminating in Churchill's government was not the result of "accidental bonds of love." Rather it was due to a carefully planned effort by the Jews who "made the British aristocracy a fifth column of world Jewry."[46] Hence, he concluded, it was no surprise that London had become the center of Zionism.

Meyer-Christian wrote that there were no common interests between those who wished for a Europe free of Jews and Zionism. National Socialism, he noted, had opposed the creation of a Jewish state precisely because it would be "nothing other than an international power center over non-Jewish peoples, a state whose citizens did not live within its borders but rather were all over the world."[47] A Jewish state would be "only a key base for world Jewry," which would enjoy citizenship in this state without giving up citizenship rights in their states in Europe and the United States. Most of the Jews would remain in other states and would "in cooperation with the false state help strengthen the power of Jewry as a world power."[48] Meyer-Christian concluded that by opposing Zionism, Germany offered the Arabs a "common enemy of the English-Jewish alliance."[49]

The Nazi regime also made explicit appeals to followers of what it understood the religion of Islam to be.[50] A directive from the Magazine Service of September 11, 1942, urged a more sympathetic understanding for "the Islamic world as a cultural factor." The editors must

> strengthen and deepen existing [Nazi, JH] sympathies in the Islamic world. We must draw this great cultural power, which in its essence is sharply anti-Bolshevik and anti-Jewish, closer to us. Through friendly, but not obsequious, presentation, we must convince the Muslims of the world that they have no better friend than the Germans. In the treatment of this theme, the words semitism and antisemitism must be avoided.[51]

Nazi propaganda sought to convince Muslims that it supported their specifically religiously based opposition to the Zionist project.

Those appeals were evident in Nazi Germany's short-wave Arabic-language radio broadcasts. During World War II, American officials in Cairo, under the direction of Ambassador Alexander Kirk from 1941 to 1944, and then Ambassador Pinckney Tuck, closely monitored these programs and produced several thousand verbatim English translations in a weekly series of reports to the State Department in Washington. The reports were entitled "Axis Broadcasts in Arabic."[52] In September 1941, Anne H. Fuller in the Overseas Branch of the United States Office of War Information in Washington summarized the themes of Nazi propaganda in these broadcasts. She found that anti-Zionism was a central component. "Interwoven into every program is the 'Jewish menace.' The Zionist question provides the basic theme." Nazi radio claimed that the Allies had promised Syria, Transjordan, and Iraq to the Zionists. For American policy, she wrote, "the Zionist problem" presented "the most difficulties in broadcasting to the Arab world."[53] German broadcasts had denounced Britain and the Balfour Declaration. In a memo on "Anti-American Propaganda in the Near East," she stated that "for the most part, this propaganda is based on American support for Zionism...."[54] The pejorative association of the United States and Britain with the Jews and Zionism remained a continuing theme of Nazi Arabic language broadcasts.

Nazi Anti-Zionism, Holocaust Policy in the Middle East, and American Responses

On November 28, 1941, Hitler met with Haj Amin el-Husseini in Berlin, thereby demonstrating publicly the convergence of Nazi anti-Jewish policy in Europe with its opposition to the Zionist project in Palestine.[55] Hitler assured Husseini that if the Germans defeated the armies of the Soviet Union on Germany's Eastern Front, they would move south from the Caucuses. "Germany's objective would then be solely the destruction of the Jewish element residing in the Arab sphere under the protection of British power."[56] In other words, he told Husseini that he intended to extend the Final Solution of the Jewish Question in Europe, which he had begun in the summer and early fall of 1941, to encompass the murder of the Jews of North Africa and the Middle East. The decision to extend the Holocaust beyond Europe was, in his mind, the logical implication of the idea that *international Jewry* was waging war against Nazi Germany.

In *Nazi Palestine*, first published in German in 2005, Mallmann and Cüppers revealed that Hitler's promise to Husseini was not an empty one. Himmler created an SS *Einsatzgruppe* under the leadership of Walter Rauff, known for his role in developing gas vans on the Eastern Front as mobile killing instruments.[57] Its purpose, in the event of German military victory in North Africa, was to extend the Holocaust to the approximately one million Jews of North Africa and the Middle East with mass shootings comparable to what the *Einsatzgruppen* had done in Eastern Europe and the occupied Soviet Union from June 1941 into spring 1942.[58] In coordination with those decisions, Nazi propaganda in the spring and early summer of 1942 denounced a supposed connection between the Allies and the Jews and praised General Rommel's victories in North Africa as heralding an era of Arab liberation from Britain. In a broadcast of July 7, 1942, with expectations high that Rommel's army would occupy Cairo, the Berlin-based Voice of Free Arabism urged Egyptians "to rise as one man kill the Jews before they kill you....The Jews aim at extending their domination throughout the Arab countries, but their future depends on a British victory."[59] In Germany, Nazi propagandists assured listeners that the Nazi regime was "exterminating" the Jews. The Arabic-language propaganda went even further in urging its listeners to participate in killing the Jews themselves.

The response of the United States Office of War Information (OWI) to this blend of anti-Jewish policy and anti-Zionism, presented in a "Weekly Propaganda Directive" of November 14, 1942, was not to fight against it. Instead, the Voice of America Arabic-language broadcasts

> must speak to the people of Palestine with greater tact and caution than elsewhere in the Middle East. Spoken and written words must alike be guided by an honest acceptance of the fact that the subject of Zionist aspirations cannot be mentioned, inasmuch as any serious outbreak of anti-Jewish feeling which might result among the Arab peoples in this area would jeopardize our strategy in the Eastern Mediterranean.[60]

The OWI officials returned to the issue in a "Basic Directive" of January 30, 1943, regarding propaganda aimed at Egypt. American political messaging was

> avoid all discussion, for the present, of those fundamental political problems which have so inflamed the Middle East in recent years. Specifically, these are three: Zionism, Pan-Arabism, and Pan-Islamism. Never take sides in these matters but preserve absolute detachment as tacit evidence that we favor a policy of 'Egypt for the Egyptians.'[61]

The OWI decision for reticence did not slow Nazi accusations that Franklin Roosevelt and American policy was dominated by Jews and Zionists.[62]

"The Jews Kindled This War in the Interest of Zionism": Nazism's Arabic Propaganda in Summer 1942

When Roosevelt sent American tanks to aid the British and ordered Operation Torch, the invasion of Northwest Africa in November 1942, Nazi propaganda attributed his decisions to the influence of American Jews. On November 16, Berlin asserted in Arabic that the Jews aimed to "encircle the Arabs.... All the Arabs should know that the victory of the Allies means the victory of the Jews."[63] On November 21, the Voice of Free Arabism claimed that "hatred of Islam and of the Arabs is the main reason for the desire of the Jews to have Palestine for their own." The Jews wished "to wipe out Arabs and Islam."[64] Unable to do so on their own, they became the allies of Britain, and then the United States. German propaganda presented Zionism as the most recent chapter in a supposed ancient Jewish animus against Islam, one that was now said to be shared by Britain and the United States, and as confirming evidence of the power of the Jews over American and British policy.

On November 3, 1943, the Voice of Free Arabism connected anti-Zionism to the Nazis' core antisemitic conspiracy theory of World War II, and this led to a call to exterminate Jews. "The Jews," it declared, especially in Britain, the United States, and the Soviet Union,

> kindled this war in the interests of Zionism.... The world will never be at peace until the Jewish race is exterminated. Otherwise, wars will always exist. The Jews are the germs which have caused all the trouble in the world.[65]

This was fantasy; in reality, the conflict over Palestine was but a small chapter in the global history of World War II. Zionists exerted no influence at all on the policies of the anti-Hitler coalition, but this fact did not stop Nazi propagandists to the Arab world from asserting that the Zionist aspiration for a Jewish state in Palestine was the cause of the entire conflict. The broadcast appeal for mass murder was one result.

On July 2, 1942, Husseini, speaking to listeners in Egypt, extolled Rommel's victories in North Africa and connected the Egyptian struggle against British imperialism with the struggle of the Palestinians against the "concentrated British power and its alliance with the Jews."[66] On December 11, 1942, he spoke in Arabic over German radio about martyrdom.[67] The Arab peoples had shed "noble blood" for the freedom and independence of Palestine, Egypt, Syria, Iraq, and the Arabian peninsula. "The spilled blood of martyrs is the water of life. It has revived Arab heroism, as water revives dry ground. The martyr's death is the protective tree in whose shadows marvelous plants again bloom."[68] The goal of "English-Jewish policy" was to divide Palestine and then to dominate the remainder of the Arab countries. "We Arabs," Husseini continued, who have fought the English,

> clearly should join the Axis powers and their Allies in common struggle against the common enemy. Doing so for us means the continuation of the fight we have fought alone for the past twenty years. Today the powerful enemies of our enemies stand on our side.[69]

If England and her allies, "God, forbid," were to win the war, "Israel would rule the whole world, the Arabian fatherland would suffer an unholy blow and the Arab countries would be torn apart and turned into Jewish colonies." The Jews would seek Jordan, Lebanon, Syria, Iraq, and the border areas of Egypt. But if England and her allies were defeated, "the Jewish danger" for the Arab countries would be defeated. Husseini thus transferred the traditional view of the all-powerful Jew to a Zionist state that "would rule the whole world." The logic of traditional Jew-hatred became a core element of his, and the Nazis' anti-Zionist propaganda and policy. The convergence between antisemitism and anti-Zionism was complete.

Husseini in Berlin on Islam and the Jews

On several occasions in Berlin, Husseini delivered versions of his core text, "Islam and the Jews." The Islamic Institute in Berlin, with government support, published a German version of his speech on November 5, 1943. The Foreign Office propaganda division presented it in shorter form in leaflets and broadcast it on radio in Arabic.[70] The speech included themes for which Husseini had become famous: The Jews had hated Islam for seven centuries. Their plans for "a Jewish "kingdom" in Palestine included destroying the Al Aksa Mosque in Jerusalem "to build a temple on its ruins." Zionism brought this centuries-long Jewish hatred of Islam into modern history. A Jewish state "would be a great danger for all of humanity" but "even more dangerous for Arabs and Muslims." It would "subject the Arab countries and all the countries of the Middle East to the danger of Jewish economic exploitation and to the Jewish world conspiracy" and colonization and occupation of "the neighboring countries."[71]

While the Americans now carried "the Jewish flag," Husseini asserted, Germany had "decided to find a definitive solution to the Jewish danger," by which he was referring to the Final Solution in Europe. The resulting "common battle against the Jewish danger" bound Arabs and Muslims to Germany. In the postwar years, apologists for Husseini suggested that his collaboration was primarily one of momentary convenience far more than ideological agreement. Husseini himself, however, insisted the

> our friendship with Germany is not at all one of opportunism that rests only on contemporary circumstances. Rather it is the result of common interests of both nations and of their unified stance toward a common enemy in a battle.[72]

The "battle" against the Jews and the Zionists was one and the same thing. The decision of the Nazi leadership to give Husseini a major propaganda platform, in print and on the airwaves, illustrated its view that anti-Jewish policy and anti-Zionism were inseparable. They comprised an ideological commonality between Nazism and Husseini's blend of Islamism and radical nationalism.

As the pages of the *VB* made clear, anti-Zionism was also a central theme in the propaganda the Nazi regime aimed at its German domestic audience. On March 20, 1943, in the midst of a major burst of anti-Jewish incitement, the *VB* led with the headline "Appeal of the Grand Mufti against the deadly enemies of Islam, Arabs will fight for their freedom on the side of the Axis" above a report about a lecture delivered in Berlin the previous evening by the Husseini on the occasion of Mohammed's birthday.[73] The story sympathetically described Hussein's appeal to the Islamic and Arab world and its fight against "occupation and cruelties by enemy oppressors."[74] To its German readers, the *VB* described the Grand Mufti as "one of the great personalities of the Islamic world who had led the struggle of the Palestinian Arabs against onrushing Jewry." In the face of "the English and American promises to world Jewry to make Palestine Jewry's exclusive property and to expel the Arabs," Palestine had become "a symbol of the Arab freedom struggle" against "British betrayal" and "the Atlantic swindle."[75]

Anti-Zionism and Denouncing "Jewish-American Imperialism"

On September 24, Voice of Free Arabism asked, "What are the aims of international Zionism?"[76] The Jews did not only want Palestine. Rather they sought "possession of all Arab countries in the east and the west" up to the Atlantic Ocean. In the west, they sought Algeria, Morocco, and Tunisia, while in the east, they wanted to connect Syria to Lebanon and then add both to Palestine. This "Jewish plan" was the "greatest danger" that would face the Arabs and Muslims if "our enemies the British, Americans, and Bolsheviks, emerge victorious." It was the "sacred duty" of Arabs to unite to "repulse this Jewish menace" and prevent "Jewish imperialism" from being established with the assistance of the British. An Allied victory would enable the Jews to realize these dreams and force the Arabs "to live as nomads."[77] Predictions of catastrophe if the "Allies and the Jews" won the war remained a key theme of Nazi propaganda and Nazi Arabic-language propaganda until the war's end. The broadcast illustrated, yet again, the convergence of Jew-hatred and anti-Zionism in Nazi propaganda.

On October 6, 1943, in response to reports of Jewish brigades in the British Eighth Army, the *VB* warned that "Palestine, Egypt and Iraq are supposed to become Jewish-American colonies."[78] Churchill "his whole life long had been dependent on the Jews." Now Churchill was returning the favor as he gave in to Jewish demands concerning Palestine and broke promises to the Arabs. In the United States, the *VB* continued, the Jews were preparing to drive the Arabs out of Palestine. "Here is the truth of Jewish-American imperialism at work which hopes to gain important bases in the far and middle Orient to aid in future world domination."[79] The focus on Zionism's links to the United States and the supposed power of the Jews in the Roosevelt administration remained a central theme of Nazi propaganda throughout the war. "World Jewry," supposedly having gained power in New York and in the Roosevelt administration, used the American government to support the establishment of a Jewish state in Palestine. The state of Israel would become the base for the penetration of the Middle East as a whole by "Jewish-American imperialism." The expansion of American power in the region would, for those who accepted this framework, appear to confirm the basic antisemitic conspiracy theory, which interpreted the expansion of American influence in the Middle East as the result of the power of American Jews, just as the Nazis such as Meyer-Christian associated British support for Zionism as the product of Jewish influence. The fact that Britain limited Jewish emigration to Palestine during the Holocaust or that Roosevelt refrained from clear support for the Zionist project did not influence Nazi propaganda in the slightest.

By 1944, reports of the mass murder of the Jews led to growing political calls in Washington to do more to rescue Europe's Jews and to urge Britain to lift restrictions on Jewish emigration to Palestine. On February 1, 1944, Senator Robert Wagner, a leading New Deal liberal from New York, joined with Senator Robert Taft, a conservative Republican from Ohio, to introduce a resolution that the United States support "free and unlimited entry of Jews into Palestine for the creation of a Jewish commonwealth."[80] General George Marshall, chief of staff of the U.S. Army, and John J. McCloy, Assistant Secretary of War, successfully urged the Senate not to support such a resolution as it would, in their view, undermine Arab goodwill and cooperation, which were needed for the war effort.

Nevertheless, on March 1, 1944, Berlin in Arabic unleashed a tirade against "criminal American Senators." The intention of Wagner and Taft's resolution was "to erase Islamic civilization from the face of the world, to eradicate the Koran from the heart of men, and to replace it by their atheism and immorality." A Jewish country in Palestine would be "a shameful crime!" The Al-Aksa Mosque in Jerusalem would be destroyed and replaced with "Solomon's Temple." The Senator's resolution was further evidence that the United States was "really a Jewish colony and that the five million Jews living there dominate the 140 million other Americans."[81] The prospect of fulfillment of Zionist aspirations in Palestine led the Nazi broadcaster to conclude in a fit of apoplectic rage and public appeals for murder. "No trace" of Arabs and Moslems would remain in "the horrible future" that awaited them. "Armies and tribes" should "drive out the menace. Men and women should fight the Allies by all means. Kill them.... God will bring you victory."[82]

On March 1, 1944, Husseini himself spoke on the Nazi station Berlin in Arabic. "Wicked American intentions toward the Arabs were now clearer." The Americans wished to "establish a Jewish empire in the Arab world.... Arabs! *Rise as one and fight for your sacred rights. Kill the Jews wherever you find them. This pleases God, history, and religion*"[83] (emphasis in original). By connecting Nazi anti-Zionism to Islam, Husseini continued to turn the dispute over land into a religious war, and thus one without compromise. Both Nazism and the Islamism of the war years nourished an uncompromising rejection of Zionism that was to have a profound impact on Arab and Islamist politics in the decades following World War II and the Holocaust.

Throughout its history, beginning with Hitler's *Mein Kampf* and continuing to the spring of 1945, Nazi Germany, in word and deed, was unequivocally opposed to the establishment of a Jewish state in Palestine. From the beginning to the end of the Nazi regime, anti-Zionism and anti-Jewish policy converged. Hitler never approved of the establishment of a Jewish state in Palestine. The Nazi regime's support for limited Jewish emigration to Palestine did not amount to support for the Zionist project. As war approached and then when Hitler started World War II, the convergence between anti-Zionism and anti-Jewish policy became even more pronounced. One result of that convergence was the alliance of radical nationalists and Islamists and the Nazi regime as they all sought to prevent the Jews from establishing a state of their own. During the war, the idea of the murderous and powerful Jew—a key theme of European Jew-hatred—evolved into attacks on the murderous and aggressive Zionist. Ironically, in the postwar decades, this latter theme of Nazi propaganda became a staple first of Soviet-bloc propaganda and later of leftist movements and states. As similar ideas percolate in the global left in the twenty-first century, recalling Nazism's vehement rejection of the Zionist project remains an important, if discomforting, imperative of historical interpretation.

Notes

Selections taken from *Nazi Propaganda for the Arab* World by Jeffrey Herf, New Haven, CT: Yale University Press, Copyright 2009. Used by permission. All rights reserved.

1 On this, see Jeffrey Herf, *Israel's Moment: International Support for and Opposition to Establishing the Jewish State, 1945–1949* (Cambridgeand New York: Cambridge University Press, 2022).

2 On the effort to extend the Holocaust to the Jews of North Africa and the Middle East, see Klaus-Michael Mallmann and Martin Cüppers, *Nazi Palestine: The Plans for the Extermination of the Jews in Palestine*, trans. Krista Smith (New York: Enigma Books, 2010); Klaus-Michael Mallmann and Martin Cüppers, *Halbmond und Hakenkreuz: Das Dritte Reich, die Araber und Palästina* (Darmstadt: Wissenschaftliche Buchgesellschaft, 2007).

3 On the clarifications of June 1936, see Jeffrey Herf, *Nazi Propaganda for the Arab World* (New Haven, CT: Yale University Press, 2009), 20–22.

4 Adolf Hitler, *Mein Kampf*, trans. Ralph Mannheim (Boston, MA: Houghton-Mifflin, 1943, 1971), 324–325.

5 "Alfred Rosenberg Biography," United States Holocaust Memorial Museum, https://encyclopedia.ushmm.org/content/en/article/alfred-rosenberg-biography.

6 Alfred Rosenberg, *Der Staatsfeindliche Zionismus* (Munich: Zentralverlag der NSDAP, Franz Eher Verlag, 1938).

7 See Alfred Rosenberg, *Der Staatsfeindliche Zionismus* (Hamburg: Deutsch-voelkische Verlagsanstalt,1922), 62–63. Also see Alfred Rosenberg, *Schriften aus den Jahren 1917–1921* (Munich: Hoheneichen Verlag, 1943); and his forward and introduction to the Nazi edition of *Die Protokolle der Weissen von Zion und*

die jüdische Weltpolitik (Munich: Deutscher Volksverlag, 1933). By this fourth edition, the publisher had brought out 25,000 copies.

8 Ibid., 73–78, 86.

9 Ibid., 86.

10 On the agreement, see Saul Friedlander, *Nazi Germany and the Jews, Volume 1: The Years of Persecution, 1933–1939* (New York: HarperCollins, 1997); and Francis R. Nicosia, *The Third Reich and the Palestine Question*, 2nd ed. (New Brunswick: Transaction, 1999).

11 Lukasz Hirszowicz, *The Third Reich and the Arab East* (London: Routledge and Kegan Paul; Toronto: University of Toronto Press, 1966), 27 and 33.

12 Ibid.

13 Antisemitismus" in *Zeitschriften-Dienst*, June 13, 1939, 6, Nr. 222.

14 Sammlung Oberheitmann, "Vertrauliche Informationen" des Reichministerium für Volksaufklärung und Propaganda für die Presse, Zeitgeschichtlich Sammlung, Nr. 215/44, September 30, 1944, Zsg. 109/51, SO, BAK.

15 On the policy shift of 1937, see Matthias Küntzel, "Kapitel II 1937: Das Jahr der Weichenstellung," in his *Nazis und der Nahe Osten: Wie der Islamische Anti-semitismus Entstand* (Berlin and Leipzig: Hentrich and Hentrich, 2019), 51–76; forthcoming as *Nazis, Islamic Antisemitism, and the Middle East: The 1948 Arab War against Israel and the Aftershocks of WW II* (London: Routledge Publishers, 2023).

16 Walter Doehle, "Abschrift Pol. VIII 309, "Inhalt: Prüfung der Frage, ob unsere Palästina gegenüber bisher verfolgte Richtlinie beibehalten werden kann oder ob sie eine Änderung erfahren muß," Jerusalem (March 22, 1937), *Politisches Archiv des Auswärtiges Amt*, PAAA R104785, Pol. VII, "Politische Beziehung Palästina zu Deutschland," E019872–E019896, E019872–E019873.

17 Ibid., E019872–E019879; and Herf, *Nazi Propaganda for the Arab World*, 27–28. On German Foreign Office awareness of Arab sympathies for Nazi Germany and the shift in German policy of 1937, also see Mallmann and Cüppers, *Nazi Palestine*, 29–55.

18 Konstantin von Neurath, "Abschrift 83–21 A 25/5," Berlin (June 1, 1937), Büro Unterstaatssekretär, Palästinafrage, June 1937–April 1938, Politisches Archiv des Auswärtiges Amt (PAAA) R29899, 37041–370142.

19 Vicco Bülow-Schwante, "Deutsche Einstellung zur Frage der Gründung eines Judenstaates in Palästina," Berlin (June 22, 1937), PAAA R29899, Politische Beziehung Palästinas zu Deutschland R104785, 37033–370138. On antisem-itism and anti-Zionism of the Foreign Office in 1937 see Eckart Conze, Norbert Frei, Peter Hayes, and Moshe Zimmermann, *Das Amt und die Vergangenheit. Deutsche Diplomaten im Dritten Reich und in der Bundesrepublik* (Munich: Karl Blessing Verlag, 2010), 99–11.

20 Ibid.

21 Ernst von Weizäcker to Generalkonsulate Jerusalem (July 20, 1937), PAAA R104787, Politische Abteilung, Betr. Plan für Verteilung Palästinas…1937.

22 Mallmann and Cüppers, *Nazi Palestine*, 46–48.

23 OKW/Aus/Abw I conversation note, June 18, 1939, IfZ, Nbg. Dok., PS-792; cited in Mallmann and Cüppers, 48–49.

24 Ibid., 49.

25 Küntzel, *Nazis in der Nahe Osten*, 63–73.

26 Anne H. Fuller, "General Argument Used in German Propaganda to the Near East," (September 29, 1941), United States National Archives, College Park, NACP RG 208, Records of the Office of War Information, Informational Files on the Near East, 1941–1946, entry 373, box 417.

27 Mallmann and Cüppers, *Nazi Palestine*, 55. The evidence of this recent scholar-ship presents an effective challenge to claims by Francis Nicosia that the Nazis did

not place value on the Arab factor. Nicosia makes that argument in *The Third Reich and the Palestine Question*; also see his *Zionism and Antisemitism in Nazi Germany* (New York: Cambridge University Press, 2008). For Mallmann and Cüpper's criticism, see *Nazi Palestine*, 54–55.

28 Heinrich Hest (Herman Erich Seifert), *Weltjuda ohne Maske, Band 2: Palästina: Judenstaat? England als Handlanger des Weltjudentums* (Berlin: Joh. Kasper and Co., 1939); and *Der Aufbruch in der arabischen Welt* (Berlin: Zentralverlag der NSDAP, Franz Eher Nachf, 1941).

29 Bucher: Juden, Engländer, Araber," *Zeitschriften-Dienst*, 17, August 26, 1939, Nr. 656:18.

30 Heinrich Hest, *Weltjuda ohne Maske, Band 2*: and *Der Aufbruch in der arabischen Welt* (Berlin: Zentralverlag der NSDAP, Franz Eher Nachf., 1941), 6.

31 On Nazi Germany's war on its Eastern Front as also a colonial project, see Shelley Baranowski, *Nazi Empire: German Colonialism and Imperialism from Bismarck to Hitler* (New York and Cambridge: Cambridge University Press, 2011).

32 Hest, *Weltjuda ohne Maske, Band 2*, 49–50.

33 Ibid., 101.

34 Alfred Rosenberg, "Die Judenfrage als Weltproblem," *Weltkampf: Die Judenfrage in Geschichte und Gegenwart 1941*, 64–72; also in *Völksicher Beobachter* (March 29, 1941), 1–2; also see the radio transcript of the speech, "28.3.1941, Alfred Rosenberg, "*Rundfunkvortrag in Berlin im Anschluß an die erste Arbeitstagung des 'Instituts zur Erforschung der Judenfrage' in Frankfurt am Main über 'Die Judenfrage als Weltproblem,*" in Walter Roller, ed., *Judenverfolgung und jüdisches Leben unter den Bedingungen der nationalsozialistischen Gewaltherrschaft, Band I, Tondokumente und Runkfunksendungen 1930–1946* (Potstam: Verlag für Berlin-Brandenburg, 1996), 181–187.

35 Rosenberg, "Die Judenfrage als Weltproblem," 64–65.

36 Ibid., 70–71

37 Hermann Erich Seifert, *Der Aufbruch in der arabischen Welt* (Berlin: Zentralverlag der NSDAP, Franz Eher Nachf, 1941).

38 Ibid., 38.

39 Ibid.

40 Ibid., 80.

41 Ibid., 91.

42 Giselher Wirsing, *Engländer, Juden, Araber in Palästina* (Jena: Eugen Diederichs Verlag, 1939). It sold 10,000 copies in four editions.

43 On the British policy during the Holocaust, see Bernard Wasserstein, *Britain and the Jews of Europe: 1939–1945* (New York: Oxford University Press, 1988).

44 Die englisch-jüdische Allianz," 3504 in Zeitschriften-Dienst (November 8, 1940). See Wolf Meyer-Christian, *die englisch-jüdische Allianz: Werden und Wirken der kapitalistischen Weltherrschaft*, 3rd ed. (Berlin-Leipzig: Nibelungen-Verlag, 1942).

45 Ibid., 11.

46 Ibid., 78.

47 Ibid., 141.

48 Ibid., 142–145.

49 Ibid., 185 and 188. Meyer-Christian offered an antisemitic interpretation of British history that placed affinities between Puritanism and Judaism at its core, associated with a pejorative association with capitalism. His writing drew heavily on Werner Sombart's 1911 work *The Jews and Economic Life*. On that work. see, "Werner Sombart: Technology and the Jewish Question," in Jeffrey Herf, ed., *Reactionary Modernism: Technology, Culture and Politics in Weimar and the Third Reich* (New York and Cambridge: Cambridge University Press, 1984), 130–151.

50 On the Nazi regime's ideological appeals and practical cooperation with Muslims in Southeastern Europe, in North Africa, and the Middle East, see David Motadel, *Islam and Nazi Germany's War* (Cambridge, MA: Harvard University Press, 2014).

51 Die islamische Welt als Kulturfactor," *Zeitschriften-Dienst* 175/44, September 11, 1942, Nr. 7514, 2.

52 On "Axis Broadcasts in Arabic," see Herf, *Nazi Propaganda for the Arab World*.

53 Anne H. Fuller, "Strategy of Propaganda to the Near East" (November 3, 1941), NACP RG 208, Records of the Office of War Information, Informational Files on the Near East, 1941–1946, entry 373, box 418, 1–4.

54 Anne H. Fuller, "Anti-American Propaganda in the Near East" (October 25, 1941), NACP 208, Records of the Office of War Information, Informational Files on the Near East, 1941–1946, entry 373, box 418, 1–5.

55 On the meeting, see Herf, *Nazi Propaganda for the Arab World*, 74–78; and Gensicke, *The Mufti of Jerusalem and the Nazis*, 66–69.

56 "No. 515, Memorandum by an Official of the Foreign Minister's Secretariat, Record of the Conversation between the Führer and the Grand Mufti of Jerusalem on November 28, 1941, in the Presence of Reich Foreign Minister and Minister Grobba in Berlin," Berlin (November 30, 1941), *DGFP, Series D (1937–1945)*, vol. 13, 881–885.

57 For an excellent biography of Rauff before, during and after the Nazi era, see Martin Cüppers, *Walther Rauff—in deutschen Diensten: Vom Naziverbrecher zum BND-Spion* (Darmstadt: Wissenschaftliche Buchgesellschaft, 2013).

58 See Mallmann and Cüppers, *Nazi Palestine*, 116–139; and Mallmann and Cüppers, *Halbmond und Hakenkreuz*, 137–164.

59 Voice of Free Arabism (VFA), July 7, 1942, 8:15 p.m., "Kill the Jews before They Kill You," Kirk to Secretary of State, No. 502 (July 21, 1942), 13–14.

60 OWI, Overseas Operations Branch, Washington, DC, "Weekly Propaganda Directive, Palestine" (November 14, 1942), NACP RG 165, MID Regional File, 1922–1944, Palestine, entry 77, box 2719, folder 2930.

61 OWI, Overseas Operation Branch, "Basic Directive for Egypt," (January 30, 1943), 2–5, Egypt 2930, NACP GR 165, MID, Regional File, 1922–1944, Egypt, entry 77, box 751, folder 3800, 6–7.

62 American diplomats and intelligence agents were reporting that Nazi Germany's primary advantage in the propaganda war in the Middle East lies in its opposition to Zionism, which found broad majority support. George Britt, "Beirut September to June," (June 1943), 3–4, NACP RG 84, Lebanon: U.S. Consulate and Legation and Embassy Beirut, 1936–1941, Classified General Records, 110.2–891, entry 2854A, box 8. Also see Herf, *Nazi Propaganda for the Arab World*.

63 Berlin in Arabic, November 18, 1942, "The Jews and the Arabs of North Africa," Kirk to Secretary of State, No. 710 (November 21, 1942), 24.

64 VFA, November 21, 1942, 8:15 p.m, "The Arabs and the War, Kirk to Secretary of State, No. 84, Cairo (December 6, 1942), Axis Broadcasts in Arabic...November 20 to 26, 1942, 1, NACP RG 84 Egypt: Cairo Embassy: General Records, 1936–1955, entry 2410, 815.4–820.02, box 77.

65 VFA, November 3, 1943, 8:15 p.m., "Palestine between the Bolsheviks and the Jews," Kirk to Secretary of State, No. 1410, Cairo (November 19, 1943), 6–7, Axis Broadcasts in Arabic...November 3 to 9, 1943, 1–2, NACP RG 84, Egypt: Cairo Embassy General Records, 1936–1955, 820.00–822.00, entry 2410, box 93.

66 Amin al Husseini, "*Nr. 18a; Rundfunkerklärung 'an das ägyptische Volk*", 3.7.1942 in Gerhard Höpp, ed., *Mufti-Papiere: Briefe, Memoranden, Reden und Aufrüfe Amin al Husainis aus dem Exil, 1940–1945* (Berlin: Klaus Schwarz Verlag, 2001), 45–46.

67 Amin al Husseini, "Nr. 42 Rundfunkrede an die Araber ("Märtyrerrede"), 11.11.1942, in Hopp, ed., Mufti-Papiere, 103.

68 Ibid., 104.

69 Ibid.

70 VFA, November 5, 1943, 6:30 p.m., "The Protests of the Moslems of Europe against the Balfour Declaration," Kirk to Secretary of State, No. 1410, Cairo (November 19, 1943), 3–4; and Haj Amin el-Husseini, *Rede S. Em* [Sein Eminenz] *Des Großmufti anlässlich der Protestkundgebung gegen die Balfour-Erklärung am 2. November 1943* (Berlin: Islamische Zentral-Institut, 1943), PAAA R27327, Grossmufti, 1942–1944, 297878–297886.

71 Ibid., 297880–297882.

72 Ibid., 297885.

73 "Aufruf des Großmufti gegen die Todfeinde des Islams, Araber werden für ihre Freiheit an der Seite der Achse kämpfen" [Grand Mufti's Call against the Deadly Enemy of Islam: Arabs Will Fight for Their Freedom on the Side of the Axis] Völkischer Beobachter (hereafter, VB) March 20, 1943, 1. The Nazi regime published a sympathetic book about the Grand Mufti. See Kurt Fischer-Weth, *Amin Al-Husseini: Grossmufti von Palästina* (Berlin-Friedenau: Walter Titz Verlag, 1943).

74 Aufruf des Großmufti,"1.

75 Ibid.

76 Voice of Free Arabism, September 24, 1943, 8:15 p.m., "What Are the Aims of International Zionism?" Alexander Kirk to Secretary of State, Cairo (October 5, 1943), "No. 1325, Axis Broadcasts in Arabic for the period September 23 to 29, 1943," NARA, RG 84, Egypt: Cairo Embassy General Records, 1933–1955, 820.00–822.00, 1943, Box 93.

77 Ibid.

78 "Englisch-amerikanischer Gegensatz im Nahen-Osten, Juda präsentiert den Wechsel, Palästina, Ägypten und Irak sollen jüdisch-amerikanische Kolonien werden" [English-American Conflicts in Middle East, Jewry Represents a Change, Palestine, Egypt and Iraq so that Palestine, Egypt and Iraq Become Jewish-American Colonies], VB, October 6, 1943, 1; also see "Englands Polizistenrolle für das Weltjudentum, Britische militärmacht soll für Ordnung und Sicherheit in Palestine sorgen" [England's Role as Policeman for World Jewry, British Military Power to Secure Order and Security in Palestine], VB, October 11, 1943, 1.

79 Ibid.

80 See discussion in Herf, *Nazi Propaganda for the Arab World*, 207–210; and Herf, *Israel's Moment*: 26–27. Also see Ronald Radosh and Allis Radosh, *A Safe Haven: Harry S., Truman and the Founding of Israel* (New York: HarperCollins, 2009), 82.

81 Berlin in Arabic, March 3, 1944, "Palestine Revolts against Decision of the Americans," Kirk to Secretary of State, No. 1642 (March 7, 1944), 8.

82 Ibid.

83 "Weekly Review of Foreign Broadcasts, F.C.C. [Federal Communications Division], No. 118, 3/4/44, Near and Middle East," NACP RG 165, MID Regional File, 1922–1944, Palestine, entry 77, box 2719, folder 2930.

4

NAZI PROPAGANDA AIMED AT ARABS AND MUSLIMS DURING WORLD WAR II AND THE HOLOCAUST

During World War II and the Holocaust, the Nazi regime engaged in an intensive effort to appeal to Arabs and Muslims in the Middle East and North Africa.[1] It did so with the assistance of Arab exiles in Nazi Berlin. The Nazis and the Arab collaborators met on a common ground of hatred for Jews and thus for the Zionist project in Palestine and of opposition to the Allies in World War II. Nazi officials, especially in the German Foreign Office, presented the Third Reich as a champion of secular anti-imperialism, especially against Britain. The Arabic language propaganda campaign was part of a broader-based effort by the Hitler regime to make a common cause with Islam as it interpreted it in Europe, North Africa, and the Middle East. Hitler, Himmler, and high-ranking officials in the German Foreign Office presented Islam as a religion that was compatible with the ideology of National Socialism.[2]

The most important immediate product of the collaboration was a flood of Arabic language propaganda, mostly on shortwave radio from Germany broadcast to North Africa and the Middle East during World War II and the Holocaust. The Nazis broadcast in Farsi to Iran as well. As a result of research in recent decades in the archives in Germany holding records of the Nazi era Foreign Office, Propaganda Ministry, and the SS, and of files of the U.S. State Department, its military intelligence agencies, and the Office of Strategic Services our knowledge of these efforts has expanded greatly beyond the already existing impressive scholarship.[3] We now have a much larger documentary record of both Nazi Germany's efforts to spread its ideology in North Africa and the Middle East as well as of the contribution to those efforts made by Arab and Islamist collaborators. During World War II and the Holocaust, the history of Nazism and Islamism intersected and left

DOI: 10.4324/9781003449669-5

an ideological and political aftermath that had an enduring and tragic impact in the Middle East. That collaboration wrote a crucial chapter in the history, and international diffusion, of antisemitism during the Holocaust and its aftermath.[4]

Before that collaboration was possible, the Nazis needed to clarify how Arabs, and Muslims in general, fit into the racist ideology of the Nazi regime. In 1936 and 1937, during preparations for the Berlin Olympics of 1936 and in response to questions from Arab diplomats, officials and lawyers in the German Foreign Ministry, the Propaganda Ministry, the Nazi Party's Office of Racial Politics (*Rassenpolitisches Amt*), and Himmler's Reich Security Main Office (SS) concluded that the Nuremberg race laws and Nazi racial legislation in general distinguished between Germans and Jews, not between Aryans and non-Aryans. Therefore, the Nazi regime's policy was correctly described as "anti-Jewish," but not "antisemitic." During World War II and the Holocaust, the Nazi Propaganda Ministry ordered the press and radio to use the term "enemy of Jews" (*Judengegner*) rather than the term "antisemitism" to describe its policy. The propaganda of the Foreign Office followed these same language rules. These policy clarifications of the mid-1930s cleared the path for a racist regime to make appeals to "non-Aryan" Arabs, Turks, and Iranians.[5]

In 1941, as became evident in its radio propaganda and choice of allies, the Orient Office in the German Foreign Office expressed empathy for the religion of Islam, a doctrine which it claimed was compatible with Nazism in its hatred of the Jews and support for authoritarian rule.[6] From the fall of 1939 to March 1945, the Nazi regime broadcast shortwave Arabic programs to the Middle East and North Africa seven days and nights a week. Most of this massive output was either never recorded or transcribed, was destroyed by Allied bombing in and around Berlin, and/or was intentionally destroyed or hidden by German officials and Arab collaborators during or after World War II. The most extensive surviving record of the propaganda campaign known to scholars was recorded by American diplomats in the U.S. Embassy in Cairo. Beginning in the summer of 1941, under the direction of Alexander Kirk, the recently arrived American Ambassador to Egypt, a staff in the U.S. Embassy in Cairo began to transcribe and translate the Axis broadcasts (that is, Italian Fascist, and Nazi German Arabic broadcasts). Kirk assumed his post in Cairo on March 29, 1941. He had been chargé d'affaires of the U.S. Embassy in Berlin in 1939 to 1940. In that capacity, he had sent informative memos to Washington about Nazi anti-Jewish persecution. He remained the American Ambassador to Egypt until March 29, 1944.

Kirk first sent summaries of Nazi radio broadcasts from September 1941 to April 1942.[7] Thereafter, every week, from April 1942 to March 1944, he sent "Axis Broadcasts in Arabic" to the Office of the Secretary of State in the State Department in Washington. The texts were then circulated in the U.S.

State Department, Department of Defense, Office of Strategic Services (OSS), and the Office of War Information (OWI). American diplomats, military leaders, intelligence officials, and presumably the Roosevelt White House as well were well informed about the flood of Jew-hatred coming from Nazi Germany's global, as well as Arabic-focused radio broadcasts.[8] "Axis Broadcasts in Arabic" was composed of verbatim transcripts in English translation of Nazi Germany's Arabic-language radio broadcasts to the Middle East. In 1944 and 1945, his successor, Pickney Tuck, continued to gather and send the reports.

Despite pleas immediately after World War II, including from prominent Senator Robert F. Wagner, for declassification of American files on Arab collaboration with the Nazis, the "Axis in Arabic" files remained sealed according to the standard 30-year rule until 1977.[9] Examination of files of American Embassies in the Middle East, military intelligence, the OSS, and the Washington offices of the State Department and Pentagon indicated that American officials were well informed about the Nazi-Arab/Islamist collaboration. For the next 30 years, the "Axis Broadcast in Arabic" files were either neglected or if scholars read them, the findings did not appear in published scholarship. I read the relevant files first in 2007 in the U.S. National Archives in College Park and then published their details first in an article in *Central European* History and in *Nazi Propaganda for the Arab World*, both in 2009.[10] The "Axis Broadcasts in Arabic" files remain an indispensable source for examination of Nazism's efforts to extend its appeals to the Arab and Muslim societies and of a key chapter in the history of Nazi and Islamist antisemitism. In addition, research in the files in archives in Germany of the Nazi Foreign Office (*Auswärtiges Amt*), the Propaganda Ministry, and the SS has made it possible to present a much fuller picture of the German officials and their collaboration with the Arab exiles who, together, produced Nazi Germany's Arabic language wartime propaganda. While officials of the Propaganda Ministry and the Reich Security Main Office/SS contributed to the campaign, its institutional core lies in the Orient Office (Office VII) of the German Foreign Office. It was there that university-educated German Orientalists worked closely with the Arab exiles to integrate propaganda and political warfare with the German three-year military campaign in Northern Africa and to continue the propaganda effort after Germany's military defeat in Tunisia in 1943. The result was a historically consequential cultural fusion, a borrowing and interaction between Nazi ideology and certain strains of Arab nationalism and Islamic religious traditions.[11]

Historians have published important works on the interaction between the main theatre of World War II and the Holocaust in Europe and Nazi policy on the important periphery of North Africa and the Middle East.[12] In 1965, the East German historian Heinz Tillmann in *Deutschlands Araberpolitik im Zweiten Weltkrieg* [Germany's Arab Policy in the Second World War] drew on then-available German archives to examine the policy of "German imperialism" in the Middle East from the 1930s to spring 1943.[13] In 1966, Lukasz Hirszowicz's *The Third Reich and the Arab East* established the chronology and key causal arguments concerning the prospects for victory by and the causes of defeat of Fascist Italy and Nazi Germany in the region, especially in Iraq and Egypt.[14] In 2006, two German historians, Klaus Michael Mallmann and Martin Cuppers, drawing on German diplomatic, military, and SS archives that had been opened and declassified in the interim, published *Halbmond und Hakenkreuz. Das Dritte Reich, die Araber und Palästina* [Crescent and Swastika: The Third Reich, the Arabs and Palestine]. An English edition, with the title *Nazi Palestine: Plans for the Extermination of the Jews of Palestine* was published in 2010.[15] Mallmann and Cuppers revealed that, in the event of German military success in North Africa, Himmler's Reich Security Main Office, the SS, planned to send one of the *Einsatzgruppe*, such as those responsible for murder by shooting of hundreds of thousands of Jews in Eastern Europe in 1941–1942, to North Africa and the Middle East to extend the Final Solution of the Jews *in Europe* to the approximately 700,000 Jews of North Africa and the Middle East. In summer and fall 1942, the fate of the Jews of the region hung on the outcome of the battles at El Alamein, in Egypt between Germany's General Erwin Rommel's *Afrika Korps* and British, Australian, and New Zealand armed forces. In the Yishuv, the Jewish community in Palestine, the fear of a German invasion of Palestine among its Jewish population was "indeed real".[16]

In wartime Berlin, radical antisemitism of European and German-speaking provenance found common ground with radical antisemitism rooted in Koranic verses and the commentaries on them in the traditions of Islam. Just as Nazi antisemitism was a radicalization of elements that already existed within European culture, so the antisemitism of the pro-Nazi Arab exiles resulted from a radicalization of elements that already existed within the traditions of Islam. In both cases, these twentieth-century extremists, in patterns familiar to historians of reception, engaged in a "labor of selective tradition."[17] That is, they actively reworked and appropriated received traditions, emphasizing some elements, and diminishing others. As a result of their shared passions and interests, they produced texts and broadcasts that they likely would not have produced on their own. Through this active labor of conserving and reworking their own while incorporating foreign traditions, the Nazis and their Arab collaborators found common ground to produce the texts and broadcasts that accompanied the Axis military and propaganda offensives in North Africa and the Middle East during the war.[18]

Cultural and intellectual historians of Nazism have long demonstrated that its ideology can neither be separated from nor reduced to its European, German, and Christian predecessors. These were necessary but not sufficient conditions for its emergence. The same was true of the radical nationalism and Islamism of the Arab exiles who joined forces with Hitler's regime. Their political outlook could neither be separated from nor reduced to its Arabic or Islamic background. They met on a common terrain of the radicalization of enmity toward Judaism and the Jews that could be gleaned from readings of the sacred texts which drew on but claimed to supersede Judaism. The historical conjuncture of World War II brought Nazis and Islamists together in the shared project of radicalizing their own past traditions.

The Nazis taught the Arab exiles the finer points of twentieth-century Jew-hatred, above all, its paranoid, conspiracy theory, and how to apply it to ongoing events. The Arab and Muslim collaborators taught the Nazis how to adapt their antisemitic conspiracy theories to Islamic idioms. The Nazis learned that they could make appeals that were in apparent contradiction to their racist ideology, while Arab and Islamic radicals in Nazi Berlin found commonalities with modern, European totalitarian ideology. The Nazi leadership sought ways to burst the bonds of nationalist German particularism and modify the doctrine of the Aryan master race in order to appeal to Arabs and Muslims. The Arabs and Muslims in Berlin engaged in a variant of what I have called "reactionary modernism" as they demonstrated a mastery of modern propaganda techniques in the interest of advocating a revival of a fundamentalist version of Islam.[19]

That said, Islamist antisemitism was not primarily due to the idea transfer of Nazi ideology into a previously benign context. Rather, the Nazi regime used its power to amplify a tradition of Islamic antisemitism that had *already emerged* especially in Egypt and Palestine and in the Muslim Brotherhood in the 1930s *before* the leading Arab exiles arrived in Berlin in fall 1941.[20] Historians have amply examined the actions and beliefs of Haj Amin el-Husseini. He was the most important public face and voice of Nazi propaganda aimed at Arabs and Muslims.[21] Four years before he arrived in Nazi Berlin, he wrote what became a standard text of Islamic antisemitism. It was delivered in 1937 in his absence to a conference Bludan, Syria. In *Islam und Judentum* (Islam and the Jews), he claimed that Jews had been enemies of Islam since the days of Mohammed and that the efforts of Zionists to establish a Jewish state in Palestine were only the latest chapter in this centuries long, religiously motivated attack. In 1938, Junker and Dünnhaupt, a Berlin publisher that evolved from promoting authors of Weimar's anti-democratic right to becoming a house promoting works celebrating Nazi ideology and policy, published *Islam and the Jews* in German translation.[22] German officials, journalists, and academics thus became aware that Husseini's opposition to the Zionist project was the direct result of his interpretation of Islam as a religion that was inherently antagonistic to Judaism and Jews. He viewed the Zionists as only the most recent of a Jewish assault on Islam that had gone on for many centuries.[23] As we will see, after his arrival in Berlin in November 1941, the Nazi regime gave him a global platform from which he could repeat and elaborate on the themes of that text. It also distributed copies of the text in relevant languages.

It was in those years that German diplomats in the Middle East realized that the Islamist tradition expressed in Husseini's *Islam and the Jews* offered a basis for cooperation in opposition to the democracies, the communists, and the Jews, and for supplementing secular appeals to Arab nationalists with religiously based appeals to Muslims.[24] In the same texts and broadcasts, the Nazis spoke the secular language of attacks on American, British, and "Jewish" imperialism while also appealing to what they depicted as the ancient traditions of hatred of the Jews in Islam itself. Nazi Germany presented itself both as an ally of Arab anti-imperialism as well as a soul mate of the religion of Islam.

Without minimizing Husseini's role, it is important to keep in mind that without the support of German officialdom, he would have been yet another powerless politician in exile bemoaning an inability to influence events. Those officials were located, most importantly in the Orient Office (Office VII) of the radio propaganda divisions of the German Foreign Office. The collaboration had the support and approval from Foreign Minister Joachim von Ribbentrop. From 1943 to 1945, Kurt Kiesinger, later a politician in the Christian Democratic Union, and Chancellor of the Federal Republic of Germany (West Germany) from 1966 to 1969, was the director of a staff of 226 in the Foreign Office Department of Radio Policy. Veteran diplomat Wilhelm Melchers directed the Political Department's Orient Office from 1939 to 1945.[25] Orientalist Kurt Munzel was the head of the team of Germans and native Arabic speakers who produced the radio broadcasts during the war. They received occasional assistance from Joseph Goebbels's Propaganda Ministry. Academically trained orientalists assisted in research institutes associated with Heinrich Himmler's Reich Security Main Office, the key institution that carried out the extermination of European Jewry also proposed ideas for leaflets and essays.[26]

By October 1939, Nazi Germany was broadcasting 15 hours a day, seven days a week, in 113 daily broadcasts around the world. By the end of 1940, about 500 people were working in various offices of German radio aimed abroad.[27] By 1943, the Nazi regime was broadcasting on 16 such stations in Arabic, Afrikan, Portuguese, Bulgarian, Dutch, English, French, Hungarian, Italian, Romanian, Serbian, Slovak, Spanish, and Turkish, however, as one historian of the program wrote "the Orient Zone had absolute priority."[28] The Arabic language broadcasts began in October 1939 and continued until February or March 1945. "Berlin in Arabic" and the "Voice of Free Arabism" and other stations broadcast a mixture of music, news, and commentary seven days and nights a week. They broadcast about two hours of news and commentary each evening. In August 1941, a U.S. OWI report estimated that there were about 90,000 shortwave radios in the region: 150 in Aden;

55,000 in Egypt; 4,000 in Iraq; 24,000 in Palestine; 6,000 in Syria; and 25 in Saudi Arabia.[29] Radios were often heard in cafes and other public places, where listening was a public and collective experience.

High rates of illiteracy in North Africa and the Middle East in this period meant that radio was crucial for propaganda campaigns. United Nations surveys conducted after World War II found illiteracy rates were still almost eighty percent in Egypt and 85 percent in Libya. In Palestine, the British mandatory government census of 1931 put the overall literacy rates among Arabs seven years and older at about 20 percent. Among Muslims, it was 14 percent (25 percent among men and only three percent among women). A UNESCO study concluded that by 1947, the literacy rate among Palestine's Arab community was 27 percent and 21 percent for Muslims (35 percent for men and seven percent for women).[30] Hence, shortwave radio reached a far larger audience than did print materials. From 1940 to 1943 when the Italian and German armies were in North Africa, the Axis distributed propaganda in Arabic-language leaflets and brochures by the German armed forces. After their defeat in the Battle of Tunisia in 1943, Nazi Germany's propaganda came overwhelmingly via the airwaves.

Content of the Broadcasts, 1939–1941

From September 1939 to fall 1941, Nazi Germany's Arabic broadcasts drew on the expertise of German Orientalists of Arabic and Islamic literature and poetry, the local knowledge gained by German diplomats in the prewar years, and on pro-Axis Arabs living in Berlin when the war began. Most of these broadcasts had the tone of a sympathetic, well-informed politically engaged scholar, one eager to please yet not familiar with local politics. These "early" broadcasts conveyed the message that Nazi Germany was a friend to both Arab nationalists and Muslims. On December 3, 1940, Munzel's Orient Office VII broadcast "a paper about the English occupation of Egypt."[31] With the incantation *"Oh, Mohammedaner"* (Oh, Muslims!), the broadcast made a direct appeal to Muslims and not only to Arab nationalists opposed to British rule in Egypt. It did so in the repetitive incantations of a religious sermon that evoked the authority of the "holy Koran" and past days of piety.

> Oh, God's servants! Above all of the other commandments, none is more important to the Muslims than piety, for piety is the core of all virtues and the bond of all honorable human characteristics. Muslims, you are now back- ward because you have not shown God the proper piety and do not fear him. You do things that are not commanded, and you leave to the side things that are. God's word has proven to be true, and you are now the humiliated ones in your own country. This has come about because you don't have the piety and fear of God as your pious forefathers did.

Of them, one can say that they "are strong against the unbelievers and merciful among themselves." Oh Muslims! Direct your gaze to the holy Koran and the tradition of the prophets. Then you will see that Islamic law is driven by piety toward God and fear of his punishment. The Koran inscribed piety as above all other commandments. Read, for example, the words, "Oh, believers, be pious and do not die without being a Muslim. Stand by God and don't be divided.[32]

Nazi broadcasts repeated that the values of Islam, which they described as piety, obedience, community, and unity rather than skepticism, individualism, and division were similar to those of Nazi Germany. That this anti-modernist assault was conveyed via the most modern means of electronic communication in 1940 was another example of the "reactionary modernist" character of aspects of Nazi ideology and policy. This and other broadcasts conveyed the message that a revival of fundamentalist Islam was a parallel project to National Socialism's political and ideological revolt against western political modernity.

The Nazi Arabic broadcasts presented the Koran as text of great relevance for events in the twentieth century. Hence the sacred texts of Islam were compatible with what the Nazis saw as the *forward-looking* nature of Nazi Germany and Fascist Italy. On December 12, 1940, for example, German radio announced that Islam

> is a religion of the community, not a religion of the individual. It is thus a religion of the common welfare [*Gemeinnutzes*] and not of self-interest [*Eigennutzes*]. Islam therefore is a just and true nationalism for it calls on the Muslim to place the general interest ahead of private interests, to live not for himself but for his religion and his fatherland. This is the most important goal that Islam follows. It is at the basis of its prayers and commandments.[33]

The priority of "the common welfare" over self-interest was a continuing and key theme of the Nazi Party before 1933 and the Nazi regime afterward.

The Nazis hoped the appeals to Islamic themes in these broadcasts would foster a willingness among Muslim listeners to respond positively to Nazism's secular political messages as well. On the same day that Radio Berlin broadcast the above message, it also sent out "A Government Statement for the Arabs."[34] The Third Reich expressed "full sympathy" for the Arabs' "struggle for freedom and independence" so that they could "take their proper place under the sun and to recover the glory and honor in service of humanity and civilization". The German government's expression of "love and sympathy" for the Arabs had "found a strong echo among the German people" while strengthening "the bonds of friendship with the Arabs which the Germans have cherished for many years". This connection was not surprising, the talk continued, because Germans and Arabs shared "many qualities and virtues," such as "courage in war ... heroism, and manly character." In other contexts, Hitler and Himmler expressed admiration for what they interpreted as Islam's martial virtues, which they contrasted with what they viewed as the anti-military and pacifist currents of Christianity.[35]

The broadcast of December 12 asserted that Germans and Muslims "both shared in the suffering and injustices after the end of the [First] World War. Both of these great peoples, the Germans, and the Arabs, had their honor insulted; their rights were denied and trampled underfoot. Both bled from the same wounds, and both also had the same enemy: namely the Allies who divided them and allowed them no claim to honor. Now Germany has succeeded in getting out from under this disgrace and regaining all of its old rights so that Germany's voice is now heard every-where and has again taken its old place."[36] It presented National Socialist Germany as a model to emulate a nation that had been humiliated yet had recovered its independence and unity. Shared antagonism, especially to Britain, remained another continuing theme of Nazi Arabic language propaganda.

The broadcasts of 1939–1941 lacked familiarity with local idioms and politics of the Middle East. The arrival in Berlin in November 1941 of Haj Amin el-Husseini and former Iraqi leader Rashid al-Khilani and their entourage ended that deficiency.[37] Both leaders had much-publicized meetings with Hitler and Ribbentrop. In the famous meeting with Husseini in Berlin on November 28, 1941, Hitler heard the Mufti lavish praise on him, express his support for Nazi Germany in the war, and request that Germany and Italy issue a strong declaration in support of Arab independence from Britain. Hitler replied that the time had not yet arrived for issuing such a declaration. However, he told Husseini that when the German armies on the Eastern Front reached "the southern exit" from the Caucuses, Hitler would "give the Arab world the assurance that its hour of liberation had arrived. Germany's objective would then be solely the destruction of the Jewish element residing in the Arab sphere under the protection of British power."[38] In other words, following the weeks and months in which Hitler had taken the decisions to launch the Final Solution of the Jewish Question *in Europe*, he also made clear to Husseini that he intended to extend it *outside Europe*, that is, at least to the Jews living in Egypt, Palestine, Trans-Jordan, and Iraq.[39] The purpose of the Arabic-language propaganda was to foster Arab support for the Axis armies fighting the Allies in North Africa and for Arab support extending the Holocaust to the Jews of the Middle East. In the postwar language of post-1945 international law, the Nazi Arabic language propaganda was an example of incitement to genocide.[40]

Alexander Kirk Sends "Axis Broadcasts in Arabic," to Washington, 1942–1944

Ambassador Kirk's dispatch to Secretary of State Hull of April 18, 1942, summarized German Arabic broadcasts of the preceding six months, that is, the period since Husseini and Kilani had arrived in Berlin.[41] German propaganda broadcasts, he wrote, attempted to convince the Arabs that the Axis countries had

> a natural sympathy with the Arabs and their great civilization, the only one comparable with the civilization introduced by the New Order into Europe, which is now being suppressed by 'British Imperialism,' 'Bolshevik barbarity,' and 'Jewish greed' and more recently 'American materialism.'

Indeed, "one of the main German war aims" was "to release Arab countries from the oppressive grip of Anglo-Bolshevik Imperialism." It was necessary for "the Arab countries to aid their liberators by uniting against the common enemy." They could do so with confidence because "the Allies 'despise but fear' the Arabs" while German victory and the break-up of the British Empire were becoming more certain. In the scramble that would follow this "imminent British collapse" when "Americans, Russians, and Jews" would "try to seize the countries now held by Britain, the Arabs may find themselves with new masters if they do not move quickly." They could never be Britain's friends because "her promises are false." Britain had "destroyed Arab unity and murdered Arab patriots; she has handed Palestine over to the Jews and loosed the Communists over Iran and Iraq." The Arabs remembered "the generous promises made by Britain in the last war." Those promises were broken while "British oppression" continued into the current period.[42] Throughout World War II, Nazi Germany presented itself to Arabs and Muslims as a champion of anti-imperialism.

Kirk noted the blend of secular and religious appeals from the Axis. Nazi radio claimed that "before Islam" the Arabs had been divided against themselves. "When Mohammed united them, they overthrew the Persians, Romans, and Jews as they can now overthrow the British, Russians, and Americans." Now they would "be led by their great leaders the Mufti [Haj Amin el-Husseini] and [Iraqi] Rashid Ali [Kilani] who are continually exchanging congratulatory messages with Hitler and Mussolini." For those Arabs who supported Britain and thus proved "false to Islam," an Axis victory in the Middle East would be "a bad day for [these] traitors when the victorious and righteous liberators of Islam arrive" assisted by "a widespread revolt throughout the entire Middle East" by the Arabs.[43] The cause of Nazi Germany, and that of Islam in the region were one. Germany's enemies were also enemies of Islam.

Kirk wrote that Nazi radio attacked the Jews "ad nauseam," claiming that the Jews, backed by Britain and the United States, were "the archenemies of Islam." The announcers claimed that the Jews controlled American finance and forced Roosevelt to pursue a policy of aggression. Roosevelt and Churchill, though criminals themselves, were "playthings in the hands of the Jewish fiends who are destroying civilization." It was known that "the White House 'is full of Jews' and most eminent figures among the Allies in the Near East are Jews." The Zionist leader Chaim Weizmann was an "aspirant to the throne of Palestine." He was "determined that Palestine, Syria, and Transjordan will be united as a pure Jewish center that will control the whole of the Middle East and, eventually, the world." America and Britain supported this plan. The Arabs who had "lost their lands and wealth to the rapacious Jewish settlers in Palestine and their liberty to the British, will now be deported to suffer famine and discomfort in lands even more barren than those palmed off on them in Palestine." Five million Jews were soon to be brought to Palestine. The Jews promised to raise an army of 20,000 men "ostensibly to assist the Allies, but in reality, to wipe out the Arabs should the Germans advance." German radio repeatedly claimed that a new Jewish state would expand into the territories of the existing Arab countries.[44]

In summer 1942, the incitement on Nazi radio to murder Jews reached a fever pitch. In the spring, summer, and fall of 1942, as General Erwin Rommel's Afrika Korps had advanced to within 60 miles west of Alexandria, Egypt, Nazi Germany's leaders thought victory in North Africa might be in their grasp. Hitler and Mussolini issued a public declaration about Arab independence that Husseini and Kilani had been requesting since their arrival in Rome and Berlin the previous fall.[50] Neither Vichy France nor Fascist Italy had gone to war in order to guarantee independence and sovereignty to the Arabs. Hitler had hesitated to make such a declaration first so as not to offend Britain when he had hopes of reaching an accommodation with it and then in order not to undermine Mussolini's hopes of expansion in the Mediterranean. Now that an uprising in Egypt might undermine British armed forces, both of the dictators agreed to go ahead with the declaration in order to assist their military operations in North Africa.

On July 3, 1942, "Berlin in Arabic" presented the Axis powers as engaged in a battle against British colonialism. Troops of the Axis powers were "victoriously advancing into Egyptian territory ... to guarantee Egypt's independence and sovereignty." The Axis forces were entering Egypt

> to dismiss the British from Egyptian territory ... and to liberate the whole of the Near East from the British yoke. The policy of the Axis powers is inspired by the principle 'Egypt for the Egyptians.' The emancipation of Egypt from the chains which have linked her with Britain, and her security

from the risks of war, will enable her to assume her position among the independent sovereign states.[45]

On July 3, 1942, "Berlin in Arabic" broadcast the following statement by Haj Amin el-Husseini

> The glorious victory secured by the Axis troops in North Africa has encouraged the Arabs and the whole East and filled their hearts with admiration for Marshall Rommel's genius, and the bravery of the Axis soldiers. This is because the Arabs believe that the Axis Powers are fighting against the common enemy, namely the British and the Jews, and in order to remove the danger of communism from spreading, following the [Allied] aggression on Iran. These victories, generally speaking, will have far-reaching repercussions on Egypt, because the loss of the Nile Valley and of the Suez Canal, and the collapse of the British mastery over the Mediterranean and the Red Sea, will bring nearer the defeat of Britain and the end of the British Empire.[46]

At 8:15 p.m. Cairo time on July 7, 1942, the Americans recorded one of the most inflammatory broadcasts of the war to that point. The "Voice of Free Arabism" (hereafter VFA) statement entitled "Kill the Jews Before They Kill You" illustrated the links between the general propaganda line in Europe and its adaptation to the Middle East context. The broadcast began with an unsubstantiated assertion that "a large number of Jews residing in Egypt and a number of Poles, Greeks, Armenians, and Free French have been issued with revolvers and ammunition" in order to "help them against the Egyptians at the last moment, when Britain is forced to evacuate Egypt".[53] The statement continued:

> In the face of this barbaric procedure by the British, we think it best, if the life of the Egyptian nation is to be saved, that the Egyptians rise as one man to kill the Jews before they have a chance of betraying the Egyptian people. It is the duty of the Egyptians to annihilate the Jews and to destroy their property. Egypt can never forget that it is the Jews who are carrying out Britain's imperialist policy in the Arab countries and that they are the source of all the disasters, which have befallen the countries of the East. The Jews aim at extending their domination throughout the Arab countries, but their future depends on a British victory. That is why they are trying to save Britain from her fate and why Britain is arming them to kill the Arabs and save the British Empire.

> You must kill the Jews, before they open fire on you. Kill the Jews, who have appropriated your wealth and who are plotting against your security.

Arabs of Syria, Iraq, and Palestine, what are you waiting for? The Jews are planning to violate your women, to kill your children, and to destroy you. According to the Muslim religion, the defense of your life is a duty which can only be fulfilled by annihilating the Jews. This is your best opportunity to get rid of this dirty race, which has usurped your rights and brought misfortune and destruction on your countries. Kill the Jews, burn their property, destroy their stores, annihilate these base supporters of British imperial- ism. Your sole hope of salvation lies in annihilating the Jews before they annihilate you.[47]

The broadcast displayed the logic of projection and paranoia that was a defining feature of Nazi antisemitism in its domestic German language propaganda. "Kill the Jews Before They Kill You" combined the political accusations of Nazism with religious demands said to stem from Islam. While antisemitic propaganda of the Nazi regime in Germany assured readers and listeners that *the regime* was making good on Hitler's threats to "exterminate" and "annihilate" the Jews, the Arabic-language propaganda appealed for *audience participation* in achieving the identical goals.

Following the British disaster at the battle of Tobruk, President Franklin Roosevelt decided to send tanks and other military supplies to aid the British in North Africa. In the spring and summer of 1942, defeating the Axis in North Africa became an American priority as well. The more the United States entered the fray, the more Axis propaganda described Roosevelt as a tool of the Jews. On July 2, Fritz Grobba, one of the leading experts on the Middle East in the Foreign Office, wrote a propaganda directive entitled "The Jews Are the Wirepullers of the Americans."[48] In light of Roosevelt's decisions, German propaganda in Arabic needed to stress that every American who "comes to the Orient comes in service of the Jews. He is sent here by the Jews, even if he does not know it. The Jews are the wire pullers of the Americans." His memo urged diffusion into Arabic propaganda of the antisemitic interpretation of Franklin Roosevelt that had been standard fare in German-language propaganda in Germany.[49]

In March 1943, officials in the Foreign Ministry in Berlin acknowledged that German propaganda in North Africa was "running into difficulties because leading Arab circles are hostile only to Britain." The Arabs still trusted the Americans. Therefore, to foster anti-Americanism,

we should again stress the necessity of using all relevant materials about Zionism. In particular, we should point to the Jews' desire to establish boundaries [in Palestine] rooted in the Old Testament, that is, [boundaries that extend] to the Euphrates River. This material can be used gradually to shatter the Arabs' confidence in the Americans' promises.[50]

Such propaganda demonstrated the convergence of the anti-Jewish and anti-Zionist policy.

American and British officials believed that some hard-to-ascertain portion of Arab opinion had become sympathetic to Nazi Germany and that a key reason for that support was Nazi Germany's attack on the Jews in Europe and equally if not more important its opposition to the Zionist aspirations in Palestine. In response, they decided that during the war, in order not to antagonize Arab opinion, they would not directly confront or refute the Nazi's anti-Arabic language Jewish and anti-Zionist propaganda. In a "Weekly Propaganda Directive" of November 14, 1942, the Overseas Operations Branch of the OWI proposed the following guidelines for Voice of America broadcasts for Palestine.[51] The Voice of America had to speak to the people of Palestine with greater tact and caution than elsewhere in the Middle East.

1 Spoken and written words must alike be guided by an honest acceptance of the fact that the subject of Zionist aspirations cannot be mentioned, inasmuch as any serious outbreak of anti-Jewish feeling which might result among the Arab peoples in this area would jeopardize our strategy in the Eastern Mediterranean.
2 Equally taboo, at present, is any mention of a Jewish army.
3 It must be remembered that, as a whole, the Jews are staunchly supporting the cause of the United Nations: the Arabs are not. Therefore, our words must be addressed primarily to Moslem and Christian Arabs, especially in view of the effectiveness of enemy propaganda.[52]

Voice of America broadcasts should "quote Hitler's own observations in regard to alien races and cultures and hold them up to ridicule and scorn" while stressing "the paganism of our enemies and embroider our comments with Biblical and Koranic phrases of denunciation." Contrasts should be drawn between "the terrible consequences of German rule upon her own allies and in the occupied countries with accounts of the benefits to be reaped by all people when victory is ours."[53] In short, in order to win and sustain support for the Allied cause in Palestine, OWI officials decided it was best *not* to directly denounce and confront the antisemitic propaganda being broadcast on Germany's Arabic shortwave radio. They assumed that Nazi propaganda was having success in gaining support for Nazi Germany among Arab nationalist and Islamist groups by linking the Allies to the Jews. Subsequent reports by the OSS and American military intelligence agents repeated this concern.[54] Although they were very well informed about its broad outlines and details, the Allies decided not to fight a war of ideas against Nazi Germany's anti-Jewish propaganda for the Arab world.

From 1943 to the end of the war, "Berlin in Arabic" and "The Voice of Free Arabism" presented constant and increasingly desperate warnings of the catastrophe that would befall Arabs and Muslims if the Allies were to defeat Nazi Germany. In Germany, Goebbels's "Do You Want Total War?" speech of February 18, 1943 offered vivid descriptions of the disasters to befall the Germans should they lose the war.[55] The Arabic-language broadcasts focused on the supposedly awful fate that the Jews had in store for Arabs and Muslims. For example, on September 8, 1943, "Berlin in Arabic" described "The Ambitions of the Jews." If the Allies won the war, the Jews would not be satisfied until they made "every territory between the Tigris and the Nile Jewish." Their goal was to "remove the Cross and the Crescent from all Arab countries." If they succeeded, "there will remain not a single Arab Muslim or Christian in the Arab world. Arabs! Imagine Egypt, Iraq, and all the Arab countries becoming Jewish with no Christianity or Islam there."[56]

On November 5, 1943, Husseini spoke at the Islamic Central Institute in Berlin to protest the Balfour Declaration.[57] The Institute published a German text, and the Foreign Ministry printed thousands of copies in Arabic and distributed them through its clandestine courier network in the Middle East.[58] The speech included key themes and whole sections of the text of his *Islam and the Jews* first delivered six years earlier in Bludan, Syria. Husseini, again, made clear that his hatred of the Jews lay in his reading of founding texts of Islam as well as in modern secular sources. He described the Balfour Declaration of November 2, 1917, whose goal was the establishment of a Jewish national home in Palestine, as "the result of a Jewish-English conspiracy in the last war." The declaration gave Palestine, which he called "an Arab-Islamic country" of great importance to Muslims, to the Jews and in so doing, broke Britain's promises to Arab leaders of postwar independence. Husseini referred to the Jews' "overwhelming egoism" that was part of their character, their "contemptible belief" that they were God's chosen people, and their claim that everything had been created for their own sake and that "other men are animals that could be used for their own purposes."[59]

As a result of these characteristics, he said that the Jews could not be loyal to another nation. Rather

> they live like a sponge among peoples, suck their blood, seize their property, undermine their morals yet still demand the rights of local inhabitants. They want every advantage, but they won't assume any obligations! All of this has brought the hostility of the world down on them and nourished the Jews' hatred that had been burning for two thousand years against all the peoples.

He believed that "God's anger and the curse on the Jews mentioned in the Holy Koran" was due to these Jewish characteristics. The Jews who had

> tormented the world for ages have been the enemy of the Arabs and of Islam since its emergence. The Holy Koran expressed this old enmity in the following words: 'You will find that those who are most hostile to the believers are the Jews.' They tried to poison the great and noble prophets. They resisted them, were hostile to them, and intrigued against them. This was the case for 1,300 years. For all that time, they have not stopped spinning intrigues against the Arabs and Muslims.

Indeed, he called the Jews "the driving forces of the destruction of the regime of the Islamic Caliphate" in the Middle East. The Jews used their power in finance, politics, and the press to this end. The Arabs and Muslims all knew of "Jewish desire" to seize the Islamic holy sites, such as the Al Aksa Mosque and "to build a temple on its ruins."[60] Husseini denounced the Balfour Declaration, and Zionist intentions to establish a Jewish home in Palestine as the latest chapter of a continuity of Jewish enmity to Islam.

The transfer of ideas that evening was from the Middle East to Nazi Germany. Nazi Germany's state-sponsored antisemitism certainly fostered its spread in other countries. Yet Husseini's hatred of the Jews was not the result of the impact of Nazi ideology on his thinking. It was due to his own Islamist interpretation of the religion of Islam. In 1937, he had made very clear that he believed that the religion of Islam was inherently anti-Jewish, or in modern terms, antisemitic. The Nazis did not create the Islamist reading of Islam, but they gave it a global platform. In Berlin, he learned how to take his ancient hatreds and adapt them to the Nazis "antisemitic" conspiracy theories of the twentieth century. Ironically, to combine the Nazi conspiracy theory with his Islamist hatreds was a way of becoming a more modern man than he was in 1937. It was his own chapter in the history of reactionary modernist ideology and politics.

This mixture of racism, Jew-hatred, and Islamist religious fanaticism found regular expression on the radio in the last year and a half of the war. On January 29, 1944, "Berlin in Arabic" broadcast "Arabs and Moslems at war with Jewry."[61] It presented Arabs and Jews as two distinct and different religions, but also a distinct and different *race*. While the Arabs were "lavishly generous," the Jews were "meanly miserly."

> While the Arabs are courageous and warlike, the Jews are cowardly and fearful. The differences between the two races were the reason for the enduring enmity which has always existed between them. We therefore believe that this enmity and strife between the Arabs and the Jews will always be maintained until one of the two races is destroyed. This struggle

or war between the Arabs and the Jews is based on beliefs, and such conflicts cannot end other than with the destruction of one party. We must also admit that the responsibility for this racial war between the Arabs and the Jews lies on the shoulders of the Jews. The characteristics of the Arabs, their generosity, unselfishness, and will to sacrifice cannot lead to war.

The broadcast presented described the difference between Judaism and Islam as a *racial* difference as well. The conflict between them was irreconcilable on both grounds. It was thus a Manichean war that had to end in the destruction of one party or another. Compromise and coexistence were impossible. In addition to its conspiracy theories, the second distinctive "modern" Nazi contribution to the cultural fusion of the broadcasts was Nazi racial ideology and the resulting view that Judaism and the Jews had irreconcilable differences with Islam and the Arabs due to their supposed inherent racial characteristics that were somehow associated with the contrasting religious identifications.

Aftereffects

American and British intelligence agencies had abundant evidence that Nazi Germany's anti-Jewish and anti-Zionist propaganda struck some responsive chords in the region. In preparing for the International Military Tribunal in Nuremberg, lead U.S. prosecutor Supreme Court Justice Robert Jackson requested that William Donovan, Director of the OSS, prepare a report about Arab collaboration with the Nazis and likely responses to placing the collaborators on trial for war crimes. The OSS report of June 23, 1945 "The Near East and the War Crimes Problem" did just that.[62] The OSS analysts concluded that

> in the Near East the popular attitude toward the trial of [Nazi] war criminals is one of apathy. As a result of the general Near Eastern feeling of hostility to the imperialism of certain of the Allied powers, there is a tendency to sympathize with rather than condemn those who have aided the Axis.[63]

In May 1945, the French army had arrested Husseini in Germany and brought him to house arrest near Paris. A year later, under relaxed surveillance, he was able to escape using an alias and disguise on a TWA flight to Cairo. The enthusiastic response to his return provided an example of what the OSS analysts had in mind.

Throughout the war, American and British intelligence agencies had been concerned about the pro-Axis sympathies of the Muslim Brotherhood in Egypt. The OSS files include the following statement by Hassan al-Banna, leader of the Muslim Brotherhood. He sent it on June 11, 1946, to officials of the Arab League.

> Al-Ikhwan Al-Muslimin [the Moslem Brotherhood] and all Arabs request the Arab League on which Arab hopes are pinned, to declare that the Mufti is welcome to stay in any Arab country he may choose, and that great welcome should be extended to him wherever he goes, as a sign of appreciation for his great services for the glory of Islam and the Arabs. The hearts of the Arabs palpitated with joy at hearing that the Mufti has succeeded in reaching an Arab country. The news sounded like thunder to the ears of some American, British, and Jewish tyrants. The lion is at last free, and he will roam the Arabian jungle to clear it of the wolves. ... What a hero, what a miracle of a man. We wish to know what the Arab youth, Cabinet Ministers, rich men, and princes of Palestine, Syria, Iraq, Tunis, Morocco, and Tripoli are going to do to be worthy of this hero. *Yes, this hero who challenged an empire and fought Zionism, with the help of Hitler and Germany. Germany and Hitler are gone, but Amin El-Husseini will continue the struggle* God entrusted him with a mission and he must succeed. The Lord Almighty did not preserve Amin for nothing. There must be a divine purpose behind the preservation of the life of this man, namely the defeat of Zionism. Amin! March on! God is with you! We are behind you! We are willing to sacrifice our necks for the cause. To death! Forward March.[64]

A plausible reading of al-Banna's statement would be that Haj Amin el-Husseini was continuing *the same* struggle that Hitler and Germany, as well as Husseini himself, had been waging during World War II, the "struggle" against the Allies, the Jews, and Zionism. al-Banna and the Muslim Brotherhood intended to continue that war in the Middle East. If so, who better to play a leading role than a political and religious leader with experience in fighting the Jewish enemy in Europe? Far from criticizing him for having sided with "Germany and Hitler," al-Banna expressed admiration for Husseini's wartime activities. Living in wartime Egypt, al-Banna and the members of the Muslim Brotherhood would have been able to hear what Husseini and others on "Berlin in Arab" and the "Voice of Free Arabism" on Nazi radio had to say about the Jews, Zionism, and the Allies. He found these words and actions admirable. Moreover, al-Banna interpreted Husseini's survival, "escape," and arrival in Cairo as proof that "the Lord Almighty" approved as well.

Conclusion

Research findings in American and German archives in recent decades extend our understanding of Nazi ideology and policy beyond a Eurocentric framework. They shed further light on the contribution that the Arab exiles made to the Nazi war effort. Haj Amin el-Husseini was an exile on the run, not a power broker in the Nazi regime. Without the technical resources and financial support of the Nazi regime, he would have remained a figure of local importance in the peripheral conflict over the future British Mandate Palestine. Hitler's regime made him a global star.

The Nazi regime failed in its efforts to achieve military victory in North Africa and the Middle East, as well as in its plans to extend the Holocaust to the Jews of that region. It succeeded however in nurturing anti-Jewish and anti-Zionist sentiments that persisted after 1945 in that region. Cultural fusion, the movement of ideas in both directions from Germany to the Middle East, and from the Middle East to Nazi Germany took place during World War II and the Holocaust. The Arab exiles taught the Nazis that the Islamists offered an interpretation of Islam as an inherently anti-Jewish religion. The Nazis taught the exiles how to integrate that Islamist Jew-hatred into the more "modern" conspiracy theories and racist ideology at the core of Nazi Germany's own anti-Jewish ideology and policy. The resulting cultural fusion and resulting incitement to genocide was evident in Nazi propaganda aimed at Arabs and Muslims.

Husseini and his fellow collaborators and their comrades in the Muslim Brotherhood in Egypt were founders of a distinctive tradition known as "Islamism," a mid-twentieth-century radical interpretation of the religion of Islam which gave anti-Judaism a centrality and intensity that it had not possessed previously. The core themes were there from 1937 on in Husseini's *Islam and the Jews*. It was not the case that his core text had "nothing to do with Islam." It had everything to do with his selective reading of the sacred texts of Islam. In that sense, Islamic antisemitism shared with its Nazi counterpart the tendency to read sacred texts in a way that accentuated—but did not invent out of thin air—long-standing stereotypes, prejudices, and hatreds about Judaism and the Jews in both Christianity and Islam. The texts examined in the preceding pages documented a crucial chapter in the history of the Islamist tradition, one that was connected to collaboration with Nazi Germany.

Nazi Germany was defeated and discredited but, as Hassan al-Banna made clear in 1946, antisemitism, that is, hatred of Judaism, the Jews, and then of the new state of Israel lived on in the Muslim Brotherhood in Egypt, in Husseini's leadership of the Palestine Arabs in the 1947–1948 war to prevent the establishment of the state of Israel, in the Islamic Republic of Iran, the Hamas Covenant of 1988, the ideology of Al Qaeda, Hezbollah, and the Islamic state. The ideological synthesis that emerged from the collaboration of Nazis and Islamists, especially in the peak years of 1941–1945 in Berlin, struck nerves among the Islamists of North Africa and the Middle East and therefore played a decisive role in the persistence and political impact of anti-Jewish and anti-Zionist politics in the aftermath of World War II and the Holocaust.[65]

Notes

1 This chapter draws on Jeffrey Herf, *Nazi Propaganda for the Arab World*. (New Haven, CT: Yale University Press, 2009), and on Jeffrey Herf, *The Jewish Enemy: Nazi Propaganda During World War II and the Holocaust* (Cambridge, MA: Harvard University Press, 2006). Also see Jeffrey Herf, "Nazi Germany and Islam in Europe, North Africa and the Middle East," *Central European History*, 49, 2 (June 2016), 261–269; and his "Nazi Propaganda to the Arab World During World War II and the Holocaust: and Its Aftereffects," in Antony McElligott and Jeffrey Herf, eds., *Antisemitism Before and Since the Holocaust: Altered Contexts and Recent Perspectives* (New York and London: Palgrave Macmillan: 2017), 183–204.

2 On Nazi Germany's policy toward Islam in general, see David Motadel, *Islam and Nazi Germany's War* (Cambridge, MA: Harvard University Press, 2014).

3 See the classic study by Lukasz Hirszowicz, *The Third Reich and the Arab East* (London: Routledge and Kegan Paul; Toronto: University of Toronto Press, 1966); and the recent important work by Klaus Michael Mallmann and Martin Cuppers, *Halbmond und Hakenkreuz. Das Dritte Reich, die Araber und Palastina* (Darmstadt: Wissenschaftliche Buchgesellschaft, 2006). Also see Robert Lewis Melka, "The Axis and the Middle East: 1930–1945" (unpublished Ph.D. diss., University of Minnesota, 1966); Francis R. Nicosia, *The Third Reich and the Palestine Question* (New Brunswick, NJ: Transaction Publishers, 1999); Josef Schroëder, "Die Beziehungen der Achsenmächte zur Arabischen Welt," in *Hitler, Deutschland und die Mächte. Materialien zur Außenpolitik des Dritten Reiches*, ed. Manfred Funke (Düsseldorf: Droste Verlag, 1976), 365–382; Philip Bernd Schroëder, *Deutschland in der Mittlere Osten im Zweiten Weltkrieg* (Göttingen: Musterschmidt, 1975); Wolfgang Schwanitz, *Germany and the Middle East, 1871–1945* (Princeton, NJ: Markus Wiener Publishers, 2004); and Heinz Tillmann, *Deutschlands Araberpolitik im Zweiten Weltkrieg* (Berlin: Deutsche Verlag der Wissenschaften, 1965).

4 On the impact of Nazism on the Middle East, and on Islamist collaboration and response see Matthias Küntzel, *Jihad and Jew-Hatred: Islamism, Nazism, and the Roots of 9/11*, trans. Colin Meade (New York: Telos Press, 2007); and his *Nazis und der Nahe Osten: Wie der Islamische Antisemitismus Entstand* (Berlin and Leipzig: Hentrich & Hentrich, 2019), English ed., *Aftershock: The Nazis, Islamic Antisemitism and the Middle East* (London: Routledge, 2023): Bernard Lewis, *Semites and Anti-Semites: An Inquiry into Conflict and Prejudice* (New York and London: W. W. Norton, 1986 and 1999); and Meir Litvak and Esther Webman, *From Empathy to Denial: Arab Responses to the Holocaust* (London: Hurst and Company 2009). For contrasting perspectives, see Israel Gershoni, ed., *Arab Responses to Fascism: Attraction and Repulsion* (Austin: University of Texas Press, 2014).

5 On these discussions, see "Zugehörigkeit der Ägypter, Iraker, Iraner, Perser und Turken zur arischen Rasse, Bd. 1, 1935–1936," Politisches Archive des Auswärtiges Amt (Berlin) R99173; and Herf, *Nazi Propaganda for the Arab World*, 15–35.

6 On Nazi Berlin's "Muslim moment," see Motadel, *Islam and Nazi Germany's War*, 38–70.

7 For example, Alexander Kirk, "Telegram Sent, September 13, 1941, 8 p.m., to Department of State from Cairo Legation, Number 1361," 1–3, NARA RG 84, Foreign Service Posts of the U.S. Department of State (hereafter RG 84), Cairo Legation and Embassy, Secret and Confidential General Records, 1939, 1941–1947, 1941, 820.02-830, Box 4, Folder 820.02 1941.

8 On Kirk and the beginnings of "Axis Broadcasts in Arabic," see Herf, *Nazi Propaganda for the Arab World*, 10–11, 69–74.

9 See Senator Robert F. Wagner's appeal to Secretary of State George Marshall in 1947 in Jeffrey Herf, *Israel's Moment: International Support for and Opposition to Establishing the Jewish State, 1945–1949* (Cambridge and New York: Cambridge University Press, 2022), 66–68.

10 Jeffrey Herf, *Nazi Propaganda for the Arab World* (New Haven, CT: Yale University Press, 2009); and "Nazi Germany's Propaganda Aimed at Arabs and Muslims During World War II and the Holocaust: Old Themes, New Archival Findings," *Central European History* 42, 04 (December 2009): 709–736.

11 Also see "Propaganda und Mitwisserschaft," in Eckart Conze, Norbert Frei, Peter Hayes, and Moshe Zimmerman, eds., *Das Amt und die Vergangenheit: Deutsche Diplomaten im Dritten Reich und in der Bundesrepublik* (Blessing Karl Verlag, 2010), 192–199. On traditions and their reworking by intellectuals, see Edward Shils, *Tradition* (Chicago, IL: University of Chicago Press, 1981), 195–261; and his *The Intellectuals and the Powers and Other Essays* (Chicago, IL: University of Chicago, 1972). David Nirenberg, in *Anti-Judaism: The Western Tradition* (New York: W.W. Norton, 2013), makes the important point that, as a reading of the Koran's intertextual commentaries on the Torah, and the New Testament makes clear, the religion of Islam and the Koran are integral parts of the Western tradition. See his Chapter 4, "'To Every Prophet an Adversary': Jewish Enmity in Islam," 135–182. The Nazis reinterpreted the Western tradition as one that was inherently and predominantly racist and antisemitic. They found in Islam as they interpreted it a parallel if culturally distinct bundle of hatreds.

12 For recent examples, see Gerhard Weinberg, *A World at Arms: A Global History of World War II* (New York: Cambridge University Press, 1994); and Horst Boog et al., *The Global War: Widening of the Conflict into a World War and the Shift of the Initiative, 1941–1943*, trans. Ewald Osers (New York: Oxford University Press, 2001). The German original is Horst Boog et al., *Das Deutsche Reich und der Zweite Weltkrieg. Vol. 6, Der Globale Krieg: Die Ausweitung zum Weltkrieg und der Wechsel der Initiative, 1941–1943* (Stuttgart: Deutsche Verlags-Anstalt, 1990).

13 Heinz Tillmann, Deutschlands Araberpolitik im Zweiten Weltkrieg.

14 Hirszowicz, *The Third Reich and the Arab East*.

15 Mallmann and Cuppers, *Halbmond und Hakenkreuz*; and *Nazi Palestine: Plans for the Extermination of the Jews of Palestine* was Published in 2010. (New York: Enigma Press, 2010); and their "'Elimination of the Jewish National Home in Palestine': The Einsatzkommando of the Panzer Army Africa, 1942," *Yad Vashem Studies* 35, 1 (2007): 111–141.

16 In a speech in Palestine in 1942, David Ben Gurion said, "The Nazis are not far away, but we are being threatened not only by Rommel in North Africa. We are also in danger of invasion from Syria and even Iraq and Turkey," cited in Tuvia

Friling, *Arrows in the Dark: David Ben-Gurion, the Yishuv Leadership, and Rescue Attempts during the Holocaust*, trans. Ora Cummings (Madison: University of Wisconsin Press, 2005), 64–65. On Nazis' anti-Jewish policies in North Africa, see Robert Satloff, *Among the Righteous: Lost Stories from the Long Reach of the Holocaust into Arab Lands* (New York: Public Affairs, 2006).

17 The phrase is from Raymond Williams, *Marxism and Literature* (New York: Oxford University Press, 1977).

18 Husseini was a central figure in Nazi propaganda. He worked with Heinrich Himmler and was collaborating with a regime he knew was implementing the Final Solution. However, he was not a decision maker in the Nazi regime. The Holocaust would have taken place without his assistance. On the importance and limits of his political power and influence in Nazi Germany, see Jeffrey Herf, "Haj Amin al-Husseini, the Nazis and the Holocaust: The Origins, the Nature and Aftereffects of Collaboration," *Jewish Political Studies Review*, 26, 3/4, (Fall 2014): 13–37; also at http://jcpa.org/article/haj-amin-al-husseini-the-nazis-and-the-holocaust-the-origins-nature-and-aftereffects-of-collaboration/

19 Jeffrey Herf, *Reactionary Modernism: Technology, Culture, and Politics in Weimar and the Third Reich* (New York: Cambridge University Press, 1984).

20 Esther Webman, "New Islamic Antisemitism, Mid-19th to the 21st Century," in Steven T. Katz, *Cambridge Companion to Antisemitism* (New York and Cambridge: Cambridge University Press, 2022), 430–447.

21 On Haj Amin el-Husseini and Nazi Germany, see Klaus Gensicke, *Der Mufti von Jerusalem und die Nationalsozialisten. Eine politische Biographie Amin el-Husseinis* (Darmstadt: Wissenschaftliche Buchgesellschaft, 2007); Zvi Elpeleg, *The Grand Mufti: Haj Amin al-Hussaini, Founder of the Palestinian National Movement*, trans. David Harvey, ed. Shmuel Himelstein (London: Frank Cass, 1993); Jeffrey Herf, *The Jewish Enemy*, 192–174, 179–180, and, 243–244; *Nazi Propaganda for the Arab World*; and "Haj Amin al-Husseini, the Nazis and the Holocaust: The Origins, the Nature and Aftereffects of Collaboration," *Jewish Political Studies Review*, 26, 3/4, (Fall 2014): 13–37: http://jcpa.org/article/haj-amin-al-husseini-the-nazis-and-the-holocaust-the-origins-nature-and-aftereffects-of-collaboration/; Matthias Küntzel, *Nazis und der Nahe Osten*; and Joseph B. Schechtman, *The Mufti and the Fuhrer: The Rise and Fall of Haj Amin el-Husseini* (New York: Thomas Yoseloff, 1965); and Anthony De Luca, "'Der Grossmufti' in Berlin: The Politics of Collaboration," *International Journal of Middle East Studies* 10, no. 1 (February 1979): 125–138. Husseini's major speeches in wartime Berlin have been published in German. See Gerhard Höpp, ed., *Mufti-Papiere. Briefe, Memoranden, Reden und Aufrufe Amin al-usainis aus dem Exil 1940–1945* (Berlin: Schwarz, 2001).

22 For a detailed list of Junker and Dünnhaupt publications from the Weimar era to the end of World War II, see https://de.wikipedia.org/wiki/Junker_und_D%C3%BCnnhaupt

23 See Haj Amin el-Husseini, "Islam-Judentum: Aufruf des Großmufti an die islamische Welt im Jahre 1937," in Mohamed Sabry, *Islam-Judentum-Boschewismus* (Berlin: Junker und Dünnhaupt, 1938), 22–32; Herf, "Preface to the Paperback Edition," *Nazi Propaganda for the Arab World* (New Haven, CT: Yale University Press, 2010), ix–xvii; and the discussion of the text in Matthias Küntzel, *Nazis in der Nahe Osten*, 63–69; forthcoming as *Aftershock: The Nazis, Islamic Antisemitism and the Middle East* (London: Routledge, 2023).

24 On the distinctive, twentieth-century Islamist interpretation of Islamic sacred texts, see Bassam Tibi, *Islamism and Islam* (New Haven, CT: Yale University Press, 2012).

25 "Personalbestand der Rundfunkpolitische Abteilung (Berlin, August 14, 1943), PAAA Rund- funkpolitische Abteilung," R67476 Referat Ru Pers. Ru HS, Bd. 1: Verwaltung Organisation 1939–1945, Bde. 1–2. On Kurt Kiesinger in Nazi Germany and in the Federal Republic, see Philipp Gassert, *George Kiesinger, 1904–1988: Kanzler zwischen den Zeiten* (Munich: Deutsche Verlags-Anstalt, 2006).

26 On the Political Department's Orient Office, and the roles of Melchers, Kiesinger, and Munzel, see Herf, *Nazi Propaganda for the Arab World*, 36–40; and "Propaganda und Mitwisserschaft," in Conze, Frei, Hayes, Zimmerman, *Das Amt und die Vergangenheit*, 192–199; and Werner Schipps, *Wortschlacht im Äther. Der deutsche Auslandsrundfunk im Zweiten Weltkrieg* (Berlin: Haude and Spenersche Verlagsbuchhandlung, 1971. On the participation of German Orientalists in the Nazi regime's propaganda campaigns, see "Martin Abel," in Ludmila Hanisch, *Die Nachfolger der Exegeten: Deutschsprachige Erforschung des Vorderen Orients in der ersten Hälfte des 20. Jahrhunderts* (Wiesbaden: Harrassowitz Verlag, 2002).

27 Schipps, *Wortschlacht im Äther. Der deutsche Auslandsrundfunk im Zweiten Weltkrieg.* 16, 45–46.

28 Ibid., 58. On the Political Department's Orient Office, and the roles of Melchers, and Munzel, see Herf, *Nazi Propaganda for the Arab World*, 38–40. On Melchers during and after the Nazi era, see Eckart Conze, Norbert Frei, Peter Hayes, and Moshe Zimmerman, eds., *Das Amt und die Vergangenheit: Deutsche Diplomaten im Dritten Reich und in der Bundesrepublik* (Blessing Karl Verlag, 2010).

29 Anne H. Fuller, "Memorandum on Radio Reception in the Near East and India" (August 18, 1941), National Archives and Record Administration, College Park (hereafter NARA), Record Group (hereafter RG) 208, Records of the Office of War Information, Informational Files on the Near East, 1941–1946, Box 417.

30 See "Egypt" and "Libya," *World Survey of Education*, vol. 1 (Paris: UNESCO, 1955), 216 and 424. On literacy in Palestine, see Ami Ayalon, *Reading Palestine: Printing and Literacy, 1900–1948* (Austin: University of Texas Press, 2004), 16–17.

31 Kult.R.Ref. VIII (VII) (Orient) Mn/P/B Kultureller Talk vom 3. Dezember 1940, "Ein Blatt über die Besetzung der Englander in Ägypten," Berlin (December 3, 1940), Bundesarchiv Berlin (BAB), R901 Auswärtiges Amt, R73039 Rundfunkabteilung, Ref. VIII Arabische und Iranische Sendungen, vorl. 39, Dez. 1940–Jan. 1941, 2.

32 Ibid., 2.

33 Bundesarchiv Berlin, [Lichterfelde] (BAB) R901 Auswärtiges Amt, R73039 Rundfunkabteilung, Ref. VIII Arabische und Iranische Sendungen, vorl. 39, Dez. 1940–Jan. 1941, Kult.R, Ref. VIII (Orient), Mu/Scha "Religio¨ ser Wochentalk vom 12. Dez. 1940 (arabisch) Die Freigebigkeit," broadcast on December 12, 1940, 14–16. Although most of the Division of Radio Policy files are in the Political Archive of the German Foreign Ministry, these files from 1940 to 1941 are in the Bundesarchiv in Berlin-Lichterfelde.

34 "Zur Regierungserklärung für die Araber," Talk vom 12. Dezember 1940 (arabisch), (BAB) R901 Auswärtiges Amt, R73039 Rundfunkabteilung, Ref. VIII Arabische und Iranische Sendung- en, vorl. 39, Dez. 1940–Jan. 1941, Kult.R, Ref. VIII (Orient), Mu/Scha, 11–13.

35 On Hitler and Himmler's views, and on Muslims serving in the Wehrmacht, see David Motadel, *Islam and Nazi Germany's War*, 63–66, and 219–245.

36 "Zur Regierungserklärung für die Araber," Talk vom 12. Dezember 1940 (arabisch).

37 On their arrival in Berlin and the Nazi's reception see Gensicke, *Der Mufti von Jerusalem und die Nationalsozialisten*; Mallmann and Cuppers, *Halbmond und*

Hakenkreuz, 105–120; and Hirszowicz, *The Third Reich and the Arab East*, 211–228.

38 "No. 515, Memorandum by an Official of the Foreign Minister's Secretariat, Record of the Conversation between the Fuhrer and the Grand Mufti of Jerusalem on November 28, 1941, in the Presence of Reich Foreign Minister and Minster Grobba in Berlin," Berlin (November 30, 1941), *Documents on German Foreign Policy (DGFP) Series D (1937–1945) Volume XIII, The War Years, June 23–December 11, 1941* (Washington, DC: United States Government Printing Office, 1949–1984), 881–882, 884. On the meeting, see Hirszowicz, *The Third Reich and the Arab East*, 218–221; and Gensicke, *Der Mufti von Jerusalem und die Nationalsozialisten*, 60–63.

39 Though Richard Breitman, and Christopher Browning, the leading historians of Hitler's decisions to launch the Final Solution differ about when Hitler did so, both agree that Hitler had taken these decisions by September 1941. See Richard Breitman, *Architect of Genocide: Himmler and the Final Solution* (New York: Knopf, 1991); Christopher Browning, *The Origins of the Final Solution: The Evolution of Nazi Jewish Policy, September 1939–March 1942* (Lincoln: University of Nebraska Press; Jerusalem: Yad Vashem, 2004). On the combination of Hitler's public anti-Jewish invective and government decision making see Saul Friedlander, *Nazi Germany and the Jews*, vol. 2: *The Years of Extermination*, esp. 272–288. On Goebbels public assertion on beginning of "gradual extermination," see Jeffrey Herf, *The Jewish Enemy: Nazi Propaganda during World War II and the Holocaust*, 120–128.

40 According to the language of the Genocide Convention adopted by the United Nations after World War II, some of the resulting broadcasts would meet its definition of "incitement" and could thus be described as part of the crime of genocide. Clause 3 in Article 3 of the "Convention on the Prevention and Punishment of the Crime of Genocide" includes "direct and public incitement to commit genocide" as acts that should be punishable. See http://www.hrweb.org/legal/genocide.html. The Reich Press Chief, Otto Dietrich, was tried and convicted in one of the successor trials of the Nuremberg Military Tribunal of "crimes against humanity." Efforts to bring a prosecution of Husseini and other Arab collaborationists for their role in Arabic-language broadcasts were unsuccessful. On the Dietrich trial, see Herf, *Jewish Enemy*, 272–274. On the failed postwar efforts to put Husseini on trial, see Herf, *Israel's Moment*, 1–130.

41 Alexander Kirk to Secretary of State, "Telegram 340, General Summary of Tendencies in Axis Broadcasts in Arabic," Cairo (April 18, 1942), NARA, RG659, United States Department of State, Central Decimal File, 1940–1944, 740.0011/ European War 1939, Microcopy No. M982, Roll 114, 21414.

42 Ibid., 1–2.

43 Ibid., 2–3.

44 Ibid.

45 "Despatch No. 502 from the American Legation at Cairo, Egypt, Axis Broadcasts in Arabic for the Period July 3 to 9, 1942, Cairo, July 21, 1942," 1, NARA, RG 84 Foreign Service Posts of the Department of State, General Records, Cairo Embassy, 1942, 815.4–820.02, Box 77.

46 Ibid., 1–2.

47 VFA, July 7, 1942, 8:15 p.m., "Kill the Jews before They Kill You," cable from Alexander Kirk to Secretary of State, No. 502 (July 21, 1942), 13–14; and discussion in Herf, *Nazi Propaganda for the Arab World*, 88–157.

48 Fritz Grobba, "Juden sind die Drahtzieher der Amerikaner," Berlin (July 2, 1942), PAAA, R60690 Kult Pol, Orient. Juden um Roosevelt, 1941–1942, Bd. 1.

49 On Nazi Germany's extensive antisemitic propaganda attack on Roosevelt, see page references under "Roosevelt, Franklin D," in Herf, *Jewish Enemy*, 387.

50 Preikecher, "Aufzeichnung für die BFP im Stabe des Herrn Reichaussenministers Herrn Dr. Magerle" (March 16, 1943), NARA, RG242, Records of the German Foreign Office, Microcopy No. T120, roll 1015. Also see "Nazi Anti-Zionism" in this volume.

51 "Office of War Information, Overseas Operations Branch, Washington, DC, 'Weekly Propaganda Directive, Palestine'" (November 14, 1942), NARA, RG165 Records of the War Department General and Special Staff, Military Intelligence Division (hereafter MID), "Regional File." 1922–1944 Palestine, Box 2719, Folder 2930.

52 Ibid.

53 Ibid.

54 See, for example, (George) Wadsworth, "United States Office of War Information, Beirut to SecState, Washington" (February 17, 1943), NARA RG84, Lebanon: U.S. Consulate and Legation and Embassy, Classified General Records, 1936– 1961, 1943: 110.2 to 1943–891 Box 8, 2–3; and George Britt, United States Office of War Information, Beirut, "Political Notes on Lebanon and Syria" (February 13, 1943), NARA RG84, Lebanon. U.S. Consulate Legation and Embassy Beirut, 1936–1941, Classified General Records 1943: 1943 110.2 to 1943 - 891, 1; and George Britt, "Beirut September to June" (June 1943) NARA RG84, Lebanon. U.S. Consulate Legation and Embassy Beirut, 1936–1941, Classified General Records 1943: 1943 110.2 to 1943 - 891, 7.

55 See Herf, *Jewish Enemy*, 192–196.

56 "Berlin in Arabic," September 8, 1943, "Talk: The Ambitions of the Jews," Alexander Kirk to Secretary of State, Cairo (September 23, 1943), "No. 1313, Axis Broadcasts in Arabic for the period September 2 to 8, 1943," NARA, RG 84, Egypt: Cairo Embassy General Records, 1933–1955, 820.00-822.00, 1943, Box 93; and Voice of Free Arabism, September 24, 1943, 8:15 p.m., "What are the Aims of International Zionism?," Alexander Kirk to Secretary of State, Cairo (October 5, 1943), "No. 1325, Axis Broadcasts in Arabic for the period September 23 to 29, 1943," NARA, RG 84, Egypt: Cairo Embassy General Records, 1933–1955, 820.00-822.00, 1943, Box 93.

57 Voice of Free Arabism, November 5, 1943, 6:30 p.m., "The Protests of the Moslems of Europe against the Balfour Declaration," Alexander Kirk to Secretary of State, Cairo (November 19, 1943), "No. 1410, Axis Broadcasts in Arabic for the period November 3 to 9, 1943," 3–4, NARA, RG 84, Egypt: Cairo Embassy General Records, 1933–1955, 820.00-822.00, 1943, Box 93.

58 Haj Amin el-Husseini, *Rede S. Em. [Sein Eminenz] Des Grossmufti anlässlich der Protestkundgebung gegen die Balfour-Erklärung am 2. November 1943* (Berlin: Islamische Zentral-Institut, 1943), PAAA R27327, Grossmufti, 1942–1944, 297878–886.

59 Ibid., 297878–879.

60 Ibid., 297880.

61 "Berlin in Arabic," January 28, 1944, "Talk: Arabs and Moslems at War with Jewry," Alexander Kirk to Secretary of State, Cairo (February 6, 1944), "No. 1581, Axis Broadcasts in Arabic for the Period January 22 to 28, 1944," NARA RG 84, Cairo Embassy General Records, 1936–1955: 1944, 820.02–822, Box 112.

62 "'The Near East and the War Crimes Problem': Office of Strategic Services, Research and Analysis Branch, R and A, No. 1090.116, 23 June 1945, Situation Report: Near East, Analysis of Current Intelligence for the Use of OSS," 1–28, in

NARA, RG 84, Syria: Damascus Legation, Confidential File, 1945: Vol. 1–2, 030-800B, Classified General Records, Box 4, Vol. II, 711-800B.

63 Ibid., "Summary."

64 "Hassan Al-Banna and the Mufti of Palestine" in "Contents of Secret Bulletin of Al Ikhwan al-Muslimin dated 11 June 1946," Cairo (July 23, 1946). NARA, RG 226, Office of Strategic Services, Washington Registry SI Intelligence, Field Files, Entry 108A, Box 15, Folder 2.

65 On Islamism after Nazism, see Paul Berman, *Terror and Liberalism* (New York: W.W. Norton, 2003); Jeffrey Herf, "What Is Old and What is New in the Terrorism of Islamic Fundamentalism," *Partisan Review* 69, 1 (Winter 2002), 25–32; also in Murray Baumgarten, Peter Kenez, and Bruce Thompson, eds., *Varieties of Antisemitism: History, Ideology, Discourse* (Newark: University of Delaware Press, 2009), 370–376; and his "Why They Fight: Hamas' Too Little-Known Fascist Charter" (August 1): http://www.the-american-interest.com/articles/2014/08/01/why-they-fight-hamas-too-little-known-fascist-charter/; Küntzel, *Jihad and Jew-Hatred*; his *Nazis und der Nahe Osten: Wie der Islamische Antisemitismus Entstand*, English ed., *Aftershock*; and Robert Wistrich, *A Lethal Obsession: Antisemitism from Antiquity to the Global Jihad* (New York: Random House, 2010). On scholarship since the 1980s, see Jeffrey Herf, "Nazi Antisemitism and Islamist Hate" (July 6, 2022): https://www.tabletmag.com/sections/history/articles/the-nazi-roots-of-islamist-hate

5

THE IMPORTANCE AND THE LIMITS OF HUSSEINI'S INFLUENCE IN NAZI BERLIN

The public and archival evidence of Haj Amin el-Husseini's eager, willing, and enthusiastic collaboration with the Nazi regime is overwhelming. Nevertheless, the Palestinian Authority has never honestly confronted the legacies of Nazi collaboration that played such a crucial personal and ideological role in the disastrous decisions to reject the UN Partition Resolution of November 1947 that would have created an Arab, as well as a Jewish state in Palestine. The failure to acknowledge the depth and ideological passion that led to Husseini's decisions to collaborate with Nazi Germany meant that his Jew-hatred found a home in the nationalism of the Palestine Arabs whom he led into the war of 1947–1948 to prevent the establishment of a Jewish state in Palestine. As the preceding chapters indicate, Husseini collaborated with Hitler's regime due to deep ideological conviction rooted in his hatred of Judaism, the Jews, and therefore of Zionism and the Zionist project in British Mandate Palestine. His collaboration went far beyond the apologetic and misleading cliché of the "enemy of my enemy is my friend." The failure of the Allied victors, both the Western democracies and the Soviet bloc states, to indict him for war crimes in the immediate aftermath of the Holocaust was one of too many examples of sweeping the Nazi past under the rug in the early postwar years.

Immediately following World War II and the Holocaust, the efforts to bring him to trial for war crimes failed as France, in particular, but also the United States and Britain, concluded that putting him on trial would undermine efforts to gain goodwill in the oil-rich Arab states.[1] Yet in the late 1940s and then again recently, some assessments of his collaboration have exaggerated his decision-making role in the Holocaust and in the Nazi regime. As the documentary record of his collaboration has deepened, so has our knowledge

DOI: 10.4324/9781003449669-6

on both the importance but also the limits of his power in Nazi Germany. On October 20, 2015, Israeli Prime Minister Benjamin Netanyahu stated in an address at the 37th Zionist Congress in Jerusalem that Husseini convinced Hitler to change his anti-Jewish policy from one of forced emigration to one of extermination. He claimed that Husseini "was one of the leading architects of the Final Solution." Fortunately, Netanyahu later retracted this exaggeration of Husseini's decision-making power in the Nazi regime.[2]

Netanyahu may have been drawing on the work of historians Wolfgang Schwanitz and Barry Rubin, who, in their 2014 work, *Nazis, Islamists and the Making of the Modern Middle East*, attributed decision-making powers regarding the Holocaust to Husseini.[3] Husseini had been urging the Nazis to end any Jewish emigration to Palestine. Rubin and Schwanitz wrote in response to Hitler's announcement of March 11, 1941, that ended Jewish emigration from Europe, that "by closing this escape route [to Palestine] for the Jews and discouraging any alternative strategy, al-Husaini helped make the 'Final Solution' inevitable."[4] The authors added that then "Germany's expulsion of the Jews was impossible and only mass murder remained."[5] Yet the end of immigration, which was a decision taken by Hitler, not Husseini, did not mean that "only mass murder remained." A continuation of the previous policy of persecution rather than extermination was a logical possibility. The key point is that it was Hitler, not Husseini, who had the power of decision-making.

The day following his then-famous meeting with Husseini's on November 28, 1941, Hitler ordered Reinhard Heydrich, Himmler's deputy in the Reich Security Main Office, to organize a conference within ten days to prepare the "final solution of the Jewish question." Rubin and Schwanitz wrote that "thus Hitler made his key decision to begin the genocide with el-Husseini's anti-Jewish rhetoric and insistence on wiping out the Jews fresh in his ears."[6] Certainly, Hitler was pleased to learn that in Husseini he had a supporter and collaborator among the Arabs and Muslims. Yet the fact that the day following their meeting on November 28, Hitler ordered Heydrich to send invitations to what became the Wannsee Conference was not evidence that Husseini had any impact on his decisions. Rather the more plausible interpretation of the aftermath of the November 28 meeting is that Hitler, having already decided to murder Europe's Jews *over the course of the previous six months*, that is, well before Husseini arrived in Berlin, wanted to inform Husseini of his desire to extend the policy to North Africa and the Middle East should the war in Europe proceed according to his hopes and plans.

The works of historians of Holocaust decision-making underscore Husseini's *unimportance* in that process. Even before the German invasion of the Soviet Union on June 22, 1941, Hitler had given orders to Heinrich Himmler who communicated them to his deputy Reinhard Heydrich who, in turn, ordered leaders of the SS *Einsatzgruppen* to murder Jews in occupied Soviet territory. The mass murders began immediately after June 22, 1941.

In mid-August 1941, having expanded the number of killers to include members of Order Police battalions, Himmler following Hitler's orders extended the policy of mass murder to include Jewish children. As Jürgen Mattäus has written, by mid-August 1941

> genocide of the Jews in the territory of the occupied Soviet Union had become a reality. No further escalation in the process was conceivable. It implied the physical elimination of all Jews, irrespective of gender, age, occupation, or behavior, and led directly to the destruction of entire communities and the 'de-Jewification' of vast areas. The question [for Nazi officials] was no longer why the Jews should be killed, but why they should *not* be killed.[7]

From June to December 1941, the SS *Einsatzgruppen* and battalions of the Order Police murdered approximately 700,000 Jews on the Eastern Front. Most of them were shot but some were gassed in newly constructed mobile gas vans. Six months before Hitler met Husseini in Berlin, his policy toward the Jews living in the Soviet Union had shifted from a policy of persecution adopted since 1933 to one of extermination.[8]

In his 1991 study, *Architect of Genocide: Himmler and the Final Solution*, Richard Breitman wrote that military victories in Western Europe in 1940 gave Hitler and Himmler "the confidence to set in motion a vast killing operation during the forthcoming campaign in the Soviet Union" planned for spring 1941. Breitman summarized his findings as follows:

> By March 1941, the Final Solution was just a matter of time—and timing. The date is months earlier than the juncture most specialists have selected, but the evidence is compelling. Hitler had rejected other, lesser plans (Madagascar, sterilization). He had already approved a liquidation plan for Jews in the Reich and Bohemia-Moravia (at the minimum). Heydrich had already started negotiations with the army regarding the *Einsatzgruppen* in the Soviet Union, and the SS Reich Security Main Office had sent "Jewish specialists" to other European countries to prepare for deportations. Emigration of Polish Jews had been banned months earlier, and closed ghettos and work camps had created the preconditions for easy disposal of Jews in Poland. Eichmann spoke of the 'final evacuation' of Jews *to* Poland at a time when Hitler was promising to remove all Jews *from* Poland. A month later Himmler referred to a new task he had for [Otto] Globocnik. Extermination in Poland was purely a technical problem. So, the argument does not rest on Hitler's rhetoric alone. None of these sources spells out everything; none is a perfect contemporary blueprint. But they are all independent sources and, taken together, form a coherent picture of far-reaching plans and fundamental decisions made during the

preparations for the campaign against the U.S.S.R. As Hitler told Hans
Frank in December 1940: 'After the victory, bind the helm faster.' Plans,
of course, are still only plans until they are implemented, but it would have
taken a political or military earthquake to have derailed the process.[9]

The earthquake did not happen. Breitman offered significant evidence that
the mass murder of the Jews of the Soviet Union in the six months before
Hitler met with Husseini was only the first phase of what was already intended to be a policy for all of Europe.

Historians, who have focused attention on Hitler's ideological motivations,
above all his radical antisemitism and the paranoid vision of an international
Jewish conspiracy see such an "early" decision as a plausible conclusion.[10]
As both his public and private statements of the summer and fall of 1941
indicated, the application of his antisemitic interpretation of the unfolding
events of World War II was central to Hitler's decision-making regarding the
Holocaust. Hitler famously had first made his "prophecy" in a speech in the
Reichstag on January 30, 1939, that if

> international Jewry inside and outside Europe should succeed in plunging
> the nations once more into a world war, the result will not be the Bolshe-
> vization of the earth and thereby the victory of Jewry, but the annihilation
> of the Jewish race in Europe.

In the view of Hitler, Goebbels, and other Nazi leaders, the events of summer 1941 appeared to confirm the truth of this conspiracy theory.[11] In their
speeches and in the regime's propaganda, the Nazi leaders interpreted the
emergence of the alliance between Britain and the Soviet Union following
the German invasion of the Soviet Union in June 1941, the declaration by
Roosevelt and Churchill of the Atlantic Charter in August, and Roosevelt's
decisions to send Lend-Lease aid to Britain across the Atlantic all to be evidence of the existence of a Jewish dominated anti-German world conspiracy. In Hitler's mind, the beginnings of the anti-Hitler coalition between the
Soviet Union and the Western democracies confirmed the validity of his radical antisemitism as a method of interpreting these aspects of world politics.
As "international Jewry" appeared intent on waging what Hitler called a
war of extermination against Germany, he would "exterminate the Jewish
race" in Europe in retaliation.[12] Goebbels reported that in a conversation
on August 19, 1941, Hitler said that his prophecy about the Jews and the
war was "coming to pass in these weeks and months with an almost ee-
rily graceful certainty."[13] Hitler's interpretation of events owed nothing to
suggestions from anyone outside the highest levels of the Nazi dictatorship.
It was embedded in ideas that he had expressed since 1919.

Christopher Browning, who since the 1980s has taken a leading role in writing the history of the decisions that led to the Holocaust, has argued for a series of decisions during the summer of 1941 that expanded the killings on the Eastern Front into a European-wide plan for genocide. He has done so in a series of works culminating in 2004 in *The Origins of the Final Solution: The Evolution of Nazi Jewish Policy, September 1939–March 1942*.[14] Browning documented the radicalization of policy to mass murder conducted by the *Einsatzgruppen* and other German killing units on Soviet territory that took place from mid-July to mid-August in 1941. In those months, Hitler and the German military leadership believed that the war against the Soviet Union would be won by fall 1941. Browning concluded that "victory euphoria in mid-July," that is, Hitler's belief that Nazi Germany was going to soon win the war against the Soviet Union,

> marked not only the conclusion of the decision-making process leading to the mass murder of Soviet Jewry but also the point at which Hitler inaugurated the decision-making process that led to the extension of the Final Solution to European Jewry.[15]

On July 31st, Heydrich obtained Herman Göring's signature on an order that authorized him to "make all necessary preparations" for a "total solution of the Jewish question" in European territories under German influence and to submit a "comprehensive draft" of a plan for a "Final Solution to the Jewish Question."[16]

Browning concluded that it was between mid-summer to mid-fall that the Nazis invented the extermination camp as the best means of perpetrating mass murder between August and October 1941. In August 1941, SS *Einsatzgruppen* leaders on the Eastern front met with experts from the Nazis' euthanasia program who possessed experience in using gas to murder the physically disabled and mental patients. By September, Walter Rauff and other SS officers had completed the development of mobile gas vans which used carbon monoxide coming from the exhaust of hermetically sealed trucks to murder victims locked inside.[17] In the first half of September, Rudolf Höss, the Commandant of Auschwitz, tested Zyklon B to murder Russian prisoners of war in sealed basement cells of the Auschwitz concentration camp. On October 1, 1941, German planning began for the construction of a second large camp at Birkenau. In late October, the engineer Kurt Prüfer of Topf and Sons engineering firm designed and contracted for the new, larger crematoria that would be necessary for the expected expansion of the camp. In mid-October, Himmler approved the construction of what became the extermination camp in Belzec. That same month construction began there as well as for a similar extermination camp in Chelmno.[18]

Browning concluded that

> inevitably, as the invention of the extermination camp passed from con-
> ception and experimentation to preparation, other people within the Nazi
> regime began to receive unmistakable signals from their colleagues in the
> SS that Nazi Jewish policy had passed a fateful divide. Mass murder and
> not expulsion awaited the European Jews.

On October 23, 1941, the Nazi regime officially ended all Jewish emigration
from Europe.[19] In mid-September 1941, Hitler approved the deportations of
Jews from Germany and Austria to German occupied territories in Poland.
On October 15, the first rail transport of Jews from Vienna for the Lodz
ghetto took place, followed by deportations from Prague, Luxembourg, and
Berlin. By November 5, twenty more transports carried Jews from Germany
and Austria to the East.[20]

Browning notes that in the months after October, "many important decisions were yet to be taken concerning how, when, where, at what rate, and
with what exceptions the task of murdering the European Jews was to be
accomplished." Yet by the end of October at the latest, "the Nazi regime had
crossed the key watershed."[21] Browning concluded that by October 1941 at
the latest, Hitler had made the fundamental decisions to shift from deportation and the murders on the Eastern Front to the implementation of a plan to
murder all the Jews of Europe. The decisions had been communicated first to
Himmler, then to Heydrich in the Reich Security Main Office and from there
to those officials needed to design and build the extermination camps and to
develop the necessary methods.

Whether we opt for the "early" decision in the spring suggested by Breitman or the "late" decision elaborated by Browning in the early fall, both
historians date the shift from deportation to extermination from between
eight months to one month before Hitler met the Grand Mufti when the latter arrived in Berlin in November 1941. Neither Husseini's name nor that of
any of his associates appears in these historical reconstructions.

The historian Christian Gerlach has argued that it was not until the week
of December 7–14, 1941, that Hitler took the decision to exterminate the
Jews of Europe.[22] He asserts that though deportations of Jews from Germany and Austria began in November, the policy of murdering them all had
not yet been implemented. He recalls Hitler's above-mentioned "prophecy"
speech of January 30, 1939. Following Hitler's declaration of war against
the United States in the Reichstag of December 11, 1941, the European war
became a world war. "Thus, the situation Hitler had envisioned in 1939 had
come about. With complete logical consistency—consistent within the framework of his anti-Semitic worldview—Hitler then proclaimed his decision to
exterminate all Jews in Europe."[23] On December 12, 1941, Hitler spoke at a

meeting of Nazi Party *Reichsleiter* and *Gauleiter* in Berlin. His speech, which was summed up by Goebbels in his diary entry, expressed the connection between the war which "the Jews" had allegedly launched against Germany to his decision to exterminate the Jews of Europe. Goebbels wrote:

> In regard to the Jewish question the Führer is determined to wipe the slate clean. He prophesied to the Jews that if they once more brought about a world war, they would be annihilated. These were not mere words. The world war is here, the extermination of the Jews must be its necessary consequence. This matter has to be envisaged without any sentimentality. We are not here to have any compassion for the Jew, but to have compassion for our own German people. As the German people has once against sacrificed some 160,000 dead in the eastern campaign, those responsible for this bloody conflict will have to pay for it with their lives.[24]

For the remainder of World War II and the Holocaust, this connection between what Nazis propagandists called "the Jewish enemy" and Hitler's decision to "exterminate" and "annihilate" the "Jewish race" in Europe remained a constantly repeated and core theme of their public pronouncements.[25] Yet Gerlach, advocate of the latest decision point among historians of the subject, focuses his attention on the same Nazi leaders as did Breitman, Browning, Friedlander, and others, namely, on Hitler and the highest ranking officials of the SS Reich Security Main Office with encouragement from Goebbels, to be sure. The name of Haj Amin el-Husseini does not come up at all in his account for a very good reason. The Mufti was not in the chain of Holocaust decision-making of the Nazi regime.

So even if, as Gerlach wrote, Hitler's ultimate decision to exterminate the Jews of Europe took place in December 1941 rather than, as Breitman argued, in the spring or, as Browning claimed, from August to October, none of them attribute any causal importance at all to Haj Amin el-Husseini and what he said to Hitler when they met in Berlin on November 28, 1941. The fundamental point on which these historians agree is that Hitler took the key decisions regarding the Holocaust and communicated them to a small but expanding concentric circle of officials in Himmler's SS Reich Security Main Office. At no point was Husseini an important figure in the decision-making process.

Hitler decided to murder the Jews of Europe as the logical outcome of his radical hatred of the Jews. He needed no encouragement from others to transform his famous hatreds into a policy of mass murder. Whether Hitler decided to kill the Jews in the spring, summer/fall, or early winter of 1941, he did not need Husseini to push his anti-Jewish policy from one of persecution to one of extermination. In other words, if the British government had managed to capture Husseini in the Middle East and prevent his arrival in Berlin, the Nazis would still have murdered 6 million Jews in Europe.

Yet if some exaggerated Husseini's role in the Holocaust, his complicity in its crimes should also not be denied. He saw Hitler and the Nazis as ideological soulmates who shared his profound hatred of the Jews, Judaism and Zionism. He expressed his enthusiasm to German diplomats in Jerusalem as early as March 1933 and then, as we have seen, eagerly used the Nazis' means of mass communication to broadcast his hatreds to North Africa and the Middle East during World War II and the Holocaust.[26]

In his *Islam and Nazi Germany's War*, David Motadel demonstrated that Husseini and other Muslim clerics contributed to "the Third Reich's pro-Islamic stance" and the resulting efforts of the German armies and the SS to mobilize Muslims on the Eastern Front war against the Soviet Union and the Jews.[27] Motadel cautions against overestimating Husseini's influence in Berlin which he viewed as "strictly limited." He was unable to "secure guarantees for Arab and Palestinian independence...His proposals were successful only insofar as they coincided with German interests. The most dramatic example was his intervention to hinder the emigration of Jews from Germany's south-eastern European satellite states to Palestine." The Mufti was best seen as "part of a more general German policy directed toward the Islamic world." In that capacity, the Nazi regime regarded him as important, as demonstrated by his "monthly salary of no less than 90,000 *Reichmarks*" as well as provision of several residences for himself and his entourage.[28] During World War II in Germany, a salary of 90,000 *Reichmarks* a month was one received only by the very wealthiest persons in Nazi Germany.[29] While Husseini's *influence* on the decision-making of the Nazi regime was limited, his *importance* to the Nazi regime was considerable, above all in his efforts offer Arab listeners an Islamist, and Arabic language variation of the Jew-hatred of the Nazi regime.

In a series of impressively documented memos in 1945 and 1946 from the American Zionist Emergency Council (AZEC) to officials of the U.S. State Department, and then to the American prosecution team in Nuremberg, Benjamin Akzin, Abba Silver, and Stephen Wise laid out the case against Husseini based on initial documentary evidence. Their "Memorandum on the Responsibility of the War Criminal Haj Amin El-Husseini, Former Mufti of Jerusalem" of July 16, 1946, focused on Husseini's role in negotiations about the possibility of allowing Jewish children to go to Palestine during the Holocaust.[30] The memos combined an exaggerated view of his role in Holocaust decision-making with a sound presentation of letters he had sent to Nazi Foreign Minister Joachim von Ribbentrop, Heinrich Himmler, and the foreign ministers of Italy, Bulgaria, and Hungary urging them not to allow the children to leave. For example, on June 5, 1943, he wrote to the foreign minister of Bulgaria to recommend that Jews be sent to places where "they will be under stringent control, as for instance in Poland." The AZEC authors wrote that "what stringent control of the Polish type meant in 1943 was an open secret both for the writer and the addressee, and *Der Mufti* could well afford the innuendo of an understatement."[31] Hence, Husseini not only sought to limit Jewish immigration to Palestine but "actively encouraged the deportation of Jews from other countries to the Polish extermination camps." The AZEC authors included Husseini's letter of June 28, 1943, to the Romanian government opposing the emigration of 1,800 Jewish children to Palestine.[32] The evidence at hand appeared "to establish that the Mufti played a role of some importance in the extermination of the Jews of Europe and that he is guilty of complicity in organized mass murder and of other crimes against humanity."[33]

The AZEC memos of 1945 and 1946 included some exaggeration of Husseini's role but included a host of plausible leads for further investigation and offered sufficient grounds for an indictment for war crimes. The U.S. government had abundant material in its diplomatic, military, and intelligence files on which to build an initial case. Unfortunately, the United States and other Allied victors decided not to bring him to trial. Such a proceeding would have brought the Allies extensive evidence of his collaboration with the Nazis to international attention. In so doing, an investigation and trial might have made it more difficult for him to emerge as the leader of postwar Palestinian nationalism and for his associates at the Arab Higher Committee to represent the Palestine Arabs at the United Nations. However, it should be recalled that the publicly well-known fact of Husseini's collaboration with the Nazis did not deter the members of the Arab Higher Committee from choosing him as its president in November of 1945. This advocate of Islamic Jew-hatred was welcomed home as a hero of anti-imperialist and anti-Zionist struggle rather than a disgraced collaborator with Nazism complicit in the crimes of the Holocaust.[34]

During World War II and the Holocaust, Husseini penned canonical texts of the tradition of Islamic antisemitism, texts that were important to a postwar policy of uncompromising rejection of the United Nations Partition Plan, Zionism, and then the state of Israel. The impact of Husseini the ideologue was as important and as destructive as Husseini the political figure. As Zvi Elpeleg has recalled, in the postwar years, before and during the war he began in 1947 in Palestine, Haj Amin el-Husseini was again able to exercise political power, shape the contours of Palestinian nationalism, and translate his ideas not only into propaganda but policy of war.[35]

Rubin and Schwanitz make a convincing case about Husseini's destructive impact on events up to and including the war of 1948. They refer to the impact of Husseini's charisma, determination to avoid any concessions to the Zionists, ability to incite his followers to violence "as well as internal pressures from Islamist and nationalist radicals who incited flammable public opinion." While acknowledging pressure from other groups that made war in 1948 seem inevitable, the war of 1948 and the Arab-Israeli conflict may not have taken place "without al-Husaini and his allies...No one individual made this outcome more likely than him...Without al-Husaini's presence as the Palestinian Arabs' and [as] a transnational Islamist leader there might have been other options." He was well-funded and

> well-armed with rifles that had been provided by the Nazis...Once al-Husaini was allowed to reestablish himself as unchallengeable leader of the Palestine Arabs, this ensured that no compromise such as Partition or the 'two-state solution' would be considered, while making certain that Arab leaders would be intimidated and driven to war.[36]

Yet Husseini was not swimming against the current of strong currents of Arab opinion. American diplomats in Cairo in November 1945 observed "the great respect and esteem" that Husseini "enjoys in all levels of society" in Palestine.[37] Upon his return to Egypt in June 1946, American Ambassador Pinckney Tuck reported that the warm welcome he received was "widespread and genuine."[38] We cannot know how events would have transpired if Husseini had been absent in the crucial years before and during the 1947–1948 war. He was, after all, only one of a number of Arab leaders who decided on war rather than compromise and partition in 1948. He had money, weapons, and followers with which to exert his will in postwar Palestine. The logical outcome of the views he expressed before during and after his collaboration with Nazi Germany, from the speech in Bludan of 1937 to the speeches from the Islamic Central Institute in Berlin and the postwar calls for war against the Zionists, was the expulsion by force of all or most of the Jews living in Mandatory Palestine.[39]

Haj Amin el-Husseini was not part of the inner circle of Nazi decision-makers. The Nazis would have conducted the Holocaust if he had never been in Nazi Germany. Yet, though an out-of-power political refugee, he sought and found protection from the Nazis and repaid the favor many times over in his work as a propagandist and recruiter of Arabs and Muslims to the Nazi cause. He knew that the Holocaust was taking place. A case was and can be made that he was complicit in supporting its implementation. He wrote a significant chapter in the history of modern hatred of Judaism, the Jews, and thus, in his mind, of Zionism and Israel as well. A frank reckoning by Palestinian leaders with the history of Haj Amin el-Husseini's collaboration with Nazi Germany during World War II and the Holocaust has not yet taken place. His political power in Berlin should not be exaggerated but neither should the importance of his choices and beliefs be minimized. He did all he could to help Hitler win World War II and supported his efforts to murder the Jews of Europe as well as Hitler's unsuccessful efforts to extend the Holocaust to the Jews of North Africa and the Middle East. His ideological legacy continues to nourish Palestinian visions of destroying the state of Israel rather than accepting a two-state solution. He was unique among Nazi collaborators in his ability to resurface in politics after the defeat of Nazi Germany without having to offer even a pretense of distancing himself from the antisemitic views for which he became world famous from 1941 to 1945. Sadly, it was because, not despite those hatreds, that he was able to achieve the political power, which, however briefly, he wielded with disastrous results for Jews and Arabs alike.

Notes

Selections drawn from Jeffrey Herf, "Haj Amin al-Husseini, the Nazis and the Holocaust: The Origins, Nature and Aftereffects of Collaboration," *Jewish Political Studies Review,* January 5, 2016: https://jcpa.org/article/haj-amin-al-husseini-the-nazis-and-the-holocaust-the-origins-nature-and-aftereffects-of-collaboration/: reprint by permission of *Jewish Political Studies Review/Jerusalem Center for Public Affairs.*

1 On the failed effort, see Jeffrey Herf, *Israel's Moment: International Support for and Opposition to Establishing the Jewish State, 1945–1949* (Cambridge and New York: Cambridge University Press, 2022), 24–130.

2 "Prime Minister Benjamin Netanyahu's Speech at the 37th Zionist Congress" (October 21, 2015), http://www.pmo.gov.il/English/MediaCenter/Speeches/Pages/speechcongress201015.aspx. On the other hand, Netanyahu's comments about Husseini's false assertions regarding Zionist and then Israeli plans to attack or destroy the Al Aksa Mosque rest on sound evidence.

3 Barry Rubin and Wolfgang G. Schwanitz, *Nazis, Islamists and the Making of the Modern Middle East* (New Haven, CT: Yale University Press, 2014).

4 Ibid., 161.

5 Ibid., 161.

6 Rubin and Schwanitz, *Nazis, Islamists,* 162.

7 Jürgen Mattäus, "Operation Barbarossa and the Origins of the Holocaust," in Christopher Browning with Jürgen Mattäus, *The Origins of Final Solution: The Evolution of Nazi Jewish Policy, September 1939–March 1942* (Lincoln: University of Nebraska; Jerusalem, Yad Vashem, 2004), 297.

8 On the two eras of persecution and extermination, see Saul Friedländer, *Nazi Germany and the Jews: 1939–1945* abridged by Orna Kenan (New York: Harper, 2009).

9 Richard Breitman, *Architect of Genocide: Himmler and the Final Solution* (New York: Knopf, 1991), 247.

10 For example, see Eberhard Jäckel, *Hitler's World View: A Blueprint for Power* (Cambridge, MA: Harvard University Press, 1981); and *Hitlers Herrschaft: Vollzug einer Weltanschauung* (Stuttgart: Deutsche Verlags-Anstalt, 1986).

11 Cited in Jeffrey Herf, *The Jewish Enemy: Nazi Propaganda during World War II and the Holocaust* (Cambridge, MA: Harvard University Press, 2006), 52. On Hitler's statements from 1939 to 1941 also see Saul Friedländer, *Nazi Germany and the Jews; and Richard Evans, The Third Reich at War* (New York: Penguin Press, 2009). Also see Richard Evans, *The Hitler's Conspiracies: The Third Reich and the Paranoid Imagination* (New York and London: Penguin, 2021).

12 Saul Friedländer drew similar conclusions about the intersection of the war, Hitler's antisemitic conspiracy theory and his decision to launch the Final Solution at some point between *August and December 1941.* See his *Nazi Germany and the Jews: 1939–1945: The Years of Extermination* (New York: Harper-Collins, 2007), 272–288.

13 Goebbels, cited by Herf, *The Jewish Enemy*, 116. See Elke Fröhlich, ed. *Die Tagebücher von Joseph Goebbels. Sämtliche Fragmente*, entry for August 20, 1941, II/2, 278 (Munich: Saur, 1987–2001).

14 Christopher Browning, *The Origins of the Final Solution: The Evolution of Nazi Jewish Policy, September 1939–March 1942* (Lincoln and Jerusalem: University of Nebraska Press and Yad Vashem, 2004). His important previous works on *Holocaust Decision Making Include Fateful Months: Essays on the Emergence of the Final Solution* (New York: Holmes & Meier, 1985); *The Path to Genocide: Essays on Launching the Final Solution* (New York: Cambridge University Press, 1992); and *Nazi Policy, Jewish Workers, German Killers* (New York: Cambridge University Press, 2009).

15 Browning, *The Origins of the Final Solution*, 314.

16 Ibid., 315.

17 On the decisions, technical details, and persons involved, see Martin Cüppers, "Mobile Gaskammern für den Völkermord," in his *Walther Rauff—in deutschen Diensten: Vom Naziverbrecher zum BND-Spion* (Darmstadt: Wissenschaftliche Buchgesellschaft, 2013), 109–144.

18 Browning, *The Origins of the Final Solution*, 309–373.

19 Browning, *The Origins of the Final Solution*, 368–369.

20 Saul Friedländer, *Nazi Germany and the Jews, 1939–1945: The Years of Extermination* (New York: Harper-Collins, 2007), 262–267; Browning, *Origins of the Final Solution*, 329.

21 Ibid., 373.

22 Christian Gerlach, "The Wannsee Conference, the Fate of the German Jews and Hitler's Decision in Principle to Exterminate All European Jews," *Journal of Modern History*, 70, 4 (December 1998), 759–812. Also see *The Extermination of the European Jews* (New York: Cambridge University Press, 2016).

23 Gerlach, "The Wannsee Conference," 784.

24 See Elke Fröhlich, ed. with the *Institut für Zeitgeschichte*, Munich and the Bundesarchiv, *Die Tagebücher von Joseph Goebbels: Sämtliche Fragmente* (Munich: Saur, 1987–2001), part 2, *1941–1945*, vol. 2, 498f (see entry for December 13, 1941); cited in Gerlach, "The Wannsee Conference, p. 785; and in Saul Friedlander, *Nazi Germany and the Jews, 1939–1945: The Years of Extermination* (New York: HarperCollins, 2006), 279–280.

25 For abundant evidence of the "paranoia and projection" of the Nazi interpretation of World War II, see Herf, *The Jewish Enemy*.

26 Herf, *Nazi Propaganda for the Arab World*, 16.

27 David Motadel, *Islam and Nazi Germany's War* (Cambridge, MA: Harvard University Press, 2014), 165.

28 Ibid., 43–44.

29 In his history of the Nazi economy, Adam Tooze writes that in 1936 "62 percent of all German taxpayers reported annual incomes of less than 1,500 *Reichmarks*." Another 21 percent reported annual incomes of between 1,500 and 2,400 *Reichmarks*. "Only 17 percent of all taxpayers recorded incomes of more than 2,400 *Reichmarks*, or 50 *Reichmarks* per week." Adam Tooze, *The Wages of Destruction: The Making and Breaking of the Nazi Economy* (London: Penguin Books, 2006), 141–142.

30 "Memorandum on the Responsibility of the War Criminal Haj Amin El-Husseini, Former Mufti of Jerusalem," (July 16, 1946), Library of Congress, Washington, DC, Robert H. Jackson Papers, Nuremberg War Crimes file, "Nuremberg War Crime s Trial, Office Files-U.S. Chief of Consul, Grand Mufti of Jerusalem (Haj Amin El-Husseini), Container 102, Reel 8. Also see discussion in Jeffrey Herf, *Israel's Moment: International Support for and Opposition to Establishing the*

Jewish State, 1945–1949 (New York and Cambridge: Cambridge University Press, 2022), 55–61.

31 Cited in Herf, *Israel's Moment*, 58.

32 "Memorandum on the Responsibility of the War Criminal Haj Amin El-Husseini," 7–9 Herf, *Israel's Moment*, 59.

33 Ibid., 10–11; Herf, *Israel's Moment*, ibid.

34 Herf, *Israel's Moment*, 60–61. On Husseini's welcome home in 1946, see "Postwar Aftereffects," in Jeffrey Herf, *Nazi Propaganda for the Arab World* (New Haven, CT: Yale University Press, 2009), 233–260.

35 On the importance of Husseini as a founding figure of Palestinian nationalism, see Zvi Elpeleg, *The Grand Mufti: Haj Amin al-Hussaini, Founder of the Palestinian National Movement*, trans. David Harvey, ed. Shmuel Himmelstein (London: Frank Cass, 1993); and Matthias Kuentzel, *Nazis und der Nahe Osten: Wie der Islamische Antisemitismus Entstand* (Berlin: Hentrich and Hentrich, 2019): forthcoming as *Nazis, Islamic Antisemitism, and the Middle East: The 1948 Arab War against Israel and the Aftershocks of WW II* (London: Routledge, 2023).

36 Rubin and Schwanitz, *Nazis, Islamists and the Makings of the Modern Middle East*, 200–201.

37 "Recent Trends in Palestine Arab Politics," (Cairo) (November 16, 1945), 3, NACP RG84, Cairo Embassy, General Records, 1936–1955, 820–820.03, entry 2410, box 134; Cited in Herf, *Nazi Propaganda for the Arab World*, 241.

38 Tuck to the Secretary of State, No. 1648, Cairo (June 24, 1946), Editorial Comment from the Cairo Press Concerning the Appearance of the Mufti in Egypt, NACP RG84, entry 1197, Damascus Legation Confidential File: 1946, vols. 304, 800–891, box 11; cited in Herf, *Nazi Propaganda for the Arab World*, 242.

39 On the logic of expulsion that emerged from Husseini's views, see Benny Morris, *1948: The First Arab-Israeli War* (New Haven, CT: Yale University Press, 2008), 406–410.

6

EAST GERMAN COMMUNISTS AND THE JEWISH QUESTION

In Memory of Sigrid Meushel (1944–2016) and for Anetta Kahane

For Communists, in the first half of Europe's and Germany's twentieth century, "the Jewish question" remained peripheral to the main drama of anti-capitalist class struggle and even to the discourse anti-fascism. Communists described Nazism to be a form of fascism, which they saw as a dictatorial version of capitalism. The Nazi persecution of the Jews in the 1930s, and then the Holocaust in the course of the Nazi assault on "Jewish Bolshevism" brought the issue of antisemitism somewhat greater attention. That shift was apparent between 1935 and 1939, the years of the popular front against fascism, from 1941 to 1945, during the Nazi invasion of the Soviet Union, and the Holocaust, and yet again from May 1947 to May 1949 when the Soviet Union and the Communist regimes in Eastern Europe supported the Zionist project in Palestine and then new state of Israel.[1] These departures from Marxist-Leninist orthodoxy proved short-lived.

From 1949 to 1953, Josef Stalin launched "anti-cosmopolitan" purges characterized by virulent antisemitism in the Soviet bloc, most famously in the Doctor's Plot in Moscow, and the Slansky Trial in Prague. Arrests and show trials featured bogus accusations of espionage and anti-communist conspiracies against Communists, mostly Jews. In Prague and Moscow, the trials ended in executions.[2] The purges also took place in East Germany, a dictatorship which the Communists called the German Democratic Republic (GDR). The arrest of Paul Merker (1894–1969), a former member of the Politburo of the German Communist Party (the *Kommunistische Partei Deutschlands* [KPD]) in December 1952 was the East German counterpart and aftereffect of the more well-known Slansky trial in Prague.[3]

Following German unification in 1991, the archives of the ruling East German Socialist Unity Party (*Sozialistische Einheitspartei Deutschlands*)

DOI: 10.4324/9781003449669-7

(hereafter SED) and of the GDR's Ministry of State Security (*Ministerium für Staatssicherheit*), known by its abbreviation, the Stasi were made accessible for research. As a result, it became possible, for the first time, to write the history of the internal purges and secret political trials of that minority among East German communists who stressed the centrality of recalled the anti-Jewish focus of Nazi policy, supported restitution to the survivors of the Holocaust, and supported the new state of Israel.[4] Paul Merker, a non-Jewish veteran Communist, and former member of the politburo of the German Communist Party was the most high-ranking member of the SED to be arrested. His case was at the center of the East German chapter of the anti-cosmopolitan purges.[5] While the Doctor's Plot and the Slansky Trial have prominent places in the history of post-1945 Communism, the Merker, and related cases in East Germany, had remained a more obscure chapter in the history of East German communism. Yet the purges of 1950–1953 had an enduring impact on East Germany's official memory of Nazi crimes. They paved the way for East Germany's rejection of financial restitution toward Jewish survivors of the Holocaust and to its policy of growing hostility to Israel and Zionism, a policy which by the 1970s had reached the point of military assistance both to Arab states and to the Palestine Liberation Organization when both were engaged in armed attacks on Israel.[6]

In part, the postwar purges were a return to Communist normalcy regarding Jewish matters. In the 1920s and 1930s, the German Communist Party or KPD extended its solidarity to Jews of the working class but denounced "Jewish capitalists." A pejorative connection between Jews and capitalism, evident in Marx's own "Essay on the Jewish Question," remained an undercurrent of German communism. Second, in accord with Stalin's 1913 essay on the national question, the Communists did not regard the Jews as a "people" or nation because they lacked the commonalities of language, territory, economic life, and cultural characteristics. Therefore, Jews as Jews did not qualify as an oppressed or persecuted nationality. Third, the communists viewed Nazism as first and foremost an attempt to crush the working class and its political organizations, and to preserve capitalism by force and violence. From that perspective, Nazism's persecution of the Jews was not its central or defining feature. German Communists expressed solidarity with German Jews following the anti-Jewish pogrom of November 1938 and denounced antisemitism. Yet the dominant view among Communists was that antisemitism was an instrument waged in the class struggle against the left.[7] As Walter Ulbricht put it, "the witch hunt (*Judenhetze)* against the Jews served to deceive the National Socialist working people about the big capitalist character of the Hitler dictatorship."[8] In their majority, German Communists did not grasp the centrality, extremism, and autonomous ideological impact of Nazi Jew-hatred.

After the November pogrom, and especially after the German invasion of the Soviet Union, the German communist response to the Jewish question was divided into two. The Communists in exile in Moscow, led by Walter Ulbricht (1893–1973), and Wilhelm Pieck (1876–1960) voiced prevailing orthodoxy.[9] The Communists in exile in Mexico City, led by Merker, dissented on "the Jewish question." The Moscow group focused on the suffering of the Soviet Union, and their own bitterly disappointed, hopes for an indigenous German revolt to overthrow the nazis.[10] The German communists returned from Moscow to Berlin in 1945 with, in Pieck's words, a "bitter, tortured consciousness that the German people did not free themselves from this band of murderers, but instead followed them to the end, and supported them in their war crimes."[11] The ambivalence of claims to form and lead a new German nation combined with a bitter intent to punish the Germans who had not overthrown the Nazis was evident in the communists' "appeal" to the German people on June 11, 1945.[12] It referred to the Germans

> shared guilt *(Mitschuld)* and shared responsibility *(Mitverantwortung)* for the war and its consequences. The greatest and most fateful of Hitler's war crimes was the malicious and treacherous attack on the Soviet Union... Day after day, in the death camps, the extermination of human beings was carried out in gas chambers and ovens.

The appeal did not mention that the vast majority of those human beings were Jews. The appeal called for restitution (*Wiedergutmachung*) for damage the nazis had done to "other peoples," meaning all of the nations which the Germans had attacked, especially the Soviet Union.[13] It was a language of generalization away from the specifics of the Holocaust that became a standard discourse in the subsequent decades.

Ulbricht published *Die Legende vom Deutschen Sozialismus* (The Legend of German Socialism) in 1945. As he was the leader of the KPD, and then General Secretary of the SED and the dominant figure in the one-party GDR regime, his account became the most important postwar East German analysis of Nazi Germany. By 1956, almost 700,000 copies of the book had been published in the GDR.[14] Ulbricht wrote that after 1933, "Hitler fascism" began with the destruction of the Communist and Social Democratic Parties, trade unions, and pogroms against the Jews which spread racial hatred "as preparation for the planned annihilation of members of other peoples in war." He referred to annihilation camps, gas chambers, ovens, and mass graves in Poland but not to Jews in particular.[15] In Ulbricht's text, the specifics of antisemitism and the Holocaust remained as marginal in early postwar memory, as Nazi anti-Jewish policies had been in prewar and wartime commentary.

Those specifics did move to the center of concern of some of the German communists who were able to escape from Hitler's Europe and find refuge in wartime Mexico City. Paul Merker was the key figure in that shift.

In Mexico City, between 1942 and 1945, and more quietly in East Berlin from 1946 to 1948, he was the one and only member of the KPD's Politburo, and after 1946, the SED's Central Committee, for whom the Holocaust and support for the Zionist project became central concerns. Merker joined the KPD in 1920 and was a member of its left wing. He was elected to the Prussian legislature in the Weimar years. In tune with communist orthodoxy, he attacked Weimar's Social Democrats as "social fascists."[16] He spent time in Moscow and was a Comintern agent in the United States from 1931 to 1933. He served in the German communist underground in Vichy France and was interned in the concentration camp at Vernet. He fled to Mexico City in the fall of 1942. From then until December 1945, he was a regular contributor to *Freies Deutschland*, [Free Germany], the bi-weekly journal published by German communists in Mexico City and was responsible for its general political line. In his published essay, such as "Hitler's Antisemitism and Us," in October 1942, Merker, in sharp contrast to the writings of the Moscow group, Merker placed Nazi antisemitism and the Holocaust at the center of communist anti-fascist politics.[17]

Merker was not Jewish. When released from prison in 1956, he penned a remarkable statement on his "Position on the Jewish Question" for the SED leadership to explain why he had taken such a prominent position on the issue.[18] He was appalled by antisemitism. He appreciated the contributions of Jews to the socialist tradition. While in the United States from 1931 to 1933, he met and worked with Jewish communists in New York and Chicago whose support of equality for American blacks and opposition to white racism within the American working class left a lasting impression. He was grateful to Jews in the communist underground in Berlin, who, in March-April 1934, hid him in their homes and apartments. After the 1938 pogrom, he concluded that "the struggle of the German working class against anti-semitism had been inadequate" and that it was "the special duty of non-Jewish people to stand up decisively against antisemitism."[19]

In his essays in Mexico City, he sought to make up for these past shortcomings. In October 1942, soon after arriving in Mexico City, he published "Hitler's Antisemitism and Us'," in *Freies Deutschland*.[20] It was the first statement by a leading German communist that placed the extermination of the Jews of Europe at the center of communist anti-fascist rhetoric. Merker wrote

if all the German rivers flowed with ink, and all the German forests were made of quill pens, they would not suffice to describe the immeasurable crimes which Hitler fascism has committed against the Jewish people...The campaign of extermination of Hitler fascism against the Jewish citizens of Germany was only the beginning. It has been extended to all the countries and areas conquered by Hitler. An unprecedented flood of antisemitic propaganda has poured over these countries and more or less also over the Western world as well. The victims of this flood number in the hundreds of hundreds of thousands. As a result, Hitler Germany will be enshrined in history as the country of the most gigantic degree of state-sponsored and cowardly murderousness. Because the German people permitted the crimes of its dominant class against the Jewish people it has taken on itself. a heavy responsibility.[21]

The essay was a departure from Communist and German Communist discourse. In contrast to Ulbricht's refusal to specifically mention the Jewish victims of Nazism, Merker wrote that the "deadly enemy" of Jews and "progressive forces" were identical. "Their struggle and their destiny correspond to one another" Resistance to fascism had brought Jews and "progressive forces" closer together in the nucleus of a future German democracy.[22]

In Mexico City, he also supported financial restitution (*Wiedergutmachung*) to Jewish victims of Nazism. Five years before Soviet diplomats at the United Nations supported the partition of Palestine into an Arab and a Jewish state, Merker expressed understanding for the growth of Jewish national feeling and the resulting desire for a Jewish state in Palestine. He sought to assure "our Jewish friends and comrades in struggle" that a new regime in Germany would find ways to "destroy antisemitism in Germany forever."[23] For Merker, financial restitution was a moral imperative, as well as practical measure to try to reconstitute Jewish life in post-Nazi Germany.

"Hitler's Antisemitism and Us" evoked critical reactions among Merker's fellow communist exiles in Mexico in the pages of *Freies Deutschland*. One critic said Merker wanted to "give back millions to Jewish bankers and big capitalists." Another responded that postwar restitution should consider the class position of victims. A third asked why only the Jews should receive restitution? Didn't those persecuted because of their political beliefs and actions, that is, communist "anti-fascist resistance fighters," have an even greater claim? Another asked why Merker focused only on the German Jews and not on the Jews of countries Hitler had invaded.[24]

Merker responded that "everything" that he said against Hitler's antisemitism and, for restitution for the German Jews, applied in equal measure for the Jewish population of the countries the nazis had invaded. He defended restitution for the Jews in a post-Nazi Germany as taking place in the context of the postwar nationalization of the German economy and as necessary for the "full, equal re-integration [of the Jews] into the economic and social life of Germany in as short a time as possible."[25] He insisted that there was a difference between the Jews and those persecuted because of their political activity. The Jews were persecuted because they were a "defenseless, national, religious or caste-like minority" that "Hitler fascism" used to divert attention from its own plans for world domination. They had the "same right to restitution of the damage done to them as do all the nations Hitler invaded and oppressed." But those who had been persecuted because of their political views were not "a national, religious or caste-like minority." They had voluntarily taken up the struggle against the nazis. "Antifascist fighters," that is, members of the Communist Party, should not "expect material compensation for the sacrifices that result." Their compensation lay in "every successful battle and the final victory, [over Nazism, J. H.] the erection of a democratic power."[26]

For his orthodox Communist contemporaries, such views entailed two ideological errors. First, his assertion that the Jews deserved restitution as did "all the *nations* Hitler invaded and oppressed" assumed, contrary to Stalin's argument, that the Jews were indeed as much a nation as the other occupied nations of Europe. Second, his argument for prioritizing the Jewish victims over Nazism's political enemies, conflicted with the communists' view that "anti-fascist resistance fighters," that is, the Communists and the Soviet Union, stood at the apex of a hierarchy of the victims of Nazism.[27]

In 1944, Merker published a two-volume work, *Deutschland – Sein oder Nicht Sein* [Germany: To Be or Not to Be]. Volume One, *Von Weimar zu Hitler* examined the path from Weimar to Hitler's entry into power. Volume Two, *Das Dritte Reich und sein Ende* [The Third Reich and Its End] examined the consolidation of the German dictatorship, Hitler's path to war, the role of Himmler and the SS, and translation of his Jew-hatred into the policy of the Final Solution. It rejected the predominant Marxist view of antisemitism as an instrument for other purposes and saw it instead as a core ideological, source Nazi policy. It was the first and remained the only work by one of the German Communist leaders to place the Nazis' Jew-hatred at the center of an analysis of National Socialism.[28]

Both Heinrich and Thomas Mann, with whom Merker had corresponded, praised the book. Thomas Mann, then in exile in Los Angeles, wrote to Merker that he was

> engrossed in the work for days. It is a shattering document, the first deeply argued and historically exact representation of the most frightful and shameful episode in German history. I think I can imagine what [a great deal) of labor of collection and organization it represents. There is no doubt that the book will find many curious readers. I only hope that it reaches Germany soon and will teach the people there who've been hit on the head, how it happened to them.[29]

Despite this praise from leading German exiles in the United States, the work remained little known in the postwar decades and was not published in East Germany. In 1972, a small leftist press in Frankfurt/Main in West Germany published the work, but it had scant influence on West German leftist discussions which continued to focus on the old link between fascism and capitalism rather than on the specifics of antisemitism and the Holocaust.[30]

In the English-speaking scholarship, Franz Neumann's *Behemoth: The Structure and Practice of National Socialism*, a work he wrote in 1942 and 1944, when he was director of the Office of Research and Analysis of the United States Office of Strategic Services in Washington, DC, long served as the canonical Marxist analysis.[31] Yet, in contrast to Neuman, Merker did not view Nazi antisemitism primarily as an instrument to protect the interest of capitalism but as a policy that the Nazis pursued for its own sake. *Deutschland – Sein oder Nicht Sein*, and especially volume two, *Das Dritte Reich und Sein Ende*, offered the preeminent analysis of the Nazi era from the perspective of left-wing communism in Germany, and the only one in which antisemitism and nazi racial ideology play central rather than marginal roles. It stood in sharp contrast to Ulbricht's marginalization of the significance of antisemitism in the Nazi regime. Merker's analysis of the instruments of terror and ideology had no equal among the communist writings of the 1940s. The work repeats orthodox Marxist analysis of links between capitalism and fascism and echoes the Communist attacks on German Social Democracy in the Weimar year. Yet his focus on Nazi persecution and extermination policies toward the Jews marks Merker's *Das Dritte Reich und Sein Ende* as one of the trenchant yet overlooked writings of the German anti-nazi emigration.

Merker returned to Berlin in 1946 in hopes of playing a leading role in the construction of what he called a new "democratic" Germany. He was elected a member of the Central Committee of the SED when it was founded in 1946. From 1946 to 1948 in East Berlin, he worked in the SED's office of labor and social welfare where he supported financial restitution for all the German Jewish survivors of the Holocaust and of placing the claims of Jewish survivors on an equal moral plane with those of "anti-fascist resistance fighters," that is the communists. As had been the case in Mexico, his more orthodox contemporaries opposed his views on Jewish questions.[32]

In the summer of 1948, during the midst of Israel's war for independence, Merker publicly supported the creation of the state of Israel and praised the Jewish struggle against British imperialism, American oil interests, and Arab "fascists."[33] The essay mirrored the arguments being made at the time by American liberals and leftists, French Gaullists, Socialists and Communists, and the diplomats of the Soviet Union at the United Nations in New York.[34] Although Merker's views in Mexico City between 1942 and 1946, his support in postwar East Berlin for restitution to Jewish survivors, and for the new state of Israel mirrored the position of the Soviet Union from May 1947 to May 1949, they were the only extended examination of the Holocaust and support for the Zionist project by a member of the KPD Politburo or the SED Central Committee in the entire history of German and East German communism. Stalin's turn against Israel in 1949, and his decision to launch the antisemitic anti-cosmopolitan purges of 1949–1953, transformed Communist policy in 1947–1949, including Merker's abundant paper trail, from an expression of a communist antifascism into an ideological heresy. Merker's political and intellectual work from 1942 to 1948 was crucial evidence that his Soviet and East German prosecutors used to denounce him in 1950, and then, following the Slansky Trial convictions and executions in Prague in 1952, to arrest and imprison him.

In August 1950, the SED leadership expelled Merker from the SED Central Committee and accused him of espionage stemming from his wartime contact with Noel H. Field, an American leftist who helped German Communists escape from Hitler's Europe.[35] In December 1952, following the Slansky trial in Prague, he was arrested, accused of being an agent of American imperialism and Zionism, and interrogated by the Stasi in preparation for a trial in Berlin. After three years in prison, he was the subject of a secret political trial in 1955 conducted by the East German Supreme Court. The court found him guilty as charged and sentenced him to eight years in prison. In January 1956, a month before Nikita Khrushchev delivered a "secret speech" in Moscow denouncing Stalin and the crimes of the Stalin era, the East German Politburo ordered Merker to be released from prison, though he did not receive the full political rehabilitation which he sought. He did not occupy a major political position again. None of his works were published in the DDR. He died in 1969, his wartime writings and his case long forgotten. The trial of Paul Merker in East Germany's Supreme Court in 1955 remained secret until the opening of the Stasi archives in 1990 and 1991. The record of the trial, of the prosecution's preparations, and of Merker's statement following his release constitute crucial documents in the history of the communist antisemitism that emerged and would persist in the decades of the Cold War.[36]

The Central Party Control Commission (*Zentralparteikontrollkommission*), abbreviated in German at ZPKK, was the name of the institution in the governing SED that policed ideological orthodoxy and conducted purges of those deviating from it, and in the Merker case those who, in its words were "spies and saboteurs" and "corrupt elements."[37] Herman Matern (1893–1971) was appointed head of the SPKK in 1946 and became a member of the SED Central Committee. He had been a member of the KPD since its foundation after World War I and a member of the Ulbricht group in Moscow. He remained in both positions without interruption until he died in 1971. As head of the SPKK, he became the SED's primary enforcer of ideological and political conformity. He wrote the texts which led to Merker's expulsion and imprisonment.[38]

Merker's expulsion from the SED was announced in a resolution of the Central Committee and the Central Party Control Commission of August 24, 1950, concerning connections between former German political emigrants and Field. The indictment read as if there had been no alliance by the Soviet

Union with the Western democracies. Merker's was mistaken in believing that "the goal of American, English and French imperialists was the liberation of Europe from fascism" and showed evidence of lack of faith in the Soviet Union in the aftermath of the Hitler-Stalin pact of 1939. The fact that Merker and the other members of the resistance fled to Mexico and did not stay in Nazi-occupied France was taken as evidence to confirm this hypothesis. Because the German immigrants had helped Field, now described as a "class enemy," they were all expelled from the SED.[39]

The SED's denunciation of Merker in the Noel Field case was only the beginning of his difficulties. As the ZPKK files indicate, between 1950 and 1952, the "Jewish question" emerged ever more prominently as the Control Commission investigated Merker's contacts with Jews in Mexico and examined his published work Jewish questions, both those involved in his analysis of Nazi Germany and the Holocaust, and his postwar policy positions regarding Israel and restitution. It was Merker's actions and writings about those matters that led the Party Control Commission to accuse the veteran communist of having been an agent of American imperialism and Zionism. By 1952, the latter had become a term of abuse in Soviet bloc communist discourse.[40]

Merker's fate was sealed by the outcome of the show trial against Rudolf Slansky and other high-ranking communist, mostly Jewish, defendants in Prague in November 1952. The fourteen defendants in Prague, eleven of whom were Jewish, were convicted of being agents of American imperialism and Zionism. Three were sentenced to life imprisonment. On December 3, 1952, four days after Stasi agents arrested Merker in Berlin, Rudolf Slansky, the second most powerful figure in the Czech Communist Party and government, Otto Fischl, the former Czech ambassador to the GDR, and Merker's friend Otto Katz (Andre Simone) were among the eleven defendants who were hanged in Prague. In the trial, confessions from the accused that were the result of torture and threats included accusations that Merker was linked to Slansky, Simone, and Fischl.[41]

On 20 December 1952, the SED Central Committee and ZPKK published "Lessons of the Trial against the Slansky Conspiracy Center."[42] It is one of the key documents of the history of antisemitism and anti-Zionism in the four decades of the East German regime. Matern, its author, denounced "the criminal activity of Zionist organizations." They had conspired with "American agents" in order to destroy the "people's democracies," that is, the communist dictatorships, in Eastern Europe. He preemptively and indignantly defended himself against the charge of antisemitism. He claimed that the Slansky trial showed that "a method of these criminals included efforts to discredit vigilant, progressive comrades by charging them with antisemitism." Yet, he continued, "the Zionist movement has nothing in common with the goals of humanity. It is dominated, directed, and organized by USA imperialism, exclusively serves its interests, and the interests of Jewish capitalists." Matern linked Merker to the Slansky conspiracy through Merker's friendship with Otto Katz. Though Merker claimed to be loyal to the Soviet Union, Matern denounced them for using "the poison of chauvinism and cosmopolitanism ... to contaminate the workers with the most reactionary bourgeois ideology."[43]

Only three years before "Lessons of the Trial Against the Slansky Conspiracy Center," the Soviet Union and the Communist regimes in Eastern Europe had offered diplomatic, and in Czechoslovakia's case, military support to the Zionists and to the new state of Israel. In so doing, they saw it as a logical outcome of leftist antifascism and a reaction against the racism or "chauvinism" of Nazism. Matern's "Lessons..." reads as if the era of Soviet bloc Zionism had never existed. Reference to cosmopolitanism as a "poison" and source of "contamination" came from the language of European Jew-hatred of right and left. The attack on cosmopolitanism, as if it were an obvious evil, once again depicted the Jews as disloyal members of any nation. Yet when the Jews created a movement of national self-determination and then established a state, Matern described the result as a form of "chauvinism," a term which in communist discourse referred to an intolerant, racist and thus "reactionary" nationalism.

For Communists with any memory of both the Holocaust and the very recent and consequential era of Soviet support for the Zionist project and the new state of Israel, the Slansky Trial in Prague and the Merker case in East Berlin came as a shocking reversal. The purges renewed and reinvigorated antisemitic currents in the communist tradition, currents which had not disappeared, but which had receded during the Popular Front, from 1935 to 1939, and the Soviet Union's war against Nazi Germany from 1941 to 1945, and in the years of Soviet bloc Zionism, from 1947 to 1949. Matern described an anticommunist conspiracy as small in numbers, linked to Jews and Zionists. As was the case in previous versions of conspiracies about the Jews, he depicted them as extremely powerful and in 1952 as a major threat to the communist states and parties. Paradoxically, while denouncing Zionism and the Jews for "chauvinism," the East German regime's attack on Zionism came in the form of a German nationalism, which defined itself in opposition to a Western, capitalist, and Jewish international conspiracy, and against the new state of Israel. The anti-cosmopolitan purges in the Soviet bloc expelled the Zionist project and Israel from the political camp of antifascism into the enemy camp of American imperialism.[44] The association of Israel with "American imperialism" was a falsehood and reversal of the realities of 1947–1948. It was one of the cornerstones of the communist face of antisemitism during the Cold War.

Matern placed Merker's views on Jewish questions at the core of the indictment by the ZPKK and Central Committee's "Lessons..." of December 1952.

He found the most compelling evidence Merker's guilt to be his published essays, along with *Deutschland Sein oder Nicht Sein*; assistance with travel funds and visas he received from the Joint Anti-fascist Refugee Committee in New York to travel to Mexico from France in 1941; his meetings with representatives of that committee and representatives of the World Jewish Congress while in Mexico City; his public efforts on behalf of financial restitution for the Jews in postwar Berlin; his support for Israel; and his friendship with Otto Katz (Andre Simone), one of the defendants found guilty and executed in the Slansky trial in Prague.

Matern wrote that under Merker's leadership, the Mexico City edition of *Freies Deutschland* defended "the interests of Zionist monopoly capitalists." There could be "no further doubt that Merker is a subject of the USA financial oligarchy which called for indemnification of Jewish property only to facilitate the penetration of USA finance capital into Germany. This is the true origin of his Zionism." The fact that Merker was not Jewish deepened the ZPKK's suspicions. Why would a non-Jew adopt his views? Its answer was that he had been bought by Jews to do so. Financial corruption, not political and moral convictions accounted for his support for "financing the emigration of Jewish capitalists to Israel" and transporting "Jewish citizens of German nationality" to a land of their choice after the war.[45] "Lessons..." recast the wartime cooperation and solidarity between German communists in Western emigration, on the one hand, and American Jewish communists, leftists, liberals, and Jewish emigres in general, on the other, into an espionage plot of "imperialists" and "Jewish capitalists."

Matern was incensed that Merker supported restitution for Jews whether they returned to Germany after 1945 or wanted to remain abroad. In so doing,

> Merker dishonestly transformed the maximum profits of the monopoly capitalists which had been squeezed out of the German and foreign workers into a supposed property of the Jewish people. In reality, the Aryanization of this capital [the expropriation of Jewish business, banks, etc. by the nazis, J. H.] amounted only to placing the profits of Jewish· monopoly capitalists into the hands of Aryan' monopoly capitalists.[46]

A pejorative association of the Jews with capitalism, and with money had been a theme of antisemitism in Europe for centuries. Since Karl Marx's 1843 essay "On the Jewish Question" that connection had been a current within Marxist and then communist anticapitalism as well. In that sense, the cosmopolitan purges and Matern's "Lessons..." were a return to an antisemitic association of Jews with money and exploitation that had moved somewhat into the background in the era of Nazism, World War II, the Holocaust, and Soviet support for Zionism from 1947 to 1949. Matern's reference to "only" shifting profits from Jewish to Aryan capitalists combined antisemitic cliches with an abysmally poor understanding of the Nazi regime's persecution and expropriation of Jewish property.[47]

Matern then raised the issue of who was Nazi Germany's primary target, the Jews, the German working class, or the Soviet Union. He claimed that Merker did not care about working class Jews, or the victims of Eastern Europe and the Soviet Union but rather and "above all the wealthy Jews, so-called economic emigrants with whom Merker, Andre Simone, and other German emigrants in Mexico were in closest touch."[48] The supposedly wealthy Jews in Mexico City were the root of Merker's support for facilitating Jewish travel to British Mandate Palestine. Matern was especially angered by Merker's wartime arguments that Nazism's political opponents, unlike the Jews, were free to participate or not to participate in the fight against Nazism, and therefore did not merit restitution payments. Matern wrote:

> With this open contempt, this agent [Merker] in effect is saying [to those who fought nazism, JH]: If you had done as I did, you would have avoided the struggle and thereby nothing would have happened to you. Therefore, your sacrifice and suffering counts for nothing compared to the sacrifices and the suffering of the Jewish people.[49]

But it was Matern, not Merker, who turned the memory of the past into a zero-sum game of competition among victims in which recognition of the Jewish tragedy had to come at the price of non-recognition of Nazism's many other victims. At the time, Matern need not have worried because it was the Jewish story, not that of the Communists, which was on the margins of memory in East Germany and in the Soviet bloc.

The anti-cosmopolitan purge affected other East German communists who fell under suspicion of sharing Merker's views. In December 1950, Alexander Abusch, who had been the editor of *Freies Deutschland* in Mexico City, was relieved of all his party functions in part because "he published Merker's false views on the question of Jewish emigration in the nationalities question and on restitution without limits."[50] In exchanges with officials of the ZPKK, Abusch insisted that, though born into a Jewish family, he had no interest at all in Jewish matters. He proved his lack of interest in testifying against Merker to the ZPKK, the Stasi, and at the secret political trial of 1955. He gained his sought-after political rehabilitation in summer 1951 and served as the GDR's Minister of Culture from 1958 to 1961.[51] Leo Zuckermann, also Jewish and a communist, a friend of Merker's in Mexico City, and his ally in bureaucratic fights over restitution in postwar East Berlin, understood how dangerous partisanship on behalf of the Jews and/or Israel was. In 1949 and 1950, Zuckermann was the chief of President Wilhelm Pieck's office. As a result of the Noel Field affair, he resigned from the post in 1950 and became a university professor. In January 1953, a few weeks after Merker's arrest, he fled with his family to West Berlin and then traveled on to Mexico, where he remained. Julius Meyer, the head of the organized Jewish community in East Berlin fled to West Germany. Meyer was a member of the SED, of the East German parliament, the *Volkskammer*, and a participant in the *Vereinigung des Verfolgten des Naziregimes* (Association of those persecuted by the Nazi regime). With Merker's arrest and the flight of Zuckermann and Meyer, three leading advocates for Jewish interests were gone from East German political life. Those Jews who remained or who recovered prominent positions in the SED, such as Abusch, and Poliltburo member, Albert Norden did so by submerging their Jewish identities and concerns in communist universalism. They did so even as East Germany supported the Arab states and the Palestine Liberation Organization in the Israeli-Arab conflict from the 1950s to 1989. The example of Merker's arrest and imprisonment demonstrated that the consequences for emphasizing the Jewish dimensions of Nazi policy, for restitution for Holocaust survivors, and for good relations with Israel included political failure, prison, or emigration.

Merker's Stasi file of over a thousand typed and handwritten pages was declassified after the collapse of the GDR regime and German unification in 1991.[52] His Stasi and Soviet interrogators asked Merker if he "was a member of Jewish-Zionist organizations."[53] According to the conversations Merker had with the Stasi's informant, his cell-mate in the early months of his imprisonment in the winter and spring of 1953, the Soviet NKVD and Stasi agents threatened Merker with death and also threatened his family. They told him that his 1942 article, "Antisemitism and Us" showed that he was a *"Judenknecht"* (servant of the Jews).[54] They mocked him as "the king of the Jews," as one who "had been bought by the Jews" and whose intention was to "sell the GDR off to the Jews."[55] The interrogators viewed Merker's contact with and assistance from Jews, both communists and non-communists, during the French and Mexican emigration as further evidence of his participation in an espionage conspiracy together with foreign Jewish capitalists, Zionists, and American imperialists.

Merker was finally brought to a trial in the East German Supreme Court in March 1955. It remained a secret until the collapse of the DDR in 1989 and the opening of the Stasi archives. The court convicted Merker of violating Article 6 of the DDR's constitution, Law Number 10, Article 10 of December 20, 1945, and Number 38 of 12 October 1946 of the Allied Control Council, laws originally intended for use against those accused of committing crimes in the nazi regime. On March 30, 1955, the judges of the *Oberste Gericht* sentenced him to an additional eight years in prison. The fifteen-page verdict of the East German Supreme Court is an important document of the history of the Jewish question in twentieth-century German communism.[56] It began by stating that as a result of the success and spread of socialism after World War II, the imperialists needed to find new ways to destroy socialism "from within" by corrupting leading members of the Communist Parties.[57] These methods had supposedly been revealed by the show trials in Bulgaria, Hungary, and especially the Slansky trial in Prague. The trials of the anti-cosmopolitan purges had shown that "renegades" had sought to replace the Communist Parties, destroy the Soviet Union, and once again establish capitalism. The judges claimed that Merker had pursued this policy "in close contact" with the Slansky group in Prague.[58] For the court, incriminating evidence included Merker's contact with organizations aiding Jewish refugees, assistance from Gaullists in the French Resistance in his flight from France, friendship with Otto Katz, who had been denounced in the Slansky trial as an "international spy, Zionist and Trotskyist," and contact with the American communist leader, Earl Browder, who, the court declared, had "decisively weakened the struggle of peoples against fascism."[59]

Merker's writings and actions on behalf of the Jews in Mexican emigration were central in the indictment. His essays in Mexico were said to confirm the story of a veteran communist seduced and corrupted into becoming an "agent of American imperialism." The judges wrote that "the leading role [of the Mexican political emigration, J H.] went to the so-called Latin American Committee of Free Germans which stood under the strong influence of capitalist Jewish emigrants." Here, Merker "played a dominant role" in shaping a postwar policy for Germany which "did not correspond to the interests of the German people but rather to those of American imperialism."[60] That is, in 1955, the Supreme Court of the GDR made a *legal* judgment that a *political* policy advocating East German support for the new state of Israel and for financial restitution to Jewish survivors of the Holocaust served the interests of "American imperialism." Further, it held it to be part of an attempt to overthrow the communist regime in East Germany, a plot that was "inspired by American monopoly capital." The judgment alleged that in Mexico Merker relied on an "emigrant capitalistic Jewish circle." He had "continuous contact with Zionist circles, especially with the organization the 'World Jewish Congress'." He had not sought his political base in Mexico in "the political but rather in the racial emigration." By "racial emigration" the court was referring to Jewish emigres in Mexico.[61]

Thus, the verdict explained Merker's efforts to place the Jewish catastrophe at the center of communist anti-fascist politics as the result of his corruption by Jewish capitalists and clever intelligence services in whose debt he supposedly stood. Further, it described giving appropriate attention to the Holocaust and its aftereffects as a ploy to restore capitalism to East Germany and the Soviet bloc. In placing the link between Jews, capitalism, and financial corruption at its core, the verdict was a key document in the history of East German governmental antisemitism.

Ten months later, on 27 January 1956, shortly before Khrushchev's Secret Speech and with a thaw after the Stalin era in the air, Merker was released from the Brandenburg-Gorden prison.[62] On April 14, 1956, Merker wrote to East German President Wilhelm Pieck to press his case for full political rehabilitation. He insisted he was innocent of all charges, and, in a sign of his unwavering communist convictions, called his persecution a "criminal aberration of Marxism-Leninism." He could demonstrate that the charges against him were without merit.[63]

By May 1956, the Central Party Control Commission, including Ulbricht and Matern, concluded that espionage accusations against Merker stemming from the Slansky trial "were insufficiently proven." The guilty verdict was rescinded. They declared Merker to be innocent and thus "rehabilitated."[64] On July 31, 1956, Ulbricht wrote to Merker that "the re-examination undertaken under new points of view led to the conclusion that the accusations made against you in the most important matters were of a political nature and do not justify judicial prosecution."[65] Merker wrote back to Ulbricht to ask what the political objections to him were, and when he would receive a full political rehabilitation.[66] His request for full political rehabilitation and the return to a leading position in the party and government was not successful. On 13 July 1956, the East German Supreme Court rescinded the guilty verdict. His actions between 1936 and 1946 were no longer "judicially significant."[67]

The SED archives offer still further evidence that "the Jewish question" was at the center of Merker's indictment, imprisonment, and political downfall. Upon his release, and in response to his efforts to obtain full political rehabilitation, the Party Control Commission asked Merker to respond in writing to the accusations it had made against him in December 1952. On June 1, 1956, Merker replied with a remarkable 38 remarkable statement on his "position on the Jewish question."[68] He wrote that his Soviet and German interrogators were convinced that he must have been an agent for the United States, Israel, or Zionist organizations because he had taken such a strong position on the Jewish question during the World War II, and because they found no evidence that he was Jewish. Why, they reasoned, would any non-Jewish German communist be so supportive of the Jews unless he was an agent of American imperialism, or Zionist and Jewish capitalists. Merker responded as follows:

> I am neither Jewish. nor a Zionist though it would be no crime to be either. I have never had the intent to flee to Palestine. I have not supported the efforts of Zionism. I have ... occasionally said that among the Jews, after having been plundered by Hitler fascism, most deeply humiliated, driven from the homelands, and millions of them murdered, only because they were Jews, the feeling of a deepest bond and the desire for their own,

Jewish country emerged among Jews of different countries. This feeling was the expression of those most deeply harmed and outraged. Moreover: Hitler fascism emerged among us. We [Germans] did not succeed through the actions of the working masses in preventing the erection of its rule and hence the commission of its crimes. Therefore, especially we Germans must not and ought not ignore or fight against what I call this strengthening of Jewish national feeling.[69]

He recalled Soviet support for a two-state solution in 1947, and the Soviet Union's UN Representative Andrei Gromyko's criticism of the influence of American oil interests on American Middle East policy. He recalled the role played by the Israeli communists in the Haganah in the fighting against the Arab Legion during World War II. While he was not an active supporter of a Jewish state, "it would be wrong actively to oppose these efforts."[70] The SED was wrong to call Zionism a tool or agent of American imperialism. Rather, it was a legitimate national movement of the Jews. He correctly pointed out that Zionist efforts to form a Jewish state in Palestine had met with "strong resistance from English as well as from American imperialists." By contrast, they received support from "the masses of Jews" in many countries, as well as from the government of the Soviet Union. "No one," Merker boldly told his former colleagues on the SED's Central Committee, "will want to claim that the Soviet government was an 'agent of American imperialism'." He wrote that Soviet victory in Stalingrad also "saved the Jews in Palestine living under Zionism from annihilation by [Wehrmacht General] Rommel's advancing army."[71] Merker argued that the logical implication of communist antifascism and was support for the Jewish state. In other words, in 1956, Merker recalled what Soviet bloc policy had been from May 1947 to May 1949. Unfortunately for Merker, in 1956, the purges which affected him, and others were the turning point away from the support for the Zionist project towards four decades of anti-Zionist policies that persisted until 1989.[72]

Merker's "Position on the Jewish Question" made clear to the SED leadership that, despite arrest and imprisonment, he had not changed his, now "incorrect" views on the Jewish question. He was readmitted to the SED but did not occupy an important political office again. The SED issued no public admission of regret for his imprisonment. When he died in 1969, the SED Central Committee published an obituary in *Neues Deutschland*. A eulogy delivered by a spokesman for the Central Committee praised Merker's contribution to the class struggle. Neither the obituary or the eulogy mentioned his years of persecution from 1950 to 1956, nor his writings and policies about antisemitism, the Holocaust, restitution, or Zionism in Mexico City and East Berlin between 1942 and 1950.[73]

Conclusion

Merker's views about antisemitism and Zionism in the 1940s belonged to a short-lived, though consequential chapter of communist solidarity with the Jews. Following the purges of 1949–1956, Jewish communists in East Germany such as Alexander Abusch and Albert Norden found places in the East German government so long as they accepted that the Holocaust would remain on the margins of the memory of the crimes of Nazism, and antagonism to the state of Israel would be official government policy. Merker's imprisonment and the executions in the Slansky trial in Prague set a clear example of the price that would be paid for deviations on this issue. The pejorative association of Jews with capitalism, "American imperialism," and Israel all evoked deep-seated and long-standing antisemitic traditions of anti-Western German nationalism.[74] Those anti-Western resentments had been central aspects of German right-wing nationalism. They persisted in Marxist-Leninist language in the GDR. The Merker case made clear that as the East German communists formed a government resting on a *German* anti-fascism, they also did their utmost to distance themselves from identification with the Jews and the familiar catalog of despised "Others" and "Outsiders" of modern German history. Paul Merker's political blunder was to continue to express solidarity with the Jews at a time when the communists were seeking to establish their credentials as leaders of the unified German nation.[75]

The Merker case and the associated purges and arrests of the "anti-cosmopolitan" campaign represented a reassertion of Marxist-Leninist orthodoxy in Jewish matters that persisted in the Soviet bloc until its collapse in 1989. East Germany, which placed antifascism at the core of its national identity, was the only Communist regime in Europe that never had diplomatic relations with the state of Israel. In contrast to West Germany, it offered no financial restitution to Jewish survivors of the Holocaust or to the state of Israel. Beginning with General Secretary Ulbricht's visit to Nasser's Cairo in 1965, the GDR became a firm ally of the Arab states. In 1974, it signed the first of annually renewed agreements of support with the Palestine Liberation Organization when Yasser Arafat's troops were engaged in armed attacks on Israeli civilians. In the 1970s and 1980s, East Germany's policy of close ties to Arab states at war with Israel, and its military and diplomatic assistance to the PLO and its splinter groups in that era of international terrorism rose to the level of an undeclared war with the Jewish state. Its propaganda compared Israel's wars of self-defense to Nazi aggression.[76]

During those decades, the East German government indignantly rejected the idea that its policies toward "Jewish questions" and toward the state had anything at all to do with the traditions of antisemitism. Yet the history of the repression of Merker and like-minded communists in the early 1950s from the purges to the undeclared wars of the 1970s and 1980s suggests a different conclusion: the East German communist regime made a significant contribution to the persistence of antisemitism. It did so, ironically, by asserting that antagonism to the state of Israel and repetition of antisemitic cliches about Jews and capitalism were essential aspects of state-sponsored antifascism.

Notes

1 On Communist antifascism and Jewish questions during the Popular Front and during World War II, see Francois Furet, *The Passing of an Illusion: The Idea of Communism in the Twentieth Century* (Chicago, IL: University of Chicago, 1999); Jeffrey Herf, "German Communism, the Discourse of 'Anti-Fascist Resistance', and the Jewish Catastrophe," in Michael Geyer and John W. Boyer, eds., *Resistance Against the Third Reich* (Chicago, IL: University of Chicago Press, 1994), 257–294; and Anson Rabinbach, "Part II, Antifascism," in Stefano Geroulanos and Dagmar Herzog, eds., *Staging the Third Reich: Essays in Cultural and Intellectual History* (New York and London: Routledge: 2020), 187–292.

2 On the anti-cosmopolitan purges in the Soviet bloc, see from an extensive scholarship, Francois Fejto, *Les Juifs et l'Antisemitisme dans les Pays Communistes* (Paris, 1960); Jonathan Brent and Vladimir Naumov, *Stalin's Last Crime: The Plot Against the Jewish Doctors, 1948–1953* (New York: Harper, 2003); Georg Hermann Hodos, *Schauprozesse: Stalinistische Säuberungen in Osteuropa 1948–1954* (Frankfurt/Main: Campus Veralg, 1988); Karel Kaplan, *Report on the Murder of the General Secretary* (Columbus: Ohio State University Press, 1990); Mario Kessler, *Antisemitismus, Zionismus und Sozialismus. Arbeiterbewegung und jüdische Frage im 20. Jahrhundert* (Mainz: Decaton, 1993); Joshua Rubenstein and Vladimir P. Naumov, *Stalin's Secret Pogrom: The Postwar Inquisition of the Jewish Anti-Fascist Committee*, trans. Laura Esther Wolfson (New Haven, CT and London: Yale University Press and United States Holocaust Memorial Museum, 2001).

3 On the Slansky trial, see Kaplan, Report on the Murder of the General Secretary.

4 On the Stasi files, see Klaus Dietmar Henke, ed., *Wann bricht schon mal ein Staat Zusammen! Die Debate iiber die Stasi-Akten auf dem 39. Historikertag 1992* (Munich: Deutscher Taschenbuch Verlag, 1993); Joachim Gauck, *'Die Stasi Akten'. Das unheimliche Erbe der DDR* (Reinbek bei Hamburg: Rowohlt Verlag, 1992). On publications soon after German unification on the East German purges, see Helmut Eschwege, *Fremd unter Meinesgleichen: Erinnerungen eines Dresdner Juden* (Berlin: Ch. Links Verlag, 1992); Olaf Groehler and Ulrich Herbert, *Zweierlei Bewältigung: Vier Beiträge über den Umgang mit der NS-Vergangenheit in den beiden deutschen Staaten* (Hamburg: Ergebnisse Verlag, 1992).

5 On the Merker case, see Jeffrey Herf, "Purging 'Cosmopolitanism'; The Jewish Question in East Germany," in *Divided Memory: The Nazi Past in the Two Germanys* (Cambridge, MA: Harvard University Press, 1997), 106–161; Jeffrey Herf, "East German Communists and the Jewish Question: The Case of Paul Merker," *Journal of Contemporary History* 29, 4 (October 1994), 627–662; Jeffrey Herf, "Dokumentation: Antisemitismus in der SED: Geheime Dokumente zum Fall Paul Merker aus SED- und MfS-Archiven," *Vierteljahrshefte für Zeitgeschichte*

(Oktober, 1994), 1–32; and Jeffrey Herf, "Der Geheimprozeß," *Die Zeit*, Dossier section, domestic edition (October 7, 1994), overseas edition (October 14, 1994), 7–8. Also see Karl Wilhelm Fricke, *Warten auf Gerechtigkeit: Kommunistische Säuberungen und Rehabilitierungen, Bericht und Dokumentation* (Cologne: Verlag Wissenschaft und Politik, 1971); Karl Wilhelm Fricke, *Politik und Justiz in der DDR: Zur Geschichte der politischen Verfolgung 1945–1968, Bericht und Dokumentation* (Cologne: Verlag Wissenschaft und Politik, 1979); Olaf Groehler, 'Integration und Ausgrenzung von NS-Opfer. Zur Anerkennung- und Entschädigungsdebatte in der Sowjetischen Besatzungszone Deutschland 1945–1946'; and Mario Kessler, 'Zwischen Repression und Toleranz. Die SED-Politik und die Juden (1949 bis 1967)," in Jürgen Kocka, ed., *Historische DDR-Forschung: Aufsätze und Studien* (Berlin: Akademie Verlag, 1993), 105–128, and 149–168; Wolfgang Kießling, "Stalinismus als Thema der gegenwärtigen DDR-Geschichtswissenschaft", in Lutz Priess, ed., *Stalins schweres Erbe – Eine unbewältigte Vergangenheit in Deutschland* (Berlin: Evangelische Akademie, Dokumentationen, 1990), 74; and Sigrid Meuschel, *Legitimation und Parteiherrschaft in der DDR* (Frankfurt/Main: Suhrkamp Verlag, 1992), 101–116.

6 On the development of East German policy from the 1950s to the 1990s, see Herf, *Divided Memory*; on the "undeclared wars," see Jeffrey Herf, *Undeclared Wars with Israel: East Germany and the West German Far Left, 1967–1989* (New York: Cambridge University Press, 2016).

7 'Gegen die Schmach der Judenpogrome! Erklärung des Zentralkomitees der KPD', *Die Rote Fahne: Sonderausgabe gegen Hitlers Judenpogrome* (November 1938), 1; Wilhelm Pieck, 'Nicht nur Entrüstung, sondern Taten! Gegen die Judenpogrome' in *Wilhelm Pieck: Reden und Aufsätze, Auswahl aus den Jahren 1908–1950*, vol. 1 ([East] Berlin: Dietz Verlag, 1950). 326–329; Waler Ulbricht, "Die Pogrome—eine Waffe der faschistischen Kriegspolitik, *Die Rote* Fahne 7 (November 1938), 2.

8 Walter Ulbricht, "Lüge und Rassenhetze als Mittel der Kriegsvorbereitung," in Walter Ulbricht, *Zur Geschichte der Deutschen Arbeiterbewegung: Aus Reden und Aufsätzen, Band 11: 1933–1946.* 2nd ed. ([East] Berlin: Dietz Verlag, 1953), 188.

9 Ulbricht's major statements from wartime Moscow are reprinted in Walter Ulbricht, *Zur Geschichte der Neuesten Zeit: Die Niederlage Hitlerdeutschlands und die Schaffung der antifaschistische-demokratischen Ordnung* ([East] Berlin: Dietz Verlag, 1955). Wilhelm Pieck's addresses on the German language edition of Moscow radio from 1942 to 1945 denouncing nazi crimes, and his appeals to the Germans to overthrow the Hitler regime were reprinted in *Wilhelm Pieck: Gesammelte Reden und Schriften, Band VI 1939 bis Mai 1945* ([East] Berlin: Dietz Verlag, 1979); and *Wilhelm Pieck: Reden und Aufsätze, Auswahl aus den Jahren 1908–1950*, vol. 1 ([East] Berlin: Dietz Verlag, 1951): 356–379. For Pieck's statements on the murders of the Jews, see his "Gegen die Hitlerbarbarei' (Rede in der deutschsprachigen Sendung des Moskauer Rundfunk, 15 September 1942)," in *Wilhelm Pieck: Gesammelte Reden und Schriften.* Band VI, 108–112.

10 See, for example, the material on the Nationalkomitee Freies Deutsch/and. Schulung Deutscher Kriegsgefangener in Wilhelm Pieck Papers NL 36/582 Stiftung Archiv der Parteien und Massenorganisationen der DDR im Bundesarchiv, Zentralpartie Archiv (hereafter) SAPMO-BA, ZPA. For lectures and course outlines from the Communist Party school in wartime Moscow see Walter Ulbricht Papers NL 182/827 SAPMO-BA, ZPA.

11 Wilhelm Pieck. 'Berlin von Hitler befreit!' in *Wilhelm Pieck: Reden und Aufsätze, Auswahl aus den Jahren 1908–1950* ([East] Berlin, 1951), 423.

12 Zentralkomitee der Kommunistischen Partei Deutschlands, "Aufruf der Kommunistischen Partei," *Deutsches Volkszeitung*1, 1 (13 June 1945), 1–2, reprinted in

Walter Ulbricht. *Zur Geschichte der Neuesten Zeit: Die Niederlage Hitlerdeutsch/ ands und die Schaffung der antifaschistische demokratischen Ordnung*, Band 1 (Berlin, 1955), 370–379. Anton Ackerman, a member of the KPD's Central Committee, wrote the appeal. Ackerman worked on propaganda aimed at the Wehrmacht by the Moscow based National Committee for a Free Germany. He became a member of SED Central Committee after the war, worked on education and media issues, and then fell out of favor in the late 1950s. See also Hermann Weber, *Geschichte der DDR* (Munich: C.H. Beck, Deutscher Taschenbuch Verlag, 1985), 47–54; and *Wer war Wer—DDR: Ein biographisches Lexikon* (Berlin: Ch. Links Verlag, 1992), 9–10.

13 Ibid.

14 Walter Ulbricht, *Die Legende vom deutschen Sozialismus: ein Lehrbuch für das schaffende Volk über das Wesen des deutschen Faschismus* ([East] Berlin: Dietz Verlag, 1945). The KPD printed 50,000 thousand copies of the book by December 1945, and 300,000 by January 1947. The SED reissued it in the 1950s under the title, *Der Faschistische Deutsche Imperialismus (1933–1945)* [Fascist German Imperialism (1933–1945)], 4th ed. ([East] Berlin: Dietz Verlag, 1956). Its third edition alone, also published in 1956, totaled 340,000 copies. See 'Verlag Neuer Weg, Plan der in Arbeit und in Vorbereitung befindliche Verlagserscheinungen, Stand am 12. Dezember 1945'; 'Aufstellung der vom 9. Mai 1945 bis 31.11 1947 im Verlag Neuer Weg bzw im Verlag JHW Dietz Nachf. GmBH erscheinen Titel', SAPMO-BA, ZPA Verlag Neuer Weg IV 2/9.13/5.

15 Ulbricht's reference to Nazi criminality without reference to the Jews is apparent here: "Himmler organized mass annihilation of the civilian population and prisoners of war in Poland and in the occupied Soviet territories. He created the annihilation camps with their gas chambers, death wagons, gallows, piles of corpses, mass graves, ovens for burning human beings in which millions of innocent men, women and children fell victim," Walter Ulbricht, *Der faschistische Deutsche Imperialismus 1933–1945, Die Legende vom 'deutschen Sozialismus'*, 24.

16 'Paul Merker', *Wer war Wer*, 308. For Merker's 'ultra-left' contributions to the attack on Social Democracy as 'social fascism' see Paul Merker, "Der Kampf gegen den Faschismus," *Die Internationale* 13, 3 (February 1930), 65–69; and 'Der Kampf gegen den Faschismus', *Die Internationale* 13, 8/9 (1930), 259–266.

17 Paul Merker, "Hitlers Antisemitismus und wir," *Freies Deutschland*, l, 12 (October 1942), 9–11. On his essays in Mexico, see Jeffrey Herf, "German Communism, the Discourse of Antifascist Resistance and the Jewish Catastrophe.;" and Herf, *Divided Memory*, 43–47.

18 Paul Merker, "An die Zentrale Kontrollkommission des ZK. Der SED, Berlin: Stellungnahme zur Judenfrage," (1 June 1956), SAPMO-BA. ZPA Paul Merker NL 102/27.

19 Ibid., 4 and 6.

20 Paul Merker, "Hitlers Antisemitismus und wir,".

21 Ibid., 9.

22 Ibid., 10.

23 Ibid., 11.

24 See Paul Merker, "Das Echo: Diskussion über "Hitlers Antisemitismus und Wir,"" *Freies Deutschland* (Mexico City) 2, 4 (March 1943), 33.

25 Ibid.

26 Ibid.

27 For a discussion of "fighters" vs "victims" of fascism in the Soviet Occupation Zone in Germany see Carl Raddatz, *Wer ist Opfer des Faschismus?* (Weimar: Thüriner Volksverlag, 1946), 3–14.

28 Paul Merker. *Deutschland — Sein oder Nicht Sein*, vol. 1. *Von Weimar zu Hitler*; vol. 2, *Das Dritte Reich und Sein Ende* (Editorial, 'El Libro Libre·', Mexico 1944;

reprint, Frankfurt/Main: Materialismus Verlag, 1972 and 1973). See, in particular, his examination in volume two of Himmler, and the SS. 58–96.

29 Heinrich Mann "Paul Merker und sein Buch," *Freies Deutschland* (Mexico City) 4, 11 (October 1945), 27–29. Also "Ernst Bloch to Paul Merker, July 15, 1944," and "Thomas Mann to Paul Merker, June 20, 1944,", SAPMO-BA, ZPA NL Paul Merker 102/31, 33 and 124. They are reprinted in Wolfgang Kießling, *Allemania Libre* 2, 353–452.

30 See Paul Merker, *Deutschland – Sein oder Nicht Sein, Das Dritte Reich und Sein Ende* (Frankfurt/Main: Materialismus Verlag, 1973). On the West German neo-Marxist 'fascism discussion' in the 1960s and 1970s, see Anson Rabinbach, "Toward a Marxist Theory of Fascism and National Socialism: A Report on Developments in West Germany," *New German Critique* 3 (Fall 1974), 127–153; reprinted in Stefanos Geroulanos and Dagmar Herzog, eds., *Anson Rabinbach: Staging the Third Reich, Essays in Intellectual and Cultural History* (New York and London: Routledge, 2022), 295–318.

31 Franz Neumann, *Behemoth: The Structure and Practice of National Socialism*, 2nd ed. (New York: Oxford University Press, 1944). On the efforts of Charles Dwork, also in the OSS, to focus on Nazi anti-Jewish policy and the Holocaust, and his differences with Neuman, see Shlomo Aronson, "Preparations for the Nuremberg Trial: The O.S.S., Charles Dwork, and the Holocaust," *Holocaust and Genocide Studies* 12, 2 (Fall 1998), 257–281; and his *Hitler, the Allies, and the Jews* (New York and Cambridge: Cambridge University Press, 2004).

32 On these controversies, see SAPMO-BA, ZPA, Sekretariat Lehmann, IV/2027/29-33 (Wiedergutmachung gegenüber den Verfolgten des Naziregimes, 1945–1950). For discussion, of the restitution issue and of the relationship of the East German state to the small (15,600 in 1945) Jewish community of East Germany see Olaf Groehler, "Integration und Ausgrenzung."

33 Paul Merker, "Der Krieg in Palästina" (probably August 1948) SAPMO-BA, ZPA NL Paul Merker 102/45. On Merker in postwar Berlin, see memoirs of the East German and Jewish historian, Eschwege, *Fremd unter meinesgleichen: Erinnerungen eines Dresdner Juden*, 51–131.

34 On the liberal, leftist, and Soviet bloc support for the Zionist project in 1947–1948, see Jeffrey Herf, *Israel's Moment: International Support for and Opposition to Establishing the Jewish State, 1945–1949* (Cambridge: Cambridge University Press, 2022).

35 On Noel Field, see Flora Lewis, *Red Pawn: The Story of Noel Field* (Garden City, NY, 1965); Maria Schmidt, "The Hiss Dossier," *The New Republic* (8 November 1993), 17–20; and Allen Weinstein, *Perjury: The Hiss-Chambers Case* (New York: Vintage Books, 1978).

36 For the documents in the German original from the trial and Merker's statement following his release from prison, see Herf, "Dokumentation: Antisemitismus in der SED."

37 See "Zu den Befugnissen der Parteikontrollkommission," in Karl Wilhelm Fricke, ed., *Warten auf Gerechtigkeit*, 131–133; "Ausführung zum Beschluß des Parteivorstandes über die Schaffung der Parteikontrollkommission," Beschluß der Parteivorstandes vom 16. September 1948, in *Dokumente der Sozialistischen Einheitspartei*, vol. II ([East] Berlin: Dietz Verlag, 1952), 97.

38 Hermann Matern, *Wer ist Wer in der SBZ; Ein biographisches Handbuch* ([East] Berlin: Verlag für Internationalen Kulturaustausch, 1958), 166; and Karl Wilhelm Fricke, *Warten auf Gerechtigkeit*, 66. For his essays and speeches see Hermann Matern, *Im Kampf für Frieden, Demokratie und Sozialismus: Ausgewählte Reden und Schriften, Band I, 1926–1956* ([East] Berlin: Dietz Verlag, 1963).

39 See Herf, *Divided Memory*, 111–126; and "Erklärung des Zentralkomitees und der Zentralen Parteikontrollkommission zu den Verbindungen ehemaliger

deutscher politischer Emigranten zu dem Leiter des Unitarian Service Committee Noel H. Field," in *Dokumente der Sozialistischen Einheitspartei Deutschlands, Band III* (Berlin: Dietz Verlag, 1952), 197–213. For the extensive documents and testimony collected while the ZPKK was preparing the denunciations in the Field affair also see Bericht des Genossen Paul Merker vom 27. Juli 1950, SAPMO-BA, ZPA (*Zentral Parteikontrollkommision*) ZPKK SED IV 2/4/117.

40 Herf, *Divided Memory*, 126–144. On the opening of the investigation into Merker following the Slansky trial verdicts, see the files of the East German Ministry of Security, the "Stasi": "Verfügung über die Einleitung eine Untersuchungsverfahrens, Merker, Paul," (November 30, 1952), *Bundesbeauftragte für die Unterlagen des Staatssicherheitsdienst der ehemaligen Deutschen Demokratischen Republik, Ministerium für Staatssicherheit Zentralarchiv* (hereafter) BStU MfSZ-Archiv, Untersuchungsvorgang no. 294/52, Paul Merker, Band I, no. 192/56, 2–3.

41 On the Slansky trial see Georg Hermann Hodos, *Schauprozesse: Stalinistische Sauberungen in Osteuropa 1948–1954*; and Karel Kaplan, *Report on the Murder of the General Secretary* (Columbus: Ohio State University Press, 1990); Meir Kotik, *The Prague Trial: The First Anti-Zionist Show Trial in the Communist Bloc* (New York: Herzl Press/Cornwell Books, 1987); and Jan Osers, "Die Spezifika des Slansky-Prozesses in der CSR im Vergleich mit den übrige Schauprozessen in Osteuropa," in Herman Weber et al., eds., *Kommunisten verfolgen Kommunisten: Stalinistische Terror und "Sauberungen" in den kommunistischen Parteien Europas seit den dreißiger Jahren* (Berlin: Akademie Verlag, 1992), 459–469. For the transcript of the trial, see *Rudolf Slansky, Defendant: Transcript of the Slansky Trial* (New York: National Committee for a Free Europe/Radio Free Europe, 1952).

42 Hermann Matern, "Lehren aus dem Prozeß gegen das Verschwörerzentrum Slansky," *Dokumente der Sozialistischen Einheitspartei, Band IV* ([East] Berlin: Dietz Verlag, 1954), 199–219.

43 Ibid., 206–207.

44 Or, as Sigrid Meuschel wrote: "In a patriotism with antisemitic and anticapitalist features, the SED saw the chance to unite the rightist and leftist critiques of Western, capitalist societies and to withdraw its own order from criticism" in her *Legitimation und Parteiherrschaft in der DDR* (Frankfurt/Main: Suhrkamp Verlag, 1992), 112.

45 Matern, "Lehren aus dem Prozeß gegen das Verschwörerzentrum Slansky," 207.

46 "Lehren aus dem Prozeß gegen das Verschwörerzentrum Slansky," 206.

47 On Nazi theft of Jewish property see Götz Aly, *Hitler's Beneficiaries: Plunder, Racial War, and the Nazi Welfare State* (New York: Henry Hold and Company, 2005); Martin Dean, *Robbing the Jews: The Confiscation of Jewish Property in the Holocaust, 1933–1945* (New York and Cambridge: Cambridge University Press, 2008); Gerald G. Feldman, *Allianz and the German Insurance Business, 1933–1945* (New York: Cambridge University Press, 2001); Peter Hayes, "Plunder and Persecution," in Peter Hayes and John K. Roth, eds., *The Oxford Handbook of Holocaust Studies* (New York and Oxford: Oxford University Press, 2010), 540–559.

48 Matern, "Lehren aus dem Prozeß gegen das Verschwörerzentrum Slansky," 207.

49 Ibid., 207.

50 See 'Betr.: Alexander Abusch, Berlin,' (11 December 1950) SAPMO-BA, ZPA ZPKK IV 2/4/111, 54.

51 Alexander Abusch, 'Ergänzungen zu meinen Mündlichen Aussage vom 10.11.1950', 42–45, and 'Skizze der innerparteilichen politischen Diskussionen in Mexiko 1942/4,' 47–51 in SAPMO-BA, ZPA ZPKK IV 2/4/111.

52 See Jeffrey Herf, "Dokumentation: Antisemitismus in der SED."

53 For example, "Vernemhungsprotokoll des Häftlings, Merker, Paul Friedrich," (3 March 1953) BStU MfS Archiv Nr. 192/56 Untersuchungsvorgang Nr. 294/52 Paul Merker, Band II, 000122.

54 BStU MfS Paul Merker, Archiv Nr. 192/56, 000167.

55 Paul Merker, "Stellungnahme zur Judenfrage," (1 June 1956) SAPMO-BA, ZPA NL Paul Merker 102/27, 1.

56 'Oberstes Gericht der Deutschen Demokratischen Republik I. Strafsenat I Zst. (I) 1/55: Im Namen des Volkes in der Strafsache gegen den Kellner Paul Merker' (29–30 March 1955), BStU MfS, Untersuchungsvorgang Nr. 294/52 Band III, Archiv Nr. 192/56, 522–536.

57 Ibid., 3. The use of the phrase 'den Kellner Paul Merker', or 'the waiter Paul Merker', refers to Merker's youthful occupation as a waiter in restaurants and hotels. Its use in the indictment of this prominent member of the Central Committee repressed his political biography at the top ranks of the KPD and then SED.

58 Ibid., 4.

59 Ibid., 9–13. Also see Merker's account of his political activities in Paul Merker, "Mein politischer Lebenslauf," 12–30, SAPMO-BA, ZPA ZPKK IV/2/llN/801.

60 Ibid., 9–10.

61 Ibid.

62 Rudi Beckert and Karl Wilhelm Fricke, 'Auf Weisung des Politburos: Der Fall Paul Merker,' 26.

63 'Paul Merker to Wilhelm Pieck, April 14, 1956,' SAPMO-BA, ZPA NL Paul Merker 102/27, 2–3.

64 See the minutes of the meetings of the ·Kommission des Zentralkomitee zur Überprüfung von Angelegenheiten von Parteimitgliedern on 19 and 25 April and 3 May 1956 in SAPMO-BA, ZPA IV/202/8 Zentralkomitee der SED.

65 'Walter Ulbricht to Paul Merker, July 31, 1956,' SAPMO-BA, ZPA NL Paul Merker 102/27, 84.

66 'Paul Merker to Walter Ulbricht, August 23, 1956,' SAPMO-BA, ZPA NL Paul Merker 102/27, 85–89.

67 Oberstes Gericht der Deutschen Demokratischen Republik 1. Strafsenat 1 Zst (I) 1/55, "In der Strafsache gegen Merker, Paul Friedrich," (13 July 1956), BStU, MfS. Untersuchungsvorgang Nr. 294/52 Merker, Paul, Band, 111 Archiv Nr. 192/ 56, 000206–000207.

68 Paul Merker, "An die Zentrale Kontrollkummission des ZK. der SED: Stellungnahme zur Judenfrage June 1, 1956," SAPMO-BA, ZPA NL Paul Merker, 102/27.

69 Ibid., 16.

70 Ibid., 18.

71 Ibid., 19.

72 On Soviet bloc support for Zionism, see Herf, *Israel's Moment.*

73 See "Nachruf des Zentralkomitee fur Genossen Paul Merker," and Kurt Seibt, "Trauerfeier fur Paul Merker" (19 May 1967), SAPMO-BA, ZPA IV 2/11V 801.

74 On this see Meuschel, Legitimation und Parteiherrschaft in der DDR.

75 On Jewish questions and antifascism in the mainstream of European communism, see Furet, *Passing of an Illusion.*

76 On the beginnings of East German connections to the Arab states, and denunciation of West German restitution efforts, see Herf, *Divided Memory.* On the 1960s to 1989 see Jeffrey Herf, *Undeclared Wars with Israel: East Germany and the West German Far Left, 1967–1989* (Cambridge and New York: Cambridge University Press, 2022). Also see Enrico Heitzer, Anetta Kahane, Martin Jander and Patrice Poutros, eds., *After Auschwitz: The Difficult Legacies of the GDR* (New York: Berghahn Books, 2021).

7

EAST GERMANY FROM ANTIFASCISM TO UNDECLARED WARS WITH ISRAEL, 1967–1989

In the years immediately following the Holocaust, other than Arab states and Islamist organizations, state-sponsored and publicly supported antisemitism became disrespectable in most of the world and in Europe in particular. From 1947 to 1949, Communists, within and outside the Soviet bloc, with fresh memories of the convergence of anti-Zionism and antisemitism in the Nazi regime, and of the Holocaust itself, were strong supporters of the establishment of the state of Israel. In word and deed, wartime antifascism of the 1940s fueled support for the establishment of the new state of Israel.[1] In those years, the Soviet Union and Soviet bloc opposed the Arabs' efforts to block the establishment of the Jewish state in Palestine. Antisemitism in those years was a kind of Arab and Islamist Sonderweg, or special path, which diverted from the sentiments of the then-young United Nations. Yet Communist and leftist antifascism of the years after World War II played a crucial role in establishing the Jewish state, so too did a redefined antifascism become central for the persistence and *global reach* of antisemitism in the subsequent decades.

The German Democratic Republic, abbreviated as GDR, was established in 1949, and thus *after* the international debate surrounding the establishment of the state of Israel, and after the war of 1947–1948 in the course of which Israel retained its independence.[2] The absence of German sovereignty of any kind meant that it had no impact on the course of events in the Middle East. However, once founded, it stood out as the only one of the Communist regimes to have never had diplomatic relations with the state of Israel. Following German unification in 1991, all of its records became accessible to historians. Those public and classified files document the *undeclared wars against Israel* waged by the Soviet bloc beginning in the 1950s, and their

DOI: 10.4324/9781003449669-8

impact on the global radical left from the 1960s to 1989.[3] The Communists in the Soviet bloc formed an anti-Zionist and antisemitic bridge between the defeat of Nazi Germany and the resurgence of the Islamists to central stage in Arab and Islamic politics in the 1980s. With the slogans and passions of antifascism, the communists rescued antisemitism from oblivion until the Islamists regained center stage to carry the mantle in the 1980s. The Soviet bloc states translated anti-Zionist propaganda into support for Arab and Palestinian Arab armed attacks on the Jewish state.[4]

East Germany from Antifascism to Anti-Zionism

In light of the crucial role that the Communists played in facilitating the creation of the Jewish state between 1947 and 1949, the four subsequent decades of Soviet bloc antagonism to Israel required a massive amount of forgetting of the era when Communist antifascism, anti-colonialism, and anti-racism all fueled Soviet bloc support for the Zionist project. The success of Communist antagonism to Israel during the Cold War lay in its propagandist's ability to place the traditions that had once led to support for the Zionist project in the service of attempting to undermine it and of presenting the Zionist project as on the "wrong side" of an era of decolonization. A distinctive feature of this chapter in the history of antisemitism was that its advocates indignantly rejected the idea that efforts to destroy the state of Israel had anything at all to do with that longer hatred. Rather, in supporting or offering justifications for armed assaults on Israel, they insisted that they were advocates of anti-racist and even anti-fascist principles. They dismissed the accusation of antisemitism as a not-very-clever Zionist trick to deflect or delegitimate necessary opposition to Israel, a state they said was born in aggression, racism, and injustice.

This shift of the tradition of leftist antifascism from support to opposition to Zionism and then Israel was crucial because it facilitated the expansion of anti-Zionism beyond the bounds of European neo-Nazi circles as well as its Arab and Palestinian or Islamist boundaries and made anti-Zionism a defining aspect of global Communist and radical leftist politics. Communist and leftist anti-Zionism became the primary vehicle through which pejorative views which had previously been applied *to the Jews* in the Western tradition came to be applied around the world to *the state of Israel*. It explains how and why that discourse of anti-Zionism became another chapter in the history of antisemitism. It did so by placing the moral and political prestige that the Soviet Union gained due to its role in the defeat of Nazi Germany in service of its assault on the Jewish state. How, the communists asked, could those who had sacrificed so much to defeat the Nazis become antisemites themselves?

Yet the contribution to the revival and global presence of antisemitism made by the Soviet Union and the Soviet bloc, including East Germany was considerable. It adapted conspiracy theories previously applied to Jews, to Israel and Zionism. In so doing, it attributed negative features to the state of Israel which previous antisemites had associated with Jews or "international Jewry," most importantly an inclination to war, aggression, and violence. Doing so culminated in what Robert Wistrich aptly called "Holocaust inversion," that is equating Israel with Nazi Germany.[5] It lent such arguments a moral and political respectability which they had lost so long as they were associated with Nazism, the far right in Europe or Islamists in the Middle East. The anti-fascist passion, once directed against Nazi Germany, now became part of the rhetorical arsenal used against the Jews. Through a combination of military power, diplomatic offensives at the United Nations, and global propaganda, the Soviet Union and its allies brought anti-Zionism into the mainstream of *international* world politics well beyond the Middle East region. For the East German regime, antagonism to Israel became a matter of ideological conviction as well as a key factor in gaining international recognition.

In the 1960s and 1970s, the memories of World War II and the Holocaust were still too fresh to permit Islamist antisemites such as Sayyid Qutb or Haj Amin el-Husseini to become respectable figures on the world stage. Their past enthusiasm for Hitler was too recent, their hatred of the Jews and Judaism too raw, too proud, and unapologetic, their origins in the religious fundamentalism of the Muslim Brotherhood too obvious to find respectability beyond their local confines. After the Holocaust, it was the Soviet Union and Soviet bloc governments who had both the power and the will to turn anti-Zionism and antisemitism from Arab or Islamist regional peculiarities into a global phenomenon. It was the historical accomplishment of Communists in the 1950s and radical and third world left in the 1960s and 1970s to burst the bonds of those geographical and cultural limitations by associating the anti-Zionist/anti-Israeli passion with the apparent universalism of the Communist regimes.

Undeclared Wars with Israel: East Germany's Contributions

All of the Soviet major bloc states supported the Arab states and the Palestine Liberation Organizaiton (PLO) during the Cold War, but East Germany took a particularly prominent role. Given the Nazi past and East Germany's self-definition as an anti-fascist regime, one might have expected that it would keep a lower profile and let the other Warsaw Pact states take the lead in the assault on Israel. The reverse was the case. In the decades in which the Soviet Union and its East European allies became the primary military and economic supporter of Israel's Arab enemies, East Germany was a willing, enthusiastic, and passionate supporter of this policy.

From the mid-1960s when it began to participate in Soviet bloc arms shipments to the Arab states to its demise in 1989, the East German government participated in the Soviet bloc's undeclared war with the state of Israel. In using the word "war" I refer to policies which, if successful, would have to the destruction of the state of Israel by force of arms. Nouns such as "criticism" or "hostility" don't capture the combination of propaganda, verbal justifications for armed attacks on Israel, deliveries of thousands of assault rifles, hand grenades, millions of bullets and other implements of war, cooperation of intelligence services, military training, and financial support for both the PLO and its affiliates and the Arab states at war with Israel. The East German government declared itself a "peace state" and never formally declared war on Israel. Nevertheless, its enthusiastic public engagement for the Arab states and the Palestine Liberation Organization took place when the PLO, whose Charter called for the destruction of Israel by "armed struggle," was engaged in military attacks on the Jewish state.

In contrast to the West German leftist terrorist organizations, such as the Red Army Faction and the Revolutionary Cells, East Germany was a state with the sinews of power that only a state possesses: armed forces, a modest arms industry, a controlled press, embassies and consulates around the world, formidable secret police and intelligence agencies, institutes for military training, hospital care for wounded soldiers, an international airport, ports and ships to deliver military assistance and government controlled universities that offered ideological messages to young students coming from third world countries. Though the West German terrorists dominated media coverage, the Soviet Union and its East European allies had a far more important impact on the conflict between Israel, the Arab states, and the PLO. Following German unification in 1991, the opening of the archives of all of the decision-making institutions of the East German regime including the Politburo, Council of Ministers, Ministries of Foreign Affairs, and Defense as well as the Ministry of State Security (MfS, that is, the Stasi), made it possible to write in detail about the East German chapter of the bloc-wide campaign.[6]

The anti-Zionist passion burned with particular intensity in East Germany. It did so from 1949 under the leadership of Walter Ulbricht, First Secretary of the Central Committee of the SED and thus leader of the East German dictatorship until 1971, and continued under his successor, Erich Honecker until 1989.[7] As was apparent during the Paul Merker case, orthodox Marxist-Leninists such as Ulbricht and Honecker did not have an adequate understanding of Nazi antisemitism and were ideologically unsympathetic to Zionism. Their perceptions of national interest also entered the equation. In its effort to undermine the East German regime, West Germany stipulated that it would refuse diplomatic recognition to any state that would recognize it. In response, East German leaders looked for ways to gain such recognition from countries outside the Soviet bloc. East Germany's hostility to Israel and its partisanship for the Arab states became the most important factor in shattering West German efforts to isolate it and in opening the path to diplomatic recognition and popularity first among the Arab states, then among other leftist regimes and organizations in Africa, Asia, and Latin America.[8]

Conversely, the East German Communist leaders understood that West Germany's support for Israel in the form of financial restitution, and then diplomatic recognition in 1965, was a vulnerability in the Arab states which they exploited by playing the anti-Israeli card. It was this *mutually reinforcing* quality of Communist anti-Zionist and anti-imperialist ideology with national self-interest and power politics conventionally understood that contributed to East Germany's eagerness to assume a high profile in the Soviet bloc campaign. As became particularly evident in the 1970s at the United Nations, East Germany's hostility to Israel won its approval from many countries around the world. All the while denying that its policies were a form of antisemitism, the East German government's antagonism to Israel brought recognition and approval, first from the Arab states, and then other "third world" states who shared their antagonism to the Jewish state.

East Germany and the Six Day War of 1967

On June 15, 1967, in a speech in Leipzig, Walter Ulbricht denounced Israel and supported the Arab states.[9] At the United Nations in New York, Soviet Ambassador Yakov Malik had compared Israel's surprise attack that began the Six Day War with the Nazis' attack on the Soviet Union on June 22, 1941, and its ensuing war on the Eastern Front in World War II. Ulbricht offered his own comparison of Israel to Nazi Germany. With allusions to Nazi Germany's Protectorate in Czechoslovakia and to the Nazis' General Government of occupied Poland during World War II, Ulbricht said that the

> world could not accept that a quarter of a century after the Second World War, the aggressor Israel and its men behind the scenes (*Hintermänner*) form a Sinai Protectorate or a General Government of Jordan for the purpose of renewed colonial oppression of the Arab peoples.[10]

In the subsequent decades, this association of Israel with Nazi Germany remained an enduring element of Communist, Arab, Palestinian, and West German, and West European leftist anti-Israeli propaganda. That link was crucial to lending anti-Zionism and antagonism to Israel's legitimacy in the global left.

East German antagonism to Israel included sending weapons to Arab states. According to CIA reports, East Germany delivered only about 3% of

Soviet bloc military assistance to the Arab states. The vast bulk of the weapons came from the Soviet Union. Yet this small country of 17 million people managed to send 50 MiG jets in spring and summer to Egypt and Syria.[11] In June 1967 alone, East German deliveries to Egypt included 35 Soviet T-34/85 tanks, 5,000 Kalashnikov 7.62 millimeter machine guns with 600,000 bullets, 6,000 MPi 41 Kalashnikov machine guns, 3,500 Kalashnikov machine guns number 43/44, as well as an additional 11 million 7.62 millimeter bullets, and 5 million 7.9 millimeter cartridges.[12]

Following the Six Day War, the Arab states waged what they called a war of attrition that included artillery exchanges with Israel's armed forces as well as terrorist raids against Israel. The files of the East German Defense Ministry indicate that while these attacks were taking place, the East Germans expanded their cost-free weapons assistance to the Arab states, primarily to Egypt and Syria.[13] The deliveries included thirty MiG-17 F and twenty MiG-17 fighter jets; 48 jet engines as well as rocket-propelled grenade launchers, recoilless rifles, 60 anti-tank rocket-propelled grenade launchers, 17,500 Kalashnikov machine guns (Mpi-41, MPi-43/44), 430 light machine guns with munitions, 150,000 land mines, 3,500 hand grenades, as well as helmets, uniforms, back packs.[14] Additional deliveries to the Saika guerilla organization in Syria included six T-34 tanks, 3,000 machine pistols, 560 machine guns, 2,000 carbines, 10,000 hand grenades, and 260 binoculars.[15] On May 13, 1969, the Politburo agreed to give—without cost—5,000 Kalashnikov's machine guns (43/44) and 12 million 7.9 millimeter cartridges to Iraq's "people's militia."[16]

The mutually reinforcing nature of ideological passion and East German national interest was apparent in June and July 1969 when Arab states granted diplomatic recognition to the GDR. On April 30, 1969, Iraq became the first non-Communist government (after Norodom Sihanouk's Cambodia) to establish diplomatic relations with East Germany.[17] The joint declaration issued by East German Foreign Minister Otto Winzer, and Iraqi Foreign Minister Abdul Karim al-Sheikhly on May 10, 1969, in Baghdad drew a clear connection between Iraq's decision to establish diplomatic relations and East Germany's position regarding Israel. The two Foreign Ministers stressed their "shared struggle...against imperialism, neo-Nazism, colonialism and Zionism" and described Israel as "racist, imperialist, reactionary and aggressive." The description of Israel as a racist state, an imperialist spearhead, and as a state similar to Nazism was thus embedded in the beginnings of diplomatic relations between the two states. Similar language accompanied the establishment of diplomatic relations between East Germany and Sudan (June 3, 1969), Syria (June 5, 1969), and Egypt as well as with South Yemen (July 10, 1969). An increase in weapons deliveries of MiG fighter jets to Syria and Egypt followed.[18] Antagonism to Israel was crucial to East Germany's successful defeat of West Germany's effort to isolate it diplomatically and to achieve recognition in the Arab world and beyond.

During these same years, the Soviet bloc deepened a state-to-state military alliance with the Arab states, a development that received less attention than that of its links to the more publicity-seeking PLO. Heinz Hoffmann (1910–1985), East Germany's Minister of Defense from 1960 to 1985, along with Ulbricht's successor as General Secretary of the SED, Erich Honecker, were the central figures in the emergence and growth of the East German component of that alliance.[19] In October 1971, Hoffmann led an East German military delegation on a trip to Iraq, Egypt, and most importantly to Syria. There he met with President Hafez al-Assad as well as with the Chief of the Syrian General Staff, Mustafa Tlass. In the course of extolling solidarity in the common struggle against Zionism, Hoffmann observed that Tlass "clearly" expressed a "tendency that existed among other leading officers of the Arab armed forces" namely an "unconditional admiration for the fascist Blitzkrieg strategy and the expert accomplishments of the bourgeois German military." Despite Tlass' admiration for the Nazi army's accomplishments, Hoffmann expressed confidence that the Syrians "will be victorious in their battle against the enemy. We are fighting the same enemy!" that is, the United States and Israel.[20] The relationship between East Germany and Syria and between Hoffman and Tlass deepened in the following decade. During the Cold War, Hafez al Assad's Syria became the lynchpin of Soviet state-to-state policy in the Middle East.

In an interview with Syrian journalists, Hoffmann said that the Syrians would "be victorious in your battle against the common enemy. We are fighting against a common enemy! The American imperialist support our enemies in Europe and give Israel money and weapons to protect their imperialist interests."[21] The East Germans and the Syrians were "conducting a common battle against the imperialist and Zionist forces." He expressed confidence that "the Arab peoples" would "be victorious over their enemy so that he will have to pull his troops back from occupied Arab territories."[22]

This mixture of antagonism against the "enemy" Israel combined with ambiguity about the meaning of victory was typical of Soviet bloc statements of the period. Did victory mean the complete destruction of Israel and its replacement with a state envisioned by the PLO? Did that mean the expulsion of the vast majority of the Jewish population as the PLO Charter of 1968 clearly implied? Or was it merely a call to reduce Israel's size to what the Israelis believed were the indefensible borders of 1967? What was the meaning of "occupied Arab territories"? Were they the West Bank and Gaza or all of Israel? The East Germans followed the Soviet lead in avoiding clarity on these issues while at the same time calling for a Geneva conference to bring about a negotiated end to the conflict. Their Arab interlocutors, who at the time rejected Israel's legitimacy, might reasonably conclude that the Soviet and East German leadership's refusal to clarify these points meant that the Communists did not preclude the possibility that victory could mean the destruction of the Jewish states. Neither the Soviets nor their East German ally stated that Israel had a right to exist, nor did they denounce Arab state and PLO calls for its destruction. On the contrary, they both attacked Anwar Sadat and others who urged the Arab world to make peace with Israel and lent "solidarity" to uncompromising and radical forces in the region.

The relationship between the GDR and Syria and between Hoffmann and Tlass deepened in the next decade. At the end of a visit to Damascus in May 1983, Hoffmann raised a toast to the Syrians and to Tlass.[23] Following the familiar denunciations of Israel, imperialism and Zionism, Hoffmann extolled the Syrian and GDR friendship as well as

> the community borne of struggle (*Kampfgemeinschaft*) of soldiers of the Syrian armed forces and of the National Peoples' Army of the GDR, to the health of all members of the Syrian armed forces and to its Minister of Defense, comrade General Mustafa Tlass![24]

That same year, Mustafa Tlass published *The Matzo of Zion*, a work that offered a Syrian version of the blood libel about Jews killing Arab children in order to use their blood to bake matzos. East German diplomats and military leaders then knew with whom they were allied but said nothing publicly to chastise the openly antisemitic, that is, Jew-hating Syrian Minister of Defense.[25] It would have been awkward to have done so as antagonism to the Jewish state was central to the GDR alliances with Syria and other Arab states in a state of war with Israel.

The connections between East Germany and Assad's Syria entailed deliveries of larger and more numerous weapons than was the case to guerilla organizations such as the PLO and its affiliates.[26] During the Yom Kippur War of 1973, West Germany adopted a stance of neutrality and joined other members of NATO in refusing to allow American planes resupplying Israel to refuel in West Germany. Conversely, East Germany loudly proclaimed its support for the Arab states and sent MiG jets and two freighters loaded with 2,000 tons of heavy weapons to Syria. While the West German government was urging Israeli ships arriving to receive American military supplies to get out of Bremerhaven harbor, the East German government sent secret shipments of weapons to the Arab states, Syria *in its own ships*. Two East German freighters delivered approximately 2,200 tons including 62 Soviet T-54 tanks with the necessary experts and ammunition; three hundred antitank rifles (RPG-7) with 24,000 shells; 75,000 grenades that were designed to function with the Syrian army's artillery systems; and 30,000 land mines capable of destroying tanks.[27]

East Germany and the PLO

Erich Honecker, General Secretary of the Central Committee of the Socialist Unity Party, and the leader of East Germany from 1971 to October 1989, continued and intensified the policies of his predecessor, Ulbricht. He adopted a high profile of "solidarity" with Communist and radical leftist armed movements in the Middle East and sub-Saharan Africa, including a very public embrace of Yasser Arafat and the Palestine Liberation Organization from the early 1970s to the end of the regime. In 1968 the PLO issued a Charter that called for the destruction of the state of Israel as a result of an "armed struggle." It stated that only Jews who came to "Palestine" before 1947 would be allowed to stay in the Palestinian state that would replace Israel. Thus, logically, it meant that approximately 1.8 million Jews who had been born in or migrated to Israel from 1947 to the late 1960s would be expelled. It was, in other words, a program to complete the expulsion of Jews from the Arab Middle East which had accelerated after the Arab-Israeli war of 1948.[28] The PLO Charter regarded all of Israel, not only the West Bank and the Gaza strip as under "Zionist occupation." It rejected any negotiated settlement that left Israel intact. The Charter justified terrorism waged against that vast majority of Jews who, it insisted, had no right to be in Palestine in the first place.[29]

For the Soviet Union, and Soviet bloc states, including East Germany, to express "solidarity" with the PLO in these years was to offer support for this policy. It was precisely in the years in which the PLO terror against Israel was most intense that Yasser Arafat's photo appeared frequently on the front page of the East German government's official newspaper, *Neues Deutschland* shown literally embracing a smiling Erich Honecker. It was in those years as well that the Soviet bloc states, including East Germany, expanded their military support for the PLO. All the while insisting that support for the Arab states and the PLO had nothing at all to do with antisemitism, Honecker, Foreign Minister Winzer, and other East German leaders did not utter a single public word of criticism of the PLO's terrorist attacks on Israeli civilians.

Following the attack on the Israeli wrestling team at the Munich Olympics by terrorists of the Black September organization on 5 September 1972, Arafat denied that the PLO was involved. On September 17, 1972, he wrote to Honecker about what he called "the action in Munich." He did so because

we [the Executive Committee of the PLO] approve, treasure, are proud of and take hope and strength from the sincere friendship for our cause and your sympathy that you have shown us as well as your recognition of our right in struggle.

He called for

understanding of the action in Munich from the viewpoint of the general problem and its historical events with all their political, national, and human dimensions. If one wants to really distinguish between the deep causes and the peripheral and secondary events, it is futile and useless to view the action apart from the stream of events and from their whole historical framework.[30]

In other words, in his letter to Honecker, Arafat justified the Munich attack.

On 27 November 1972, Honecker sent a public letter of greetings to the "Arab People's Conference in Support of the Palestinian Revolution" taking place in Beirut.[31] In the name of the SED's Central Committee and "of the whole people" of the GDR, he sent "warm greetings" to the conference which was an expression of "strengthening of the unity and determination of broad strata of the Arab peoples in struggle against imperialism, Zionism and reaction." He did not mention the Munich massacre. Instead, he referred to what he called "the string of recent Israeli acts of aggression against the Republic of Lebanon and the Syrian Arab Republic." They had demonstrated "yet again that Israel, with the support of the United States and other imperialist states is not ready to agree to a peaceful settlement of the Middle East conflict."[32] The "history of the worldwide confrontation with imperialism" had shown that the unity of the "anti-imperialist front" led by the Soviet Union and the "socialist community of states" lay behind "every success in the struggle for self-determination and social progress." East Germany, "in the future as in the past" stood "firmly on the side of the Arabic-Palestinian people, its resistance movement" and supported its right to self-determination.[33] Honecker never deviated from this pattern of solidarity with the PLO which entailed silence about its terror aimed at Israelis combined with denunciations of Israeli retaliation.

Arafat visited East Berlin for the first time from October 30 to November 2, 1971.[34] On several more visits in 1973, he met Politburo members Herman Axen and Gerhard Grüneberg.[35] In August 1973, the East Germans celebrated Arafat as a major attraction of the "World Youth Festival" in East Berlin. He then held the first of many meetings with Erich Honecker. In August 1973, East Germany became the first of the Communist states to open a PLO Consulate in its capital. It did so a year before the Soviet Union did.[36] The consular agreement extolled a common "struggle against imperialism and Zionism."[37] The agreement signed by Arafat and Grüneberg on 2 August 1973 included provisions for the delivery of "solidarity goods in the civilian and non-civilian area." Similar agreements for civilian and military deliveries were signed on an annual basis over the next 15 years.[38]

The opening of the PLO office caused consternation in the small Jewish community in West Berlin. On September 21, 1973, Heinz Galinski, its titular head, published an open letter to Honecker to express the "growing concern and anxiety in the Jewish community" about the establishment of the PLO office in East Berlin.[39]

With astonishment, we see that the stance of the GDR towards Israel is more hostile than other socialist countries…Now and then we hear from your side the assurance that you have nothing against Jews. Rather it is only Zionism that you condemn and fight. We have had negative practical experiences with such theories. There is no doubt that that the biased, uninformed, and hate-filled reporting about Israel in the press, radio, and television in the GDR in recent years again awakens anti-Semitic resentment. In so doing, it accords with the intentions of neo-Nazi elements. People, such as yourself, who belonged to the circle of those persecuted by the Nazi regime, must be especially conscious of such effects. It especially pains us that people [such as yourself] who suffered with us under National Socialism and fought against it, foster such destructive emotions and sentiments.[40]

Honecker did not reply to Galinski's letter.

During the 1970s, the East German-PLO relationship grew into a full-scale alliance that included military training, delivery of weapons, and cooperation between East Germany's MfS, the Stasi, and the PLO's intelligence service. One result was the formulation of a distinctive East German definition of counterterrorism. It amounted to simultaneously attempting to prevent Arab and Palestinian terrorist attacks in West Germany and Western Europe that could be traced back to East Germany while supporting and facilitating the PLO's terrorist attacks on Israel.[41] In June 1979, East Germany's MfS signed a formal agreement of cooperation with the PLO intelligence services based on their shared interest in preventing the use of East Germany as a base for terrorist operations against Western Europe but also using it as a base for terrorist operations against Israel.[42]

The smiling faces of Arafat and Honecker on the front pages of *Neues Deutschland*, the government's official newspaper, and on East German television, became a ubiquitous feature of the East German-PLO alliance. The alliance became a point of pride for the regime. The Stasi files reveal further elements of its operational dimensions. From 1957 to the end of the regime in 1989, Erich Mielke was the director of the MfS. He was a member of the SED's Central Committee from 1950 to 1989 and of the Politburo from 1976 to 1989. In May 1979, Mielke commissioned a study of "Information about Activities of Representative of the Palestine Liberation Movement in Association with International Terrorists to Include the GDR in the Preparation of Acts of Violence in the Countries of Western Europe."[43] The Stasi had learned that "groups within the Palestinian liberation movement in association with anarcho-terrorist groups have intensified their efforts to use the territory of the GDR as a logistical base and starting point for the implementation of acts of violence in Western Europe." East Germany's "generous stance of solidarity toward the national liberation movement of the Arab peoples is seen by these groups as offering favorable conditions for the planning and implementation of operations." So did East Berlin's "communications possibilities." In the wake of " the separate peace," that is, the Camp David Accords between Israel and Egypt of 1979 of April 1979,

> the Palestinian Liberation Movement activated the planning and preparation of acts of violence seen as acts of war against Western countries. Such activities that are based on the territory of the GDR create political dangers and damage our national state security interests.[44]

Since the beginning of March 1979, the Stasi was aware that practitioners of terrorism such as Ilich Ramirez-Sanchez better known as "Carlos" had been a guest of the First Secretary of the Embassy of the Peoples' Democratic Republic of Yemen in East Berlin. Other persons that concerned the Stasi residing in East Berlin were PLO officials Abu Hisham, an aide to Salem Kalef, alias Abu Ayad, the head of the PLO's intelligence service, Nabil Kouleilat, the director of the PLO's office in East Berlin, and members of the West German June 2nd Movement.[45] Moreover, the Stasi knew that Arab, Palestinian, West German, and West European terrorist organizations had been using East Germany and the Soviet bloc states as a base from which to attempt to launch terrorist attacks in Western Europe and that these groups had plans to continue to do so in the future. The report viewed such actions which Western intelligence agencies could trace back to East Germany and the Soviet bloc as harmful to East Germany's national interests.[46] Mielke decided to intensify cooperation between the Stasi and the PLO's intelligence services both to prevent the attacks with such origins in West Germany and Western Europe while also aiding the PLO in its campaign against Israel. In June and August 1979, he held discussions about these issues with Abu Ayad, the head of the PLO intelligence service.[47] In February 1980, they agreed that a permanent representative of the PLO security services would be stationed in East Berlin and that a Stasi officer would be a contact officer with the PLO in Beirut, Lebanon.[48] From then until the collapse of the regime in 1989, Ayad or his second in command Amin al-Hindi met several times a year with Mielke or with Gerhard Neiber, the director of Division XXII, the office for "Fighting Terrorism" (*Terrorismusbekämpfung*). The agreement called for "operational cooperation" between the Stasi and the PLO intelligence service in East Germany.[49]

On July 15, 1980, Ayad discussed "terrorist forces and their activities" with Stasi officials in Division XXII.[50] Before offering a 20-page-long assessment of various terrorist organizations, Ayad candidly explained the meaning of some important terms. The PLO, he said, distinguished between "right-wing terrorism," "left-wing adventurers," and "terrorist forces that are active in the interest of the Palestinian resistance movement." While it rejected both "right-wing terrorists" and "left-wing adventurers," the "PLO supported the other terrorist forces and at times worked together with them."[51] Ayad

avoided euphemism. He understood terrorism to be the intentional target-
ing of civilians, and that it was distinct from acts of war carried out against
military forces. In relevant United Nations committees, the PLO, the GDR,
and the Soviet bloc dismissed Western attacks on "international terrorism"
as imperialist propaganda. However, when speaking to one another, the Stasi
and PLO officials abandoned public euphemism and were frank about the
nature of terrorism and their support for it.

The Stasi officials, probably Mielke and Neiber, replied that they

> could support a certain toleration of left-oriented terrorist forces so long
> as it preserves strict secrecy, obeys [East German, JH] law, and the pre-
> cludes any kind of political or any other kind of damage for the GDR and
> its allies.

Ayad assured his counterparts that the PLO agreed with the MfS on this
matter. He suggested that agreement about these issues was a basis on which
"the exchange of information could continue to be improved." Ayad then
offered "details about terrorist groups and forces to which the PLO had contacts and connections."[52] The groups in question included the Carlos group,
Abu Nidal, Iraq's Saddam Hussein, former members of the Wadi Haddad
group, the Armenian Liberation Front, and the Japanese Red Army. Regarding "terrorist groups in the FRG," that is, in West Germany, he said that the
PLO had no contact with the June 2nd Movement or the Red Army Faction,
but it had developed contacts to the Revolutionary Cells, the group which
participated in the hijacking of an Air France flight to Entebbe, Uganda in
1976. In 1981, Ayad told the Stasi officials that the PLO was working with
the Revolutionary Cells and "intended to expand the connections to the so-
called 'Revolutionary Cells' in the Federal Republic and eventually to use it
to carry out particular armed actions."[53]

The Stasi leaders raised no concerns either about those connections or
about Palestinian terror attacks on Israel. Their primary concern was to prevent Arab and Palestinian terrorists from using East German territory as a
base from which to launch attacks in West Germany and Western Europe.
The Stasi knew that radical Arabs and Palestinians had traveled to East
Berlin from the Middle East and from other Warsaw Pact countries with
false passports and had then proceeded to West Berlin and from there to West
Germany and Western Europe where they could conduct terrorist attacks.
East Germany's problem lay in reconciling its self-presentation as an advocate
of peace, détente, and better relations with the West with toleration and perhaps active support of terrorist groups waging attacks in West Germany and
Western Europe.[54] The Stasi sought to square a circle. At the same time that
it was sending arms and offering military training to the PLO (as well as to
the Popular Front for the Liberation of Palestine and the Democratic Popular

Front for the Liberation of Palestine) who were carrying out terrorist attacks against Israel and perhaps elsewhere in the world, it also worked with the PLO to prevent terrorist attacks in West Germany and Western Europe that could be traced back to East Germany, the Soviet Union, or other Communist regimes in Eastern Europe. Shifting terrorist attacks away from Europe and toward Israel was part of the Stasi's definition of "counterterrorism."

The files of the Stasi's Division of Weapons and Chemical Services (*Abteilung Bewaffnung und Chemische Dienst or BCD*) indicate that the Stasi also played a key role in delivering weapons to the PLO. On August 4, 1980, shortly after their conversations about the meaning of terrorism, the MfS delivered the following weapons to the PLO: 2000 MPi, a modernized version of the famous Kalashnikov machine gun, 5,000 hand grenades, 750 explosives of 200 grams each, 372 explosives of 400 grams each, along with detonators and wire, all with a value of 1,296,000 Marks.[55] On April 11, 1980, the MfS sent the following to the PLO: 5,000 hand grenades, as well as explosives, detonators, wire, and ammunition valued at 114,102.38 Marks.[56] In February 1981, the Stasi's Division of Weapons and Chemical Services BCD sent 3,500 Kalashnikovs and 350 palettes of ammunition. In 1981, when the PLO was building up its arsenal in Lebanon, the Stasi weapons deliveries were worth 2,269,190 Marks.[57] On April 6, 1982, the MfS sent the PLO 564,400 bullets and 1,400 Kalashnikovs. On April 23, 1982, it sent ten rocket-propelled grenade launchers and five heavy machine guns costing 18,905 and 35,225 marks, respectively.[58]

Israel invaded Lebanon in June 1982 in order to destroy a then sizable PLO arsenal and army that had emerged there. On July 1, 1982, the GDR sent the PLO 900 Kalashnikovs (MPi KMS-72) worth 583,000 marks; 720 hand grenades worth 11,260.80 marks, 297,480 bullets worth 121,907.30 marks, 15 anti-tank rifles (RPG-7) worth 67,410.75 marks, and two light machine guns (lMG RPK Kal. 7.62).[59] On July 7, 1982, it sent 96 HL-grenades, designed for attacking tanks worth 46,694.40 marks.[60] The cost of weapons deliveries for this one week in July 1981 was over 720,000 marks. In sum, from 1980 to 1982, the Stasi sent 8,300 Kalashnikovs and 10,896 hand grenades to the PLO, presumably as "solidarity goods" and thus cost-free. The Stasi officials were well aware that the purpose of the weapons was to wage war and terror campaigns against the citizens of Israel.

Beginning in the mid-1960s, the East German Defense Ministry played a major role in delivering heavier weapons including tanks, planes, larger artillery to Egypt and Syria.[61] As the CIA assessments indicated, after Egyptian President Anwar Sadat broke with the Soviet bloc in 1975, Hafez al-Assad's Syria moved even more to the center of Soviet bloc military and economic assistance. The records of East Germany's weapons deliveries to Syria during the Yom Kippur War of October 1973 offer striking evidence of the depth of its relationship with Assad's regime. Honecker approved sending a squadron of twelve MiG 21 jet fighters to the East German Air Force along with the necessary ammunition and experts.[62] East German pilots flew the plans to Budapest and from there they were delivered to Syria in Soviet transport planes. Two East German freighters, the Freyburg and Klosterfelde, departed from Rostock harbor in mid-October and arrived at the Syrian port of Tartus on November 1 and 2, 1973. Their cargo of approximately 2,200 tons of military equipment included 62 Soviet T-54 tanks with the necessary experts and ammunition, 300 anti-tank rifles (RPG-7) with 24,000 shells, 75,000 grenades that were designed to function with the Syrian army's artillery systems, and 30,000 land mines capable of destroying tanks.[63] Heinz Hoffmann ordered that all German language markings on the tanks were to be erased and replaced with Russian language markings and accompanying documentation.[64] Two thousand and two hundred tons of military equipment was a fraction of what the Soviet Union was sending to Syria and of the massive American resupply operation to Israel, "Operation Reforger," that President Nixon ordered and which was crucial for Israel's ability to recover from the initial Arab surprise attacks on Yom Kippur. Yet it was important enough to Honecker that he received 30 daily reports on the journey of the Freyburg and Klosterfelde and the unloading operation in Tartus, Syria.[65] East German solidarity with the Arab states contrasted with the official West German position of neutrality during the war.

The United Nations General Assembly became the central political institution through which anti-Zionism expanded beyond the limits of regional Arab politics and became a key element of the political culture of world politics. The Soviet Union and its allies played a key role in that process of internationalization. After it became a member of the United Nations in 1973, East Germany placed itself in the midst of the huge anti-Israel majority in the UN General Assembly.[66] In 1975, it was one of the twenty co-sponsors of the UN resolution that created the PLO's anchor at the UN, the Committee for the Exercise of the Inalienable Rights of the Palestinian People (CEIRPP). It joined the majority of seventy-two nations in the General Assembly that voted in favor of the "Zionism is racism resolution" of November 10, 1975. Chaim Herzog, Israel's Ambassador to the UN, told the General Assembly at the time that as a result of the resolution the UN had become "the world centre of antisemitism. Hitler would have felt at home on a number of occasions during the past year, listening to the proceedings in this forum, and above all, to the proceedings during the debate on Zionism."[67]

In his response on November 10 to the passage of the Zionism as racism resolution, the American Ambassador to the UN Daniel Patrick Moynihan declared that "the resolution was a lie," that "a great evil has been loosed upon the world. The abomination of antisemitism....has been given the appearance of international sanction." Moynihan added that if, as the Soviet delegate declared "racism is a form of Nazism, and if, as this resolution declared, Zionism is a form of racism, then we have step by step taken ourselves to the point of proclaiming that Zionism is a form of Nazism." This was a lie "scarcely exceeded" in the twentieth century's "annals of untruth and outrage. The lie is that Zionism is a form of racism. The overwhelmingly clear truth is that it is not."[68] Yet it was this lie, that Zionism was, in fact not only a form of racism but also "a form of Nazism" which was so devastatingly effective for the globalization of antisemitism in the halls of the United Nations. East Germany joined in placing the traditions of Communist antifascism and anti-imperialism in the service of this attack on Zionism and the state of Israel. It enthusiastically followed the lead of the Soviet Union and voted in favor of this and many other anti-Israeli resolutions at the UN. In so doing, it made a significant contribution to the globalization of antisemitism embedded in the rhetoric of anti-Zionism.

On October 14, 1974, Yosef Tekoah, Israel's Ambassador to the United Nations, in opposing a resolution to give the PLO observer status in the organization, referred to the PLO's program to destroy the state of Israel and its use of "the most despicable of methods witnessed by mankind in recent decades—the deliberate murder of guiltless civilians."[69] Peter Florin, East Germany's UN Ambassador replied that "we fully support" the "just struggle to ensure the people of Palestine their legitimate rights." Referring to Tekoah's comments he added that

> the slander of the Israeli representatives against the PLO is simply a desperate effort to distract attention from Israel's continuing aggression against neighboring Arab States and shows that Israel is still not inclined to acknowledge the rights of the Arab peoples of Palestine.[70]

It was in these same years as the PLO and its various affiliates (Popular Front for the Liberation of Palestine, Popular Democratic Front for the Liberation of Palestine) carried out attacks on Israeli citizens in northern Israel that East Germany's support for those organizations engaged in terrorism deepened.[71]

The response of the Soviet Union and East Germany to Israel's invasion of Lebanon in 1982 offered an example of how anti-Zionism crossed the line to antisemitism. The war took place following almost a decade of terrorist attacks on the towns of northern Israel from PLO bases in southern Lebanon, hence its name, "Peace for Galilee." Within Israel and abroad, the war was controversial. The distinguishing feature of Soviet bloc, including East German propaganda during the war was, as *Neues Deutschland* blared on June 28, 1974, a "war of extermination" (*Ausrottungskrieg*), a term associated with the Nazi war on Germany's Eastern Front in World War II. On June 29, East German Foreign Minister, Oskar Fischer wrote to UN General Secretary Pere de Cuellar to repeat the charge of a "war of extermination." On July 6, 1974, *Neues Deutschland* reprinted an article from *Pravda* which claimed that "the Zionists solve the 'Palestinian Question' exactly as the Nazis solved the 'Jewish Question,'…through total extermination and genocide. The 'Great Israel' was built with the same methods as was the 'Great Germany' that is, "by territorial conquest" at "the cost of the blood and bones of other peoples." In July, *Neues Deutschland* described Israel's war in Lebanon with nouns made infamous by their association with Nazi Germany— *Sonderkommando* (special commandos) *Mordfeldzug (*campaign of murder), *Ausrottungskrieg* (war of extermination) and *Völkermord* (genocide).[72] That summer, *Neues Deutschland* published wildly inflated numbers of civilian deaths, figures which it did not correct when accurate and far lower figures were reported by Lebanese as well as Israeli sources. While the Soviet press repeated the "Israeli as Nazi" theme that emerged in the UN debates in 1967, the East Germans were a bit more reserved, merely describing the Zionists as mass murderers and practitioners of genocide.[73] According to the Soviet bloc including East German propaganda organs, Israel's war in Lebanon confirmed what Moynihan had called the lie that Zionism was a form of Nazism. For the Soviet bloc propaganda organs, Israel's war in Lebanon confirmed what Moynihan had called the lie that Zionism was a form of Nazism.[74]

Conclusion

Following the Iranian revolution of 1979, the publication of the Hamas Charter in 1988, the revolutions of 1989 in Eastern Europe, and then the collapse of the Soviet Union in 1991, Islamists emerged again as a leading force in the war against the Jewish state. In contrast to the Communists and the radical left, the Islamists proudly declared their hatred of Jews and Judaism, offered religious, not secular justifications for this hatred, dispensed with rhetoric about diplomatic and peaceful solutions, and proudly declared that they intended to destroy the state of Israel by armed force. Islamism revived the classic public convergence of antisemitism and anti-Zionism that was present in Nazi Germany. Yet the habits of thought of the secular Communist and leftist era survived the collapse of the Soviet Union and the East European Communist states because the Communists had been successful in associating falsehoods about Israel with the causes of antifascism, anti-imperialism, and then anti-racism.

We return to the point made at the outset about Soviet bloc communism as an anti-Zionist bridge. In the four decades following the Holocaust, Communism and the radical left did for antisemitism what Islamism could not do. Even in the 1960s and 1970s, the memories of Haj Amin el-Husseini's radio broadcasts from Nazi Berlin or Sayyid Qutb's justifications of the Holocaust in his *Our Struggle with the Jews* were too close to the letter and spirit of Nazism to appeal beyond the radical nationalist Arab or Islamist milieus of North Africa and the Middle East. An anti-Zionism which insisted that it had nothing to do with antisemitism, which spoke in the name of antifascism and anti-imperialism and which came from a power, the Soviet Union, that had played a decisive role in defeating Nazi Germany proved to be a powerful carrier of a set of ideas and factual claims about the state of Israel that denied its legitimacy and justified armed attacks on its citizens. It was this Communist and radical leftist anti-Zionism that contributed to repeated defeats of Israel in the United Nations General Assembly and turned it into what Chaim Herzog called the world's center of antisemitism. These were ideas that fostered indifference to terrorist attacks launched against Israelis, justified those attacks as part of a legitimate struggle for national liberation, and offered excuses for expressions of open Jew-hatred when it came from Arabs and Palestinians. The anti-Zionism of the Communist era during the Cold War also made hatred of the Jewish state respectable among those who spoke the language of human rights, anti-racism, and anti-colonialism. Through the global competition with the United States and its allies, the Soviet Union and its allies spread falsehoods about and hatred toward Israel and the Israelis beyond the limits of the Middle East. The most important arena of that globalization was the United Nations where East German diplomats collaborated intensively in the anti-Zionist effort.

Communist anti-Zionism described the state of Israel's place in world politics in ways that European antisemites had viewed the Jews in European history, that is, as violent, aggressive, murderous, and a great danger to the entire world. It presented Israel as both a manifestation of an evil modernity, now called Western imperialism, as well as an anachronism whose national liberation struggle was somehow not acceptable while nationalisms of Palestinians and the Arab states were to be extolled. The repeated falsehood that the Israelis behaved like the Nazis was central to Communist anti-Zionism. By associating the Jewish state with the embodiment of radical evil in modern history, Communist anti-Zionism made a major contribution to the persistence of antisemitism. For if the Jewish state was practitioner of genocide, gross violations of human rights, and wars of extermination, did this not have something to do with the character of the Jews who had created state of Israel?

On March 11, 1978, Yasser Arafat laid a wreath at the memorial to "victims of fascism and militarism" in East Berlin. The photo of the event shows Arafat walking between Gerhard Grüneberg, the member of the East German Politburo who negotiated and signed the agreements with the PLO, and an East German military officer who bears resemblance to Minister of Defense Heinz Hoffmann. Units of East Germany's National People's Army stand at attention in the background.[75] By associating honoring the memory of victims of fascism with honoring the leader of the Palestine Liberation Organization then engaged in war with Israel, the image captures the essence of Soviet bloc and East German propaganda aimed at the state of Israel, namely that the war against Israel was another chapter in the history of antifascism.

In East Germany, the Soviet bloc's undeclared war with the Jewish state offered a sort of national liberation from the burdens of German history in the Nazi era. It was of a piece with the East German Communist conviction that as an officially "anti-fascist" regime it had no particular obligations or responsibilities to Jewish survivors of the Holocaust. The leaders of East Germany believed that solidarity with the Arab states and the PLO lifted them out of the continuities of German history and placed them instead on the correct side of a historical dialectic of global anti-imperialist revolution. In the process, the East German Communists became oblivious to the fact that they were the second German dictatorship in the twentieth century that adopted policies that would bring death and injury to Jews. East Germany's support for the Arab states and Palestinian terrorist organizations was not comparable to Nazi Germany's Final Solution yet it did constitute support for governments and organizations whose clear goal was the destruction of the Jewish state and with it the death and suffering of many Jews, including Jewish survivors of the Holocaust.

Following the collapse of the Communist dictatorship in fall 1989, the first democratically elected parliament (*Volkskammer*) in Eastern Germany since 1932 met from April 5 to October 2, 1990. On April 12, 1990, the *Volkskammer* unanimously passed a resolution supported by all of the political parties in the parliament.[76] The resolution drew particular attention to the Nazi genocide of the Jews of Europe and expressed shame in the face of this burden of German history. It asked

> the Jews in the entire world for forgiveness. We ask the people in Israel for forgiveness for the hypocrisy and hostility of official GDR policy toward the state of Israel and for the persecution and humiliation of Jewish fellow citizens in our country.[77]

The parliament looked forward to establishing diplomatic relations with Israel, something the GDR never did. On July 2, 1990, the *Volkskammer* passed another resolution, one that rejected East Germany's support of the United Nations Resolution 3379 of November 10, 1975, that condemned Zionism as a form of racism. Twenty-three members of the parliament spanning the spectrum of all the parties except the successor party to the East German Communists were its signers. They included its leading proponent, Konrad Weiss; a future President of the Bundestag, Wolfgang Thierse; and a future President of a unified Germany, Joachim Gauck.[78] The *Volkskammer* distanced

> itself from all forms of the anti-Israeli and anti-Zionist policies that were practiced in this country [East Germany, JH] for decades and from their domestic and foreign policy consequences. It distances itself in particular

from [East Germany's] agreement to Resolution 3379 of the 30th United Nations General Assembly of 10 November 1975

and from the "equation of Zionism with racism" in that resolution.[79] In spring and summer 1990, caught up in momentous events of the peaceful revolutions that brought down the Communist dictatorships in Europe, the members of the short-lived, democratically elected *Volkskammer* grasped the importance of events discussed in this chapter. Now, due to the opening of the archives made possible by the peaceful East German revolution of 1989, we have been able to give adequate scholarly attention to the Soviet bloc and to East Germany's undeclared war on Israel and the anti-Zionist and antisemitic bridge it helped to build.

Notes

Selections reprinted with permission from Jeffrey Herf, *Undeclared Wars with Israel: East Germany and the West German Far Left, 1967–1989* (Cambridge University Press), Copyright 2016, reproduced with permission of Cambridge University Press [the Licensor] through PLSclear. All rights reserved; Herf, Jeffrey, "'At War with Israel': East Germany's Key Role in Soviet Policy in the Middle East," *Journal of Cold War Studies* Summer 16, 3 (2014), ©2014 by the President and Fellows of Harvard College and the Massachusetts Institute of Technology, 129–163; Jeffrey Herf, "The Anti-Zionist Bridge: The East German Communist Contribution to Antisemitism's Revival after the Holocaust," *Antisemitism Studies* 23, 1 (Spring 2017): 130–156. Copyright Indiana University Press. 2017. Reprinted with permission. All rights reserved.

1 See Jeffrey Herf, *Israel's Moment: International Support for and Opposition to Establishing the Jewish State, 1947–1949* (New York: Cambridge University Press, 2022).

2 The official title of the country known as the "German Democratic Republic" and its common abbreviation "GDR" is an example of Orwellian double speak. It was a regime that was neither democratic nor was it based on republican principles that imply checks and balances, and the peaceful transfer of power in free and fair elections. The government was a one-party dictatorship. The parliament was a rubber stamp. It was a "communist" not a "socialist" experiment. The repetition of "GDR" in academic and journalistic commentary contributes to obfuscation of realities. I prefer the term "East Germany" though at times, to save time and space, I will occasionally refer to the "GDR."

3 Jeffrey Herf, *Undeclared Wars with Israel: East Germany and the West German Far Left, 1967–1989* (New York: Cambridge University Press, 2016). The official name of the regime is East Berlin was the "German Democratic Republic," hence the initials, "GDR." While it was certainly a German government, it was neither democratic nor was it a republic.

4 This essay draws on Jeffrey Herf, "The Anti-Zionist Bridge: The East German Communist Contribution to Antisemitism's Revival After the Holocaust," *Antisemitism Studies* 23, 1 (Spring 2017): 130–156; and "At War with Israel: East Germany's Key Role in Soviet Policy in the Middle East," *Journal of Cold War Studies* 16, 3 (Summer 2014): 129–163; and Herf, *Undeclared Wars with Israel*.

5 Robert Wistrich, "Holocaust Inversion," in Anthony McElligott and Jeffrey Herf, eds., *Antisemitism Before and Since the Holocaust: Altered Contexts and Recent Perspectives* (London: Palgrave/Macmillan, 2017), 37–49.

6 See Herf, *Undeclared Wars with Israel.*

7 For biographical details about Walter Ulbricht and Erich Honecker, see "Ulbricht, Walter," and "Honecker, Erich," Bernd-Rainer Barth, et al., *Wer war Wer in der DDR: Ein biographisches Handbuch* (Frankfurt/Main: Fischer Taschenbuch Verlag, 1996), 750, and 321–322. On Honecker up to 1945, also see Martin Sabrow, *Erich Honecker: Das Leben davor, 1912–1945* (Munich: C.H. Beck, 2016).

8 Herf, "Diplomatic Breakthrough to Military Alliance: East Germany, the Arab States, and the PLO, 1969–1973," in *Undeclared Wars with Israel,* 119–157; Alexander Troche, *Ulbricht und die Dritte Welt: Ost-Berlins 'Kampf gegen die Bonner 'Alleinvertretungsanmaß* (Erlangen: Palm and Enke, 1996).

9 "Sicherheit für die Friedliche Arbeit unseres Volkes: Kernsätze aus der Rede Walter Ulbrichts," *Neues Deutschland,* June 15, 1967, 1 and 3; see "Walter Ulbricht's Leipzig Speech of June 15, 1967," in Herf, *Undeclared Wars with Israel,* 55–58.

10 Ibid., 118.

11 See Herf, "East Germany and the Six Day War of June 1967," in *Undeclared Wars with Israel,* 33–74. "Anlage Nr. 1 zum Protokoll Nr. 7/67 vom 7.8. 1967; Betr.: Maßnahmen im Zusammenhang mit der Situation im Nahen und Mittleren Osten," BAB SAPMO DY 30/J IV 2/2/1117, 7. The Politburo members included Walter Ulbricht, Friedrich Ebert, Gerhard Grüneberg, Fritz Hager, Erich Honecker, Herman Matern, Gunter Mittag, Albert Norden, and Will Stoph.

12 Klaus Storkmann, "Tabelle 14: Aufstellung der vom MvNV am 14. Juni 1967 gemeldeten Hilfslieferungen und die VAR (Auszüge)," Geheime *Solidarität: Militärbeziehungen und Militärhilfen der DDR in die 'Dritte Welt'* (Berlin: Ch. Links Verlag, 2012), 600.

13 "Kostenlose Hilfslieferungen, GVS-Nr.: A 76 938," BAMA DVWI 115671, MfNV Sekr. D. Ministers. Unterlagen zur Vorbereitung d. Militärdelegation in den arabischen Staaten, 6–7.

14 Ibid., 31.

15 "Kostenlose Hilfslieferungen,GVS-Nr.: A 76 950" BAMA DVWI 115671, MfNV Sekr. D. Ministers. Unterlagen zur Vorbereitung d. Militärdelegation in den arabischen Staaten, 30–31.

16 Generaloberst (Colonel General) Heinz Keßler to Generalleutnant Borning, [East] Berlin (July 9, 1970), BAMA, MfNV, DVW1 115537, 105. Also see Herf, "Diplomatic Breakthrough to Military Alliance"; Heinz Keßler to Paul Markowski, [East] Berlin (July 27, 1970), BAMA, MfNV, DVW1 115537, 107–108. See "Weiss, Gerhard," in Bernd-Rainer Barth, et al., *Wer war Wer in der DDR: Ein biographisches Handbuch* (Frankfurt/Main: Fischer Taschenbuch, 1996), 779–780.

17 See Angelika Timm, *Hammer, Zirkel, Davidstern: Das gestörte Verhältnis der DDR zu Zionismus und Staat Israel* (Bonn: Bouvier Verlag, 1997), chs. 7–9. See the documents in Wolfgang Bator and Angelika Bator, eds., *Der DDR und die arabischen Staaten* ([East] Berlin: Staatsverlag der Deutschen Demokratischen Republik, 1984).

18 See Herf, "Diplomatic Breakthrough to Military Alliance," also "Arabische Republik Ägypten (ARÄ): Beziehungen der speziellen Außenwirtschaft zu den militärischen Organen der ARÄ," BAMA DVWI 115671, MfNV Sekr. D. Ministers. Unterlagen zur Vorbereitung d. Militärdelegation in den arabischen Staaten, 37–38.

19 "Hoffmann, Heinz," Barth, et al., *Wer war Wer in der DDR.*

20 Heinz Hoffmann, "Bericht über den Aufenthalt einer offiziellen Militärdelegation der Deutschen Demokratischen Republik in der Republik Irak, der Syrischen Arabischen Republik und der Arabischen Republik Ägypten in der Zeit vom. 13.-31. Oktober 1971, BAMA DVWI 115673, MfNV Sekr. D. Ministers, 4.

21 Heinz Hoffman interview with Jaych-Ach-Chaab, Damascus (October 1971), MfNV. Schriftverkehr des Ministers. Militärdelegation der DDR nach Syrien, Ägypten, Irak, BAMA DVW1/115673, 4.

22 Ibid., 5–6.

23 Heinz Hoffmann, "Empfang in der Botschaft der DDR," MfNV Sekr. des Ministers. Militärdelegation der DDR nach Syrien, Ägypten, Irak., BAMA DVW1/115673.

24 Ibid., 4 and 10.

25 On the meetings between Heinz Hoffmann and Mustafa Tlass, and the latter's *Matzo of Zion* see Herf, *Undeclared Wars with Israel*, 142–144, 371–372, 377–380.

26 On military deliveries to the Arab states during the Yom Kippur War see "East German Arms Deliveries to Syria" in Herf, *Undeclared Wars with Israel*, 234–238.

27 Generalleutnant Fritz Streletz, "VS-Nr.: A 360 179, Informationsbericht Nr. 15 zur Lage im Nahen Osten: Stand: 20.10.1973, 0500 Uhr," BA-MA, VA-01 32899, 65–75.

28 On this see Georges Bensoussan, *Juifs en Pays Arabes: Le grand Déracinement, 1850–1975* (Paris: Editions Tallandier, 2012); and Georges Bensoussan, ed., "Les Juifs d'Orient face au nazisme et a la Shoah (1930–1945)," *Revue D'Histoire de la Shoah*, No. 205, October 2016 (Paris: Centre de Documentation Juive Contemporaine, 2016); Martin Gilbert, *In Ishmael's House: A History of Jews in Muslim Lands* (New Haven, CT: Yale University Press, 2010); Shulewitz Hillel, ed., *The Forgotten Millions: The Modern Jewish Exodus from Arab Lands* (New York: Continuum, 1999); Lyn Julius, *Uprooted: How 3,000 Years of Jewish Civilization in the Arab World Vanished Overnight* (London: Vallentine-Mitchell, 2018).

29 "The Palestinian National Charter: Resolutions of the Palestine National Council 1–17 July 1968," Yale Law School, The Avalon Project Documents in Law and Diplomacy, http://avalon.law.yale.edu/20th_century/plocov.asp. For a close reading of the PLO Charter see Yehoshafat Harkabi, *The Palestinian Covenant and Its Meaning* (London: Valentine, Mitchell, 1979).

30 Yasser Arafat to Erich Honecker (17 September 17, 1972), "Notizen und Schreiben außenpolitischen Charakters zwischen der DDR und der Palästinensischen Befreiungsbewegung zur Unterstützung der PLO durch die DDR, 1972, 1974, 1978–1979," Politisches Archiv des Auswärtiges Amt, Berlin, PAAA, MFAA, Abt. Naher-und Mittlerer Osten, MfAA, C 7.667 (ZR 2040/01), 48–49.

31 Abteilung Internationale Verbindungen, "Entwurf eines Grußschreibens: An die arabische Volkskonferenz zur Unterstützung der palästinensischen Revolution", Berlin (24 November 1972), 1–2. Also see "*Kongreß zur Unterstützung des palästinensischen Volkes eröffnet: Delegation der DDR überbrachte Grüß des ZK der SED*," *Neues Deutschland* (28 November 1972), Bundesarchiv Berlin, BAB ZK der SED, DY 30 9529, 1.

32 Ibid., 1–2.

33 Ibid., 2.

34 Timm, *Hammer, Zirkel, Davidstern*, 269–275. Also see Lutz Maeke, *DDR und PLO (Studien zur Zeitgeschichte)* (Berlin: De Gruyter Oldenbourg, 2017).

35 "Grüneberg, Gerhard," Barth et al., *Wer war Wer in der DDR: Ein biographisches Handbuch*, 252.

36 See "Formalizing the East German Alliance with the PLO and the Arab States: 1973," in Herf, *Undeclared Wars with Israel*, 198–238. In 1965 Mao's China agreed to open the first of the PLO's foreign bureaus.

37 Ibid., 276.

38 Gerhard Grüneberg and Yassir Arafat, "Vereinbarung zwischen der Sozialistischen Einheitspartei Deutschlands und der Palästinensischen Befreiungsorganisationen (PLO) für die Jahre 1976/1977," [East] Berlin (December 1, 1975), Bundesarchiv Berlin SAPMO DY 30/ 9529, "Büro des Politburo des ZK der SED 1972-1989," 1–3.

39 "Galinski bedauert feindselige Haltung der 'DDR' gegen Israel," West Berlin, *Die Welt* (September 22, 1973), BStU, Archiv der Zentralstelle, MfS ZAIG, Nr. 11048, 398.

40 Ibid.

41 On East Germany's Eurocentric counterterrorism policies see "An Alliance Deepens: East Germany, the Arab States, and the PLO, 1978–1982," in Herf, *Undeclared Wars with Israel,* 342–385.

42 Stellvertreter des Ministers, Genossen Generalmajor Neiber, "Vorlage zum Einsatz eine Vertreters der Vereinigen PLO-Sicherheit in der DDR," Berlin (April 1, 1980), BStU, Archiv der Zentralstelle, Ministerium für Staatssicherheit (MfS) Hauptverwaltung (HA) XXII, Nr. 17508, 67–69.

43 "Information über Aktivitäten von Vertretern der Palästinensischen Befreiungsbewegung in Verbindung mit internationalen Terroristen zur Einbeziehung der DDR bei der Vorbereitung von Gewalttakten in Ländern Westeuropas." [East] Berlin, (8 May 1979), Z 3021, BStU, Archiv der Zentralstelle, Ministerium für Staatssicherheit, MfS, 1–16.

44 Ibid., 1–2.

45 Ibid., 2 and 7.

46 "Information über Aktivitäten von Vertretern der Palästinensischen Befreiungsbewegung in Verbindung mit internationalen Terroristen zur Einbeziehung der DDR bei der Vorbereitung von Gewalttakten in Ländern Westeuropas." [East] Berlin (8 May 1979), Z 3021, Bundesbeauftragte für die Unterlagen des Staatssicherheitsdienstes der ehemaligen Deutschen Demokratischen Republik, BStU, Archiv der Zentralstelle, Ministerium für Staatssicherheit (MfS) Hauptverwaltung, 1–16.

47 Stellvertreter des Ministers, Genossen Generalmajor Neiber, "Vorlage zum Einsatz eine Vertreters der Vereinigen PLO-Sicherheit in der DDR," Berlin (1 April 1980), BStU, Archiv der Zentralstelle, Ministerium für Staatssicherheit (MfS) Hauptverwaltung (HA) XXII, Nr. 17508, 64–69.

48 "Vorlage zum Einsatz eine ständigen Mitarbeiters der Vereinigten PLO-Sicherheit in der DDR," [East] Berlin (29 February 1980), BStU, Archiv der Zentralstelle, Ministerium für Staatssicherheit (MfS) Hauptverwaltung (HA) XXII, Nr. 17508, 70–85.

49 Gerhard Neiber "Vorlage zum Einsatz eines Vertreters der Vereinigten PLO-Sicherheit in der DDR," [East] Berlin (1 April 1980), 64–74. Amin El-Hindi replaced Abu Ayad as Chief of the Palestinian Security Services. He was a member of the General Union of Palestinian Students (GUPS) in Frankfurt/Main in the late 1960s. See Isabel Kershner, "Amin al-Hindi, Former Palestinian Intelligence Chief, Dies at 70," *The New York Times* (18 August 2010); and Abdallah Frangi, *Der Gesandte: Mein Leben für Palästina: Hinter den Kulissen der Nahost-Politik* (Munich: Wilhelm Heyne Verlag, 2010).

50 "Bericht über das Gespräch mit dem Leiter der 'Vereinigten PLO-Sicherheit"—ABU AYAD—am 15.7.1980 zu terroristischen Kräften und ihren Aktivitäten," [East] Berlin (18 June 1980), BStU MfS ZA HA XXII, Nr. 17508, Teil 2, 304–323.

51 Ibid., 304.

52 Ibid., 305.

53 Ibid., 319.

54 On the connections between the Stasi and West German terrorists in the 1970s and 1980s see Martin Jander, "Differenzen im antimperialistischen Kampf: Zu den Verbindungen des Ministeriums für Staatssicherheit mit der RAF und dem bundesdeutschen Linksterrorismus," in Wolfgang Kraushaar, ed., *Die RAF und der linke Terrorismus,* (Hamburg: Hamburger Edition, 2006), 696–713; and Tobias Wunschik, "Die 'Bewegung 2. Juni' und ihre Protektion durch den Staatssicherheitsdienst der DDR," *Deutschland* Archiv 40 (2007), 1014–1025; and "Baader-Meinhof international?" *Aus Politik und Zeitgeschichte* 40–41 (2007),

23–29. On the connections of West German terrorists to Arab, including Palestinian terrorist organizations, see Wolfgang Kraushaar, *München 1970*; and Thomas Skelton Robinson, "Im Netz verheddert: Die Beziehungen des bundesdeutschen Linksterrorismus zur *Volksfront für die Befreiung Palästinas (1969–1980)*, in Kraushaar, ed. *Die RAF und der linke Terrorismus*, 905–931. On the Stasi in West Germany in general see Hubertus Knabe, *Die unterwenderte Rebublik: Stasi im Westen.* 2nd ed. (Munich: Ullstein Verlag, 2001).

55 "Lieferungen 1980 gesamt"), BStU, AZ, MfS, BCD (Abteilung Bewaffnung und Chemische Dienst) Nr. 2802, 73–75.

56 Ibid., 76.

57 "Lieferungen 1981-gesamt"), BStU, AZ, MfS, BCD Nr. 2802, 80. That same year it sent also sent weapons to Iran (1,718,817), Yemen (400,000), Mozambique (451,970) and Yemen (443,324).

58 Aufstellung über Abgabe 1982 DDR Erzeugnisse: Beleg-Nr. 18306 v. 23.4. 1982," [East] Berlin (21 October 1982), BStU, AZ, MfS, BCD Nr. 2802, 97.

59 "Aufstellung über Abgabe 1982 DDR Erzeugnisse: Beleg-Nr. 00211 v. 1.7.1982," [East] Berlin (21 October 1982), BStU, AZ, MfS, BCD Nr. 2802, 96 and 98.

60 "Aufstellung über Abgabe 1982 DDR Erzeugnisse: Beleg-Nr. 00212 v. 7.7.82," [East] Berlin (21 October 1982), BStU, AZ, MfS, BCD Nr. 2802, 98.

61 Heinz Hoffmann, Sekretariat des Ministers UA Militärpolitik, Bundesarchiv-Militärarchiv Freiburg, DVW 1/114478 VS-Akte. Hoffmann referred to weapons deliveries to Egypt, Syria and Yemen that began in 1965. On this see Storkmann's *Geheime Solidarität*, 183–243.

62 "Bericht über die Unterstützungsmaßnahmen für die SYRISCHE ARABISCHE REPUBLIK: Stand: 16.10.1973, 04,30 Uhr," BA-MA, VA-01/32899, Militärarchiv der Deutschen Demokratischen Republik: Nationale Volksarmee Ministerium für Nationale Verteidigung Stellv. des Chefs des Hauptstabes für operative Fragen Verw. Gefechtsbereictschaft u. op. Ausbildung, 30–35.

63 Generalleutnant Fritz Streletz, "VS-Nr.: A 360 179, Informationsbericht Nr. 15 zur Lage im Nahen Osten: Stand: 20.10.1973, 0500 Uhr," BA-MA, VA-01 32899, 65–75.

64 "Heinz Hoffmann to Generalleutnant Stechbarth," Berlin, 14.10.1973, BA-MA, VA-01/ 32899, 265.

65 "Informationsbericht Nr. 30 zur Lage im Nahen Osten: Stand: 04.11.1973, 05.00 Uhr," BA-MA, VA-01/ 32899, 218–224.

66 On East Germany and the Soviet bloc at the United Nations, see "Political Warfare at the United Nations During the Yom Kippur War of 1973," and "The United Nations 'Zionism is Racism' Resolution of November 10, 1975," in Herf, *Undeclared Wars with Israel*, 239–253, and 288–316.

67 Chaim Herzog, United Nations General Assembly (UNGA), 30th Session, 2400 Plenary Meeting, New York (November 10, 1975), UN Official Documents System (ODS), A/PV.2400, 773–776; cited in Herf, *Undeclared Wars with Israel*, 295–296.

68 Cited in Herf, *Undeclared Wars with Israel*, 298–299. Also see Daniel Patrick Moynihan, UNGA, 30th Session, 2400 Plenary Meeting (November 10, 1975), UN ODS A/PV.2400, 796.

69 Yosef Tekoah, "Question of Palestine," UNGA, 29th Session, 2267 Plenary Meeting (October 14, 1974), UN ODS A/PV.2267, 665–667; cited in Herf, *Undeclared Wars with Israel*, 277.

70 Peter Florin, "Agenda Item 108: The Question of Palestine," UNGA, 2268 (October 14, 1974), UN ODS, A/PV.2269, 671; cited in Herf, *Undeclared Wars with Israel*, 278.

71 On the PLO terrorist attacks on northern Israel from its bases in southern Lebanon, see Herf, *Undeclared Wars with Israel*, 386–414.

72 On these assertions, see Herf, *Undeclared Wars with Israel*, esp. 417 and 425–426.

73 See Herf, *Undeclared Wars with Israel*, ch. 12.

74 These extremely negative views of Israel also became important aspects of the West German and West European radical left. See Chapters 3, 10 and 13 in Herf, *Undeclared Wars with Israel*. Also see Andrei Markovits, "'The Twin Brothers': European Antisemitism and Anti-Americanism," in his *Uncouth Nation: Why Europe Dislikes America* (Princeton, NJ: Princeton University Press, 2007), 150–200. On the way Soviet era antisemitism and false charges of Nazism persists in Putin's Russia see Jeffrey Herf, "Putin's Continuities: From 'Israelis as Nazis' to "Denazifying Ukraine," *Times of Israel* (March 11, 2022): https://blogs.timesofisrael.com/putins-continuities-from-israelis-as-nazis-to-denazifying-ukraine/.

75 Photo in Herf, *Undeclared Wars with Israel*, 343.

76 "Antrag aller Fraktionen der Volkskammer der Deutschen Demokratischen Republik zu einer gemeinsamen Erklärung," Deutscher Bundestag, *Protokolle der Volkskammer der Deutschen Demokratischen Republik 10 Wahlperiode (5. April bis 2. Oktober 1990), Band I, Protokolle der 1. Sitzung bis 9. Sitzung, Nachdruck* (Bonn: Deutscher Bundestag; Leske and Budrich, 2000), 23–24. On the *Volkskammer* resolution see Jeffrey Herf, *Divided Memory: The Nazi Past in the Two Germanies* (Cambridge, MA: Harvard University Press, 1997), 364–365.

77 Ibid., 23. The second part of the statement expressed similar sentiments towards the peoples of the Soviet Union, the third about East German support for the suppression of the "Prague Spring" in 1968, and the fourth spoke of a "special responsibility" to the peoples of Eastern Europe in the course of German unification and affirmed that the German-Polish border lay on the line of the Oder-Neisse rivers, 23–24.

78 "Antrag von 23 Abgeordneten über die Distanzierung von der Resolution Nr. 3379 der UNO-Vollversammlung vom 10. November 1975 und ihren Aussagen über den Zionismus durch die Deutsche Demokratische Republik," Deutscher Bundestag, *Protokolle der Volkskammer der Deutschen Demokratischen Republik 10 Wahlperiode (5. April bis 2. Oktober 1990), Band 3, Protokolle der 26. Sitzung bis 38. Sitzung, Nachdruck* (Bonn: Deutscher Bundestag; Leske and Budrich, 2000), 1280–1283. The 23 signers were: Johannes Gerlach (SPD); Jörg Brochnow (CDU/DA); Sabine Bergmann-Pohl (CDU/DA); Harald Ringstorff (SPD); Hans GEisler (CDU/DA); Konrad Weiß (Bundnis 90/Grüne); Werner Schulz (Bundnis 90/Grüne); Wolfgang Ullmann (Bundnis 90/Grüne); Stefan Gottschall (DSU); Nikolai Tschalamoff (CDU/DA); Bertram Wieczorek (CDU/DA); Boje Schmuhl (CDU/DA); Uwe Grüning (CDU/DA); Hans-Dirk Bierling (CDU/DA); Joachim Steinmann (CDU/DA); Reinhard Höpper (SPD); Eberhard Brecht (SPD); Joachim Gauck (Bundnis 90/Grüne); Ibrahim Böhme (SPD); Rainer Ortleb (Liberale); Wolfgang Thierse (SPD); Helmut Krause (Liberale); and Lothar Klein (DSU), "Antrag der Abgeordneten, Volkskammer der DDR 10.

79 Ibid. "Wahlperiode, Drucksache Nr. 169," http://webarchiv.bundestag.de/volkskammer/dokumente/drucksachen/100169.pdf.

8

THE WEST GERMAN LEFT AND ISRAEL, 1967–1977

In the two decades after the Holocaust, sympathy for Israel was one defining feature of liberals and Social Democrats in the Federal Republic of Germany (West Germany). It was of a piece with support for war crimes trials, for journalism and scholarship about the crimes of the Nazi regime, and for financial restitution to the Jewish survivors. It was a dissent against a widespread, West German, and West European, inclination to look away from the crimes against the Jews to focus on economic reconstruction and the threat from the Soviet Union. In a society whose armies had fought to the very end in World War II, West German liberals believed that sympathy for Israel along with the tradition of "coming to terms with the Nazi past" were important dissents from a conservative mood of silence and avoidance in the first decades of the Cold War. The moral aspirations of the dissenters were modest but important: the Federal Republic should do no harm to the Jews and to the Jewish state. Despite their differences, this was one dictum upon which Konrad Adenauer, the conservative Christian Democratic Chancellor, Theodor Heuss, the liberal Federal President, and Kurt Schumacher, the leader of the Social Democratic Party agreed.[1]

In the 1950s and 1960s, empathy and support for Israel were also a component of leftist politics among students in West Germany. SDS, the *Sozialistische Deutscher Studentenbund* (Socialist German Student Association), favored West German diplomatic relations with Israel and support for restitution (*Wiedergutmachung*) payments to individual Jews and to the state of Israel.[2] In 1957, at the Free University in Berlin, the first "German-Israeli Study Group" was established. In 1962, it opened a campaign to support the establishment of diplomatic relations with Israel at a time when West German business leaders and parts of the German Foreign Office saw a

DOI: 10.4324/9781003449669-9

formal relation with Israel as coming at the cost of markets and oil access in the Arab states.[3] West German liberals and leftists were vocal in their criticisms of the Egyptian government's decision to employ West German missile engineers and scientists, many of whom had worked on the V2 missile programs for the Nazi regime, to build missiles to be aimed at Israel.[4] When Ludwig Erhard, Adenauer's Christian Democratic successor, decided to establish diplomatic relations with Israel in 1965, he did so with strong support from his left-of-center political opponents.[5] Up to the June days of 1967, the support for Israel was a defining element of the West German non-communist left. Sympathy for Israel seemed like the self-evident and logical response both to the crimes of the Nazi regime and to residues of antisemitism in postwar Germany and Europe.

Between June and September 1967, leaders of SDS and thus the West German new left rejected these fundamentals of the liberal tradition of "coming to terms with the Nazi past" (*Vergangenheitsbewältigung*), upended the meaning of anti-fascism, replaced empathy with hostility to Israel, and became partisans of the Arab states but even more so of the Palestinian armed organizations waging war against Israel.[6] The West German New Left was not unique in that regard as a similar radicalization took place in the global New Left movements in Europe, the United States, as well as in Asia, Africa, and Latin America. Under the impact of the war in Vietnam in particular, the juxtaposition of "US imperialism" versus "the third world" loomed far larger in the minds of the generation coming of age than did the lessons and memories of World War II and the Holocaust.[7] Yet though the West German left was part of this global change which tended to place Israel on the "wrong" side of the epic battle between imperialism and the third world, the fact that Nazism and the Holocaust were ineradicable parts of *very recent German* history meant that, in one way or another, they would also loom larger in the radical left in West Germany than in any other of the radical leftist movements in Western-style democracies. The prevalence in the West German left of theoretical abstractions about capitalism and imperialism ran into the stubborn realities of historical specificities about Nazi Germany and the Jews, and the consequences of the Holocaust including the establishment of the state of Israel.

A conjuncture of two simultaneous but causally unrelated episodes of international and local politics in June 1967—war in the Middle East and the shooting death of a student protester by police in West Berlin—precipitated and accelerated the shift of loyalties in the West German New Left. On June 2nd, a demonstration to protest the visit to West Berlin by the Shah of Iran turned into a violent confrontation between police and demonstrators in the course of which a West Berlin police officer, Karl-Heinz Kurras, shot and killed 26-year-old Benno Ohnesorg, a student at the Free University of Berlin. The shooting reinforced a belief in the New Left that the West German government was an authoritarian or even fascist regime. Research in the files of East Germany's Ministry of State Security (the Stasi) has subsequently revealed that Kurras had been an agent of Communist East Germany's Ministry of State Security, the Stasi, since 1955.[8] So far, no evidence has been found that indicates that Kurras was ordered to shoot one of the demonstrators in order to lend credence to East German and Soviet accusations about the "neo-fascist" nature of the West German government and to thereby radicalize the student left in the Federal Republic.[9] Such, however, was the result of Kurras action. Had Kurras' connection to the Stasi been known at the time, the political results would likely have been dramatically different for they would have focused attention on Communist efforts to subvert the West German government by depicting it as a neo-fascist regime. Indeed, one of the three major West German leftist terrorist organizations of the 1970s decided to call itself "the June 2nd Movement," named for the date when Kurras shot Ohnesorg.

In West Berlin and in West Germany, the newspapers of the conservative Axel Springer press, especially its tabloid *Bild-Zeitung*, took a leading role in denouncing the New Left. Yet the same papers also were leading voices in support of Israel in West German journalism. The association of the Jewish state with this tribune of West German tabloid conservatism became embedded into the outlook of the 1960s radical left, all the more deeply because of another accident of timing. Ohnesorg was shot just three days before the Six Day War began. Reimut Reiche, the president of West German SDS, wrote on June 9, 1967 that

> we [in SDS] cannot give emphatic support to the state of Israel when the whole [West German] press celebrates this conduct of war with the same concept, 'Blitzkrieg,' with the which Nazis conquered Poland in three days and massacred its Jewish and non-Jewish population.[10]

For the young left, the simultaneity of the Six Day War and the Ohnesorg shooting linked support for Israel with their West German conservative antagonists.

From September 4–9, 1967, 70 SDS delegates from 48 West German universities meeting on the campus of Johan Wolfgang Goethe University in Frankfurt/Main passed a resolution that codified SDS' turn against Israel.[11] The assembled elected a new National Council and a new president, Karl Dietrich Wolff.[12] The other members of the National Council in power as the organization consolidated its anti-Israeli position were leading and prominent members of SDS, including Hans-Jürgen Krahl, a Marxist theorist and student of Theodor Adorno, and Bernd Rabehl from West Berlin.[13] Rudi Dutschke, the West German New Left's most famous and charismatic figure, also participated, though in unpublished notes at the time he wrote that the founding of the state of Israel was "the political emancipation of Jewry. It must absolutely be preserved."[14] Dutschke's view became a minority one in SDS after 1967.

Varieties of Marxism, Marxism-Leninism, and enthusiasm for revolutions in the global south, not discussions of the Nazi past or the Holocaust, dominated the political atmosphere of the SDS conference.[15] Yet the Nazi past, the geographical proximity of the Middle East, the West German government's "special relationship" and diplomatic relations with Israel, and their own contacts and discussions with Arab students in West German universities made everything connected with Israel a far more pressing for the West German New Left than it was for similar movements elsewhere. The SDS statement of fall 1967 was an early and influential statement of leftist anti-Zionism. It stated that the Six Day War could "only be analyzed against the background of the anti-imperialist struggle of the Arab peoples against their oppression by Anglo-American imperialism." The resolution called for the "rehabilitation of hundreds of thousands of Arab refugees back to their motherland." The authors of the resolution were confident that doing so would "not mean the new expulsion of the Israeli masses living there, but it would mean the end of the Zionist immigration law, that is, it means repatriation and material restitution of the Palestinians." That in turn required the socialist transformation of both the Arab states "and in Palestine and thus the formation of a socialist unity front in the Middle East."[16]

The SDS September resolution criticized Israel for a "policy of expulsion and oppression of Palestinian Arabs." Therefore,

> the recognition of the right of existence of the Jews living in Palestine by the revolutionary movement in the Arab countries must not be identical with the recognition of Israel as a bridge of imperialism and as a Zionist state form.[17]

SDS reassured Jews that they had a right to exist "in Palestine" but not to have a state of their own, i.e., Israel. The problem would be resolved by a "revolutionary socialist movement" that "overcomes imperialism" and creates unity between socialists in the Arab countries and "socialist Israel." The delegates rejected an alternative resolution that called on the "anti-imperialist forces in the Arab world to respect Israel's prewar borders."[18]

The Palestine Liberation Organization and its student organization on West German university campuses, the General Union of Palestinian Students (GUPS), found supporters in the West German New Left. In the summer of 1968, the PLO issued a National Charter.[19] Its call to destroy the state of Israel by force of arms expressed the radicalism of the global left of that iconic year. It denied moral legitimacy to the state of Israel. It designated a geographical area called Palestine, which included all of what was then

Israel, as "the homeland of the Arab Palestinian people." The "Palestinian people" had a "legal right" to this territory. Article 6 stated that the Jews who had resided in Palestine "until the beginning of the Zionist invasion will be considered Palestinians." The date of the beginning of that "invasion" was a source of uncertainty. If, as was often the case, the "invasion" was said to have begun in 1917 with the signing of the Balfour Declaration, then only 60,000 of the approximately 2.5 million Jews living in Israel in 1968, would be considered Palestinian. If the "invasion" was dated from 1947, then about 700,000 Jews would be so defined and could thus remain in the Palestinian state to be created. The rest would not be considered "Palestinians" in a new state and thus presumably would be expelled. Article 8 asserted that in the "national struggle for the liberation of Palestine," those "in the national homeland or in diaspora," that is in the Middle East and in Europe, constituted "one national front working for the retrieval of Palestine and its liberation through armed struggle." Article 9 stated that "armed struggle is the only way to liberate Palestine. This is the overall strategy, not merely a tactical phase. According to Article 10, "commando action constitutes the nucleus of the Palestinian popular liberation war."

Article 20 denied that there was any historical connection between the Jewish people and Palestine or that there even was such a thing as the Jewish people. Hence,

> the Balfour Declaration, the Mandate for Palestine, and everything that has been based upon them, are deemed null and void. Claims of historical or religious ties of Jews with Palestine are incompatible with the facts of history and the true conception of what constitutes statehood. Judaism, being a religion, is not an independent nationality. Nor do Jews constitute a single nation with an identity of its own; they are citizens of the states to which they belong.[20]

This denial of the elementary aspects of Jewish history and of the connection of the Jews to the land of Israel, both ancient and modern, became an enduring element of anti-Zionist propaganda in the ensuing decades.

Article 22 was the opening salvo in a propaganda campaign that reached fruition seven years later in November 1975 when the United Nations General Assembly declared Zionism to be a form of racism.

It read as follows:

> Zionism is a political movement organically associated with international imperialism and antagonistic to all action for liberation and to progressive movements in the world. It is racist and fanatic in its nature, aggressive, expansionist, and colonial in its aims, and fascist in its methods. Israel is the instrument of the Zionist movement, and geographical base

for world imperialism placed strategically in the midst of the Arab homeland to combat the hopes of the Arab nation for liberation, unity, and
progress. Israel is a constant source of threat vis-a-vis peace in the Middle
East and the whole world. Since the liberation of Palestine will destroy the
Zionist and imperialist presence and will contribute to the establishment
of peace in the Middle East, the Palestinian presence and will contribute
to the establishment of peace in the Middle East, the Palestinian people
look for the support of all the progressive and peaceful forces and urge
them all, respective of their affiliations and beliefs, to offer the Palestinian
people all aid and support in their just struggle for the liberation of their
homeland.[21]

For the West German New Left to voice "solidarity" with the PLO in those
years, was to lend support for these very public, very clear positions which
amounted to a declaration of a war the purpose of which was the destruction
of the state of Israel by force of arms. Though the Charter appealed to "all
progressive and peaceful forces" around the world, it struck a nerve in the
West German radical left because, as we will see, the rhetoric of anti-fascism
and anti-imperialism offered another kind of apparent liberation, that is, liberation from the burdens of German history after the Holocaust.

The subsequent political impact of the PLO Charter of 1968 in the half
century after it was written was remarkable. In 1975, its arguments were
crucial for convincing a majority in the United Nations General Assembly
that Zionism was a form of racism. Remarkably, it did so while offering a
justification for the expulsion, by armed force, if necessary, of the vast majority of the approximately 2.3 million Jews then living in Israel. Depending
on how one read the PLO Charter, Jews who arrived in Palestine either after
1917 or 1947 did not qualify to be Palestinian citizens. Hence, they would
have no right to remain in a state of "Palestine." It follows logically that a
PLO victory would have then led to the expulsion of at least 2.3 million and
at most 2.9 million of the Jews living in Israel in 1968. As this would have
been the consequence of a military defeat, the number of dead and wounded
would have been considerable as well. For those able or willing to think
through these implications of the PLO Charter, it was clear that it envisaged a
Palestinian chapter of the expulsion of the Jews from most of the Arab world
that had taken place following the establishment of Israel in 1948. To express
solidarity with the PLO and its Charter was to express agreement with these
views, policies, and their clearly foreseeable consequences. The PLO Charter
served as a justification for terrorist attacks against the citizens of the state of
Israel. It was the preeminent twentieth-century political document of a form
of leftist antisemitism that insisted it was nothing of the sort and of a racism
and bigotry which projected its hatreds and intolerance onto "the Zionists,"
that is, the citizens and government of Israel. Indeed, it became one of the

most influential political statements of the radical left in the many decades since it was first issued.

Radicalization of the West German New Left, 1968–1969

The destruction of German Jewry during the Holocaust meant that the Jewish community in West Germany after the war was very small. In 1970, according to figures of the Central Council of Jews in West Germany, there were about 26, 799 Jews living in the Federal Republic; in 1980, the number had risen to 28,173. Judging from those figures, the number of Jewish students in West German universities from the 1960s and 1970s would have been modest and probably less of a presence than the approximately 16,000 students from Arab countries, of whom 3,000 were Palestinians.[22] The shift of the New Left's sympathies from Israel to the PLO and its affiliates was in part the result of interaction with Arab, including Palestinian, students at West German universities as well as workers from the Middle East in the West German economy, and the very small number of Jewish fellow students.[23] In these years, the "GUPS" fostered political mobilization among Palestinian students in the West Germany.[24] The GUPS was an arm of Al Fatah and the Arab League with headquarters in Cairo.[25] Its purpose was to open a political front in West Germany in the PLO's war against Israel. For the PLO, the West German front became the most important in Western Europe.

Jewish students in the West German universities had formed the National Association of Jewish Students in Germany (*Bundesverbandes Jüdischer Studenten in Deutschland*). In the spring of 1968, they invited Asher Ben-Natan, the Israeli ambassador to West Germany, to speak about the Middle East conflict at West German universities. Over the course of the next year, he spoke at nineteen campuses to large audiences, mostly without incident. On June 9, 1969, at the Johann Wolfgang Goethe University of Frankfurt, members of SDS, together with supporters of Al Fatah in the GUPS and an anti-Zionist "Israel Revolutionary Action Committee Abroad" (ISRACA), interrupted Ben Natan's lecture with chants such as "[West German Chancellor] Nazi Kiesinger and Ben Natan, a clique with [Moshe] Dayan" and "Zionists out of Palestine." Natan left the session after two hours because he could not be heard over the tumult. He called the leftist anti-Zionism at the event a "hidden antisemitism."[26]

Ten days later, Theodor Adorno, along with Max Horkheimer, the leading figure of the left-liberal Frankfurt Institute for Social Research, co-author of the classic *Dialectic of Enlightenment*, of other studies on the nature of anti-semitism, and mentor to prominent figures in the New Left, wrote to his old friend and fellow Frankfurt School luminary Herbert Marcuse, who at this point was teaching in the United States and had become an intellectual hero of the young left. Adorno reported that left-wing students had interrupted his lectures twice in the summer (March to July) semester and that he had to call the police to evict students occupying the Institute of Social Research. He wrote that

> the danger that the students will turn toward fascism is one I take more seriously than you do. After people here in Frankfurt screamed at the Israeli Ambassador, I'm no longer convinced of the assurance that this has nothing to do with antisemitism....You must once look into the manic, cold eyes of those who, even when appealing to us [Frankfurt School theorists], turn their rage against us.[27]

On August 6, 1969, at the age of 66, Adorno died of a heart attack. As the coming years in Frankfurt/Main indicated his warnings about "their rage against us" proved prescient.[28]

That summer about fifty members of West German SDS accepted invitations from Al Fatah and the Democratic Front for the Liberation of Palestine to spend time during July and August at an "Al Fatah Summer Camp" in Jordan.[29] In a public letter said to be written from Amman, Jordan on August 15, 1969, the West German SDS travelers wrote that the people they met,

> whether political militants of Al-Fatah or other organizations...are all aware of the difference between Zionists and Jews and make it clear that their fight is against Zionism and imperialism and not against the Jews. Indeed, the point was made to us more than once that the Palestinian revolution seeks to 'liberate the Jews from Zionism.'[30]

The travelers expressed support for "the Palestinian revolutionary struggle," which was fighting against "the same enemy" as were the members of West German SDS. They adopted the PLO's view of events past and present:

> In the specific case of Palestine, a whole people were thrown out of their homeland by Zionism supported by British and American imperialism. More and more people are beginning to realize that the so-called state of Israel, created by Zionism and imperialism, is racialist and imperialist. It is a colonial state and is fiercely opposed to the liberation struggle of the Palestinian and Arab people. The Palestinians are therefore right to fight for the creation of a democratic state in Palestine, and to pursue the method of armed struggle and peoples' war to achieve this end. All members of the camp unconditionally support the Palestinian revolutionary struggle....Our experiences in the past month [in Jordan, JH] have strengthened our solidarity and support for the Palestinian cause. We return to our countries knowing more than ever that we are fighting the same enemy.[31]

The SDS travelers adopted the PLO's view that Israel was an example of racism and imperialism and that "the Palestinians" were right to adopt "armed struggle" to achieve "a democratic state in Palestine." SDS and the PLO, in fighting the West German government, and the state of Israel, were fighting "the same," that is reactionary imperialist "enemy." In the coming years, this presumed common struggle evolved into a consequential alliance between West German leftist terrorists and Palestinian terrorist organizations.

SDS dissolved in 1970 but its hostility to Israel and enthusiasm for the Palestinian armed organizations persisted in a plethora of Marxist-Leninist sectarian organizations, so-called "K-Gruppen" (Communist groups). They included local "Palestine Solidarity Committees"; the three major West German leftist terrorist groups, the Red Army Faction (RAF), Revolutionary Cells (*Revolutionäre Zelle*, henceforth RCs), and the June 2nd Movement, as well as in the GUPS and related leftist political organizations of Arab and Iranian students in West Germany. All described Israel as a racist and imperialist state. Due to their political activism, those organizations created a significant presence in West German universities. Though small in numbers, they loomed large in discussions of Israel and the Middle East in what the German historian Gerd Koenen termed West Germany's "the red decade" from 1967 to 1977.[32]

Though not imbued with the spirit of the New Left, the East German-oriented, orthodox Marxist-Leninist *Deutsche Kommunistische Partei* [German Communist Party], with 36,000 members in 1972, became the single largest of the organizations of the radical left.[33] The persistence and, in many cases, the reemergence of Marxist-Leninist orthodoxy in so-called "*K-Gruppen*," that is, Communist groups, was one of the most striking features of West German leftist politics after the 1960s. This network of organizations, along with their many local versions, mobilized scores of activists who wrote and distributed leaflets and brochures and attended demonstrations and rallies.[34] The annual reports of the West German Office for Protection of the Constitution (*Verfassungsschutz*) for 1970, 1971, and 1972 reported 117, 79, and 62 terrorist attacks by leftist groups including two murders, 33 explosions and 27. In 1972, there were as well seven death threats and 1,556 threats of bombing and arson.[35] Jewish organizations in West Germany and in Europe observed these developments in the universities with increasing concern.[36]

On November 9, 1969, the thirtieth anniversary of the Nazi pogrom of November 1939, a bomb was placed at the Jewish Community Center in Berlin. It failed to explode.[37] Four days later, unnamed members of a radical leftist group that called itself the "Black Rats, Tupamaros West Berlin" (*Schwarze Ratten TW*), claimed responsibility for placing the bomb in a statement entitled "Shalom and Napalm." The authors published their statement in *Agit 883*, a magazine of the West Berlin leftist scene.[38] They supported the "armed struggle" of the Palestinians who were striking "the Zionists in their own country," that is, in Israel. At the same time, they called on German "anti-imperialists" to play an active role in the battle against supporters of Israel in West Germany.[39] That is, the authors of "Shalom and Napalm" supported attacks on Jews in West Germany, especially those who publicly supported Israel. At the time, *Agit 883* had a circulation of about 20,000.[40]

The "Shalom and Napalm" authors also attacked the West German tradition of *Aufarbeitung der Vergangenheit*. They denounced West German restitution payments (*Wiedergutmachung*) and development aid as a contribution to the Zionist defense budget. "Under the guilt-laden pretext of coming to terms with the fascist atrocities against the Jews, they [West German government and industry] make a decisive contribution to Israel's fascist atrocities against Palestinian Arabs." Using an evasive passive voice, the leaflet's authors both coyly accepted responsibility for placing the bomb and declared war on the government of West Germany.

In West Berlin, on the 31st anniversary of the fascist Kristallnacht "Shalom and napalm" and "Al-Fatah" were painted on several Jewish memorials. A bomb was placed in the Jewish Community Center. No longer are both actions to be defamed as an outgrowth of right-wing radicals. Rather, these actions are a decisive link of international socialist solidarity. The previous silence and theoretical paralysis of the left regarding the conflict in the Middle East is a result of the German guilty conscience *(Schuldbewußtsein)*. "We gassed the Jews and must protect the Jews from a new genocide." The neurotic-historicist examination of the historical lack of legitimacy of an Israeli state does not overcome this helpless anti-fascism. True anti-fascism is the clear and simple expression of solidarity with the fighting fedayeen. No longer will our solidarity remain only with verbal-abstract methods of enlightenment as [with opposition to the American war] in Vietnam. Rather, in concrete actions, we will mercilessly fight against the close intertwining of Zionist Israel with the fascist Federal Republic of Germany. Every hour of memory in West Berlin and in the FRG suppresses the fact that *Kristallnacht* of 1938 is today repeated every day by the Zionists in the occupied territories, in the refugee camps and in Israeli prisons. The Jews who were expelled by fascism have themselves become fascists who, in collaboration with American capital, want to eradicate the Palestinian people. By striking the direct support for Israel by German industry and the government of the Federal Republic, we are aiding the victory of the Palestinian revolution and serve to bring about the renewed defeat of world imperialism. At the same time, we expand our battle against the fascists in democratic clothes and begin to build a revolutionary liberation front in the metropole. BRING THE BATTLE FROM THE VILLAGES INTO THE CITIES! ALL POLITICAL POWER

COMES FROM THE BARREL OF A GUN. Black Rats, *TW Schwarze Ratten, TW[Tupamoros West Berlin]*[41]

In contrast to their "guilt-ridden" contemporaries, whose political judgment was supposedly clouded by emotion and sentimentality, the West Berlin Tupamaros presented themselves as the voice of reason and political clarity. Presumably, having overcome unjustified guilt complexes, they could attack the "fascist" Israelis with a clear conscience. The Zionists, along with an allegedly neurotic tradition of West German memory of the Holocaust, had victimized the West Germans with unjustified accusations and bad memories. The "Shalom and Napalm" statement, and the attack on the West Berlin Jewish Community Center stood for an attempted psychological liberation from those burdens. As the Federal Republic was complicit in supporting an evil state, Israel, it was time to aim guns at "the fascists in democratic clothes" in the Federal Republic.

Several days later, the West Berlin Tupamaros sent a taped confession and justification for the attempted bombing of the Jewish Community Center. A woman's voice declared that

> [Axel] Springer, the West Berlin Senate and [Heinz] Galinski [the leader of the organized West Berlin Jewish Community and Chairman of the Central Council of Jews in Germany] want to sell us their *Judenknacks* [Jewish complex] We won't join that business… learn from the Tupamaros, Che lives! Vietnam is not here. Vietnam is in America. But listen: Palestine is here, we are fedayeen. This afternoon we fight for the revolutionary Palestinian liberation front, Al-Fatah. Strike now.[42]

On November 27, 1969, Dieter Kunzelmann, the leader of the West Berlin Tupamaros and a key figure in the West German left's turn towards support for Palestinian guerrilla organizations, published a "Letter from Amman" in *Agit 883*. In fact, at the time, he was in West Berlin.[43]

> For the FRG and Europe, Palestine is what Vietnam is for the Amis [slang for Americans] The left has not yet understood that. Why? [Because of] the Jewish complex (*Judenknax*). "We gassed six million Jews. The Jews today are called Israelis. Whoever fights fascism is for Israel." It's as simple as that but that's all wrong. When we finally learn to understand the fascist ideology of Zionism, we will no longer hesitate to replace our simple philosemitism with an unambiguous and clear solidarity with AL FATAH. In the Middle East, it has taken up the battle against the Third Reich. What is the meaning of solidarity? It means taking up our battle.[44]

Kunzelmann regretted that a local Palestine committee had failed to "use the opportunity of the bomb [placed at the Jewish Community Center] to start a campaign."[45] With these statements and actions in the fall of 1969, Kunzelmann and the West Berlin Tupamaros redefined the meaning of West German leftist anti-fascism to mean both verbal antagonism to Israel as well as support for terrorist attacks against Israelis and against their Jewish and non-Jewish supporters in West Germany. In so doing, they echoed the transformed meaning of anti-fascism that emerged in the anti-cosmopolitan purges in the Soviet bloc, including in East Germany almost two decades earlier.

In February 1970, Palestinian terrorists carried out a wave of terrorist attacks against civil aviation to and from West Germany and Israel and against Jews in West Germany. On February 10, the "Action Organization for the Liberation of Palestine" used hand grenades and automatic weapons to attack passengers waiting for an El Al flight in Munich's Reim airport. On February 13, 1970, someone poured gasoline on the stairs of a Jewish home for the aged located in a Jewish community center in Munich and set it on fire. Seven residents died, six in the flames and smoke of the fire, and one from injuries suffered after jumping from an upper story window to escape the flames. Six more suffered serious injuries. It was the worst attack on Jews in Germany since 1945. No one claimed responsibility and the case remains unsolved, though circumstantial evidence pointed to the involvement of West German leftist and/or Palestinian terrorists. On February 21, a bomb on an Austrian Airlines flight departing from Frankfurt/Main exploded in mid-air but the damaged plane was able to return safely to the airport shortly after take-off. Later that day, another bomb was placed on Swiss Air Flight 330, departing from Zurich for Tel Aviv. It exploded in mid-air, causing the plane to crash. All 38 passengers and nine crew members were killed.[46] A representative of the Popular Front for the Liberation of Palestine-General Command (PFLP-GC) led by Ahmed Jibril claimed responsibility. George Habash, leader of the PFLP announced his support for such actions while Yasser Arafat denounced them.[47] At that time, Arafat was the head of the PLO's "Unified Command" of its Executive Committee, one that included many Palestinian guerilla organizations including the PFLP and PFLP-GC. The proliferation of such groups conveyed the impression that they acted independently of Arafat, thus giving the most public face of the PLO a fig leaf of plausible deniability.

On April 3, 1970, Kunzelmann sent another statement "from Amman" that implicitly addressed the attacks on El Al and other airlines flying to Israel as well as on the Jewish home for the aged in Munich. He expressed impatience with his leftist "comrades on the home front."

When are you finally going to begin the battle against the holy cow, Israel? When will we relieve the fighting Palestinian people with practical internationalism? The grenades at the [Munich, JH] Riem airport permit only this criticism: to replace the desperate death commandos with better organized, more clearly focused commandos that we, ourselves will carry out and therefore can be better organized and arranged…We have never had such an opportunity to advance the revolution in our own country by direct support of a peoples' liberation war [in Palestine.][48]

He was urging his fellow West German leftists to engage in similar attacks in West Germany which could be "better organized and arranged." Collaboration with the Palestinian armed organizations and overcoming "the Jewish complex" was, he argued, crucial for making a communist revolution in West Germany. The sentiments of Kunzelmann's statements in 1969 and 1970 were repeated in the coming years radical leftist terror and antisemitism in the West Germany.

By 1969, the gap between the Jewish leadership in West Germany and the West German radical left had become an abyss. While aware of the shortcomings of judicial reckoning in West Germany, leaders of the organized Jewish community did not think that the Federal Republic was an authoritarian or "fascist" state. On the contrary, they saw the West German national, regional, and local judicial and police authorities, and the stability of the country's liberal democratic institutions as indispensable for the protection of the very small Jewish community and its synagogues, schools, and community institutions. They welcomed West German policies of restitution agreements for Jewish survivors and the opening of diplomatic relations with Israel in 1965.

On the occasion of Rosh Hashonah in 1970, Heinz Galinski, leader of the Jewish community in West Berlin, expressed concern about anti-Zionism that came "from circles that regard themselves as progressive," that is, from the student left. "Whether or not those who spread and advocate this anti-Zionism understand it or intend to do so, it has the function of awakening anti-Semitic prejudices."[49] The issue was not only about antisemitic words, but terrorism aimed at Israelis. In January 1973, the Jewish Press Service published a list of forty-four acts of Arab terrorism aimed at Israelis in Israel as well as at Jewish institutions in Europe that had been perpetrated since 1968. They included airplane hijackings, attempts to murder Israeli diplomats, bomb attacks on Israeli embassies, the deaths of 47 passengers and crew on a Swiss Air Flight blown up in mid-air on February 21, 1970, the Lod Airport massacre of May 30, 1972, during which three members of the Japanese Red Army machine guns and hand grenades to murder 24, wound 80 people in the airport luggage area, and, most famously, the Black September attack on the Munich Olympics in September 1972 which resulted in the deaths of eleven members of the Israeli Olympic team. Less well known in these years were letters bombs send to Israeli Embassies and to Jewish institutions including synagogues, Zionist youth groups, and a home for the aged. Officials in the Offices for the Protection of the Constitution had been warning of letter bombs sent to Israeli and Jewish addresses since 1967.[50]

The Central Council of the Jews in Germany kept close track of threats to Jewish schools and community centers and sent instructions to them about how to recognize letter bombs and the efforts of West German police and intelligence authorities to convey warnings. On October 12, 1972, Hendrik Van Dam, secretary general of the Central Council, wrote to the leaders of larger Jewish communities that they should "take special care to ensure security measures to protect Jewish children. With cooperation from the police, all kindergartens, daycare centers, schools and school buses should be secured." These added security measures to protect Jewish children were necessary in view of a recent attack on a Jewish school in Belgium and in the face of "repeated threats of an Arab terrorist organization to use all means, including hostage taking to force the release of the terrorist who were involved in the crime in Munich." He requested that directors of various Jewish organizations inform him about their security measures.[51]

On September 22, 1972, Heinz Galinski on the front page of the Central Council's newspaper, the *Jüdische Allgemeine* responded to the attack on Israeli athletes at the Munich Olympics attacks and drew attention to what he saw as a developing alliance between "Arab extremists" and West German leftists.[52] He referred to the

> dangerous circumstances…in the activity of Arab extremists that have developed in the first place in the colleges and universities. They have distributed anti-Jewish, German language malicious propaganda literature, organized demonstrations, meetings, and actions together with radical leftist elements. We [the Central Council] have drawn attention to the fact that when such things happen in Germany, they objectively amount to fostering neo-Nazi antisemitism.[53]

In these same weeks, Ulrike Meinhof, while awaiting trial due to her activities with the RAF terrorist organization, responded to the attack on the Olympics by writing "The Action of Black September in Munich, On the Strategy of Anti-Imperialist Struggle."[54] She wrote that "the action of Black September in Munich…was simultaneously anti-imperialist, anti-fascist and internationalist."[55] The Munich "action" was one against "Israel's Nazi fascism."[56] "Just as the essence of imperialism is fascist, so anti-fascism is in its tendency anti-imperialist." Thus, the attack on the Israeli athletes was anti-imperialist and hence anti-fascist. The Palestinians were the victims of "Israel's policy of extermination."[57] The goal of the West German government was "not to be in any way inferior to the Moshe Dayan fascism–Dayan this Himmler of Israel."[58] Following the death of its athletes, "Israel cries crocodile tears. It used its athletes as the Nazis used the Jews–as fuel to be burned for its imperialist policy of extermination."[59]

In her view, the Black September perpetrators were without blame for the deaths of the athletes. "They took hostages from a people that has pursued a policy of extermination against them…They did not want to kill." She falsely claimed that "the German police massacred the revolutionaries and their hostages."[60] The statement ended as follows: "The action of Black September in Munich will not be extinguished from the memory of anti-imperialist struggle. Solidarity with the liberation struggle of the Palestinian people! Solidarity with the revolution in Vietnam! Revolutionaries of all lands, unite!"[61] Meinhof's essay, like Kunzelmann's *Shalom und Napalm*, were early West German examples of what the historian Robert Wistrich called "Holocaust inversion," that is, the description of Israel's policies toward the Palestinians as comparable to that of Nazi Germany's toward the Jews of Europe.[62] Meinhof joined Kunzelmann as another prominent member of the radical left to move from rhetorical solidarity with the Arabs and Palestinians to public support for terrorist violence aimed at Israelis who they now described as Nazis and fascists.

The alliance between the West German leftist terrorist organizations and the Palestinian counterparts, especially the PFLP, found its clearest expression in their joint effort in June-July 1976 to hijack an Air France plane to Entebbe, Uganda, and there to hold Israeli and Jewish passengers' hostage at gunpoint.[63] The two West German participants, Wilfried Böse and Brigitte Kuhlmann, had adopted the ideas about Israel, Zionism, and the Palestinian armed organizations that had emerged in the West German left since 1967. By 1976, Holocaust inversion and the redefinition of Zionism as a form of racism and fascism had become common themes in their circles and for the West German far left.

In 1970, Böse co-founded *Roter Stern Verlag* [Red Star Press], a leftist publisher in Frankfurt/Main. He and Kuhlmann lived and worked amid Frankfurt/Main's leftist intellectual and political milieu. He was also a co-founder of the RCs organization that claimed responsibility for 67 fire-bombings and explosions in West Germany that took place from 1973 to 1980.[64] The PFLP, responsible at the time for attacks on Israeli civilians of northern Israel, aided the RC and the RAF by offering escape routes, training, weapons, and even money to the West German leftist terrorist groups. To cooperate with the PFLP in those years was to collaborate with an organization that unified word and deed in an effort to destroy Israel by force of arms and engaged in armed attacks on Israeli civilians.

In the hijacking to Entebbe in 1976, the RCs and the PFLP also collaborated with Uganda's dictator Idi Amin. As they did so in the name of anti-fascism, and anti-racism, it is important to recall Amin's very public views about Hitler and Nazism. After the Black September attack on the Munich Olympics, Amin wrote to United Nations Secretary-General Kurt Waldheim with copies to Golda Meir and Yasser Arafat.[65] He denounced Israel for having "occupied Palestine for twenty-five years." He urged that Israel be expelled from the United Nations. He wrote that

> Germany is the right place where when Hitler was the prime minister and supreme commander, he burnt over six million Jews. This is because

Hitler and all German people knew that the Israelis are not people who are working in the interest of the people of the world and that is why they burnt the Israelis alive with gas in the soil of Germany.[66]

He added that the Palestinians should be offered assistance "to remove all the Israelis from the Middle East and take them to Britain which was responsible for taking them to Palestine."[67] As of September 13, 1972, Amin's antisemitism, justification of the Holocaust, praise for Hitler, for the terrorists who killed the Israeli athletes in Munich, and support for removing "all Israelis" from "Palestine" was public knowledge around the world. This was the man with whom the PFLP and thus the PLO and Arafat, as well as *RC* members Böse and Kuhlmann claimed to be fighting fascism.

On June 27, 1976, members of the West German RCs together with the PFLP comrades hijacked an Air France plane with 248 passengers on board and forced the pilots at gunpoint to land the plane at the airport in Entebbe, Uganda. Amin greeted them warmly at the airport. The hijackers separated the Israelis and Jews from the larger group of hostages. In the next two days, they released 148 non-Israeli and non-Jewish passengers, keeping more than one hundred Israelis and the non-Jewish pilot, as hostages. The RC and PFLP issued demands for the release of terrorists held in prisons in France, Israel, France, Kenya, and West Germany and threatened to kill the hostages unless their demands were not met. Israel ended the episode by carrying out a military raid that freed all the hostages held at the airport and killed all of the hijackers. Böse and Kuhlmann, who were both killed in the gunfight with the Israelis, became the first Germans since the Holocaust to point machine guns at unarmed Jews and, as far as we know, the first Germans to exchange fire with Israeli armed forces. Their participation in the Entebbe attack remains one of the most important and widely publicized examples of the cooperation between the West German terrorist organizations and the PFLP.[68] In the hijacking to Entebbe, the German participants demonstrated the consequences of the redefinition on the West German far left of the meaning of anti-fascism and support for the PLO's efforts to destroy the Jewish state. The reality of West Germans pointing assault weapons at Jews etched another chapter in the history of German antisemitism.

As the discussion about the Entebbe hijacking at the United Nations took place only in the Security Council, East German diplomats at the UN did not have an opportunity to comment on the official record about those events. Coverage of the events in the East German press remained low-key.[69] On July 5, *Neues Deutschland* reported on "Israel's Bloody Attack on Airport in Uganda."[70] A July 10, *ND* article, "Israel's Zionist Policy Again Shows its Racist Essence: TASS Commentary on the Act of Aggression Against the Republic of Uganda," asserted that Israel's raid demonstrated that it viewed Africans as "second-class" countries, a view that stemmed from Israel's "ever closer alliances with South Africa and Rhodesia." *Neues Deutschland* reported nothing about the cooperation of the Ugandan government with the hijackers, the separation of Jewish and non-Jewish passengers, Idi Amin's praise for Hitler, the Holocaust and the Munich massacre, or the disappearance and probable murder of one of the elderly Jewish hostages, Dora Bloch. East Germany's State Security Service, the Stasi, commissioned an eighteen-page report that denounced "Israel's aggression against the African Republic of Uganda." The Stasi report called Israel "a serious danger to world peace" and a blow to "the moral norms of cooperation and relations between states." [71]

The RCs then attacked Israeli-identified institutions in West Germany.[72] In a 1978 communique, it offered a justification for these attacks which obliterated the distinction between Zionists, Israelis, and Jews. "Zionist" and "Israeli" institutions in West Germany that supported and gathered funds to send to Israel were supporting its "campaign of expulsion and extermination" against the Palestinians.

> These institutions have made a principle of placing Jewish cultural and social establishments (homes for the aged, day care centers, etc.) in their immediate vicinity or even in a normal home filled with families. They do this so that if there are attacks on their offices, as many people will be affected and injured so that the affected Jewish institutions can use an age-old and proven Zionist strategy of denouncing such attacks as "anti-Semitic incidents." This form of barricading, the systematic misuse of uninvolved people as a living protective shield who do not know who has placed them in the middle, is one of Zionism's most despicable and inhuman "specialties."[73]

The RC regarded the offices, schools, homes for the aged, and day care centers associated with the Jewish community in West Germany—that is, perfectly legal activities having nothing to do with military activities—to be legitimate military targets. Hence, presumably, the RC viewed "attacks of this sort," that is, on the offices of "Zionist" institutions, to be morally acceptable. It was "not enough to say" that Israel's policies "correspond to the Nazis' blood and soil policies."[74] As Israel's policies corresponded to those of the Nazis, then attacking Jewish institutions in West Germany was a form of fully justified anti-Nazism or anti-fascism that had nothing to do with anti-semitism. On the contrary, the RC communique asserted that

> the battle against Zionism is the decisive battle against any antisemitism. For just as this battle was one fought against fascist crimes, so it is fought against the crimes of the Israeli state against the Palestinians, who are themselves semites.[75]

In other words, for the RC, killing Jews in West Germany in 1978 was a way to fight against antisemitism. This was a logical outcome, in deeds, of the ideas that had percolated in the West German far left in the preceding decade.

In 1979, Hans Joachim Klein, a former member of the RC, published *Rückkehr in die Menschlichkeit: Appell eines ausgestigenen Terroristen* (Return to Humanity: The Appeal of a Terrorist Who has Abandoned Terrorism).[76] Western intelligence reports had long viewed the PFLP as the PLO's key instrument to open a "front" with West German and West European leftist terrorists. Klein's assertions confirmed those assessments. He stressed the importance of the PFLP for the survival and persistence of the leftist terrorist organizations in West Germany. He also revealed, and thereby thwarted, an RC plan to assassinate Heinz Galinski, as well as Ignatz Lipinski, then head of the Jewish community in Frankfurt/Main. Klein wrote that the plan to murder them "was and is fascist, even if the killers call themselves 'revolutionaries.'" Klein's RC comrades told him that though they had no "political interest" in killing Galinski and Lipinski, they had to show their Arab counterparts that they remained an effective force after Entebbe. They needed "countries where they could take hostages, weapons and above all," they "needed money." Murdering the two Jewish leaders would satisfy the demands of their PFLP contact and enhance their prospects for future assistance.[77]

Klein placed these planned "murders in the sequence of the disastrous history of German Nazi-fascism." He also revealed that members of the RC were contemplating murdering Simon Wiesenthal, director of an organization in Vienna that focused on bringing ex-Nazis to trial, at times assisting the Mossad. The *Jüdische Allgemeine* on May 13, 1977, wrote that "leading Jewish personalities" as well as other public figures were fully aware of

> the dangers that come with open opposition to murder and deadly attacks, to anarchist bands of murderers and their henchmen, to left-wing and right-wing extremists and their press organs which include attacks on Jews, Jewry, democracy and freedom in every issue.[78]

Conclusion

The terror in Entebbe may not have surprised those West German leftists who had participated in the anti-Zionist passion since 1967. In any case, expressions of regret or second thoughts remained private. Entebbe was not a turning point that ushered in a period of de-radicalization. That became apparent when the RAF conducted a wave of terrorist attacks in the "hot autumn" of 1977, 15 months after the hijacking to Entebbe. The ideas that emerged in the nine years from 1967 to 1977, ideas about Holocaust inversion, about the fascist and Nazi-like nature of Israel, about justifications for Palestinian terrorism aimed at Israelis, and about the fundamental illegitimacy and immorality of Zionism and the state of Israel dominated the radical left in West Germany. West German leftists such as Kunzelmann, Meinhof, and Böse imagined themselves to be breaking with the Nazi past, even as they repeated new forms of old stereotypes about Jews. In so doing, they replaced the nightmare of the murderous and evil Jew, so central to the antisemitic traditions of centuries past, with that of the aggressive, imperialist, and fascist Zionist and Israeli. "Jewish questions" had a greater centrality in West Germany than elsewhere but what first emerged with greatest clarity in that country found counterparts in the convergence of antisemitism and antagonism to Israel in many others in the following decades.

During these years, Jean Amery, essayist, novelist, survivor of Nazi concentration camps, and self-described advocate of liberalism and the democratic left, wrote extensively about the emergence of leftist "anti-Zionism as the new antisemitism" in West Germany.[79] After the Six Day War, Amery wrote that familiar cliches and stereotypes about the Jews were evident in "the pamphlets of Arab propaganda" circulating on West German university campuses. The antagonism to Israel had expanded beyond the Palestinian organizations to a much broader "intellectual left." It became respectable and chic. The "guilt feelings" had become "boring." The Jews were not "being burned" but after the Six Day War had become victors and then occupiers. "Napalm and so forth. Relief spread through the country." Amery thought that in West Germany the new antisemitism in the form of antagonism to Israel was inseparable from a psychological effort to be unburdened by the memory of the crimes of Nazism. Kunzelmann's urging to overcome the "guilt complex" had struck nerves well beyond the bohemian neighborhoods of West Berlin.

Amery was convinced that "antisemitism was present in anti-Israelism or anti-Zionism as thunder belonged to clouds." Referring to Israel as a "criminal state" had become part of the "ordinary speech." He was having none of it. There was, he wrote, "no honorable antisemitism," despite the efforts of those years to drape it in the language of the left.[80] In 1969, he asked how it was that West German New Leftists had become supporters of the "Arabic *Freikorps*, above all Al Fatah…How has it come about that Marxist dialectical thinking lends a hand to the preparation of a future genocide."[81] Why was the New Left in West Germany so indifferent and dismissive of the existential threats to the citizens of Israel? Despite their frequent assertions of antifascist credentials, Amery thought that the young left actually "understood nothing about Nazism." Of the Holocaust, it had "only indirect knowledge." To understand the need for the existence of Israel one had to have what the West German New Left lacked, namely "a comprehensive understanding of the Jewish catastrophe." The preoccupations of the New Left were those of the global left of the late 1960s, of imperialism and anti-imperialism, not with the historical realities of Nazi Germany and the Jews, and the aftermath. Too much of the young left did not understand that Israel's notion of the future was inseparable from "the dark background of catastrophe."[82]

Amery was not convinced by assertions that the anti-Zionism of the young left was not also a form of antisemitism. The Marxists, who focused on objective consequences of actions more than individual intentions, did not think about the likely consequences for the Jews in Israel of victory of the Arab and Palestinian armed organizations. The indifference to consequences of leftist anti-Zionism in Germany and Europe drew on "dangerous ground" of an antisemitism that had not been overcome. "In the collective unconscious of the peoples of Europe, an antisemitism drawing on the error of the deicide accusation is as virulent as ever" and was apparent in the new antisemitism aimed at Israel. For, Amery wrote, "ultimately it is *the Jews*" who yet again in the form of the hated "Zionist" emerge as the world enemy and oppressor and in this manner the young left was connecting to old traditions of antisemitism.[83]

In the process, he thought an antisemitism draped in the language of anti-Zionism was becoming respectable in progressive circles.[84] In the 1970s, the old antisemitism of the right of the *Protocols of the Elders of Zion* or of the Nazis remained beyond the pale in the world of intellectuals, universities, politics, and the press. The new antisemites of the mid-1970s insisted that as "anti-Zionists" they were nothing of the sort. In their view, Israel was a state based on the expulsion of the Arabs. It was an occupying power comparable to the Nazis between 1940 and 1945. The Palestinian cause was a "generally good, progressive cause" like other national liberation struggles. Therefore, why not be suspicious of Jews in West Germany and Europe who expressed solidarity with this "unjust state of Israel"? It was an "undoubted fact that the most rabid anti-Zionists" were in a leftist milieu that encompassed a spectrum from young Socialists to orthodox Soviet-oriented Communists, Maoists, Trotskyists, and the fringe groups of left-wing radicals. Common to them all was an "indifference to the Jewish catastrophe."[85] Ironically, the young left was making common cause with sentiments of the "bourgeoisie" concerned first with access to oil and foreign markets. In the West German left of the 1970s, the "honorable antisemite (*ehrbare Antisemite*) has a clear conscience" as he fights against an Israel he views as expansionist and colonialist. Amery dissented: "Antisemitism, also when it calls itself anti-Zionism, is not honorable."[86]

The views of the fringe, of Kunzelmann, Meinhof, the leaders of SDS in Frankfurt/Main in 1967, and the PLO Charter of 1968 had filtered more broadly into the West German left. By the early 1970s, antagonism to Israel had become a prominent, and for some, a defining feature of the West German left. Böse and Kuhlmann's pushed those more widely shared ideas in their world to a terrorist conclusion, one that, but for Israel's military intervention, could have led to a massacre of Jews by Germans at the airport in Entebbe.[87]

Contrary to a widely held assumption, the leading voices of the leftist generation of "1968" in West Germany—and elsewhere—did not, at the time, make a significant contribution to "coming to terms with the Nazi past." On the contrary, the leftist radicalism of those years ignored the specificities of antisemitism during the Holocaust and displayed little understanding of or empathy for the state of Israel.[88] The generation of Kunzelmann, Meinhof, Böse, and Kuhlmann, of the RAF, RCs, Marxist-Leninist groups, and the Palestine Solidarity Committees cared about and knew less about both the Holocaust and the links between liberal and leftist anti-fascism and the establishment of the state of Israel than did an older generation of liberals and leftists such as Adorno and Amery who had lived through the years of the Holocaust and Israel's beginnings.

On the contrary, their view of "anti-fascism" did more to foster antisemitic hatreds in new forms than to challenge and defeat them. The leftist anti-Zionist antisemitism was not unique to West Germany. It had counterparts in the New Left around the world. Yet it was only in Germany, both East and West, that the antagonism to Israel offered its advocates a psychological liberation, however illusory, from the burdens of facing their own country's criminal past with integrity, responsibility, and honesty. As the references in this essay indicate, a significant body of scholarship and commentary by historians, both within and outside Germany, has deepened our understanding of the era of the "new antisemitism" that Adorno, Amery, Galinski, and others criticized at the time. In so doing, it continued the founding West German tradition of an honest reckoning with the Nazi past. Yet much damage had been done. Antisemitism couched as anti-Zionism achieved a certain intellectual respectability. The blend of antisemitism with anti-Zionism once introduced many decades ago into the discourse of the West German and global left, has remained one of its important, and too often, defining features.

Notes

1 On the West German tradition of coming to terms with the past, see Jeffrey Herf, *Divided Memory: The Nazi Past in the Two Germanys* (Cambridge, MA: Harvard University Press, 1997); and Magnus Bretchken, ed., *Aufarbeitung des Nationalsozialismus: Ein Kompendium* (Göttingen: Wallstein Verlag, 2021).
2 On the history of West German restitution policy see from an extensive scholarship, Constantin Goschler's *Schuld und Schulden: Die Politik der Wiedergutmachung für NS-Verfolgte seit 1945* (Göttingen: Wallstein Verlag, 2005); and Herf, *Divided Memory*.
3 Martin Kloke, "Oppositioneller Proisraelimsus vor 1967," in his *Israel und die deutsche* Linke (Frankfurt/Main: Haag + Herchen, 1994), 70–105; and Willy Albrecht, *Der Sozialistische Deutsche Studentenbund (SDS): Vom parteikonform*

Studentenbund zum Repräsentanten der neuen Linken (Bonn: Friedrich Ebert Stiftung, 1994).

4 On former Nazis in Egypt, see Ulrike Becker, ""Unsere Nazis in Ägypten": Westdeutsch-ägyptische Beziehungen zwischen 1951 und 1965 im Spannungsfeld von Neuanfang und nationalsozialistischer Kontinuität," doctoral dissertation, Friedrich Schiller Universität Jena, 2020.

5 From the extensive scholarship on West German Israeli relations, see Inge Deutschkron, *Israel und die Deutschen: Das schwierige Verhältnis*, rev. ed. (Cologne: Verlag Wissenschaft und Politik, 1991).

6 On the shift in 1967, see Herf, *Undeclared Wars with Israel*, 33–74.

7 See Shulamit Volkov, "Readjusting Cultural Codes: Reflections on Antisemitism and Anti-Zionism," and Andrei Markovits, "An Inseparable Tandem of European Identity? Anti-Americanism and Antisemitism in the Short and Long Run," in Jeffrey Herf, ed., *Convergence and Divergence: Antisemitism and Anti-Zionism in Historical Perspective* (London and New York: Routledge, 2007), 38–49, and 71–90.

8 "Stasi Archive Surprise: East German Spy Shot West Berlin Martyr," http://www.spiegel.de/international/germany/stasi-archive-surprise-east-german-spy-shot-west-berlin-martyr-a-626275.html; Nicholas Kulish, "Spy Fired Shot That Changed West Germany," *New York Times* (May 26, 2009): http://www.nytimes.com/2009/05/27/world/europe/27germany.html?_r=0.

9 "'Die 68er waren betrogene Betrüger': Der Historiker Peter Horvath untersucht die Kontakte der Studentenbewegung zu SED und Stasi. Für ihn handelt es sich um eine "inszenierte Revolte"," *Die Welt* (June 12, 2009): http://www.welt.de/welt_print/article3910491/Die-68er-waren-betrogene-Betrueger.html. Also see Peter Horvarth, *Die inszenierte Revolte: hinter den Kulissen von '68* (Munich: Herbig, 20120).

10 Cited in Kloke, Israel und die deutsche Linke, 115; and in Jens Benicke, *Von Adorno zu Mao: Uber die schlechte Aufhebun der antiauritaren Bewegung* (Freiburg: ca ira, 2010).

11 See "An Anti-Israeli Left Emerges in West Germany: The Conjuncture of June 1967," in Herf, *Undeclared Wars with Israel*, 33–74; and "Deligiertenliste der XXII. ODK (4–9 September 1967), Archiv Apo FU Berlin, Sammlung BV 1967 SDS, Archiv Apo FU Berlin, Sammlung BV 22.DK 1967 SDS.

12 Wolff was also the co-founder of the leftist publisher, *Roter Stern Verlag* (Red Star Press). On K.D. Wolff and other connections and interactions between the American and West German New Left, see Martin Klimke, *The Other Alliance: Student Protest in West Germany and the United States in the Global Sixties* (Princeton, NJ: Princeton University Press, 2010).

13 "Sozialistischer Deutscher Studentenbund, 22. Delegiertenkonferenz des SDS, 4–9 September 1967, Neuwahlen," SDS Bundesvorstand (n.d.) Archiv Apo FU Berlin, Sammlung BV 1967 SDS; and "(Zweite) vorläufige Tagesordnung der 22. Ordentlichen Delegiertenkonferenz des SDS," Frankfurt/Main (September 4–8, 1967), Bundesvorstand, Sozialistische Deutscher Studentenbund (SDS), (hereafter BV SDS), Archiv des Hamburger Instituts für Sozialforschung, (Arch HIS) SDS 140, Diskussionspapiere, Organisationsdebatte, Politische Initiativen, Box 01, Blattsammlung, Presse, Flugblätter, Entwicklung des SDS in Jahr 1967.

14 Rudi Dutschke, "Notizen," Mappe 2, Blatt 2, June 1967, K21/48, Archiv des Hamburger Instituts für Sozialforschung, cited in Wolfgang Kraushaar, "Rudi Dutschke und der bewaffnete Kampf " in Wolfgang Kraushaar, Karin Wieland, and Jan Philipp Reemtsma, eds., *Rudi Dutschke, Andreas Baader und die RAF* (Hamburg: Hamburger Edition, 2005), 48; emphasis in the original text. On Dutschke's public rejection of terrorism a decade later Rudi Dutschke, "Toward

a Clarifying Criticism of Terrorism," trans. Jeffrey Herf, *New German Critique* (Fall 1977), 9–10.

15 "Sozialistischer Deutscher Studentenbund, 22. Delegiertenkonferenz des SDS, 4.-9 September 1967, "V. Dem SDS von der 22. ODk als Material überwiesen: 24. Der Konflikt im Nahen Osten," 48-54, Archiv Apo FU Berlin, Sammlung BV 1967 SDS.

16 Ibid., 49–50.

17 Ibid., 52.

18 Ibid., 53.

19 "The Palestinian National Charter: Resolutions of the Palestine National Council July 1–17, 1968," Yale Law School, The Avalon Project, Documents in Law, History and Diplomacy, http://avalon.law.yale.edu/20th_century/plocov.asp.

20 "Article 20, Article 15, The Palestinian National Charter the Avalon Project, http://avalon.law.yale.edu/20th_century/plocov.asp.

21 "Article 22, The Palestinian National Charter: Resolutions of the Palestine National Council July 1–17, 1968," The Avalon Project, http://avalon.law.yale.edu/20th_century/plocov.asp.

22 "Tabelle 2: Mitgliederzahlen der jüdischen Gemeinden," in Erica Burgauer, *Zwischen Erinnerung und Verdrängung—Juden in Deutschland nach 1945* (Reinbek bei Hamburg: Rowohlt Taschenbuch, 1993), 356. The figures for the tiny and declining size of Jewish population in East Germany in 1970, 1976, 1982 and 1987 were 1078, 728, 470 and 370, respectively, ibid., 359. On the immediate postwar years se Howard Geller, *Jews in Post-Holocaust Germany, 1945–1953* (New York and Cambridge: Cambridge University Press, 2005); and Herf, *Undeclared Wars with Israel*, 96–97.

23 On the migration and to trans-national links in the 1960s left in West Germany, see Klimke, *The Other Alliance*; and Quinn Slobodian, *Foreign Front: Third World Politics in Sixties West Germany* (Durham, NC: Duke University Press, 2012).

24 On GUPS, see the memoir of its director in West Germany: Abdallah Frangi, *Der Gesandte: Mein Leben für Palästina: Hinter den Kulissen der Nahost-Politik* (Munich: Heyne, 2011).

25 The annual reports of the *Verfassungsschutz* examined the role of foreign student political organizations in West Germany.

26 Herf, *Undeclared Wars with Israel*, 97–98.

27 Theodor Adorno, "Nr. 338 Brief an Herbert Marcuse, 19 Juni 1969," in Wolfgang Kraushaar, ed. *Frankfurter Schule und Studentenbewegung: Von der Flaschenpost zum Molotowcocktail, 1946–1995*, vol. 2, *Dokumente* (Hamburg: Rogner and Bernhard bei Zweitausendeins, 1998), 651–652. Also see Herf, *Undeclared Wars with Israel*, 98. Kraushaar's three volume work is a remarkably comprehensive and important source. Also see the chronology in volume one and essays by participants in volume three. Adorno's and the Frankfurt School's works on antisemitism, see, from an extensive scholarship, Lars Rensmann, *The Politics of Unreason: The Frankfurt School and the Origins of Modern Antisemitism* (Albany, NY: SUNY Press, 2017).

28 On Adorno and the West German student left, see Detlev Claussen, *Theodor W. Adorno: Ein Letzes Genie* (Frankfurt/Main: S. Fischer Verlag, 2003), 391–401; and Stefan Müller-Doohm, *Adorno: Eine Biographie* (Frankfurt/Main: Suhrkamp Verlag, 2003), 679–729.

29 Wolfgang Kraushaar, "17.Juli.1969," Frankfurter Schule und Studentenbewegung: Von der Flaschenpost zum Molotowcocktail, 1946–1995, Band I: Chronik (Hamburg: Rogner and Bernhard, 1998), 445–447.

30 "Statement by participants in the Al Fatah Summer Camp, Jordan, July to August 1969," Archiv Apo FU Berlin, R80, Internationalismus, Palästina, L Amerika, Afrika, Asien.

31 Ibid.

32 Gerd Koenen, *Das Rote Jahrzehnt: Unsere kleine deutsche Kulturrevolution, 1967–1977* (Frankfurt/Main: Suhrkamp, 2002).

33 Ibid., 83.

34 Ibid., 93–94. One study concludes that between 1970 and 1975, there were over sixty organizations in West Germany with the word "*Kommunist*" in the title. See Jürgen Schröder, *Ideologischer Kampf vs. Regionale Hegemonie: Ein Beitrag zur Untersuchung der 'K-Gruppen'* (Berlin: Berliner Arbeitshefte und Berichte zur Sozialwissenschaftlichen Forschung, Nr. 40, 1990), Institut für Sozialforschung, Hamburg.

35 Ibid., 62.

36 Dan Diner, "Bericht über die arabische Propaganda und ihre Auswirkungen in der Bundesrepublik Deutschland," December 1969, *Zentral Archiv zur Erforschung der Geschichte der Juden in Deutschland (ZA-Heidelberg)* Bestand B.1/7 468, Nah Ost Krise, 1969–1973.

37 See Herf, *Undeclared Wars with Israel*, 102–105. Also see Wolfgang Kraushaar, *Die Bombe im jüdischen Gemeindehaus* (Hamburg: Hamburger Edition, 2005); and Wolfgang Kraushaar, ed., *Die RAF und der linke Terrorismus* (Hamburg: Hamburger Edition, 2006).

38 The noun "Tupamaros" came from the name of a terrorist group in Uruguay composed of students inspired by the Brazilian legislator and Communist Carlos Marighella. See his *Urban Guerilla Minimanual* (Vancouver, CA: Pulp Press, 1974).

39 Herf, *Undeclared Wars with Israel*, 103. "Schalom + Napalm," *Agit 883*, November 13, 1969, 1. Jg., Nr. 40, 9. The original is available online at: http://www.agit883.infopartisan.net/.

40 Martin Kloke, *Israel und die deutsche Linke* (Frankfurt/Main: Haag + Herchen, 1990), 163–164.

41 Herf, *Undeclared Wars with Israel*, 103–104.

42 Ibid., 105. Also cited in Kraushaar, *Die Bombe im jüdischen Gemeindehaus*, 62–64. The "Tupamaros" were an urban guerilla organization of the 1960s in Uruguay. "Che" was a reference to the Cuban Communist leader, Che Guevara.

43 Dieter Kunzelmann, "Brief aus Amman (I), *Agit 883*, Nr. 42 (November 27, 1969), p. 5; cited in Herf, *Undeclared Wars with Israel*, 105. On Kunzelmann's political activities see "Dieter Kunzelmann," in Wolfgang Kraushaar, *"Wann endlich beginnt bei Euch der Kampf gegen die Heilige Kuh Israel?" München 1970: Über die antisemitischen Wurzeln des deutschen Terrorismus* (Hamburg: Rowohlt, 2013), 785–786; and Aribert Reimann, *Dieter Kunzelmann—Avantgarde, Protest und Radikalismus nach 1945* (Göttingen: Vandenhoeck and Ruprecht, 2009).

44 Ibid.

45 Ibid.

46 For a detailed account of these attacks on the planes and the investigations into them, see Wolfgang Kraushaar, *München 1970*, 37–81 and 169–250. On the attack on the Jewish home for the aged in Munich, see 86–162.

47 See Wolfgang Kraushaar, *München 1970*, 184–185.

48 Dieter Kunzelmann, "Brief aus Amman (II) Das palästinensische Volk wird in seinem bewaffneten Kampf siegen," *Agit 883*, Nr. 55 (April 3, 1970), 11; cited in Herf, *Undeclared Wars with Israel*, 108.

49 Heinz Galinski, "Zu Rosch Haschanah 5731," Für unsere Mitglieder, Vorstand der Jüdischen Gemeinde zu Berlin West Berlin (September 1970), ZA Heidelberg; Herf, Undeclared Wars with Israel, 111.

50 "Dokumentation arabischer Terrorakte 1968–1972," ZA Heidelberg, *Jüdischer Presse Dienst: Informationen des Zentralrats der Juden in Deutschland*, Dusseldorf, Nr. 1 (January 1973), 5–8; "Gift-Briefe aus Karlsruhe" (October 23, 1972), BAK, B443/641; "Informationsaustausch zur Sicherheitslage—Duesseldorf—Sprengstoffbrief eingegangen beim juedischen altersheim in Duesseldorf," BAK 443/641.

51 Hendrik van Dam, "an die Mitglieder des Direktoriums Landesverbände und die Gemeinden Berlin, Frankfurt, Hamburg, Köln und München, Jüdischen Organisationen in der Bundesrepublik," Dusseldorf (September 4, 1972), ZA Heidelberg, B.1/7.93, Politisch Divers, 1974–1976; "Bericht: Versand von Sprengstoffbriefen durch arabische Terroristen an israelische Personen," BAK, 443/641; and Bundeskriminalamt Abt. II—Sicherungsgruppe to Bundesamt für Verfassungsschutz, "Versand von Sprengstoff in Briefen an israelische Missionen" (September 26, 1972), BAK 443/ 641; Herf, *Undeclared Wars with Israel*, 188–189.

52 Heinz Galinski, "Unausweichliche Alternative: Das Verbrechen von München mahnt," Allgemeine unabhängige jüdische Wochenzeitung, Dusseldorf (September 22, 1972), 1.

53 Ibid.

54 Ulrike Meinhoff, "Die Aktion des Schwarzen September in München. Zur Strategie des Antiimperialistischen Kampfes," *Rote Armee Fraktion: Texte und Materialien...*, pp. 151–177. Cited in Herf, *Undeclared Wars with Israel*, 189–193. On the Baader-Meinhof group see Stefan Aust, Der Baader-Meinhof Komplex, rev. ed. (Munich: Goldmann Verlag, 1998); Jeffery Herf, "An Age of Murder: Ideology and Terror in Germany," Telos, No. 144 (Fall 2008): 8–38; Butz Peters, *Tödlicher Irrtum: Die Geschichte der RA*, 3rd ed (Frankfurt/Main: Fischer Taschenbuch, 2007); and Willi Winkler, *Die Geschichte der RAF* (Berlin: Rowohlt Verlag, 2007).

55 Ibid., 151–152.

56 Ibid., 159.

57 Ibid., 171.

58 Ibid., 173.

59 Ibid., 173.

60 Ibid., 177.

61 Ibid., 177. For an analysis of the text by the Bundeskriminalamt, see "Bericht: Illegal Druckschrift der RAF mit dem Titel 'Die Aktion des Schwarzen September in München—Zur Strategie des antiimperialistischen Kampfes,'" BAK B106/83804 Bundeskriminalamt, Bonn (January 15, 1973).

62 See Robert Wistrich, "Antisemitism and Holocaust Inversion," in Anthony McElligott and Jeffrey Herf, eds., *Antisemitism Before and Since the Holocaust: Altered Contexts and Recent Perspectives* (London: Palgrave/Macmillan, 2017), 37–50.

63 See the discussion in "The Entebbe Hijacking and the West German 'Revolutionary Cells,'" Herf, *Undeclared Wars with Israel*, 317–341.

64 Prof. Dr.[Kurt] Rebmann, [Generalbundesanwalt] Beim Bundesgerichtshof to Bundesminister der Justiz, "Ermittlungsverfahren gegen Johannes Weinrich und andere Mitglieder einer terroristischen Vereinigung 'Revolutionäre so: Zellen (RZ) wegen Verdachts eine Vergehens nach para. 129a StGB und andere Straftaten," Karlsruhe, (March 19, 1980), Bundesarchiv Koblenz (BAK) Bundesministerium des Innern, Bundesgerichtshof, B106/403104.

65 Embassy Kampala to SecState Wash DC, "Subject: Amin's Position on ME" (September 13, 1972), United States National Archives, College Park, NACP RG 59 General Records of the Department of State, SNF, 1970-73, Political and Defense, From Pol. 27 Arab ISR 7/172 to Pol 27 Arab ISR 1/1/73, NWDPH-2 1997, Box 2060. Also see "Amin Praises Hitler for Killing of Jews," *The New York Times* (September 13, 1972), 4; cited in Herf, *Undeclared Wars with Israel*, 170–172.

66 "Subject: Amin's Position on ME" (September 13, 1972); Also in "Non-Arab Africa: Uganda: Amin's Message to the UN, Mrs. Meir and Yasir Arafat: Kampala home service in English 1700 gmt 11Sept 72," BBC, *Summary of World Broadcasts (SWB): Part 4: The Middle East and Africa* (September 13, 1972), ME/4091/B/1.

67 Ibid.

68 On the connections between West German leftist terrorist organizations with the Popular Front for the Liberation of Palestine, see Thomas Skelton Robinson, "Im Netz verheddert: Die Beziehungen des bundesdeutschen Linksterrorismus zur Volksfront für die Befreiung Palästina (1969–1980)," in Wolfgang Kraushaar, ed., *Die RAF und der linke Terrorismus* (Hamburg: Hamburger Edition, 2006), 828– 904; and Martin Jander, "German Leftist Terrorism and Israel: Ethno-Nationalist, Religious-Fundamentalist, or Social-Revolutionary?," *Studies in Conflict and Terrorism*, 8, 6 (2015), 456–477.

69 "Entführtes französisches Flugzeug in Uganda gelandet," *Neues Deutschland* (June 29, 1976), 7; and "Flugzeugentführer in Entebbe ließen 47 Geiseln frei," *ND* (July 1, 1976), 15.

70 "Blutiger Überfall Israels auf Flughafen in Uganda," *ND* (July 5, 1976), 6.

71 "Zum Ablauf und den Begleitumständen der Entführung eine Flugzeuges der 'Air France' durch Terroristen nach Entebbe sowie den Israelischen Aggressionshandlungen gegen die Republik Uganda," ["On the course of events and related circumstances of the hijacking of an Air France plan by terrorists to Entebbe as well as the Israeli aggressive actions against the Republic of Uganda."] *Bundesbeauftragte für die Unterlagen des Staatssicherheitsdienst der ehemaligen Deutschen Demokratischen Republik, Ministerium für Staatssicherheit Zentralarchiv (hereafter)* BStU MfSZ-Archiv, MfS-HA XXII, Nr. 105418, Teil 1 von 2, 5.

72 ID-Archiv im IISG Amsterdam, eds., "Aktion gegen die Israelische Import-Gesellschaft Agrexco," Frankfurt (June 1978), *Die Früchte des Zorns: Texte und Materialien zur Geschichte der Revolutionären Zellen und der Roten Zora, Band I* (Edition ID-Archiv: Berlin, 1993), 131–132.

73 Ibid., 132; cited in Herf, *Undeclared Wars with Israel*, 333–334.

74 Ibid.

75 Ibid., 132–133; cited in Herf, *Undeclared Wars with Israel*, 334.

76 Hans-Joachim Klein, Rückkehr in die Menschlichkeit: Appell eines ausgestigenen Terroristen (Reinbek bei Hamburg: Rowohlt Verlag, 1979), 80–81; see Herf, *Undeclared Wars with Israel*, 340–341.

77 Klein, *Rückkehr in die Menschlichkeit*, 87–88.

78 Hermann Lewy, "Ein Terrorist gibt auf: Hans-Joachim Klein enthüllt weitere Mordpläne." *Berliner Allgemeine jüdische Wochenzeitung*, Dusseldorf (May 13, 19787), 1.

79 Jean Amery, *Werke, Band 7: Aufsätze zur Politik und Zeitgeschichte* (Stuttgart: Klett-Cotta, 2005); and Marlene Gallner, ed., *Jean Amery, Essays on Antisemitism, Anti-Zionism, and the Left* (Bloomington: Indiana University Press, 2022).

80 Jean Amery, "Der ehrbare Antisemitismus," in *Aufsätze zur Politik und Zeitgeschichte*, 131–135, 140.

81 Jean Amery, "Die Linke und der 'Zionismus,'" in *Aufsätze zur Politik und Zeitgeschichte*, 141–142.

82 Ibid., 144.

83 Ibid., 148.

84 Jean Amery, "Der neue Antisemitismus," in *Aufsätze zur Politik und Zeitgeschichte*, 159–171.

85 Ibid., 167.

86 Ibid., 175, 196.

87 The journalist and essayist Henryk M. Broder wrote extensively about the convergence of antisemitism with anti-Zionism. See his: *Der ewige Antisemite: Über Sinn und Funktion eines beständigen Gefühls* [The Eternal Antisemite: On the Meaning and Function of a Persistent Sentiment] (Berlin: Berliner Taschenbuch Verlag, 2006); *Vergesst Auschwitz: Die deutsch Erinnerungswahn und die Endlösung der*

Israel Frage [Forget Auschwitz: The German Illusion of Memory and the Final Solution of the Israel Question] (Munich: Knaus Verlag, 2012).

88 The scholarly confrontation with the Holocaust in West Germany and the gradual movement of such issues from the margins to the center of scholarly and intellectual life was a preoccupation of West German liberals, more than it was of Marxists of the 1960s and 1970s. On this, see Karl Dietrich Bracher, *The German Dictatorship* (New York: Praeger, 1970); "The Role of Hitler: Perspectives of Interpretation," in Walter Laqueur, ed., *Fascism: A Reader's Guide* (Berkeley: University of California Press, 1976), 211–225; his *Zeitgeshichtliche Kontroversen: Um Faschismus, Totalitarismus, Demokratie* (Munich: Piper Verlag, 1976); and Lucy Dawidowicz, *The Holocaust and the Historians* (Cambridge, MA: Harvard University Press, 1981).

9

ANTISEMITISM AND WHITE RACISM

Similarities and Differences

When historians in the United States examine ideologies of race and racism, the overwhelming preoccupation concerns skin color.[1] In view of the history of white racism toward African Americans within the United States and of the racism that accompanied colonialism and imperialism, the focus is understandable. However, antisemitism, by which I mean hatred of Jews and Judaism, and in recent years often if not always, the state of Israel as well, does not fit this conventional understanding. Neither anti-Judaism with Christian or Islamic theological origins nor racial antisemitism based on presumed biological differences derive from distinctions of skin color. The fact that antisemitism does not fit into the conventional categories became obvious after neo-Nazis and right-wing extremists in Charlottesville on August 11–12, 2017, marched through the streets and past a synagogue carrying torches and chanted "the Jews will not replace us." The chant derived from antisemitic ideology that blamed Jews for planning and implementing a "great replacement" of whites with non-white immigrants. The right-wing extremists also defended monuments to white supremacy and the Confederacy.[2] In other words, they were simultaneously racists against people of color, as well as antisemites. However, much of the press commentary focused on the former and more familiar form of racism that dealt with issues of color, but not the specifically antisemitic dimension of their hatred. In so doing, journalists reflected the conventional American and Western understanding of race and racism, as well as its deficiency in understanding antisemitism.

A comparative historical perspective can be helpful in sorting out similarities and differences between these forms of hatred and intolerance. We can do so by examining three issues: first, the commonalities and differences between white racism and antisemitism; second, distinctions between the

DOI: 10.4324/9781003449669-10

antisemitism of the 1930s in Nazi Germany, what Saul Friedlander called the era of persecution, on the one hand, and the radical antisemitism of the years of the Holocaust, on the other[3]; and third, the continuities and breaks between Christian theological anti-Judaism of the preceding 1,900 years and the Nazis' radical antisemitism in the twentieth century.[4]

First, the ideologies of white racism and antisemitism share in the dehumanization of their victims. They are the ideological inspiration of two massive crimes. Historians estimate that over the course of three centuries of the approximately ten million Africans seized and forcibly deported from Africa to the Americas, North and South, up to half, that is, up to five million people, died from the point of capture, on the transoceanic voyage or through mistreatment on slave plantations.[5] As we know, in the four years from 1941 to 1945, the Nazi regime murdered six million of Europe's Jews. Comparing the mass murder of European Jews compressed into a four-year spasm with the deaths and suffering of enslaved Africans and then African Americans suggests a starting point for a grim comparative analysis.

The core of white racism toward African Americans was the imputation of inferiority due to what racists claimed was an ineradicable *biological* connection between skin color and character. Contrary to what modern science has repeatedly demonstrated, white supremacists asserted that black skin was evidence of biologically determined intellectual and moral inferiority, an inferiority that justified drastic political, social, and economic subordination. The subordination and denial of human rights to African Americans in the era of slavery rested on these imputations of inferiority and denial of humanity that had everything to do with color.[6] As human rights were the rights of human beings, white racists argued that Black people were not fully human or not as human as whites. The inferiority that slave owners imputed to their slaves meant that the latter were fit only for burdensome and simple labor always controlled by whites. While the outcome of the Civil War destroyed slavery, the conviction of white racists regarding the racially determined inferiority of African Americans fueled the counter-revolution against reconstruction governments and then the imposition of a century of legalized segregation and denial of citizenship rights and to a mythic retelling of the meaning of the war itself.[7]

Leon Poliakov, Benzion Netanyahu, and more recently David Nirenberg have emphasized the role of the Spanish Inquisition in the fifteenth and sixteenth centuries in the history of racism. It was then that the old religious antagonism of Judaism and Jews first assumed the dimensions of biological racism in the form of the "purity of blood" statutes.[8] So when Europeans first encountered black Africans, they came up with ideas that connected race and biology that ironically first emerged in a Spanish context in which color was not an issue. The scientifically discredited notion that humanity is divided into distinct biological races emerged first in the Inquisition when anti-Judaism for the first time in its longer history became hatred of Jews as a distinct race. As Winthrop Jordan pointed out, Europeans who had long associated the color black with a host of pejorative qualities, including evil, dirt, filth, licentiousness, and unrestrained sexuality, brought with them the habits of racial biology first articulated in the Inquisition's anti-Jewish persecutions.[9]

In 1978, in his important work on the history of European racism and antisemitism in the nineteenth and twentieth century, *Toward the Final Solution: A History of European Racism*, George Mosse drew attention to the commonalities and differences between European white racism of the modern era toward blacks and European racial hatred of the Jews.[10] Both the European pseudo-scientists and racial ideologues such as Houston Stewart Chamberlain and then various Nazi racial ideologues, like the ideologists of white supremacy in the United States, claimed to find connections between external appearances and body type with pejorative features of mind and character. Culminating in the caricatures that filled the pages of Julius Streicher's *Der Stürmer*, they depicted a stereotyped Jewish body held to be physically inferior in every way to an idealized Aryan vision of the beautiful body. They viewed Jews' alleged physical ugliness to be evidence of moral inferiority.[11] The antisemites Mosse examined depicted a stereotypical Jewish body but not one distinguished by skin color.

The strand of antisemitism that imputed moral inferiority to the Jews based on the assertion that Jews were a distinct biological race in conflict with another Aryan race found clearest expression in the Nuremberg race laws of 1935, especially "The Law for the Protection of German Blood and Honor." These laws broke with traditional Christian anti-Judaism which held out the hope that Jews, who were not viewed as a distinct biological race, would redeem themselves by converting to Christianity. The biological racism at the heart of the Nuremberg race laws precluded that possibility. The laws transformed the Jews from a distinct religious group into a racial, that is, biological, other. They included detailed reflections on the dangers of "mixing" German and Jewish "blood" and elaborate rules defining who was and was not Jewish. It forbade Germans to marry or have sexual relations with Jews as well as with persons of "alien blood," that is, "Gypsies, Negroes, and their bastards."[12] James Whitman has pointed out that the German lawyers involved in drafting these laws found helpful models in American miscegenation legislation.[13] The consequences of the Nuremberg race laws were immediate: Jews lost their civil and political rights. In December 1935, a supplementary decree ordered the dismissal of Jewish professors, teachers, physicians, lawyers, and notaries who were state employees and had been granted exemptions. This German era of persecution and denial of citizenship rights to Jews bears close comparison with the racial persecution based on imputation of inferiority to African Americans. In both cases, obsessions with racial biology and notions about racial superiority and inferiority led to discrimination, denial of citizenship rights, unequal treatment in the courts, impoverishment, and periodic violence.

In Nazi Germany in the 1930s, racial antisemitism, again one that had no connection to skin color, included elements of physical revulsion, sexual panic, and assumption of seemingly clear, easily recognizable physical differences. In that manner, it had similarities with European and then American racism toward Africans and then African Americans. Like these other forms of racism, this antisemitism associated pejorative qualities of inward character with alleged specific physiological appearances. The Jewish body implied a Jewish character associated with cowardice, sexual rapacity, crime, murderous attacks on women and children, lack of patriotism, and subversion of the nation.[14] Pornographic and biological antisemitism of this sort certainly fostered a climate of hatred and revulsion in which mass murder was a possibility. It was central to the murders of the mentally ill and physically handicapped and to barbaric "medical experiments" undertaken by Nazi physicians.[15] It played an important role in the development of techniques of mass gassing, lent the prestige of science to inhumanity and in so doing contributed to a climate of opinion in which a genocide could take place.[16] The Nazi antisemitism of the 1930s was similar in its outcomes to the white racism that justified slavery before the Civil War and legalized segregation and discrimination afterward.[17] Ideological assertions about the supposed physical and moral inferiority of the Jews, like comparable assertions about African Americans, were components of both eras of persecution associated with both of these forms of racism.

Yet, the antisemitism of the era of persecution in Nazi Germany, the racial hatred that assigned inferiority to the Jews, did not lead to mass murder. It certainly spread a climate of hatred and indifference toward the fate of the Jews and in that sense facilitated a climate in which genocide could take place, but the antisemitism of the Nuremberg race laws was not the core of the ideology that accompanied the Holocaust. The now well-known terms—*völkisch* ideology, politics of cultural despair, redemptive antisemitism, the hour of authoritarian biology, and reactionary modernism—bring us to the ideological world of the Nuremberg race laws and the November pogrom of 1938.[18] The racial biological dimension of anti-Jewish hatred in Germany, that is, what it had in common with a racism focused on issues of color, does not explain why that form of antisemitism led to an unprecedented spasm of mass murder the purpose of which was to exterminate all the Jews of Europe and anywhere else in the world that Nazism could have them in its grasp. It accounted for massive persecution, slave labor, impoverishment, and denial of rights but not for genocide. Friedlander's term "redemptive antisemitism" comes closer, but it too refers to a Germany "redeemed" by expelling the Jews to some other part of the world. In suggesting that the entire world would be redeemed if Judaism and the Jews were exterminated, it prefigured but did not yet demand the genocidal option.

The leap from persecution to extermination and the Nazi regime's *radical antisemitism* from 1939 to 1945 brought the conspiratorial and paranoid elements that lurked in Hitler's thinking and in the Nazi Party to the center of its ideological outlook. The Nazis attack on what they called "the Jewish enemy" did not allege Jewish inferiority and stupidity. On the contrary, it imagined an enormously powerful, clever, and evil international conspiracy aimed at the extermination of Germany and the Germans.[19] It was a radicalization of the antisemitism of the Nuremberg race laws and was also distinct from the white racism familiar to historians of slavery and colonialism. Its key component, what Norman Cohn called "the warrant for genocide" had been prefigured in the famous forgery of Russian intelligence services, *The Protocols of the Elders of Zion.*[20] The Nazis brought the lurid tale of Jews plotting to wage wars and cause economic crises up to date and peopled it with living personalities in public life in the Soviet Union, Britain, and the United States of the years before and during World War II. Nazi wartime propaganda and the major speeches by Hitler and Goebbels did not dwell primarily on biological obsessions about blood, race, and sex of the Nuremberg race laws. Rather it focused on an imagined conspiracy allegedly controlled by a political subject called "world Jewry" which it accused of waging a war of extermination against Nazi Germany. On numerous occasions, Hitler and other leading officials publicly threatened to and then proudly announced that they were in the process of exterminating the Jews of Europe as an act of retaliation against the war of extermination which, they claimed, "the Jewish enemy" had launched against Germany and the Germans. When they spoke in this manner and justified mass murder, they had in mind *a racially defined political subject active in contemporary history far more than a biologically defined subject.* To be sure, images of Jewish inferiority were also ubiquitous but the ideological spur to genocide came from a paranoid fear of the consequences of an alleged Jewish *superiority* during World War II. This accusation about the Jews's supposed evil deeds comprised the distinctively genocidal component of Nazism's antisemitic ideology. In the minds of Hitler and his associates, this accusation, and the rage that it fostered, justified and legitimated the leap from persecution to genocide.

While Southern slaveholders lived in fear of slave revolts, real, and imagined, American pro-slavery ideology did not present African Americans as members of a global conspiracy who were willing and able to wage war against the United States as a step on the path to global black domination and the extermination of whites. Rather, they viewed slaves as the Germans viewed the Poles and Slavs, that is, as intellectual inferiors incapable of organizing anything so massive as an international political conspiracy. Just as enslavement for purposes of labor was the logical consequence of pro-slavery ideology, so the Holocaust was the logical consequence of the conspiracy theory of radical antisemitism. The radical antisemitic accusation, the ideological element that called for a complete extermination of the Jewish people in Europe and everywhere on the globe did *not* lie in racial biology. Rather it was the direct consequence of a *political* accusation made against the Jews who the Nazis had transformed from merely a religious other into a threatening and powerful *race*. Throughout World War II and the Holocaust, paranoia and projection remained handmaidens of Nazi aggression and mass murder.

In the jargon of historians of the Holocaust and Nazi Germany, this approach is one of *modified intentionalism*. Nazi ideology was a central causal factor, but it emerged in Nazi decision-making in the context of events and circumstances created by Hitler's decisions to start World War II between 1939 and 1941. In the minds of the Nazi leaders, the connection between World War II and the Holocaust was inherent in their radical antisemitism. It was not a contingent result of timing, geography, and opportunity, although all of those factors were present.[21] Such a view avoids the teleological determinism in the realm of ideas that presents German and European history as the pre-history of the Holocaust but it does attempt to do what historians must do, connect preconditions in long-term trends to short-term contingencies. It seeks to move historical writing away from an exclusive search for origins to an examination of ideas, intentions, and circumstances that produced a novel event.[22]

In this vast outpouring of words and images, the Nazi leadership interpreted World War II as a war begun and waged by "international Jewry" the purpose of which was to exterminate the German people. It described "Jewry" as a political subject, no less real than the governments of the Allied powers. According to the Nazis, "Jewry" was the power behind the scenes in "London, Moscow and Washington" and the "glue" that held together this unlikely coalition of "Jewish Bolsheviks" and "plutocrats." On many occasions, Hitler and his associates said publicly that the Nazi regime would respond to this alleged prior act of Jewish aggression and attempted mass murder by "exterminating" and "annihilating" the "Jewish race" in Europe. From the perspective of the Nazi leadership, "the war against the Jews" was not only the Holocaust.[23] It was also the war against Britain, the Soviet Union, the United States, and their allies. The Final Solution was, in their view, an act of fully justified retaliation. The denial of the uniqueness of the Holocaust was embedded in the propaganda that accompanied it.

This argument calls for a revision of our understanding of what the Nazis meant by the phrase "the war against the Jews." Since the publication of Lucy Dawidowicz's classic work with that title, the phrase became synonymous with the Holocaust.[24] Dawidowicz's work succeeded in drawing attention to the Holocaust, which in 1975 still stood in the shadows of the main historical event, World War II. Yet the evidence of the public assertions of Hitler and other Nazi leaders is clear. When they spoke of the war against the Jews, they were not referring only to the Final Solution. Rather in their public statements, private diary entries, and personal conversations, they asserted that the "war against the Jews" comprised the war against the Allies led by the United States, Great Britain, and the Soviet Union *as well as* the murder of Europe's Jews. They believed that these policies were two parts of one imagined war to the death between Nazi Germany and international Jewry or sometimes between the "Aryan race" and the Jewish "race."

There were contemporary observers who grasped the centrality or radical antisemitism in the above sense of the term. The literary scholar and diarist Victor Klemperer strongly hinted at this thesis when he wrote in his diary in June 1944, soon after D-Day: "However much I resisted it, *the Jew* is in every respect the center of the language of the Third Reich, indeed *of its whole view of the epoch*."[25] The young E.H. Gombrich, who subsequently gained fame as an eminent art historian, worked at the British Broadcasting Corporation (BBC) translating and analyzing German wartime propaganda. In a lecture in London in 1969, he concluded that what was characteristic of Nazi propaganda was "less the lie than the imposition of a paranoiac pattern on world events."[26] Though Gombrich put his finger on the core issue, his insights remained on the margins of subsequent historical scholarship. By far the most dangerous, indeed the distinctively genocidal component of Nazi antisemitism lay in this *overwhelmingly political* accusation, namely that a real existing political subject, "international Jewry," had started and escalated the World War II in order to exterminate Germany and the Germans. The regimes frequently discussed biological racism was important primarily because it pointed to a bond said to exist among all Jews, yet racial biology was not central to the justification for mass murder.

While caricatures of the Jewish body filled the pages of *Der Stürmer* and fascinated the pseudo-science of Nazi eugenics, the distinctively genocidal components of radical antisemitism dealt above all with what "international Jewry" was alleged to have done, not how Jews looked. The Jews, as Goebbels asserted in one of his most important antisemitic tirades, practiced "mimicry," that is, they were experts at camouflaging their actual identity and passing as non-Jews.[27] It was precisely because the Nazis did not believe that they could tell who was and was not a Jew by reference to biological features that they required Jews in Nazi-occupied Europe to wear the yellow star. Again, it was the Nazi accusation of what "Jewry" was alleged to be doing to the Germans, not their presumed physical features that stood at the center of the Nazi commitment to mass murder.

The interpretation of modified intentionalism offered here pushes analysis beyond the search for origins and draws out the intrinsic connections between World War II and the Final Solution in the minds of the Nazi leadership.

It recasts the meaning of the war against the Jews and offers an explanation as to why the Holocaust happened when it did. It contributes to understanding why, for the first time in its long history, antisemitism became an ideology that justified mass murder and not "only" as it had before, another era of persecution. The radical antisemitism of the Holocaust was not only distinct from the racism that accompanied American slavery. It was a new and the most lethal chapter in the history of antisemitism.

Nazi racial prejudices toward Poles and the peoples of Eastern Europe bore similarities with pro-slavery and then segregationist views in the United States. In the Nazi racial imagination, the "Asiatic hordes" and "Slavic subhumans" were frightening due to sheer numbers and the destructive outcomes said to result from "race-mixing." The mark of inferiority extended to assertions about limited mental capacity. For the Nazis, Poles and other Eastern Europeans were fit to be enslaved because they were lesser human beings. Yet the ultimate goal of *Lebensraum* in the East was to create a territory cleansed and cleared of much of its native inhabitants. It had genocidal implications. Those who remained would be colonial subjects dominated by Germans who settled in the East. Had the Nazis won World War II, many millions more of the citizens of Eastern Europe would have been classified as "excess eaters," died of starvation or at best reduced to the status of colonial subjects.[28]

Nazi *Lebensraum* policies on its Eastern front combined expulsions and murder of the native population, starvation, enslavement, and elimination of education to a level of minimally educated manual laborers fit only for menial tasks. During the first years of the German occupation of Poland, the SS Einsatzgruppen murdered an estimated 60,000 Polish nobles, clergy, and members of the professional middle classes. It intended to the country to one of menial laborers.[29] As Ulrich Herbert has recently stressed, Nazi Germany also wrote a large chapter in the history of slave labor as it imported foreign labor from multiple European countries into Germany during the war. [30] By the end of 1942, there were 1.7 million Soviet civilians or prisoners of war at work in Germany.[31] By 1944, foreign conscript labor in Germany accounted for 20.8 percent of the work force with a far higher percentage in agriculture.[32] As Christian Gerlach's studies have documented, the intersection of the racist ideology of *Lebensraum* led to forced labor, enslavement, and mass starvation.[33] Three million non-Jewish Poles, seventeen million Soviet civilians, and eight million Red Army soldiers, almost three million of whom were in German captivity, died during World War II. Nazi occupying authorities, as Gerlach has documented, actively planned the mass starvation and deaths of millions of "excess eaters." Germany's racist "war of extermination" (*Vernichtungskrieg*) on its Eastern Front demonstrated that a conventional racism based on distinctions of superiority and inferiority fueled policies that went far beyond those of the era of persecution within Germany from 1933 to 1939.

The reality of antisemitism as a cultural tradition and ideological outlook that has its own autonomous history and is thus not primarily a tool, instrument, or function for achieving other purposes has eluded leftist interpreters from Marxist and Communist interpretations since the 1920s to the more recent discussion of post-colonial theories. Hitler's public statements that he was in the process of "exterminating" the Jews of Europe were a fanaticism that did not fit into the categories of generations of leftists accustomed to see ideas as the instruments of dominant classes. In his 1942 study, *Behemoth: The Structure and Practice of National Socialism*, Franz Neumann, then director of the Office of Research and Analysis of the Office of Strategic Services (OSS) of the U.S. Government, viewed antisemitism as a "spearhead" in the service of other goals of German imperialism. Walter Ulbricht in his *Der Faschistische Deutsche Imperialismus (1933–1945)*, also published with the title *Die Legende vom 'deutschen Sozialismus* devoted hardly any space at all to the specifics of antisemitism and the murder of the Jews.[34] In response to a revival in 1970s West Germany of such Marxist interpretations that interpreted Nazism and antisemitism primarily as agents or tools of the capitalist class, the historian Karl Dietrich Bracher wrote that such views reproduced the "illusions and fictions" that, in Weimar and Nazi Germany, "led to the fatal underestimation of Hitler and his movement."[35] With few exceptions, those historians who first drew attention to the central role of antisemitic ideology, did so outside, and in opposition to interpretations influenced by Marxist economic reductionism.[36]

The neglect of antisemitism as a core topic of inquiry is evident as well in recent "post-colonial" writings which view the Holocaust as a form of colonial violence that has returned from overseas back to the European continent.[37] In so doing, such interpretations avoid examination of the distinctive history of antisemitism in European history, and thus also miss what distinguishes antisemitism from the forms of racism that accompanied colonialism. Along these lines, one historian has recently argued that "all Nazi extermination policies were expressions of permanent security" and that "redemptive antisemitism was a function of a broader project: redemptive imperialism."[38] While, as noted in previous chapters, the Nazis justified their policy of mass murder by asserting the existence of dangerous "Jewish enemy," the reality was that such fears were completely delusional because the Jews of Europe posed no threat whatsoever to Nazi Germany or anyone else.

The hatred of the Jews in Europe was not, as Aime Cesaire wrote in his *Discourse on Colonialism*, the importation of colonial racism back to the continent of Europe.[39] Rather, as a now very large historical scholarship has demonstrated, anti-Judaism was a core element of European and Christian culture many centuries before the era of colonialism and imperialism. As noted above, the older Christian anti-Judaism first became a racial hatred in the fifteenth century in the Spanish Inquisition and then again among racial ideologies in the nineteenth and early twentieth centuries Western and Central Europe, and in both cases was a "racism" that had nothing to do with the color line.[40] Rather Europe's antisemites offered pseudo-biological arguments about blood lines and genealogies that secularized and modernized older religious Christian regarding the power, the evil and the murderousness of the Jews. In the Spanish Inquisition, they did so before the era of colonialism had begun.[41]

The various forms of racism, those that do and do not have to do with color, were and are inhumane, immoral, and evil. The historian's task is not to present one as "worse" than others. Such efforts are those of political activists, not scholars. While there are relationships between different traditions, each also has its own autonomous history that cannot and ought not be reduced to something external to it or viewed as a "function" or "instrument" for other purposes. The historian, this historian in any case, seeks to clarify the connection between ideas and politics, or for governments, between ideology and policy, and to draw attention as well to the connections between the long-term cultural traditions, and the form they have taken in the short-term contingencies of the twentieth- and twenty-first centuries.[42]

The radical antisemitic conspiracy theory of the Nazi regime had its "logical" and evil conclusion in the effort to wipe the Jews off the face of the earth, first in Europe and then everywhere else they could be found. In seeking to "exterminate world Jewry," Hitler and his associates were convinced they would eliminate the source of evil in the world and heroically defend Germany against a threatening enemy which, in their imagination, was both powerful and evil. The link between their antisemitic conspiracy theory and their determination to implement "the Final Solution of the Jewish Question in Europe" distinguished radical antisemitism from all other forms of racism and hatred. That distinctiveness is still insufficiently understood in a world that thinks of racism as primarily to do with distinctions of color.

Notes

Selections taken from Jeffrey Herf, "A Comparative Perspective on Antisemitism, Radical Antisemitism in the Holocaust and American White Racism," *The Journal of Genocide Research* 9, 4 (December 2007): 575–600: Reprinted by permission of the publisher (Taylor & Francis Ltd, http://www.tandfonline.com; and from Jeffrey Herf, "The Roots of Hitler's Hate: The Anatomy of Antisemitism," *The National Interest* (May–June 2018), http://nationalinterest.org/feature/the-roots-hitlers-hate-25411: Reprinted by permission of *The National Interest Magazine*.

1 This chapter revises "Antisemitism and Racism: Sources, Similarities and Differences," at the Annual Meetings of the American Historical Association, Saturday, January 6, 2018, Washington, DC; "A Comparative Perspective on Antisemitism, Radical Antisemitism in the Holocaust and American White Racism" *The Journal of Genocide Research* 9, 4 (December 2007), 575–600; and "The Roots of Hitler's Hate: The Anatomy of Antisemitism," *The National Interest* (May–June 2018), http://nationalinterest.org/feature/the-roots-hitlers-hate-25411.

2 See Wald, "The New Replacement Theory: Anti-Zionism, Antisemitism, and the Denial of History," in Alvin H. Rosenfeld (ed), *Anti-Zionism and Antisemitism: The Dynamics of Delegitimation* (Bloomington: Indiana University Press, 2019), 3–29.

3 Saul Friedlander, *Nazi Germany and the Jews: Volume One: The Era of Persecution, 1933–1939* (New York: Harper, 1998).

4 For a valuable comparison of antisemitism and white racism see George M. Fredrickson *Racism: A Short History* (Princeton, NJ: Princeton University Press, 2002, and 2015).

5 See Ira Berlin, *Many Thousands Gone: The First Two Centuries of Slavery in North America* (Cambridge, MA: Harvard University Press, 1998); Joseph C. Miller, *Way of Death: Merchant Capitalism and the Angolan Slave Trade 1730–1830* (Madison: University of Wisconsin Press, 1988); and the discussion of slavery in David Landes, *The Wealth and Poverty of Nations: Why are Some so Rich and Some so Poor* (New York: W.W. Norton, 1998), 116–119.

6 David Brion Davis, *The Problem of Slavery in the Age of Revolution, 1770–1823*, 2nd ed. (New York: Oxford University Press, 1998). On race, slavery and the U.S. Constitution see Sean Wilentz, *No Property in Man: No Property in Man: Slavery and Antislavery at the Nation's Founding* (Cambridge, MA: Harvard University Press, 2019).

7 The attack on the reconstruction governments and the emergence of legalized apartheid in the South thereafter see, among much else, David Blight, *Race and Reunion: The Civil War in American Memory* (Cambridge, MA: Harvard University Press, 2001); W.E.B. Du Bois, *Black Reconstruction in America* (New York, 1935); Eric Foner, *Reconstruction: America's Unfinished Revolution, 1863–1877* (New York: Harper and Row, 1988); C. Vann Woodward, *The Strange Career of Jim Crow* (New York: Oxford University Press, 2002 [1966]).

8 David Nirenberg, *Anti-Judaism: The Western Tradition* (New York: W.W. Norton, 2013); and his "Was There Race Before Modernity? The Example of 'Jewish' Blook in Late Medieval Spain," in Miriam Eliav-Feldon, Benjamin Isaac, and Joseph Ziegler, eds., *The Origins of Racism in the West* (Cambridge: Cambridge University Press, 2009); Leon Poliakov, "The Cult of the Purity of Blood, or Iberian Racism," in his *The History of Antisemitism: From Mohammed to the Marranos*, trans. Natalie Gerardi (Paris: Calmann-Lévy, 1961; Philadelphia: University of Pennsylvania, 2003), 222–232; Benzion Netanyahu, "The Rise of Racism," in his *The Origins of the Inquisition in Fifteenth Century Spain* (New York: Random House, 1995), 975–1004.

9 Winthrop Jordan, *White over Black: American Attitudes toward the Negro, 1550–1812* (New York: W.W. Norton, 1968).

10 Notably, George Mosse, *Toward the Final Solution: A History of European Racism* (New York: Howard Fertig, 1978). I have commented on Mosse's crucial impact on historical scholarship. See Jeffrey Herf "George Mosse's Recasting of European Intellectual and Cultural History," *German Politics and Society* 18, 4 (Winter 2000), 18–29; "The Historian as Provocateur: George Mosse's Accomplishment and Legacy," *Yad Vashem Studies*, XXIX (2001), 7–26; and "Reflections on George Mosse's Work on Antisemitism," forthcoming in *Antisemitism Studies*, 2023.

11 See, for example, George Mosse, *Towards the Final Solution*. Also see Michael Burleigh and Wolfgang Wippermann, *The Racial State: Germany 1933–1945* (New York: Cambridge University Press, 1991); Benno Müller-Hill, *Murderous Science: Elimination by Scientific Selection of Jews, Gypsies and Others, 1933–1945*, trans. George Fraser (New York: Oxford University Press, 1988); Alan Steinweis, *Studying the Jew: Scholarly Antisemitism in Nazi Germany* (Cambridge, MA: Harvard University Press, 2006).

12 Saul Friedlander, *Nazi Germany and the Jews, vol. 1: The Years of Persecution* (New York: Harper Collins, 1997), 152–153.

13 James Whitman, *Hitler's American Model: The United States and the Making of Nazi Race Law* (Princeton, NJ: Princeton University Press, 2017).

14 Sander L. Gilman, *The Jew's Body* (New York: Routledge, 1991).

15 The evolution from antisemitism based on Christian religious traditions to that of modern racial antisemitism is a large topic that extends beyond the bounds of this paper. See Robert Chazan, *Medieval Stereotypes and Modern Antisemitism* (Berkeley: University of California Press, 1997); Susannah Heschel, *Transforming Jesus from Jew to Aryan: Protestant Theologians in Nazi Germany* (Tucson: University of Arizona, 1995); and Friedlander, *Nazi Germany and the Jews, Vol. 1*; John Weiss, *The Ideology of Death: Why the Holocaust Happened in Germany* (Chicago, IL: Ivan Dee, 1996).

16 On the role of doctors in the murders of the mentally ill and its significance for the Holocaust, see Henry Friedlander, *The Origins of Nazi Genocide: From Euthanasia to the Final Solution* (Chapel Hill: University of North Carolina, 1995).

17 Saul Friedlander, *Nazi Germany, and the Jews: Volume I, The Years of Persecution, 1933–1939* (New York: Harper Collins, 1997), 145–176. Also see Saul Friedlander, *Nazi Germany and the Jews: The Years of Extermination* (New York: Harper Collins, 2007).

18 George Mosse, *The Crisis of German Ideology* (New York: Grosset and Dunlap, 1964; Howard Fertig, 1998); Fritz Stern, *The Politics of Cultural Despair* (New York: Anchor Books, 1964); Saul Friedlander, *Nazi Germany and the Jews;* Helmut Plessner, *Die Verspätete Nation* (Frankfurt/Main: Suhrkamp, 1964); Jeffrey Herf, *Reactionary Modernism: Technology, Culture and Politics in Weimar and the Third Reich* (New York and Cambridge: Cambridge University Press, 1984); Walter Laqueur, *The Changing Face of Anti-Semitism: From Ancient Times to the Present Day* (New York: Oxford University Press, 2006).

19 Jeffrey Herf, *The Jewish Enemy: Nazi Propaganda During World War II and the Holocaust* (Cambridge, MA: Harvard University Press, 2006).

20 Norman Cohn, *Warrant for Genocide: The Myth of the Jewish World Conspiracy and the Protocols of the Elders of Zion* (New York: Harper and Row, 1967). The scholarship on antisemitism in Russia in the era of pogroms is extensive. On its emergence and opposition to it, recently see Laura Engelstein, *The Resistable Rise of Antisemitism: Exemplary Cases from Russia, Ukraine, and Poland* (Waltham, MA: Brandeis University Press, 2020); and Steven Zipperstein, *Pogrom: Kishinev and the Tilt of History* (New York and London: W.W. Norton, 2018).

21 My view draws both on Christopher Browning's "Beyond 'Intentionalism' and 'Functionalism': The Decision for the Final Solution Reconsidered," in *The Path to Genocide: Essays on the Launching of the Final Solution* (New York: Cambridge University Press, 1992), 86–121, as well as Richard Breitman, *The Architect of Genocide: Himmler and the Final Solution* (Hannover and London: Brandeis University Press, 1991).

22 On these methodological issues see Francois Furet, *Interpreting the French Revolution*, trans. Elborg Forster (New York: Cambridge University Press, 1981).

23 Lucy S. Dawidowicz, *The War Against the Jews: 1933–1945* (New York: Holt, Rinehart and Winston, 1975). Also, see On Dawidowicz, see Nancy Sinkoff, *From Left to Right: Lucy S. Dawidowicz: The New York Intellectuals and the Politics of Jewish History* (Detroit: Wayne State University Press, 2020).

24 Saul Friedlander has implicitly stressed this distinction. See his *Nazi Germany and the Jews, Vol. 1: The Years of Persecution, 1933–1939* (New York: HarperCollins, 1997).

25 Victor Klemperer (July 20, 1944), *I Will Bear Witness, 1942–1945*, trans. Martin Chalmers (New York: Knopf, 2000), 335; and Victor Klemperer, *Tagebücher 1944* (20. Juli 1944) (Berlin: Aufbau Verlag, 1995), 85.

26 On paranoia and Nazi wartime propaganda, see E. H. Gombrich, *Myth and Reality in German War-Time Broadcasts* (London: The Athlone Press, 1970). On paranoid politics among the Jacobins in the French Revolution see Francois Furet, *Interpreting the French Revolution*, trans. Elbourg Forster (New York: Cambridge University Press, 1981); and in American politics see Richard Hofstadter, *The Paranoid Style in American Politics and Other Essays* (New York: Knopf, 1965; reprint ed. Cambridge, MA: Harvard University Press, 1996); and the discussion of antisemitism and paranoia in Max Horkheimer and Theodor Adorno, *The Dialectic of Enlightenment*, 1944 trans. John Cumming (New York: Herder and Herder, 1972; orig. 1944), 187–200.

27 Joseph Goebbels, "*Mimikry*," July 20, 1941, in Goebbels, *Die Zeit ohne Beispiel: Reden und Aufsätze aus den Jahren 1939/40/41* (Munich: Zentralverlag der NSDAP, 1941), 526–531.

28 On German colonialism in Africa, and Nazi policy in Eastern Europe, see Shelley Baranowski, *Nazi Empire: German Colonialism and Imperialism from Bismarck to Hitler* (New York and Cambridge: Cambridge University Press, 2011); Robert Gerwarth and Stephan Malinowski, "Hannah Arendt's Ghosts: Reflections on the Disputable Path from Windhoek to Auschwitz," *Central European History* 42, 2 (June 2009), 279–300; Wendy Lower, *Nazi Empire Building and the Holocaust in the Ukraine* (Chapel Hill: University of North Carolina, 2005); Jürgen Zimmerer, *Deutsche Herrschaft über Afrikaner: Staatlicher Machtanspruch und Wirklichkeit im kolonialen Namibia* (Munster: Lit, 2004).

29 On this see Ian Kershaw, *Hitler 1936–1945: Nemesis* (New York: Norton, 2000); and Jan Gross, *Polish Society under German Occupation: The General Gourvernment, 1939–1944* (Princeton, NJ: Princeton University Press, 1979).

30 Ulrich Herbert, *Hitler's Foreign Workers: Enforced Foreign Labor under the Third Reich*, trans. William Templer (New York: Cambridge University Press, 1997); and ed. *National Socialist Extermination Policies: Contemporary German Policies and Perspectives* (New York: Berghahn Books, 2000).

31 Adam Tooze, "Labor, Food, and Genocide," in his *Wages of Destruction: The Making and Breaking of the Nazi Economy* (London: Allan Lane/Penguin, 2006), 513–551; Michael Burleigh, *The Third Reich: A New History* (New York: Hill and Wang, 2000), 479.

32 Kershaw, *Hitler*, 713.

33 Christian Gerlach, *Kalkulierte Morde: die deutsche Wirtschafts- und Vernichtungspolitik in Weissrussland, 1941–1944* (Hamburg: Hamburger Edition, 1999).

34 Franz Neumann, *The Structure and Practice of National Socialism* (New York: Oxford U.P., 1944; reprint, Ivan Dee, 2009); and Walter Ulbricht, *Der Faschistische Deutsche Imperialismus* (1933–1945), also as *Die Legende vom 'deutschen Sozialismus*, 4th ed. (Berlin: Dietz Verlag, 1956).

35 Karl Dietrich Bracher, "The Role of Hitler: Perspectives of Interpretation," in Walter Laqueur, ed., *Fascism: A Reader's Guide* (Berkeley: University of California Press, 1976), 213. Also see his classic and still essential, *The German Dictatorship* (New York: Praeger, 1970); and his essays in *Zeitgeshichtliche Kontroversen: Um Faschismus, Totalitarismus, Demokratie* (Munich: Piper Verlag, 1976).

36 However, in recent decades, economic historians of the Nazi regime have acknowledged the central role of ideology. See Peter Hayes, *Industry and Ideology: I.G. Farben in the Third Reich* (New York and Cambridge: Cambridge University Press, 2000); and Adam Tooze, *The Wages of Destruction: The Making and*

Breaking of the Nazi Economy (New York and London: Allen Lane/Penguin, 2006), xxv–xxvi.

37 Michael Rothberg, *Multidirectional Memory: Remembering the Holocaust in an Age of Decolonization* (Stanford, CA: Stanford U.P., 2009). Also see Aime Cesaire, *Discourse on Colonialism* (New York: Monthly Review, 2001). While Rothberg favors "noncompetitive" memory, he does not engage either the scholarship on the history of antisemitism and the form it took in Nazi Germany or the extensive postwar discussions of the Holocaust in West Germany. There is no entry for "antisemitism," "anti-Judaism," or "Jew-hatred" in his index.

38 Dirk Moses, *The Problems of Genocide: Permanent Security and the Language of Transition* (Cambridge: Cambridge University Press, 2021).

39 Aime Cesaire, *Discourse on Colonialism* (New York: Monthly Review Press, 2001).

40 On the emergence of hatred of Judaism and the Jews as a form of racism, see "Book Four: The Origins of the Inquisition," in Benzion Netanyahu, ed., *The Origins of the Inquisition in Fifteenth Century Spain* (New York: Random House, 1995), 925–1092.

41 On the emergence of hatred of Judaism and the Jews as a form of racism, see "Book Four: The Origins of the Inquisition," in Benzion Netanyahu, ed., *The Origins of the Inquisition in Fifteenth Century Spain* (New York: Random House, 1995), 925–1092. In the long term in the Western traditions of Christianity, secular antisemitism and, in Islam (also a Western tradition), see David Nirenberg, *Anti-Judaism: The Western Tradition* (New York: W.W. Norton, 2014).

42 Jeffrey Herf, "The Long Term and the Short Term: Antisemitism and the Holocaust," in Robert Williams, James Wald, and Mark Weitzman, eds., *The Routledge History of Antisemitism* (New York and London: Routledge, 2023), 277–283.

10

ANTISEMITIC CONSPIRACIES YET AGAIN

White Racism, Holocaust Denial, and Ideological Assaults on Israel

In the May 2021 issue of the London journal *The Jewish Quarterly*, Deborah Lipstadt, then Professor of Modern Jewish History at Emory University known for her publications on Holocaust denial and for challenging Holocaust deniers such as David Irving, published "White Insurrections: Antisemitism in America."[1] In the summer of 2021, President Biden nominated her to be the U.S. State Department's Special Envoy to Monitor and Combat Antisemitism. In March 2022, the U.S. Senate confirmed the nomination.[2] The editors of *The Jewish Quarterly* asked me to respond to "White Insurrections" and to its arguments concerning the connection between antisemitism and white racism. The following draws on my reply, published in *The Jewish Quarterly* of August 2021.[3]

Deborah Lipstadt's "White insurrection" draws attention to the significant role that antisemitism plays in contemporary right-wing extremism and its bizarre but important connection to white racism. In Charlottesville in August 2017, the American Press was perplexed that demonstrators opposed to dismantling monuments to Confederate leaders chanted "Jews will not replace us" and used torches reminiscent of Nazi parades as they marched past a synagogue.[4] Lipstadt's important essay explores the connection between these two hatreds and presents the thesis that "antisemitism is the ideological foundation stone of the far right's racism." It is a challenge to the notion, voiced on American campuses in recent years, that Jews who raise the issue of antisemitism do so as an expression of their "white privilege" and as a Zionist tactic to deflect criticism of Israel. Yet, to establish her theory more firmly, additional historical perspective is required.

For most of their histories, antisemitism and white supremacy constituted distinct and causally unrelated cultural traditions, each with its own

DOI: 10.4324/9781003449669-11

autonomous history and cultural components. Beyond the obvious fact that hatred of "others" reinforces xenophobia and prejudice, neither formed an ideological foundation for the other. Racism toward peoples of color and the belief in a connection between skin color and intellectual inferiority—whether in the United States or in Britain and the European colonial powers—had multiple causes unrelated to the traditions of antisemitism.[5] Likewise, the radical antisemitism of the Holocaust did not have origins in racism towards peoples of color, or in the practices of German and European colonialism in Africa.[6] Rather, before and during the Holocaust, antisemitism was part of a Western—first religious, then secular—tradition that was distinct from racism based on skin color.[7] Lipstadt argues that in recent years, and for the first time, antisemitism offers an ideological foundation for white racism.

Lipstadt's "White insurrection" essay suggests the following hypothesis: The distinguishing feature of radical antisemitism before, during, and since the Holocaust is a paranoid conspiracy theory that depicts first the Jews, and then the state of Israel, as powerful and evil, and engaged in efforts to dominate world politics in order to bring harm to millions of non-Jews.[8] Those who apply this paranoid scheme to American history begin with the fact that American Jews and Jewish organizations and leaders, to an extent far greater than Americans of other religious denominations, and other white Americans, supported African-American efforts to overcome the legacy of white racism. Jews are the only ethnic group among white Americans who have, in their considerable majority, voted for the Democratic Party, especially as the Republican Party adopted the "Southern strategy" and increasingly became a party articulating the grievances of white voters.

White racists link black skin to intellectual and moral inferiority. They refuse to attribute the advance of African Americans into the professional middle classes, to elective offices, and then Barack Obama's election as president, to the merits and qualifications of the individuals concerned. The political rise of Donald Trump, fueled by Trump's lies about Obama's birth certificate, illustrated the appeal of such racist convictions. Right-wing antisemites interpreted the broad Jewish support for Obama as evidence in support of their view that "the Jews," conspiratorially operating behind the scenes, were responsible for this, in their view, otherwise inexplicable, and threatening, African-American advance.

This intersectional, causal link connected antisemitic images of powerful and evil Jews with racist convictions about Black inferiority. The antisemitic interpretation of black advance links the presumed unity of Jewish power and evil with the bundle of ideas that justified slavery and segregation. Trying to explain why the Allies were at war with Nazi Germany, Nazi propaganda minister Joseph Goebbels screamed that "the Jews are guilty." For the Nazis, antisemitism explained the inexplicable alliance of the Britain and the United States with the Soviet Union. Lipstadt's right-wing ideologues find that "the

Jews are guilty" of something else altogether—the fact that African Americans have made significant social, economic, and political advances in the last seventy years, that Hispanic and Asian immigration has expanded in recent decades, and that the United States has become an increasingly multi-ethnic and multi-racial democracy.

For its advocates, this antisemitic interpretation of recent history solves the riddle of African-American advance and offers a simple explanation to account for immigration flows around the world. It, again, personalizes and locates a "perpetrator," an identifiable set of persons, who can be "held responsible" for complex economic and social developments. It is the Jews who are "guilty" yet again and who, in programs such as affirmative action, and defending rights to asylum, have "betrayed" whites by seeking to "replace" white men especially, from their accustomed positions of power or privilege. The political implication of this paranoid fantasy is that violent attacks on Jews and Jewish institutions are necessary because, without the sinister power of the Jews, Black Americans would be restored to the unequal status of second-class citizenship that racists believe should be and is the natural order of things, and immigrants fleeing persecution would somehow be prevented from arriving in the United States. The Lipstadt thesis is a starting point for further examination of these sensitive and crucial issues. It draws our attention to what seems at first a paradox. The clear implication of "White insurrection" is that to fight against white racism, we need also to fight against what has in recent years become one of its ideological foundations, antisemitism, and its conspiracy theories about sinister Jewish power.

Holocaust denial, that is, assertions that it either did not happen or that Jews have vastly exaggerated the numbers of those murdered, became an important element of antisemitism after the Holocaust. Lipstadt and other scholars writing about Holocaust denial have addressed the conspiratorial elements that have been and remain central to repetition of its falsehoods.[9] Richard Evans examined the right-wing extremist forms in the work of David Irving.[10] Valerie Igounet and Elhanan Yakira have analyzed the bizarre meeting of the minds of left-wing and right-wing conspiracy theorists and Holocaust deniers in France.[11] Meir Litvak and Esther Webman have examined Holocaust denial in Arab countries.[12] Litvak has pointed out that leaders of the Islamic Republic of Iran claim that Zionists used "the Holocaust myth" to solicit support for the establishment of the state of Israel.[13] In its various political forms and geographical locations, Holocaust deniers, both on the far left and far right, in Europe, Iran, and the Middle East dismiss the vast evidence produced at the Nuremberg and other war crimes trials as victor's justice, assert that the state of Israel and its Jewish enablers in other countries has spread the "hoax" about the murder of six million Jews in Europe in order to extort millions of dollars in undeserved restitution funds.

These forms of Holocaust denial impute to Jews and to Israel a conspiracy of great power and evil which spreads a lie for the purpose of financial gain and political power. In doing so, these assertions recycle core elements of the same antisemitic conspiracies that were central to the ideological justifications that the Nazi leaders offered during the years of extermination of European Jewry. Holocaust denial found advocates in the Arab states and with particular importance in the Islamic Republic of Iran. In the process, it contributed to the fusion of antisemitism and anti-Zionism.[14] As Robert Wistrich argued, when pushed to its logical extreme, the imputation of such conspiracy theories to the state of Israel leads to "Holocaust inversion," that is, the assertion that the spreading of such lies for financial gain and political interest is just one of the sins of the Jewish state that justify comparing it to Nazi Germany. Wistrich points out that such "inversion" and its resulting ideological transformation of Nazism's primary victims into the powerful and evil perpetrator of the state of Israel serves as a second warrant for genocide.[15]

Notes

Selection taken from "Response to Deborah Lipstadt's 'White Insurrections," *The Jewish Quarterly* (August 2021), 101–103. Reprinted with permission of the publisher (https://jewishquarterly.com/).

1 Deborah Lipstadt, "White Insurrections: Antisemitism in America," *The Jewish Quarterly* 244 (May 2021), 53–66. Also see Deborah Lipstadt, *Antisemitism: Here and Now* (New York: Schocken, 2019).

2 On her position as Ambassador in the State Department, see https://www.state.gov/biographies/deborah-lipstadt/.

3 Jeffrey Herf, "Correspondence," *The Jewish Quarterly* 245 (August 2021), 101–103.

4 Jeffrey Herf, "Lessons from German History After Charlottesville," *History News Network* (September 10, 2017), https://historynewsnetwork.org/article/166864.

5 An adequate discussion of the origins of racism lies beyond this comment. It should be kept in mind that the view of Jews as a "race" linked to biology began in the religiously inspired persecution of the Spanish Inquisition. This "racist" linkage of biology to character was then later applied to persons of color.

6 The claim that the Holocaust was a transfer of the violence of colonialism back to Europe was first made by Aime Cesaire's in his 1950 and 1955 work *Discourse on Colonialism* (New York: Monthly Review Press, 2001). In recent years, the connection between German colonialism in Africa, and the Holocaust became a topic of debate in Germany. Shelly Baranowski, *Nazi Empire: German Colonialism and Imperialism from Bismarck to Hitler* (New York and Cambridge: Cambridge University Press, 2010) for a judicious assessment of these issues.

7 From the large literature, see David Nirenberg, *Anti-Judaism: The Western Tradition* (New York: W.W. Norton, 2013).

8 On the Nazis' radical antisemitism that accompanied and offered their justification for the Holocaust, see Jeffrey Herf, *The Jewish Enemy: Nazi Propaganda during World War II and the Holocaust* (Cambridge, MA: Harvard University Press, 2006). On subsequent conspiracy theories about Israel, see essays by Robert Wistrich, Meir Litvak, and Deborah Lipstadt in Anthony McElligott and Jeffery Herf,

eds., *Antisemitism Before and Since the Holocaust* (London: Palgrave/Macmillan, 2017).

9 See Deborah Lipstadt, *Denying the Holocaust: The Growing Assault on Truth and Memory* (New York: Plume, 1994); and her "A Few Observations on Holocaust Denial and Antisemitism," 23–36.

10 Richard Evans, *Lying About Hitler* (New York: Basic Books, 2002).

11 Valerie Igounet, *Histoire du négationisme en France* (Paris: Seuil, 2000); Elhanan Yakira, *Post-Holocaust, Post-Zionism: Three Essays on Denial, Forgetting and the Delegitimation of Israel* (New York and Cambridge: Cambridge University Press, 2009); and his "Five Reflections on Holocaust Denial, Old and New Forms of Hatred of Jews and the Delegitimation of Israel," in Anthony McElligott and Jeffrey Herf, eds., *Antisemitism Before and Since the Holocaust: Altered Contexts and Recent Perspectives*, 335–352.

12 On denial in Arab countries, see Meir Litvak and Esther Webman, "Denial of the Holocaust," *From Empathy to Denial* (London: Hurst, 2009), 155–192.

13 Meir Litvak, "The Islamic Republic of Iran and the Holocaust: Anti-Semitism and Anti-Zionism," in Jeffrey Herf, ed., *Anti-Semitism and Anti-Zionism in Historical Perspective: Convergence and Divergence* (London and New York: Routledge/ Taylor and France, 2007), 250–267; and his "Iranian Antisemitism and the Holocaust," in McElligott and Herf, eds., *Antisemitism Before and Since the Holocaust*, 205–230.

14 On this see Richard Evans, *Lying About Hitler* (New York: Basic Books, 2002); Valérie Igounet, *Histoire du négationism en France* (Paris: Seuil, 2000); and Elhanan Yakira, *Post-Zionism, Post-Holocaust: Three Essays on Denial, Forgetting, and the Delegitimation of Israel* (New York and Cambridge: Cambridge University Press, 2009); Meir Litvak, "Iranian Antisemitism and the Holocaust,"; and Elhanan Yakira, "Five Reflections on Holocaust Denial, Old and New Forms of Hatred of Jews and the Delegitimation of Israel," in Anthony McElligott and Jeffery Herf, eds., *Antisemitism Before and Since the Holocaust: Altered Contexts and Recent Perspectives* (London: Palgrave Macmillan, 2017), 23–36, 205–230, and 335–352.

15 Robert Solomon Wistrich, "Antisemitism and Holocaust Inversion," in McElligott and Herf, eds., *Antisemitism Before and Since the Holocaust*, 37–49; and his "Lying About the Holocaust," *A Lethal Obsession*, 631–661. On Iran's nuclear program and its antisemitism, see Jeffrey Herf, "What Does Coming to Terms with the Past Mean in the Berlin Republic in 2007," *Telos* (February 4, 2008): https://www.telospress.com/what-does-coming-to-terms-with-the-pastmean-in-the-berlin-republic-in-2007/; and *Dissent/Democratiya* (Spring 2008): https:// www.dissentmagazine.org/democratiya_article/what-does-coming-to-terms-with-the-past-mean-in-the-berlin-republic-in-2007.

Essays on Antisemitism and Contemporary History Since September 11, 2001

To work, as I have for decades, on the history modern German history, including the era of Nazism and the Holocaust, fosters awareness that what happened once, can happen again, albeit in different forms. Genocides and gross violations of human rights did not stop with the defeat of the Nazis in 1945. As Theodor Adorno wrote, the purpose of education after Auschwitz is to see that "it," namely an effort yet again to exterminate the Jews or anyone else, must never reoccur. In addition to my work as a historian, I have written essays on contemporary events, including on the simultaneous resurgence of antisemitism's three faces in recent years. In so doing, I have tried to challenge the polarization of our intellectual and scholarly life that too often stands in the way of exploring antisemitism not only in its most familiar and famous form, that of the Nazis but also when it has emerged from the radical left, and from Islamists.

DOI: 10.4324/9781003449669-12

11

WHAT IS OLD AND WHAT IS NEW IN THE TERRORISM OF ISLAMIC FUNDAMENTALISM?[1]

This essay draws on remarks delivered at a faculty-student forum about 9/11 on October 8, 2001, at the University of Maryland, College Park.

Mass murder inspired by Islamist fundamentalism and fanaticism differs from the secular totalitarian ideologies and regimes of Europe's twentieth century: fascism and Nazism, on the one hand, and Communism, especially in the Stalin era, on the other. Like the twentieth-century totalitarians, today's Islamic fundamentalist fanatics are convinced that they possess the absolute "Truth" which is immune to refutation or criticism. And, like the reactionary modernists of the 1930s and 1940s, they despise Western modernity yet borrow its technological accomplishments in an effort to destroy it. They believe that force and terror are necessary to establish a utopia in place of the current decadent and corrupt world, and they explain history on the basis of a conspiratorial construct in which the United States, more than "international Jewry" or global capitalism, plays the central role.

Unlike the followers of the past century's secular religions, today's terrorists draw inspiration from an apocalyptic vision rooted in religious radicalism. Osama bin Laden and al Qaeda emerge in a global political culture in which elements of leftist anti-globalization discourse and reruns of fascist and Nazi visions of Jewish conspiracies merge with religious passions. Because al Qaeda knows how to speak the language of leftist anti-imperialism of the past century, it suggests a mood that overlaps with secular third-world radicalism. Yet in crucial matters, such as its view of death and suicide and its stance on rationality, it appears closer to the fascist and Nazi philosophy than to the Communist past. The stand-off with Soviet Communism ended in the peaceful revolutions of 1989–1990, and then the implosion of the Soviet empire and union. Yet, as was the case with the defeat of fascism and

DOI: 10.4324/9781003449669-13

Nazism, the only way the threat of terrorism inspired by radical Islam can end is through its military defeat.

By terrorism, I meant the intentional murder or attempted murder of any person, civilian or military, man, woman, or child, old or young, who is not engaged in military combat. In this sense, civilian deaths caused by stray bombs and missiles or preemptive killings of those who are actively engaged in acts of terror, neither of which intentionally target the innocent, are not acts of terrorism. In the modern European context, terrorism is rooted both in the Jacobin and Communist traditions, on the one hand, and in the fascist and Nazi movements and regimes, on the other. At all times and in all places in modern European history, terrorism's many targets have always included a frontal attack on the institutions and principles of liberal democracy, which rests on the principle that all conflicts should be resolved by discussion, debate, and compromise. Terrorists, however, believe they are in possession of absolute truths and thus have the right and obligation to kill those who disagree with them and who stand in their way. In every instance, terrorists are persons with an ideological rationale that facilitates murdering the innocent with a clean conscience fueled by self-righteous indignation. In many cases, their targets have been political leaders who sought compromise or nonviolent solutions to complex problems.

The emergence of terrorism during the French Revolution represented a regression to the normal practice of war during the wars of religion in the seventeenth century. During the Thirty Years War, Europeans did not distinguish between combatants and civilians but between believers and apostates, Protestants and Catholics. The resulting devastation led to efforts to codify rules of war that would establish such distinctions, put limits on war and political violence, and establish in the Treaty of Westphalia of 1648 the principle that peace required toleration of differing religious beliefs. The American Constitution rests in part on the bitter European recognition that civil peace required the separation of religion from the state. By inventing the new category of "enemy of the people" during the French Revolution, the Jacobins again blurred the distinction between combatant and noncombatant and gave renewed justification to murder as a political weapon. Since the Jacobins, terror has remained an important component of European history when Left/Right and nationalist tensions reached a boiling point.

Terrorism in modern Europe has been the practice of those who believe that reform and diplomacy are undesirable. As Georges Sorel argued in *Reflections on Violence* (a work that influenced the subsequent apostle of the virtues of violence, Frantz Fanon), violence has an extra-political dimension in supposedly invigorating otherwise sleeping oppressed classes and shattering the complacency of bourgeois society. Apologists for terrorism suggest that it is the result of conditions of social injustice. Violence in the Sorelian tradition is a response to the growing success of working-class integration in Europe and the popularity of peaceful reformism as opposed to revolutionary sentiment within the working classes. Terrorists have repeatedly attacked those who seek to find negotiated and non-catastrophic solutions to difficult problems. The assassination of the Austrian Archduke Ferdinand in June 1914 by the Serbian terrorist Gavrilo Princip, which was the immediate but not deeper cause of World War I, illustrates this enduring feature of terrorism. Ferdinand was among those in the Hapsburg Empire who sought a negotiated solution to the dilemma of nationalism within a multinational empire. Hence, it was the key to murder him in order to rule out all but the most radical possibilities.

Probably, the single most consequential assassination of recent history was the murder of Israeli Prime Minister Yitzhak Rabin by a right-wing Israeli religious fundamentalist. Rabin's murder, as well as the earlier murder of Anwar Sadat by precursors of the al Qaeda terrorists in Egypt, illustrate that the terrorists' traditional preference for apocalypse and destruction in place of diplomacy, compromise, and reform has become a sad fixture in the Middle East as well. Through the delivery of violent and apocalyptic shocks to the world of reason and discussion, terrorists hope that it will retaliate in new waves of repression and/or simply collapse under the weight of tragedy. Should it strike out in rage, as the Austrians did in August 1914, the repression will, according to the terrorists, radicalize the masses, leading to further war and violence and the eventual overthrow of the existing order. In Western Europe and Japan in the 1970s and 1980s, this terrorist tradition continued in the hopes that by revealing the "fascist" core behind the "illusions" of liberal democracy, a revolutionary apocalypse would ensue.

Terrorism's murderous hostility to reform must be kept in mind to understand the atrocities of September 11, 2001. Like the murderers of Sadat and Rabin, the al Qaeda planners, following the policies of their counterparts in Hamas and Hezbollah, began their planning in the period in which the labor government of Ehud Barak in Israel was making unprecedented offers of a Palestinian state to Arafat's PLO (Palestine Liberation Organization) in the context of the Oslo Peace process. A negotiated settlement to the IsraeliPalestinian conflict would have been a devastating blow to Islamic fundamentalists. It would lend Arab legitimacy to the very existence of the Jewish state in the Middle East, something which Islamic fundamentalists find intolerable. Osama bin Laden and al Qaeda propagandists claim that Israel's occupation of the West Bank and Gaza is one source of the attacks of September 11th. Yet, like European and Middle Eastern predecessors, bin Laden and al Qaeda launched the attacks to further undermine any efforts at a negotiated peace in the Israeli-Palestinian conflict.

Another possible political rationale recalls the apocalyptic scenarios that Sorel envisaged and links the mass murder of September 11th to past terrorist practices. Islamists hoped that the United States would indeed treat this as a "clash of civilizations," denounce Islam in general, launch indiscriminate attacks on Arab populations, and thus generate a massive Islamic uprising in nuclear-armed Pakistan and in oil-rich Saudi Arabia. Then, with oil, nuclear arms, and ideological fanaticism, Islamic radicalism could finally emerge as a major player on the world stage to challenge and then attack the "Great Satan"—the United States. Just as World War I ushered in Europe's decline and the Soviet invasion of Afghanistan preceded the implosion of the Soviet Union, a massive and monstrous attack on New York's symbol of world capitalism, democracy, female emancipation, homosexuality, and the Jews would hopefully lead the enraged United States to strike out wildly and indiscriminately. In the short run, this expectation has met with disappointment, though clearly the prospect of instability in the region is a long-term concern. Yet, along with this crazed "rationale," we should keep in mind that, as Dostoevsky understood so well in *The Demons*, at the core of every terrorist movement lurks the nihilistic pleasure in destruction. Bin Laden's celebratory statements following the attacks of September 11th stand in a long line of terrorist exultation over death and destruction.

Such arguments played a key role in the development of fascism and Nazism. Both Mussolini and Hitler were able to combine respectability with brute force on the path to power. The intellectual and cultural atmosphere in which fascism and Nazism emerged in the first third of the century, one shaped by Sorel's *Reflections on Violence*, Friedrich Nietzsche's denunciation of a complacent European middle class and its rationality, Ernst Jünger's ecstatic celebrations of the masculine male community of the trenches in World War I, as well as the violence of the Great War itself created a critical mass of angry, middle and lower-middle-class men for whom the distinction between war and politics blurred to insignificance. Like many of the terrorists in al Qaeda, un- and underemployed "intellectuals" and youth of the professional middle classes in post-World War I Europe were attracted to fascism and Nazism in the belief that a violent assault on liberal democracy and bourgeois society by a new movement of hard and disciplined heroes would replace the decadent present with a vital future.

The Holocaust stands as the ultimate act of terror of the twentieth century, the pristine case of the murder of innocents on a vast scale. In the fevered Nazi imagination, the Jews of Europe and the world were not innocents at all. Instead, they were members of a giant global conspiracy which was always referred to by a singular noun: "international Jewry." This vast, unseen yet all-powerful group was, in the Nazis' view, responsible for all of Germany's misfortunes: the loss of World War I and the Versailles Treaty, the Great Depression, and the threat from the East of what Hitler called "Jewish Bolshevism" or "the Mongol storm." Hence, mass murder, far from constituting an unprovoked act against a defenseless civilian population, was merely one front in Germany's fully justified war of defense and retaliation against the supposed previous acts of Jewish aggression. This was a lunatic explanation that had no relation to actual events; nevertheless, millions of Germans came to believe it. Today, in the fevered imagination of Islamic fundamentalists, the United States and Israel—what bin Laden calls the "Zionist-Crusader alliance"—have replaced this older conspiracy theory, though clearly there are elements of continuity in the lasting importance of the United States, capitalism, and the Jews as leaders of the conspiracy. As in the 1930s and 1940s, such conspiracy theories invariably lead to mass murder, for only if the powerful international conspiracy is crushed can an ideal world be brought into existence. Communism having been vanquished in 1989–1990, Islamic fundamentalism now focuses its rage on old and familiar targets, capitalism, and the Jews.

As noted earlier, despite the similarities of its language with that of the anti-imperialist Left of the past century, Islamic fundamentalist terror today is closer to the fascist and Nazi past than it is to Communism. (Saddam Hussein's Baath Party and the Iraqi regime have origins in French fascist ideologies of the 1930s, but that is a discussion for another time.) Twenty years ago, I described Nazism as a form of "reactionary modernism" in which a secular, fundamentalist movement embraced modern technology yet rejected Enlightenment modernity. Flying Boeing 757s loaded with fuel into the World Trade Center and the Pentagon is a terribly clear act of reactionary modernist rage. Just as fascism and Nazism were movements that emerged in societies challenged by rapid modernization and seeking to find a way to blend modernity with tradition, Islamic fundamentalism borrows the West's technology in order to destroy it.

A second similarity to the fascist and Nazi experience evident in Islamic fundamentalism today is contempt for women and rejection of their equality, a stance which exceeds, yet recalls, the exaggerated masculinity and backlash against female emancipation of the fascist and Nazi movements. Like the paramilitary organizations of fascist and Nazi street fighters of the 1920s and 1930s, the Islamic terrorist organizations are militant "brotherhoods." (Mohammed Atta, one of the hijackers who flew a plane into the World Trade Center, apparently left a request that no women attend his funeral.) Where fascism and Nazism sought to restore the position of women to their subordinate status before the advances made in the wake of World War I, the Islamic fundamentalist vision of the position of women regresses well beyond that point to Europe's premodern times. While Communism's economistic roots precluded an adequate understanding of the position of women in society, its declared support for women's equality stood in complete contrast to that of radical Islam. Indeed, from the Communist point of view, radical Islam must be regarded as counter-revolutionary and reactionary in the extreme.

Third, and most importantly, Islamic fundamentalism is closer to the fascist and Nazi traditions in its celebration of values which depart from

rationality. Marxism-Leninism was a doctrine whose erroneous interpretation of history, politics, and economics nevertheless contained elements of
rationality and possibilities of empirical assessment. Moreover, while Communists certainly fostered a cult of martyrdom, they did not make death a
virtue. The elements of rationality within Marxism-Leninism combined with
the self-interest associated with possession of the huge state of the Soviet
Union. As a result, Soviet leaders believed that they had more to lose than to
gain by unleashing a nuclear war with the United States. Because the Communists possessed this minimum of rationality, it was possible for the West
to arrive at a nuclear stalemate with Moscow for half a century. Nuclear
deterrence rested on the assumption that both players preferred survival to
self-destruction. Given Hitler's fundamental contempt for rationality and his
celebration of the will, combined with the paranoid structure of his interpretation of international politics, the chances that such a peaceful nuclear
stalemate could have been sustained with Nazi Germany for half a century
would have been far less likely. A Nazi leadership would have been far more
likely to go over the brink to war, even if that meant the nuclear devastation
of Nazi Germany.

However enamored Hitler and the Nazis were of an apocalyptic end, Nazism as an ideology celebrated the victory of the "master race," not its death
and revival in heavenly paradise; that is, it was a secular totalitarianism.
On the other hand, terrorists inspired by Islamic fundamentalism have an
attitude toward their own death which is quite different precisely because
it is inspired by a religious radicalism that envisages a heavenly paradise in
the next world. Radical Islam convinces its adherents that a martyr's death
is a prelude to this paradise. Their otherworldly visions clearly inspired the
murderers of September 11th just as they have inspired the hundred suicide
bombers who have attacked Israel since 1993, thirty in the past year. These
visions have a profound consequence for the future of world peace and security. Should a radical Islamic group or state come to possess weapons of
mass destruction (chemical, biological, or nuclear) and the means to deliver
them, there is no reason to assume that the prospect of nuclear retaliation by
the United States would deter war. This is so because, in their view, their own
death is a prelude to certain entry to a better life in the heavenly paradise
to come. For people with such belief, nuclear retaliation may be a blessing
rather than a threat.

Hence, as in World War II, we are in a race against time. However complex, long-term, and multi-faceted our assault on terrorism will be, it must
include, as the Bush administration has made clear, the military defeat of this
network. In contrast to the response of the authoritarian Austro-Hungarian
Empire to the assassination of June 1914 in Sarajevo, the United States is re-
sponding to the mass murder of September 11th as it should, namely by seeking to isolate the terrorists from the rest of the Islamic world, to underscore

that they have no solutions to any of the problems they mention, that the era in which they can kill others with impunity has come to an end, and that the democracies which they regard as decadent and weak are in fact capable of a judicious and powerful capacity to make a war which will end in their destruction. Terrorists in the twentieth century repeatedly made the error of assuming that liberal democracies were weak and vulnerable. Al Qaeda is making the same mistake of believing its own propaganda about our reluctance to fight and defeat them.

After World War II, European intellectuals turned away from the orgy of violence that prevailed from 1914 to 1945. This is evident in Albert Camus's *The Rebel* and in Jurgen Habermas's work on the priority of discussion over force. In the late 1970s and 1980s, another generation again turned away from the romance of revolution and cults of violence of the 1960s New Left. A key question of the months and years to come will be whether and to what extent the opinion-shaping elites of the Islamic world will offer a similar liberating discourse of disillusionment with ideological fanaticism and a realistic assessment of the values of reform and compromise. As the experience of twentieth-century Europe following the defeats of Nazism and Communism suggests, sobriety and common sense may very well be the consequence rather than the cause of the defeat of the fanatics and terrorists now claiming to speak for Islam. Regardless, it is important that in our country, intellectuals and scholars do what they can to eliminate the last pathetic shreds of legitimacy to the terrorist tradition that contributed to the crimes of September 11th in New York and Washington.

Notes

Jeffrey Herf, "What Is Old and What Is New in the Terrorism of Islamic Fundamentalism?" *Partisan Review* 69, 1 (Winter 2002), 25–31: *Partisan Review* Collection, Boston University Libraries, Howard Gotlieb Archival Research Center.

1 Jeffrey Herf, "What Is Old and What Is New in the Terrorism of Islamic Fundamentalism?" *Partisan Review* 69, 1 (Winter 2002), 25–31; reprinted in Murray Baumgarten, Peter Kenez and Bruce Thompson, eds., *Varieties of Antisemitism: History, Ideology, Discourse* (Newark: University of Delaware Press, 2009), 370–376. Also see Jeffrey Herf, "Reframing the Enemy after France's 9/11," *Times of Israel* (January 5, 2015): https://blogs.timesofisrael.com/reframing-the-enemy-after-frances-911/; and Herf, "Radical Islam, Euphemisms, and the Labor of Selective Tradition," *The American Interest* (June 27, 2016): https://www.the-american-interest.com/2016/06/27/radical-islam-euphemisms-and-the-labor-of-selective-tradition/.

12

WHY THEY FIGHT

Hamas' Too-Little-Known Fascist Charter[1]

Given all the ink spilled about the current Gaza War, and the innumerable tragic photos, it is strange that the Western press hasn't inquired into why one of the parties is fighting. That would be Hamas, of course; the turgid psychologizing about Israel's motives is quite familiar. But what about its Islamist enemy, penned up in a barren territory from which it launches rockets and digs tunnels under Israeli kibbutzim and kindergartens? Why was all that concrete poured into the ground as part of the offensive, instead of above ground as the foundation of schools, factories, and homes?

It's not exactly difficult to find out. Hamas published a "Covenant" of 36 articles on August 18, 1988, that details its aims and ideology precisely.[2] Its philosophy is rooted in the totalitarianism and radical antisemitism that has undergirded Islamism since its rise in the 1930s and 1940s. Far from moderating its core ideology, Hamas's seizure of power in 2007 gave it the opportunity to make policy based on its guiding goal—namely, the destruction of the state of Israel.[3] Yet even though the Covenant clearly presents the declaration of intent of a group now governing millions of people, it goes unnoticed by reporters, editors, and pundits who race to comment on Hamas' war with Israel. In 2017, the Hamas leadership accepted the idea of a Palestinian state within the boundaries that existed before 1967 but rejected recognition of Israel yet retained the core of the 1988 document.

There is no reason for ignorance about the basic text. The briefest Google search brings one to an English translation of the Covenant, provided by the Avalon Project of the Yale Law School over a decade ago.[4] Hamas has not fundamentally revised or modified the document, and the public statements of its leaders and its continued terror offensive against Israel provide clear evidence that the Hamas of 2014 remains inspired by the ideas expressed in

DOI: 10.4324/9781003449669-14

founding text. This should be every policymaker's, and every journalist's, first stop in their efforts to understand Hamas, and it is of utmost importance that they read the text itself, as any student of literature will tell you. There is no substitute; to understand a person one must read him in his/her own words, noting everything from the cadence and syntax to the allusions to key figures of his ideological tradition. The Gaza War of 2014 will be incomprehensible to anyone who refuses to take Hamas at its word—these words.

The Covenant's first words place it into the longer tradition that historians call "Islamism," that is, a distinct twentieth-century interpretation of the religion of Islam that emerged in the 1930s and 1940s in Egypt and Palestine. Islamism's key figures included the Nazi sympathizer Haj Amin-el Husseini, the founder of the Muslim Brotherhood, Hassan al-Banna, and the Brotherhood's leading ideologue of the 1950s and 1960s, Sayyid Qutb. According to them, Islam was an inherently anti-Jewish religion. Through selective quotations from the Koran and various commentaries, they claimed Islam's holiest book supported their racist and anti-Jewish views. The Islamists also opposed liberal democracy, celebrated terrorism, supported the Nazis during World War II, and have been the most implacable enemies of Zionism since long before Israel's founding in 1948.[5] The authors of the Hamas Covenant traced their origins to "the struggle against the Zionist invaders" in 1939, to the Muslim Brotherhood and its role in the 1948 war and to the "Jihad operations of the Moslem Brotherhood in 1968 and after." The Hamas Covenant is one variation of an Islamist tradition that also drives al Qaeda, Hezbollah, the government of Iran, Boko Haram in Nigeria, and, most recently, ISIS (Islamic State of Iraq and Syria). These terrorist organizations have fought one another at times, but they share the views that the religion of Islam is at its core hostile to the Jews and that the state of Israel should be destroyed by force.

The authors of this charter make their allegiance to Islamism clear from the outset, distinguishing themselves from other, secular, anti-Zionist groups. They cite Hassan al-Banna, the iconic founder of the Muslim Brotherhood in Egypt, who said, "Israel will exist and will continue to exist until Islam will obliterate it, just as it obliterated others before it." Furthermore, the Covenant claims that the destruction of Israel is a religious obligation—that is, for Muslims; it is a "response to Allah's command." In contrast to the secular radicalism of the Palestine Liberation Organization (PLO), the Covenant offered an unambiguously religious justification for hating Jews. While the PLO Charter of 1968 also called for the destruction of Israel by force, the eventual collapse of the Soviet bloc deprived it of its major arms supplier and military adviser, not to mention its champion at the United Nations. As secular anti-Zionism was losing its key support, the religious wave was cresting in the wake of the Iranian Revolution in 1979 and the failure of the secular anti-Zionists to destroy Israel.

Hamas, like all varieties of Islamist politics, dispensed with the PLO's dubious assertion that anti-Zionism was not identical to hatred of the Jews as Jews. On the contrary, the writers of the Covenant declare, "our struggle against the Jews is very great and very serious"—the ultimate goal, not merely a tactic. To Hamas, this cause is both great and serious because it is explicitly religious. The Covenant is a Manichean document; it divides politics into true or false, just or unjust, alternatives. It promises to remake the world in the name of Islam, which, it regrets, has been wrongly driven from public life. This is its slogan: "Allah is its target, the Prophet is its model, and the Koran is its constitution: Jihad is the path and death for the sake of Allah is the loftiest of its wishes." This celebration of martyrdom and death had been a key theme in Hassan al-Banna's writings and subsequently became a commonplace for Islamists.

Not only is it fighting the Jews themselves; Hamas is devoted to destroying their nation, Israel. It strives to "raise the banner of Allah over every inch of Palestine, for under the wing of Islam followers of all religions can coexist in security and safety with their lives, possession and rights are concerned." It goes without saying that no one, least of all the Jews, would take seriously Hamas' promise that all religions would "coexist" under Islam. The Arab nations expelled their Jewish populations after Israel's founding in 1948. But leaving aside its risible attempt at reassurance, this excerpt illustrates that from the outset Hamas sought to recover "every inch of Palestine," in other words, the entire state of Israel. The Covenant states, "the land of Palestine is an Islamic Waqf [an inalienable religious endowment of property] consecrated for future Moslem generations until Judgment Day. It, or any part of it, should not be squandered: it, or any part of it, should not be given up." For Hamas, a two-state solution that left any part of Israel intact would constitute religious apostasy.[6]

If you had any doubts about what the conquest would entail, the Covenant's Article 13 makes clear the political implications of these religious demands. Diplomatic efforts such as "peaceful solutions, initiatives and international conferences" are "in contradiction to the principles of the Islamic Resistance Movement." In fact, there is "no solution for the Palestinian question except through Jihad. Initiatives, proposals, and international conferences are a waste of time and vain endeavors." Nor, according to the document, can any individual Muslim abstain from warfare. Article 15 declares, "Jihad for the liberation of Palestine is an individual duty. In the face of the Jews' usurpation of Palestine, it is compulsory that the banner of Jihad be raised." Many anti-Zionist assaults have been bloody, but Hamas's distinctive contribution has been the theological sanction of violence.

Though Islamism owes a considerable debt to Nazism, the Hamas Covenant claims that it is *Israel* that is the equal of Nazi Germany. In Article

20, the authors write that they confront "a vicious enemy which acts in a way similar to Nazism, making no differentiation between man and women, between children and old people...."[7] "Israelis as Nazis" canard has been a staple of both secular and religious anti-Zionist propaganda since the 1960s. When secular anti-Zionists such as Nasser, Arafat, and Assad, Sr. spoke about global conspiracies against the Arabs, they attributed a mythical conspiracy against the Arabs to "U.S. imperialism" and its Israeli "spearhead"—echoing the propaganda of their patrons, the Soviets.[8] Indeed, the Hamas Covenant of 1988 notably replaced the Marxist-Leninist conspiracy theory of world politics with the classic antisemitic tropes of Nazism and European fascism, which the Islamists had absorbed when they collaborated with the Nazis during World War II. That influence is apparent in Article 22, which asserts that "supportive forces behind the enemy" have amassed great wealth:

> With their money, they took control of the world media, news agencies, the press, publishing houses, broadcasting stations, and others. With their money they stirred revolutions in various parts of the world with the purpose of achieving their interests and reaping the fruit therein. They were behind the French Revolution, the Communist revolution and most of the revolutions we heard and hear about, here and there. With their money, they formed secret societies, such as Freemason, Rotary Clubs, the Lions and others in different parts of the world for the purpose of sabotaging societies and achieving Zionist interests. With their money they were able to control imperialistic countries and instigate them to colonize many countries in order to enable them to exploit their resources and spread corruption there.[9]

The above paragraph of Article 22 evokes themes and phrases from Nazi Germany's anti-Jewish propaganda texts and broadcasts. Echoing not only the European, but also American, antisemites of the twentieth century, Hamas repeated the assertion that the Jews used their money to control both "the world media" and the established social order. At the same time, these Jewish scions of the status quo were "behind" the French and Communist revolutions—one of the European fascists' favorite theories during their heyday. In the same manner as their antisemitic predecessors, the authors of the Hamas Covenant claimed that the Jews "control imperialistic countries" and advocate colonization and exploitation of other nations. Notably, it is Israel that controls the United States in this account, a reversal of the Soviet-era anti-Zionist propaganda. This paranoid vision of powerful, wealthy, and evil Jews echoes such works as *The Protocols of the Elders of Zion*, Hitler's *Mein Kampf*, and the daily diet of Nazi newspapers and Arabic-language radio broadcast from Nazi Berlin by Arab collaborators.[10] The Covenant is so devoted to the fantasy that Jews engineer every world event that it blames the Jews for starting World War I:

> You may speak as much as you want about regional and world wars. They were behind World War I, when they were able to destroy the Islamic Caliphate, making financial gains and controlling resources. They obtained the Balfour Declaration, formed the League of Nations through which they could rule the world. They were behind World War II, through which they made huge financial gains by trading in armaments and paved the way for the establishment of their state. It was they who instigated the replacement of the League of Nations with the United Nations and the Security Council to enable them to rule the world through them. There is no war going on anywhere, without their having their finger in it.[11]

For anyone with the slightest knowledge of modern European history and the causes of World War I, the assertion that the Jews, a stateless minority scattered among many nations of Europe, had anything at all to do with its outbreak is preposterous. Moreover, it is a depressing confirmation of the intellectual backwardness and historical ignorance of the authors of this document and of the Muslim Brotherhood's success in diffusing antisemitic propaganda in the decades after World War II. The charge that Jews masterminded the League of Nations is no less befuddling; it hardly needs saying that the Jewish people were in no position to found a conference of international heads of state. These delusions have next to nothing to do with actual events; whatever path history takes, in the antisemitic imagination, it is the Jews who are dictating it. According to this fantasy, the powerful Jew is timeless; indeed, his power is as total today as it was in past centuries.

It should come as no surprise, then, that the fevered minds who wrote this document claim the Jews were behind World War II, from which they supposedly made huge amounts of money. This, too, was an idea they adopted from their forebears, the Nazis. It was the central assertion of German propaganda from 1939 to 1945, one that Hitler, his Propaganda Minister Joseph Goebbels, and other Nazi leaders repeated endlessly on radio and in the press. The charge that an actual political actor called "the Jew" or "International Jewry" had launched the war against Nazi Germany played a large role in Hitler's justification for murdering Europe's Jews. As had been the case for the Nazis, the description of the Jews as evil and powerful led Hamas to promote genocide against them.[12] If Jews were responsible for all wars, as it claimed, the path to peace demanded their extermination.[13]

If the previous sections articulated Hamas' theory that the Jews control the world and foment all wars, the later articles make that supposed threat personal: the Jews' first order of business, states Article 22, is to wipe out the Arab countries one by one, starting with Palestine. That appears to be

Hamas' characterization of the Camp David Accords. Naturally, Hamas is the first to stand against the Zionists: it seeks "to prevent the success of this horrendous plan.... Today it is Palestine, tomorrow it will be one country after another. The Zionist plan is limitless. After Palestine, the Zionists aspire to expand from the Nile to the Euphrates." In this as well, Hamas is indebted to Nazis, who also promoted the idea that Zionists coveted a land empire stretching from "the Nile to the Euphrates." Via short wave radio from Berlin, Arab-language Nazi propaganda not only claimed that the Jews were responsible for the war in Europe, but that in addition "the Jews kindled this war in the interest of Zionism."[14] Again, the influence of the famous forgery *The Protocols of the Elders of Zion* is apparent. For the Muslim Brotherhood in 1948 and Hamas 40 years later, the sheer existence of the state of Israel was sufficient evidence to confirm the truth of antisemitic conspiracy theories.

We do not know whether Hamas would have been weakened and war avoided if the political leaders of the West had spoken out against this poisonous declaration in 1988 or in any way considered its likely effect on Hamas' governance later in 2007. Like any other movement, Hamas has core beliefs, chillingly on display in its Covenant, yet they are far too frequently ignored. A misplaced reticence and a condescending desire not to offend have only made it easier for Hamas to grow stronger and more dangerous. Now is a good time for anyone with an interest in understanding Hamas to read its founding document and see its debt to Nazism and European fascism presented in its own words. Only then will an observer know why Hamas started this and previous wars and why peace demands that its odious ideology be examined and delegitimated.

Postscript 2023

Hamas, with support from Iran, has continued to fire rockets at Israel and has not departed from the fundamental antisemitic convictions expressed in its Covenant of 1988.

Notes

"Why They Fight: Hamas' Too-Little-Known Fascist Charter," Jeffrey Herf, originally in *The American Interest* (August 1, 2014): https://www.the-american-interest.com/2014/08/01/why-they-fight-hamas-too-little-known-fascist-charter/. Reprinted with permission.

1 Jeffrey Herf, "Why They Fight: Hamas' Too-Little-Known Fascist Charter," *The American Interest* (August 1, 2014): https://www.the-american-interest.com/2014/08/01/why-they-fight-hamas-too-little-known-fascist-charter/. Also see my "A Pro-Hamas Left Emerges," *The American Interest* (August 26, 2014): http://www.the-american-interest.com/articles/2014/08/26/a-pro-hamas-left-emerges/; and "Fascism with a

Religious Face. Hamas at War with Israel. Forever," *American Purpose* (May 26, 2021).

2 References to the "covenant" or "charter" in this essay are from "The Hamas Covenant: The Covenant of the Islamic Resistance Movement, 18 August 1988," The Avalon Project, Documents in Law, Diplomacy and History, Yale Law School: https://avalon.law.yale.edu/20th_century/hamas.asp

3 On this issue see the excellent essay by Tzipi Livni, Israel's Minister of Justice, "Three Boys, One Terrorist Group and a Message for Democracies," *Wall Street Journal*, June 25, 2014. On the use of democracy to destroy democracy, see the now-classic work by Karl Bracher, *The German Dictatorship* (New York: Praeger, 1970); and more recently, Ian Kershaw, *Hitler: A Biography* (New York: W.W. Norton, 2010).

4 "The Hamas Covenant: The Covenant of the Islamic Resistance Movement."

5 On Islamism, see Paul Berman, *Terror and Liberalism* (New York: W.W. Norton, 2003); Bassam Tibi, *Islamism and Islam* (Yale University Press, 20012); Matthias Kuentzel, *Jihad and Jew-Hatred: Nazism, Islamism and the Roots of 9/11* (New York: Telos Press, 2007); Jeffrey Herf, *Nazi Propaganda for the Arab World* (New Haven: Yale University Press, 2009). On the Western reluctance to speak frankly about Islamism, see Paul Berman, *The Flight of the Intellectuals* (New York: Melville House, 2010).

6 Hamas leaders have repeated such views in recent years. For example on August 10, 2012, Ahmad Bahr, Deputy Speaker of the Hamas Parliament, stated in a sermon that aired on *Al-Aqsa TV*: "If the enemy sets foot on a single square inch of Islamic land, Jihad becomes an individual duty, incumbent on every Muslim, male or female. A woman may set out [on Jihad] without her husband's permission, and a servant without his master's permission. Why? In order to annihilate those Jews.... O Allah, destroy the Jews and their supporters. O Allah, destroy the Americans and their supporters. O Allah, count them one by one, and kill them all, without leaving a single one." "Hamas Official Ahmad Bahr Preaches for the Annihilation of Jews and Americans," Middle East Media Research Institute MEMRI, Clip No. 3538, August 10, 2012.

7 On the history of the comparison of Israelis to Nazis in postwar Arab political and intellectual life, see Meir Litvak and Esther Webman, *From Empathy to Denial: Arab Responses to the Holocaust* (London: Hurst, 2009).

8 On the place of Israel in the conspiracy theory of the secular left in the Cold War, see Jeffrey Herf, " At War with Israel: East Germany's Key Role in Soviet Policy in the Middle East," *Journal of Cold War Studies* 16, 3 (Summer 2014): 129–163; and *Undeclared Wars with Israel: East Germany and the West German Far Left, 1967–1989* (New York and Cambridge: Cambridge University Press, 2016).

9 Article 22, "The Hamas Covenant."

10 See Jeffrey Herf, *Nazi Propaganda for the Arab World* (New Haven, CT: Yale University Press, 2009); and in this collection, Chapter 3, "Nazi Anti-Zionism."

11 Ibid.

12 On Islamist Holocaust "justification," see Litvak and Webman, *From Empathy to Denial*; and Wistrich, *A Lethal Obsession*.

13 Leaders of Hamas repeated such views in recent years. In an interview with Al-Aqsa TV in September 12, 2012, Marwan Abu Ras, a Hamas MP, who is also a member of the International Union of Muslim Scholars, stated (as translated by MEMRI): "The Jews are behind each and every catastrophe on the face of the Earth. This is not open to debate. This is not a temporal thing, but goes back to days of yore. They concocted so many conspiracies and betrayed rulers and

nations so many times that the people harbor hatred towards them…. Throughout history—from Nebuchadnezzar until modern times…. They slayed the prophets, and so on… Any catastrophe on the face of this Earth – the Jews must be behind it." Hamas MP Marwan Abu Ras: "The Jews Are Behind Every Catastrophe on Earth," MEMRI TV, September 12, 2012.

14 See, for example, "Palestine between Bolsheviks and the Jews," November 3, 1943, cited in Herf, *Nazi Propaganda for the Arab World*, 184.

13

IS DONALD TRUMP A FASCIST?[1]

Is Donald Trump, now with the results of Super Tuesday the Republican presidential nominee-apparent, a fascist? It is stunning even to pose the question in the context of a national-scale American election, but many people are posing it, and they are not entirely wrong to do so. The short answer to the question is "no, but...." But the "but" begs a historically tutored explanation, the conclusion to which should not make us feel too good about the "no" part of the answer.

When a historian asks a question like this, methodological fragilities rush to consciousness. Context is critical, so much so that in some ways it is impossible to state in any simple fashion what the similarities and differences are between Donald Trump and the fascist and Nazi dictators of Europe's twentieth century. But we can sketch out the domains in which a comparison might make sense. Those domains include most prominently attitudes toward democracy, political violence, press freedoms, and the role of the state within society and culture.

When Trump asserts that politicians are "all talk and no action," he casts doubt on a great virtue of elected legislatures in democracies—namely, the creation of a public sphere in which people with divergent views can talk with and to one another. Trump does not, as Hitler and Mussolini did, openly denounce the institutions of liberal democracy. Yet like them, he accuses those institutions of failing to adequately address political and economic crises. The classic dictators denounced democracy itself, especially the peaceful democratic competition among political parties, as a formula for national weakness. Trump has not done so, but his dictatorial personality suggests that he can do singlehandedly what American political institutions have failed to do for many years running. He postures as the man on the white

DOI: 10.4324/9781003449669-15

horse, as someone who would make Carl Schmitt, the reactionary modernist and authoritarian legal theorist of Weimar and Nazi Germany, proud. The fascists and the Nazis combined violent rhetorical attacks and insults with well-organized paramilitary organizations that inflicted violence, leading to injuries and deaths among their political opponents. Trump has mastered the art of the bruising insult but has not made organized violence a part of his campaign. While he thrills his audiences with rhetorical flourishes about wanting to punch opponents in the face, he hasn't organized a paramilitary organization that would inflict physical harm on his opponents.[2]

The fascist movements were schizophrenic about the relationship of society to the state. As they sought political power, fascists and Nazis pointed with pride to mass movements that, in their view, gave them a democratic mandate beyond the supposed fakery of the voting process. Trump has begun to refer to his candidacy as a political movement, and some of his supporters, like Alabama Senator Jeff Sessions, have explicitly done so. Fascists and Nazis wanted to create a new man and a new woman by abolishing the distinction between public and private life through a network of totalitarian institutions. In other words, they wanted to merge society into the state. Trump wants to make "America great again," but he has never expressed a totalitarian aspiration to create a new and presumably better American. Still, his demeanor and his taunts are those of the "strong man" who will fix problems. Trump's insults preclude any serious effort at building consensus. His vision of politics is that of the one-man rule he has enjoyed in his "great, terrific business." Trump's confidence about the ease with which our problems can be solved reflects an authoritarian impulse.

As to the panoply of liberal freedoms, the right-wing dictators of the twentieth century learned to use the means of mass communications, especially the radio, to good effect. Trump emerged as a public figure on television, has received massive publicity on cable and network news, and uses Facebook and Twitter to communicate—almost for free, too. Though Trump has threatened to diminish freedom of the press through the use of libel suits against leading newspapers, he is not yet running on a platform of substituting dictatorship for democracy or rescinding the First Amendment.

Mussolini and Hitler vastly expanded the role of the state in the economy and in all spheres of life. They celebrated state power, which initially confused large parts of the Italian and German business elites. A few industrialists turned to the fascists as a presumed bulwark against the vastly exaggerated danger of a Communist revolution. Most initially were skeptical of Mussolini, who began his career as a radical socialist, and of Hitler, who led a party with the word "Socialist" in its name. They did not understand that the fascists intended to use the state to remake society itself, specifically to make a "revolution from the right" that would, so they claimed, replace economic fragmentation and the alienating dimensions of bourgeois society with new national unity established by the primacy of politics of a more powerful state.

Trump remains vague regarding the role of the government, but he tends to repeat conservative mantras about the sins of big government. He has given no indication that he even understands, let alone plans to use, the state to remake American society or to stimulate some kind of Cultural Revolution. Thus, his movement lacks any explicit goal, except to elect Trump in order to expiate an accumulated mountain of anger against a tenured political class that, in its view, has only its own elitist interests in mind. Trump points to no "third force" beyond capitalism and communism. There is not the slightest hint of the anti-bourgeois impulse of the fascists and the Nazis. He promises capitalism on steroids—wealth for all. In this sense, Trump's authoritarianism is quintessentially American. Far from denouncing business, money, and materialism in the name of a new post-materialist national community, his tasteless narcissism knows no bounds.

Indeed, Trump exudes not an ounce of the anti-bourgeois cultural radicalism of the right-wing extremism of Europe's mid-twentieth century. In contrast to the structures of the multinational corporation, Trump owns a family business that is not accountable to anyone but himself. He boasts that his wealth creates the economic foundation for his ability to defy political correctness and say whatever he wants about anything. His reminders to his followers that he is funding his own campaign underscore his distinctive message about the connection between money, power, and the freedom to say whatever he pleases.

Trump's petty, narcissistic form of authoritarianism emerges from different experiences than those of Hitler and Mussolini. Hitler's radicalism had much to do with the fact that he was a veteran of World War I, while Mussolini early on expressed belief in the utility of political violence in politics. Hitler, in particular, expressed bitterness and disappointment about defeat and what was, in his view, an unjust peace. The two dictators and their leading associates sought to remake Italy and Germany in the image of a mythologized masculine community of World War I trenches. They spoke to and for disillusioned veterans who yearned to militarize civilian politics. In place of defeat and unjust peace, they promised a glorious future of national grandeur that demanded geographical expansion, through war if necessary. Trump's authoritarianism, by contrast, is utterly civilian in origins. It is not a transfer of the culture of the military (of which he has no personal experience) to the realm of civilian politics. Rather, he translates his own extensive experience of complete control over an almost archaic institution, the family-owned large business, into the political realm.

Trump displayed the distinctively civilian roots of his authoritarianism, as well as his contempt for the officer corps of the armed forces, when, at an early point in his campaign, he said that there was nothing heroic about Senator John McCain's imprisonment in North Vietnam. He found nothing noble in McCain's decision to turn down an offer for early release in order to maintain solidarity with his fellow American prisoners of war and the fact that he endured terrible torture as a result. Instead, he dismissed McCain's sacrifice, commenting "I like people who weren't captured"—a kind of callow flippancy made all the more shameless by the fact that, at that same moment in history, Trump was in college, followed by numerous draft deferments, and a stint in the family real estate business in New York.

There is another important difference between Trump and fascists like Mussolini and Hitler. It concerns their views of Islam. Trump's call for a temporary ban on Muslim immigration to the United States reflects the undifferentiated fear of Islam that has become a staple of the far Right in Europe. Hitler, however, admired Islam because he viewed it as a warrior religion that had much in common with National Socialist authoritarianism and its celebration of war. He viewed the pacifism that Christianity inspired as weakness. Also, of course, Hitler was at one with the Arab and Muslim hatred of the Jews and Zionism.

Trump probably remains unaware of the fact that Nazis and Islamists of an earlier time met on a common terrain of contempt for weakness and liberal democracy. Trump and his supporters think of themselves as being at least cultural Christians, if not more. It's part of their identity, not necessarily their faith. More importantly, after 15 years of war and terror around the world waged in the name of Islam, Trump senses that millions of Americans are fed up with euphemisms and efforts to make fine distinctions. Faced with a president who has refused to state the obvious about the connection between Islamism and terror (whether this is a good or bad idea is beside the point), Trump thrills his followers by dispensing with all distinctions between Islam and Islamism.

The idea that politics in liberal democracies is a massive swindle, that money rules everything, and that all politicians are corrupt and can be bought is as old as democracy itself. Far from promising a new, uncorrupted politics, Trump is distinctive in openly celebrating his intention to buy politicians and expect them to give him a good return on his investment. For someone whose name once hung over casinos in New Jersey and Las Vegas and who owns real estate across New York City, buying politicians is just part of doing business. Trump apparently has never met a politician he could not buy, and thus he takes pleasure in expressing his contempt for the breed. He does not promise an end to the swindle but its ultimate expression. He is, in other words, selling cynicism, along with his supposed capacity to operate within and beyond it.

Fascism and Nazism combined elements of a desire for respectability with hints of violence; Trump recalls that blend. He reminds his audiences that he attended "the Ivy League" Wharton School of Finance, where there were many "smart" people, including himself. Yet he is that Ivy Leaguer who either will not or cannot speak the English language properly. He takes pleasure in using a limited vocabulary, relying on non-descriptive words such as "nice," "beautiful," "good," "great," "bad," and "very bad." At the same time, he assumes a kind of pseudo-propriety, feigning horror at the thought of women's bodily functions, such as Hillary Clinton's use of a bathroom during a debate or Megyn Kelly's putative menstruation.

Trump's insults of the patrician Jeb Bush were a crucial aspect of his campaign's success. He succeeded in reinterpreting Bush's decency and civility as "low energy," a form of "weakness." Trump's followers took pleasure in his attacks on Bush not primarily because they disagreed with this or that policy, but because Trump gave them a way to dismiss Bush's obvious strengths. Bush's style, his intelligence, the size of his vocabulary, his seriousness, and his ability to speak knowledgeably about the details of problems—these were a constant challenge to those like Trump who lack the ability to do any of these things. Such strengths stir resentment and envy, reminding listeners of what they themselves do not understand. Trump's insults made it possible for his followers to dismiss their discomfort over not understanding policy questions. They could be "big guys" despite their ignorance. This was very liberating.

This combination of elite background and unsophisticated airs recalls a feature of fascist orators. Mussolini and Hitler differentiated themselves from traditional European conservatives by their willingness and ability to speak in the idiom of the common man, to speak crudely and profanely in the service of their goals. Where conservative parties had previously feared "the masses," fascism and Nazism focused on building a "movement" composed of them. The absurdity of a New York billionaire who claims to be "anti-establishment" is lost on his followers, who instead marvel at his willingness to insult a member of the family that had led the Republican Party for the past quarter century. Trump's *ad hominem* attacks on McCain and then Bush signaled that it was now open season on the old elites defined by taste, erudition, and public service. Like the fascists of old, he combined an authoritarian style with a populist bad-boy rebelliousness. In breaking the taboos of civility and civilization, a Trump speech and rally resembles the rallies of fascist leaders who pantomimed the wishes of their followers and let them fill in the text. Trump says what they want to say but is afraid to express. In cheering this leader, his supporters feel free to say what they really believe about Mexicans, Muslims, and women. The bond between leader and follower created by his willingness to fulfill wishes, both conscious and unconscious, constitutes a key element of the whiff of fascism that surrounds the Trump phenomenon.

Italian Fascism and German National Socialism celebrated highly conventional notions of masculinity associated with strength and force, and associated liberal democracy with weakness and weakness with feminine qualities of listening as well as talking. In this way, they suggested that there is a link between masculinity and authoritarianism. Their call for a new leader was for a *strong man*. Yet Hitler and Mussolini presented themselves as men of the people who sought and won respectability. Hitler sought to reassure the German elites that though he was from the people, he really shared some of the values of the old elites. Trump, coming as he does from wealth, disdains respectability. He flaunts his tastelessness, vulgarity, and, in the Detroit debate, the size of his genitals. That tastelessness is of a piece with an even more key point he made in Detroit. Asked what he would do as President if the military leadership refused to obey orders to engage in torture or to kill the families of terrorists, he insisted they would do as they were told. Here was *the strong man* dismissing the irritating details of the rule of law and the rules of war.

Another element of Trump's appeal is the message of freedom from political correctness. This, too, carries echoes of twentieth-century authoritarianism. Trump, of course, has no monopoly on criticism of leftist and liberal political correctness. It has existed for decades within parts of the universities, the media, and in the Washington establishment of the Republican Party that Trump despises. But Trump's rejection of political correctness is distinctive in its cruelty. As Richard Cohen in the *Washington Post* has astutely observed, Trump does not merely disagree; he needs to demean and disparage those who have the nerve to criticize him.[3] It is this very cruelty, his contempt for compassion and disdain for the weak, and his rejection of the norms of good sportsmanship, that his followers *admire*. For his followers, Trump's cruelty liberates them from the no-longer-tolerable self-censorship of the era of political correctness.

After seven years of Obama, Trump understands that compassion fatigue is a mass sentiment. Social Darwinism, the idea that the survival of the fittest is and should be the law that governs relations in society and between states, was a key source of fascism and Nazism. Trump's contempt for "losers" and his self-description as a "winner" stand in this longer Social Darwinist tradition. For the fascists, the Nazis, and for Trump, victory and defeat were and are not merely the result of contingent circumstances; they comprise a moral judgment as well. That is why some of his fiercest criticism of his opponents has nothing to do with their actual policy positions, but focuses instead on their low poll numbers, as if the latter were themselves evidence of the devalued moral worth of "losers."

Both Mussolini and Hitler were careful to attack those whom they believed were weak and vulnerable. Their blunders and downfall were due partly to the fact that their own ideologies blinded them to the true power of their adversaries—the major powers who ultimately won World War II. They rode high so long as they were confident bullies, sure to attack only those who were unable to defend themselves. When Mussolini waged war on the Italian Left, it had already been divided between Communists and Socialists and posed no realistic threat of revolution. Hitler also benefited from a German Left that was split into warring democratic versus communist factions and from conservatives who invited him into power. The Jews in Europe lacked a state and a means to defend themselves. Ethiopia in the 1930s was defenseless against the Italian Air Force. Trump's promise to deport eleven million undocumented immigrants recalls those earlier attacks on vulnerable minorities.

For his followers, Trump's cruelty is inseparable from the message of freedom from the norms of civility and political correctness. His cruelty was in plain view in his effort to humiliate the Fox News reporter Megyn Kelly, his nasty sarcasm about the physical handicap of *New York Times* reporter Serge Kovaleski, in the obvious pleasure he takes in commenting about the real or imagined personal shortcomings of his competitors, and in the outrageous mass deportation plan. Such a step would inflict untold suffering on millions of families, but he talks about carrying out such cruelty with pride. Doing so signifies that he and his followers will no longer be taken for suckers and that the hour of justified revenge has arrived against all the alien murderers and rapists supposedly in our midst. Yet the same cruelty that arouses disgust and anger among those who see it as a clear violation of elementary moral principles excites his followers. To them, the threatened violence and expulsion stand for a return of freedom and the recovery of their country.

Extreme nationalism, along with the temptation toward the transgressive, was central to the appeal of fascism and Nazism. The fascists and Nazis divided the world into Italians and Germans who were wonderful in various ways, and the rest of humanity, which existed on a sliding scale of depravity and inferiority. The fascists and Nazis extended humanity and camaraderie to their fellow Italians or in Germany to members of the "people's community" or the Aryan race, but not to the vast majority of humanity outside the charmed circle of the nation. Trump's nationalism echoes that mixture of nationalist self-love and disdain for various "others." While he is not calling for concentration camps or planning to go abroad in search of foreign enemies to destroy, he claims his intention to build a physical wall on the Mexican border and an economic and cultural wall of protectionism against the rest of the world economy. He and his followers have heard that many people around the world do not like the United States. His followers cheer when he tells them the feeling is mutual; he and his followers don't much like the rest of the world.

How his disdain for other nations could be compatible with the continued American leadership of the liberal democracies and market economies around the world is a mystery that Trump leaves unsolved. His followers are so filled with rage at other nations that it does not occur to them that electing Trump as President would mean the collapse of American alliances worldwide. How could Trump make America great again yet display no understanding of the meaning of American political, military, economic, and diplomatic leadership? It's a question that is not allowed to arise. In their combined anger and fear, Trump and his supporters have lost their common sense and this too accounts for his appeal. It doesn't even bother his followers that Trump, a man who as president would have the U.S. nuclear arsenal under his control, has not a clue about what the nuclear triad is.

Conspiracy theorizing also links Trump to the fascists and the Nazis. Trump offers no pretensions to intellectual seriousness. He does not offer a conspiracy theory as the explanatory key to modern history. He has repeated stereotypically antisemitic remarks about Jews, but he gives no indication of believing in the antisemitic canards that were at the core of Nazi appeals. Yet although he does not cite *The Protocols of the Elders of Zion* or, at least so far, repeat the falsehood that the "Israel lobby" was responsible for the war in Iraq, he does present the United States, the most powerful country on earth, as a hapless victim of China, Mexico, and Japan. A differing cast of nations, a diffuse "they" or "them," is somehow able to run rings around the "stupid" politicians and trade representatives of the U.S. government, and presumably the CEOs of major American corporations. He presents America's fall from greatness as a story of an innocent—and "stupid"—victim of dark forces who manipulate its goodwill for their own benefit. This story of the good nation victimized by evil conspirators recalls the pathos of national innocence and victimization that fueled the fascist and Nazi demagogues.

Trump's conspiratorial mentality is evident in the lies he repeats. When he asserts, against all evidence to the contrary, that "thousands" of Muslims stood on rooftops in New Jersey and cheered as the World Trade Center towers collapsed on 9/11 or that President Obama was not born in the United States, he is not only fanning racist sentiments toward Muslims and blacks or undermining the legitimacy of the first African American President; he is also asserting the existence of a massive conspiracy to conceal these facts, one composed of hundreds if not thousands of journalists and politicians who presumably know the real truth but refuse to reveal it. When pressed to reveal evidence about these assertions, Trump either simply repeats the charges or points to dubious sources on the internet. Normal standards of verification do not apply. The implicit message of these accusations is that the media are part of a conspiracy of silence. It is as if the leftist postmodernism of the universities, which for decades has cast doubt on the existence of fact, has found its mirror image in the billionaire capitalist's dismissal of evidence. The irony here is that the very media he blames for suppressing the truth have failed miserably to inform the public about how a man whose companies have declared bankruptcy four times manages to present himself as a paragon of business acumen and solid leadership.

Yet Trump's conspiracy theorizing is not a subject for humor. Nothing is more dangerous to politics in a liberal democracy, or in any other system for that matter, than conspiracy theories. It is difficult if not impossible to convince believers in conspiracy theories of their falsehood because they refuse to be dissuaded by normal standards of empirical verification and refutation. The idea of a conspiracy offers believers the blessings of simplicity and clear targets for their rage and hatred. Conspiracy theorizing fosters a contempt for facts and thus undermines possibilities for compromise about complex issues. Because conspiracy theories divide the world into good and evil between which no common ground is possible, they preclude the give-and-take of democratic politics. If the evil is great enough, conspiracy theories always contain the possibility of "altruistic violence"—possibly massive violence against alleged conspirators that are always characterized as an act of self-defense. Trump inculcates a conspiratorial habit of mind in his followers that contains enormous dangers, especially if and when levels of unemployment actually do increase to the alarming levels he falsely claims already exist.

On February 8, 2016, in New Hampshire, Jeb Bush said, "It's not strong to insult women. It's not strong to castigate Hispanics. It's not strong to ridicule the disabled. And it's not strong to call John McCain…who spent six years in a POW camp in Hanoi a loser because he got caught." In that one eloquent statement, Bush the patrician captured the whiff of fascism, the false understanding of strength and weakness, and the essential bully that is Donald Trump. None of this seemed to mean anything to many of the Republican primary voters in New Hampshire, however—a fact that ought to send shivers up the spine of any decent American. Bush, and earlier Senator Lindsey Graham, seemed to stand alone in the Republican Party in their willingness to confront Trump when his campaign was still in its early stages. They were abandoned by their fellow Republicans, who wrongly thought they could ignore him. When fascism and Nazism emerged in Italy and Germany, their rise to power was also accompanied by an astonishing series of political blunders and misjudgments by the elites of the time. Hitler was underestimated by his opponents on the Left, who thought he was merely a tool of the capitalists, and by the industrialists, who thought he would become their own pliable tool. In both cases, the political establishments failed to take the danger seriously enough and then descended into cynical opportunism borne of partial agreement and lack of principle, now evident in the stunning decision of New Jersey Governor Chris Christie to support Trump.

History does not repeat itself in simple ways. Trump is not a carbon copy of Hitler or Mussolini. Yet he has now threatened the owners and editors of the *New York Times* and the *Washington Post* with libel suits if they continue to criticize him. He (absurdly) pretended not to know who David Duke is and, in an interview, appeared to refuse to disavow him and the Ku Klux Klan thereby shamelessly pandering to votes from the extreme racist Right. He subsequently did disavow them, but without clarifying why he was doing so. His cynism was transparent. Whether or not Trump gains the nomination of the Republican Party, he has already done enormous damage to American politics. The poisons he has unleashed and the taboos he has smashed with such glee have created a new, dangerous field of rhetorical violence and insult in American public life. He has revealed that large numbers of our fellow citizens are willing to follow a demagogue who voices contempt for basic principles of liberal democracy, offers simple explanations of complex issues, and draws on racism, religious bigotry, and extreme nationalism to "make America great again." Trump's mixture of wealth and authoritarianism, and the underestimation of his potential power by the establishment, also evokes comparisons to Italy's former Prime Minister Silvio Berlusconi and the damage he did to Italy while he served as Prime Minister. Berlusconi's launching pad in private wealth is similar to Trump's. Yet Trump is less the buffoon and more of a bully than Berlusconi. Given the role of the United States in world affairs, the damage he could do should he become President would be far greater.

Despite the significant differences between the Trump phenomenon and the extreme Right of Europe's twentieth century, his campaign recalls dangerous echoes from the past. We know what can happen when politicians who speak and act like Donald Trump gain power, even if they do so by using the instruments of democracy. With fear and anger unloosed in the land, much can happen, nearly all of it very bad. Trump can be stopped, but for that to happen we need to take the threat he poses seriously and to remember the lessons of the not-so-distant past.

2023 Postscript

By January 6th at the latest, Trump and Trumpism had evolved into a distinctively American form of fascism, that is, an attack on the institutions of liberal democracy and the rule of law. The essay underestimated the speed of the collapse of substantial opposition to Trump and Trumpism within the Republican Party. The rapid reversal by Senator Graham from Trump critic to Trump supporter was representative of this broader trend. Trump's flirtation with antisemitic themes was apparent in his 2016 campaign denunciations of then familiar Jewish figures in the world of finance. His comment about "fine people on both sides" after the neo-Nazi attack in Charlottesville revealed his willingness to connect with the racist, and antisemitic extreme right, and to echo conspiracy theories, most importantly the falsehood about the "stolen election" of 2020. Notwithstanding his enthusiasm for right-wing politics in Israel, Trump's attack on America's alliances would not be "good for Israel" as the erosion of those alliances would, eventually also erode that alliance as well.[4] The essay was prescient in arguing that the release of emotions, resentments, hatreds, and pleasures that Trump fostered in 2016 would remain a potent factor in American politics.

Notes

"Is Donald Trump a Fascist?," Jeffrey Herf, originally in *The American Interest* (March 7, 2016): https://www.the-american-interest.com/2016/03/07/is-donald-trump-a-fascist/. Reprinted with permission.

1 Jeffrey Herf, "Is Donald Trump a Fascist?," in *The American Interest* (March 7, 2016): https://www.the-american-interest.com/2016/03/07/is-donald-trump-a-fascist/. For my other essays on Trump and Trumpism, see: "Postscript to Is Donald Trump a Fascist?," *The American Interest* (August 8, 2016): http://www.the-american-interest.com/2016/08/08/postscript-to-is-donald-trump-a-fascist/; "Elements of Conspiracy," *The American Interest* (October 31, 2016): http://www.the-american-interest.com/2016/10/31/elements-of-conspiracy/; "Lessons from German History after Charlottesville," September 17, 2017: https://historynewsnetwork.org/article/166864; "Trump Doesn't Understand How Antisemitism Works: Neither Do Most Americans?," *Washington Post* (October 27, 2018): https://www.washingtonpost.com/outlook/2018/10/28/trump-doesnt-understand-how-anti-semitism-works-neither-do-most-americans/?utm_term=.e512d3887a0d; "The 2020 National Elections: An American Reckoning," *Israel Journal of Foreign Affairs* (September 10, 2020), 169–182: https://www.tandfonline.com/doi/abs/10.1080/23739770.2020.1810405; "Trump's Refusal to Acknowledge Defeat Mirrors the Lie that Fueled the Nazi Rise," *Washington Post, MadebyHistory* section, November 23, 2020: https://www.washingtonpost.com/outlook/2020/11/23/trumps-refusal-acknowledge-defeat-mirrors-lie-that-fueled-nazi-rise/; "The January 6th Assault on Congress and the Fate of the GOP's Faustian Bargain with Trump: Notes from German History," *History News Network*, January 31, 2021: https://historynewsnetwork.org/article/178983.
2 See Chapter 6, "Be There, Be Wild," in Select Committee to Investigate the January 6th Attack on the United States Capitol, *The January 6th Report: Findings form the Select Committee to Investigate the January 6th Attack on the United States Capital* (New York: Random House, 2023), 499–574.
3 Richard Cohen, "Donald Trump's Intolerable Cruelty," *Washington Post* (February 22, 2016): https://www.washingtonpost.com/opinions/donald-trumps-intolerable-cruelty/2016/02/22/c3e72a04-d992-11e5-81ae-7491b9b9e7df_story.html
4 "The 2020 National Elections: An American Reckoning," *Israel Journal of Foreign Affairs* (September 10, 2020), 169–182: https://www.tandfonline.com/doi/abs/10.1080/23739770.2020.1810405

14

IDEOLOGICAL EXCEPTIONALISM

Taking Iran's Antisemitism Seriously[1]

Radical, theologically based hatred of Judaism, Zionism, and the state of Israel, is part of the core ideological beliefs of the leaders of the Islamic Republic of Iran. Yet U.S. policymakers all too rarely consider Iran's endemic antisemitism. In fact, it is hardly ever discussed outside of Israel and a few Western intellectual circles. To be sure, the Iranian regime's radical antisemitism is of deepest concern to Israel, but a regime driven by such violent hatred also endangers the world, especially modern, Western, and democratic nations.

While the U.S. Congress has held hearings about the technical details of Iran's nuclear programs and the impact of economic sanctions, as far as I know, it has never publicly discussed the core ideology of the Iranian regime and how it affects Iran's quest for nuclear weapons. Such hearings are long overdue. The radical antisemitism voiced by Iranian leaders is a worldview so delusional, so removed from actual realities, that those who advocate it will almost certainly not operate according to the customary norms of what constitutes reasonable behavior in international affairs. Indeed, U.S. policymakers cannot assume that Iran will value its own survival more than it does the goal of eliminating the hated Jewish enemy.

The scholarship on the history of antisemitism has not yet had a significant impact on the policy discussions in Washington about Iran. Perhaps too many of our policymakers, politicians, and analysts still labor under the mistaken idea that radical antisemitism is merely another form of prejudice or, worse, an understandable (and hence excusable?) response to the conflict between Israel, the Arab states, and the Palestinians. In fact, it is something far more dangerous, and far less compatible with a system of nuclear deterrence, which assumes that all parties place a premium on their own survival.

DOI: 10.4324/9781003449669-16

Iran's radical antisemitism is not in the slightest bit rational; it is a paranoid conspiracy theory that proposes to make sense (or rather nonsense) of the world by claiming that the powerful and evil "Jew" is the driving force in global politics. Leaders who attribute enormous evil and power to the thirteen million Jews in the world and to a tiny Middle Eastern state with about eight million citizens have demonstrated that they don't have a suitable disposition for playing nuclear chess.

Iranian antisemitism has been well-documented, by Meir Litvak of the Dayan Center for Middle East Studies at the University of Tel Aviv and the Middle East Media Research Institute (MEMRI). They have offered abundant evidence that hatred of the Jews and a determination to destroy the state of Israel are paramount goals for the Islamic Republic and have been ever since its founder, Ayatollah Ruhollah Khomeini, gave such views theological sanction. Like his fellow Islamists, Haj Amin al-Husseini and Sayyid Qutb, Khomeini asserted that Jews were bent on destroying Islam, a mission he claimed found modern expression in the establishment of Israel. Indeed, he saw no difference between his hatred of Jews and Judaism and his hatred of Israel.[2] His successor shares Khomeini's views: as reported by the Islamic Republic News Agency (IRNA), Ayatollah Ali Khamenei stated in 2001 that

> the occupation of Palestine [by the Jews] is part of a satanic design by the world domineering powers, perpetrated by the British in the past and carried out today by the United States, to weaken the solidarity of the Islamic world and to sow the seeds of disunity among nations.[3]

As Meir Litvak writes, both Khomenei to Khamenei see Jews and Judaism as a threat to Islam and the Muslims. Khomenei made uncompromising, theologically based assertions that Israel and Zionism were enemies not only of Islam but of humanity in its entirety, and Khamenei has said the same. Such evil enemies, they believe, must be wiped out for the good of all.

As a historian of modern German history, specializing in the Nazi era and the Holocaust, I know the pitfalls of misplaced historical analogies. Israel's enemies commonly make such analogies; the Soviet Union, the Arab states, Palestinian organizations, Islamist terror groups, and the government of Iran has all compared Israel to Nazi Germany. Yet our current policy debates suffer from the opposite problem. Policymakers have been unwilling to discuss radical antisemitism openly and frankly when it comes from Islamist sources. Despite their differences, we must remember that the Islamic Republic of Iran is the first government since Hitler in which antisemitism constitutes a central element of its identity. An Iran with nuclear weapons would thus be the first government since Hitler's to be both willing and able to threaten a second Holocaust.

No high-ranking member of the Obama Administration has admitted that this is the case—neither the President nor his Secretaries of State and Defense have ever publicly discussed Iran's antisemitism. The issue has faded into the background, replaced by a preoccupation with technical details about centrifuges, percentages of uranium enrichment, and lengths of "break-out times." When policymakers fail to consider the core beliefs of the Iranian leadership, they foster the impression that Iran is a smaller, Islamic version of the Soviet Union—that is, a state that would act in its own self-interest if it had nuclear weapons. Yet the Soviet Union was governed by atheists who disdained notions of life after death and would have laughed at the idea of a "12th Imam" descending to earth after an apocalyptic disaster. If Iran acquires nuclear weapons, it would likely be the first such state not to be deterred by the prospect of nuclear retaliation. Yet the irrationality of Iran's government has received scant attention in the United States government, which seems unable to believe that people could put their faith in a post-apocalyptic messiah. That is both a failure of imagination and a failure of policy.

It is not clear why there has been such consistent disinclination to publicly examine and discuss what the Iranian leaders believe. Part of the blame may lie with the tendency of realist scholars of international relations and politics to dismiss the importance of ideology. Or perhaps it is the fact that Israelis have done the best and most careful work on Iran's ideology that leads some foreign policy analysts to ignore it. President Obama's repeated assertions that "the tide of war is receding," his decision to leave Iraq and Afghanistan and his refusal to intervene in Syria suggest a different explanation. A close and honest look at the beliefs of Iran's leaders would undermine the hope that the Islamic Republic is a normal, rational actor in world affairs. For if the Iranians do believe what they say, then the unavoidable conclusion is that they are lying about the purposes of their nuclear program and have been playing Western leaders, including the President, for fools. Further, it means that they will not cease their pursuit of the bomb unless, at the very least, they are threatened with more severe damage to their economy—though more likely not, unless the United States credibly threatens military action against them. Since no one knows how such a military campaign—not an invasion but a naval and air campaign—would end, policymakers understandably wish to consider Iran a "normal" state and tend to neglect the inconvenient evidence of its ideological fanaticism. Yet denying the reality will not make it disappear.

There are other and more familiar reasons why the United States does not want Iran to get the bomb. A nuclear Iran could deter military action against its terrorist proxies, Hamas and Hizballah, and threaten to disrupt the flow of energy in the Persian Gulf. If Iran were to acquire the bomb after several American Presidents had asserted that this must not happen, America's credibility would be damaged. Without the U.S. as a reliable guarantor, the nuclear non-proliferation treaty would seem less stable, and many other states might begin to develop their own nuclear weapons programs—not least Japan and South Korea.

On February 6, 2014, Senator Robert Menendez, Chairman of the Senate Foreign Relations Committee delivered a historic yet underreported speech on the Senate floor about the state of the negotiations with Iran. Stating his opposition to the relaxation of economic sanctions by the Geneva Agreement of November 2013, the Senator said that "years of obfuscation, delay, and endless negotiation have brought the Iranians to the point of having— according to the Director of National Intelligence—the scientific, technical, and industrial capacity to eventually produce nuclear weapons." The Iranian's strategy of using "these negotiations to mothball its nuclear infrastructure program just long enough to undo the international sanctions regime" has "brought them to a nuclear threshold state."[4] The Obama Administration must surely know this to be true as well. Policymakers must understand that Iran has not invested billions of dollars and weathered years of international isolation only to change course and stop pursuing nuclear weapons. Perhaps the officials involved in the P5 + 1 (representatives of China, France, Russia, the United Kingdom, and the United States, plus Germany) talks know that the most likely outcome of the current policy is that Iran will get the bomb it claims not to want. If the plan is to contain and deter a nuclear Iran rather than to prevent it from getting the bomb in the first place, then the refusal of the President and other European leaders to consider the Iranians' ideology makes a certain sense. Such a policy can only rest on a willful ignorance of the regime's core beliefs.

The United States has the economic and military resources to prevent Iran from getting the bomb. If it becomes necessary to use force to achieve that end, the Administration must present the full range of reasons for that decision. A regime animated by radical antisemitism not only poses a threat of a second Holocaust but, due to its dangerous irrationality, poses a threat to the entire world. President Obama and his leading officials insist that their policy remains one of prevention, yet they do not seem to understand the very people they are seeking to deter. Iran's ideological extremism has become lost in the fog of technical details. If we are to have an effective policy on Iran, we must first understand what makes the country tick, as well as its bombs.

Notes

"Ideological Exceptionalism: Taking Iran's Anti-Semitism Seriously," Jeffrey Herf, originally in *The American Interest* (June 2, 2014): https://www.the-american-interest.com/2014/06/02/taking-irans-anti-semitism-seriously/. Reprinted with permission.

1 Jeffrey Herf, "Ideological Exceptionalism: Taking Iran's Antisemitism Seriously," *The American Interest* (June 2, 2014): https://www.the-american-interest.

com/2014/06/02/taking-irans-anti-semitism-seriously/. Also see "What does coming to terms with the past mean in the Berlin Republic in 2007," first delivered to the 35th Römerberg Conversations (35. *Römberberg Gespräche*) Frankfurt/Main, November 16/17, 2007 then published in *Telos* (February 4, 2008): https://www.telospress.com/what-does-coming-to-terms-with-the-pastmean-in-the-berlin-republic-in-2007/; and *Dissent/Democratiya* (Spring 2008): https://www.dissentmagazine.org/democratiya_article/what-does-coming-to-terms-with-the-past-mean-in-the-berlin-republic-in-2007; "The Iran Deal and Antisemitism" (April 6, 2015): http://blogs.timesofisrael.com/the-iran-deal-and-anti-semitism/; and other blog essays at my *Times of Israel* blog (https://blogs.timesofisrael.com/author/jeffrey-herf/) dealing with the Joint Comprehensive Plan of Action (JCPOA) deal intended to prevent Iran from acquiring nuclear weapons; and "Times Is on Iran's Side: There's no more kicking the can if we are to prevent a nuclear Iran," *American Purpose* (January 14, 2022): https://www.american-purpose.com/articles/time-is-on-irans-side/. "Where Are the Anti-Fascists?" *The New Republic* (December 04, 2007): https://newrepublic.com/article/64109/where-are-the-anti-fascists

2 Meir Litvak, "Iranian Antisemitism: Continuity and Change," in Charles Asher Small, ed., *Global Antisemitism: A Crisis of Modernity, Volume IV, Islamism and the Modern World* (Institute for the Study of Global Antisemitism, 2023), 60' and his "The Islamic Republic of Iran and the Holocaust: Anti-Semitism and Anti-Zionism," in Jeffrey Herf, ed., *Anti-Semitism and Anti-Zionism in Historical Perspective: Convergence and Divergence* (London and New York: Routledge/Taylor and France, 2007), 250–267; and "Iranian Antisemitism and the Holocaust," in McElligott and Herf, eds., *Antisemitism Before and Since the Holocaust*, 205–230.

3 Ayatollah Ali Khamenei, cited in Litvak, "Iranian Antisemitism," 60.

4 Robert Menendez, "Chairman Menendez Speech on Iran" (February 6, 2014): https://www.menendez.senate.gov/newsroom/press/2014/02/06/chairman-menendez-speech-on-iran

15

ANTISEMITISM AND THE ACADEMY SINCE 9/11

In the months following the terrorist attacks of 9/11, the proponents of leftist conventional thinking of the past half century were momentarily thrown into a state of confusion and uncertainty. The Islamists were obviously reactionaries who made those who presented them as anti-imperialist heroes of the global left look like fools or worse—as apologists for Jew-hatred, misogyny, totalitarianism, and mass murder. The year before, at negotiations in Camp David hosted by President Bill Clinton, Israel's Labor Party Prime Minister Ehud Barak had agreed to a deal that offered Yasser Arafat, the leader of the Palestinian Authority (successor to the Palestine Liberation Organization) a Palestinian state on the West Bank and Gaza. Arafat turned it down and instead launched a terror campaign, "the Second Intifada."

Then a very strange thing happened. Instead of sympathizing with the Israelis as suicide bombers attacked them on the campus of Hebrew University, in bus stations, and in restaurants, voices in the intellectual and academic worlds turned against them. As Paul Berman wrote in *Terror and Liberalism*, "the high tide of the terrorist attacks in the early months of 2002 proved to be the very moment when around the world, large numbers of people felt impelled to express their fury at the Israelis."[1] Rather than cast a firm gaze at the ideological fanaticism inspiring the terrorists, a mood spread among prominent liberal and leftist intellectuals that the cause of the terror, whether secular or Islamist in inspiration, was to be found in a combination of the policies of the state of Israel, its sheer existence, or the economic problems of the Arab and Muslim world presumably caused by the Western democracies. The conventional leftist analysis that had been emerging in the universities since the 1960s about the sins of the West obscured the reality that the leaders of the terrorist organizations came from middle class or, in the case of Osama

DOI: 10.4324/9781003449669-17

bin Laden, very wealthy backgrounds. Within the universities and colleges, in the non-governmental organizations and the liberal media, the intellectual shock of 9/11 was short-lived. The liberal repudiation of Islamist terror and antisemitism that Berman articulated so brilliantly, and which Israelis had been warning about for decades, met a barrier in the form of the by-then well-established antagonism to Zionism and Israel which had emerged in the global left after the Six-Day War of 1967 and found institutional and political support in world politics at the United Nations in the 1970s.[2] In the intervening decades, the ideas about the racist and oppressive essence of the Jewish state that was common in the diplomacy and political warfare of the Soviet bloc, the Palestine Liberation Organization, and an anti-Israeli majority in the United Nations entered the academy, achieved tenure, and scholarly respectability. Advocates of these ideas were to be found not only among many scholars working on the Middle East but also in departments with no scholarly claim to expertise in the history of Israel or the Middle East, such as English, American studies, anthropology, and women's studies.[3]

Yet another odd factor, the decision by President George Bush to invade Iraq in 2003, contributed to the antagonism to Israel in the academy. Israel's leaders across the political spectrum had focused Iran's efforts to acquire nuclear weapons combined with its denial of the Holocaust and threats to "wipe out the Zionist entity." Nevertheless, in March 2006, two American political scientists, John Mearsheimer, of the University of Chicago, and Stephen Walt at Harvard, published an article in the *London Review of Books* in which they blamed what they called "the Israel lobby" inside and outside the Bush administration for the American decision to invade Iraq. They expanded on the thesis in a book published by the New York Prestige Press, Farrar, Strauss, and Giroux in 2008.[4]

My colleague, the University of Michigan political scientist Andrei Markovits, and I wrote a letter to the editor following the publication of Mearsheimer and Walt's article. We wrote in part that "accusations of powerful Jews behind the scenes are part of the most dangerous traditions of modern anti-Semitism," and that it was

> not true that the United States went to war in Iraq due to the pressure of a Jewish lobby…Whatever Israel or its supporters in the United States may or may not have wanted, American and British leaders decided to go to war for their reasons grounded in their interpretation of the respective national interest.[5]

Mearsheimer and Walt's article and then book was an example of what Berman noted: the worst the terror against Israel became, the more they aimed criticism at Israel. Their attack on "the Israel lobby" came eight years after the attacks of 9/11, six years after Barak's compromise offer, and Arafat's response with a terrorist campaign of his own, after numerous terrorist attacks all over the world by Al Qaeda and its sympathizers, repeated statements by Iranian leaders calling for Israel to be eliminated, and an electoral victory in 2006 by Hamas, an openly antisemitic terrorist organization. The authors ignored Israel's withdrawals from Lebanon in 2000 and from Gaza in 2005, statements by Iranian officials Israel should be wiped out and that the Holocaust was a myth, and the continuing rejection by both radical Islamist and secular Palestinian militants of a compromise peace.[6]

Mearsheimer and Walt did not write from the perspective of leftist opponents of American imperialism but as "realists" speaking up for the American national interest and against an "Israel lobby" that was, in their view, undermining American national security. The authors insisted that they had no antisemitic intent. That was irrelevant because their argument that an "Israel lobby" had led the United States into an unnecessary war of choice familiar aspects of antisemitic conspiracy theories about Jewish War mongers operating behind the scenes to advance their own interests in contrast to the interest of the country of which they were citizens.

Within the universities, the primary support for the campaign of boycotts, divestment, and sanctions (BDS) against Israel did not come from those, such as Mearsheimer and Walt, who worried about American national security. Rather it came from academics on the left who accepted the Palestine Liberation Organization's version of the history of its conflict with Israel, according to which the state was founded on the expulsion of native inhabitants and had no moral or political legitimacy. The alternative was not only an end to the post-1967 occupation of the West Bank but also an end to "foreign occupation" that was said to have begun in 1948 and establishment of a "Palestine from the river to the sea," that is, from the Jordan River to the Mediterranean that would replace the existing state of Israel. In the United States and in Great Britain, BDS advocates asserted that Zionism, and then Israel, were forms of racism or settler colonialism. As has been the case since 1975 in the United Nations, the accusation that Zionism was a form of racism and Israel a form of apartheid put Israel's supporters, especially among undergraduates, on the defensive.[7] These accusations were the result of a remarkably successful campaign by the Palestine Liberation Organization (PLO) which largely succeeded in diverting attention to the racism, antisemitism, and Nazi collaboration of the leaders of the Palestine Arabs who rejected the UN Partition Resolution of 1947 and from their advocacy of "racial homogeneity" in doing so.[8]

As was the case in the Communist and leftist political assaults on Israel during the Cold War, their successors in the universities in recent decades also claim that they are not antisemites at all. The Nazis were proud of their Jew hatred. The Islamists viewed their efforts to destroy the state of Israel similarly. The antisemitism of the left, from Marx's essay "On the Jewish

Question" of 1843, the PLO Charter of 1968, the United Nations Zionism is racism resolution of 1975, and the "Declaration and Program of Action of the World Conference Against Racism, Racial Discrimination, Xenophobia and Related Intolerance," of August 31 to September 7 in Durban, South Africa, rejects the suggestion that it is in any way at all antisemitic.[9] That is a novelty in the history of antisemitism. BDS advocates describe efforts to label their efforts as forms of antisemitism as nothing more than a form of "Zionist" political warfare or simply a form of racism masquerading as a fight against antisemitism. David Hirsh has described what he calls "the Livingston formulation," named after Ken Livingston, the former Mayor of London. Hirsh writes that "the counter allegation of Zionist conspiracy which treats discussion of antisemitism as though it were a vulgar, dishonest tribal fraud" comprises an important form of "contemporary antisemitism."[10] The accusation further implies that even the examination of antisemitism in its leftist and Islamist forms is itself a form of racism or "Islamophobia." The consequence of such accusations, and one of their purposes, is to discourage essential scholarship into antisemitism's two non-Nazi forms.

In 2013, BDS activists in the United States gained victories in the American Studies Association, and oddly Asian American Studies, when they achieved majorities in favor of resolutions to boycott Israeli academics. These votes came from disciplines, the scholars of which had no scholarly expertise in the history of the state of Israel and its conflict with Arab states and Palestinian organizations. In response, my fellow historian Sonya Michel and I wrote to Wallace Loh, the President and Mary Ann Rankin, the Provost of the University of Maryland, College Park, that "the boycotters' obsessive focus on Israel's alleged sins in the midst of a world of sinners indicates that this very old prejudice [antisemitism] is at work here in a new guise."[11] We wrote that the boycott was an effort to turn a scholarly organization, in this case, the American Studies Association, into a political instrument, that a boycott constituted a form of blacklist since it was directed against particular people due to their connections to Israeli academia, and thus "in its consequences this is an act of anti-Semitism--that is, a racist act." It broke with the norms of the academy and undermined universities' claims to support diversity and inclusion. We urged the President and Provost to reject and denounce the boycott efforts and to reaffirm that support for diversity and inclusion is incompatible with advocacy of antisemitism.[12]

On December 21, 2013, Loh and Rankin issued a "Statement of the University of Maryland President and Provost Opposing the Boycott of Israeli Academic Institutions." They wrote that "any such boycott is a breach of the principle of academic freedom" and faculty, students, and staff needed to "remain free to study, do research, and participate in meetings with colleagues from around the globe...The University of Maryland has longstanding relationships with several Israeli universities. We have many exchanges of scholars and students. We will continue and deepen these relationships."[13] The statement was one of many by university and college presidents and provosts but was particularly emphatic in asserting the intention to "continue and deepen" relationships with Israeli universities. In the following years, most BDS campaigns on American campuses failed to win majorities but nevertheless succeeded in making the association of Israel with racism a theme when discussions of that issue were intense in American public life.

In response to the American war in Iraq, an organization of left-leaning historians called "Historians Against the War" or "HAW" emerged in American departments of history. On July 31, 2014, during the second of the wars launched by Hamas against Israel, HAW posted on its website an open letter to President Obama calling for an end to American military assistance to Israel which, it asserted, was committing "war crimes" in its retaliation against Hamas firing of rockets into Israel. HAW asserted that by August 13th, 1,000 historians, including a considerable number from Mexico and Brazil, had signed the statement.[14]

On August 26, I responded in the online pages of *The American Interest* with "A Pro-Hamas Left Emerges."[15] With the reactionary nature of Hamas ideology in mind, I wrote that "the leftism of the Historians Against the War statement reflects an opposition to some reactionary movements but not others." Although Hamas had made clear that it was an antisemitic, sexist, homophobic, and, of course, anti-democratic organization, these historians of the left chose to accept its factual assertions about events during the war. The Hamas Covenant had been easily available on the internet for a decade. Its repetition of the classic reactionary antisemitic conspiracy theories common in Nazi Germany was there for all to see. Its determination to destroy the state of Israel, and its proud and religiously justified rejection of any compromise settlement was equally public knowledge. I wrote that this was "an historically significant event" for it represented a break

> with both the self-understanding and public image of a Left that carried a banner of anti-fascism. It rests on a double standard of critique, a critical one applied to the extreme Right in the West and another, apologetic standard applied to similarly based rightist Islamist movements.[16]

In 2015 and 2016, BDS efforts were defeated in the American Historical Association (AHA). The issue of antisemitism largely remained in the background of the debates.[17] In the debate at the AHA meeting to consider the resolution, those opposed to the BDS efforts expressed skepticism about the factual claims about Israeli policy, asserted that the resolutions rested on political opinions, not scholarship, and thus amounted to collapsing the distinction between scholarship and politics. Moreover, with injustices and crimes of dictatorships around the world, some AHA members commented on the selective outrage and double standards which, in effect if not intent, amounted to antisemitism.[18]

While the historical profession's main organization has, so far, resisted boycott efforts, 80 percent of the participating members of the Middle East Studies Association (MESA), the main scholarly organization dealing with the region, voted overwhelmingly to do so in March 2022.[19] The logical implications of acceptance of the boycott resolutions is to refuse to offer academic position to "Zionists," a sentiment that, in practical matters, would extend to Jews who do not agree with the boycott resolution. The irony of boycotts against alleged Israeli "racism" would be to foster a renewed era of job discrimination against Jews. Some Israeli scholars claim that "a silent boycott" of the absence of invitations to conferences, refusals to publish articles, or be in contact with them had already begun.[20] In 2007, Bernard Lewis and Fouad Ajami, joined with others to establish the Association for the Study of the Middle East and Africa (ASMEA) as an alternative to MESA. Smaller, and with few members who are tenured professors at universities with doctoral training programs, it serves the invaluable purpose of offering scholars the opportunity to gather, discuss, and debate many issues underexamined in MESA, including the nature of antisemitism in the Arab states, in Iran, and in Islamist organizations.[21]

In 2016, the International Holocaust Remembrance Alliance (IHRA) adopted a "working definition of antisemitism." Many governments have since adopted it. Its distinctive feature is to examine when legitimate criticism of Israel's policies crosses a line and becomes a form of antisemitism. Those line-crossing features include the following

Denying the fact, scope, mechanisms (e.g., gas chambers) or intentionality of the genocide of the Jewish people at the hands of National Socialist Germany and its supporters and accomplices during World War II (the Holocaust).

Accusing the Jews as a people, or Israel as a state, of inventing or exaggerating the Holocaust.

Accusing Jewish citizens of being more loyal to Israel, or to the alleged priorities of Jews worldwide, than to the interests of their own nations. Denying the Jewish people their right to self-determination, e.g., by claiming that the existence of a State of Israel is a racist endeavor.

Applying double standards by requiring of it a behavior not expected or demanded of any other democratic nation.

Using the symbols and images associated with classic antisemitism (e.g., claims of Jews killing Jesus or blood libel) to characterize Israel or Israelis.

Drawing comparisons of contemporary Israeli policy to that of the Nazis.

Holding Jews collectively responsible for actions of the state of Israel.[22]

The above accusations have figured, at one time or another, in antagonism to Jews and to Israel since the Holocaust. The IHRA definition left abundant room for criticism of the policies of the government of Israel, but it captured a deep truth about the nature of antisemitism since the establishment of the state of Israel. It is that the stereotype of the murderous, and evil individual Jew so deeply embedded in the Western tradition of anti-Judaism in Christianity, Islam, and then in modern secular antisemitism had reappeared in the depiction of Israel as a racist, imperialist, and even Nazi aggressor.

The IHRA definition rests on the assertion that Israel was not a state founded on racism and expulsion of the native inhabitants of British Mandate Palestine.[23] Obviously, if the state of Israel was a racist, apartheid state, then, like apartheid South Africa, it too would deserve "regime change" and the end of the Zionist project. If Israel fits the descriptions offered by the Palestine Liberation Organization, the Hamas Charter, or the various United Nations resolutions denouncing it, then describing it as such would not be a form of antisemitism. It would simply be telling the truth about a terrible reality.

Therefore, in discussions of what is and is not a form of antisemitism, issues of truth, fact, and evidence are unavoidable, and the role of historians is crucial. Recalling the realities of the establishment of the state of Israel and of its conflict with the Arab states, and Palestinian organizations is essential to respond to the primarily leftist and Islamist forms of antisemitism. The fact is that the Zionist project emerged from and was devoted to fighting against racism and colonialism and that, in the crucial years of 1947–1949, it was violently opposed by leaders, some of whom had collaborated with Nazi Germany, and who saw no distinction between antisemitism and anti-Zionism. On a number of famous occasions since 1947, the Palestinian leadership rejected proposals that would have replaced conflict with the Jewish state by the establishment of two states, one Jewish and one of the Palestine Arabs. The racism and antisemitism on the part of the founders and their successors of Palestinian nationalism that accompanied these repeated rejections was public, unabashed. Far too often, they have been overlooked, excused, or even justified in the United Nations, and then in the BDS efforts of recent years. Whether secular leftist or Islamist in inspiration, they shared the fundamental goal of replacing the existing state of Israel with another form of government which at best would eliminate Jewish sovereignty and at worst entail a massive war of destruction.[24] Recollection of the historical realities of the late 1940s is essential to challenge this most recent incarnation of the longest hatred.

Notes

Selections taken from Jeffrey Herf, "Historians Reject Anti-Israel Resolutions," originally in *The American Interest* (January 19, 2015): http://www.the-american-interest.com/2015/01/19/historians-reject-anti-israel-resolutions/. Reprinted with permission.

Jeffrey Herf, "How BDS Failed in the American Historical Association" (January 26, 2015): http://blogs.timesofisrael.com/how-bds-failed-in-the-american-historical-association/: reprinted with permission; and Jeffrey Herf, "Yet Again: The American Historical Association Rejects a Resolution Denouncing Israel," *Times of Israel* (January 13, 2016): http://blogs.timesofisrael.com/yet-again-the-american-historical-association-rejects-a-resolution-denouncing-israel-3/: reprinted with permission.

Jeffrey Herf, "Yet Again: The American Historical Association Rejects a Resolution Denouncing Israel," *History News Network* (January 15, 2016): http://historynewsnetwork.org/article/161729: reprinted with permission.

Jeffrey Herf, "IHRA and JDA: Examining Definitions of Antisemitism in 2021," *Fathom Journal* (April 2021): https://fathomjournal.org/ihra-and-jda-examining-definitions-of-antisemitism-in-2021/: reprinted with permission.

1 Paul Berman, *Terror and Liberalism* (New York: W.W. Norton, 2003), 142.

2 On the resistance to addressing the links between Islamism and antisemitism, see Paul Berman, *The Flight of the Intellectuals* (Brooklyn: Melville Press, 2010). On the leftist consensus, see Jeffrey Herf, "1967: The Global Left and the Six Day War," *Fathom Journal* (Spring 2017): https://fathomjournal.org/1967-and-the-global-left-the-case-of-the-east-german-regime-and-the-west-german-radicals/.

3 On this see Cary Nelson, *Israel Denial: Israel Denial: Anti-Zionism, Anti-Semitism, & the Faculty Campaign Against the Jewish State* (Bloomington: Indiana University Press, 2019); and Cary Nelson and Gabriel Noah Brahm, eds., *The Case Against Academic Boycotts of Israel* (Detroit: Wayne State University Press, 2015).

4 John Mearsheimer and Stephen Walt, "The Israel Lobby," *London Review of Books* 28, 6 (March 23, 2006): https://www.lrb.co.uk/the-paper/v28/n06/john-mearsheimer/the-israel-lobby; also as *The Israel Lobby and U.S. Foreign Policy* (New York: Farrar, Strauss and Giroux, 2008).

5 Jeffrey Herf and Andrei Markovits, "Letter to the Editor about John Mearsheimer and Stephen Walt on 'the Israel Lobby,'" *London Review of Books* 28, 7 (April 6, 2006): https://www.lrb.co.uk/the-paper/v28/n07/letters. On the Bush administration's focus on preventing "a second attack" as central to Bush's decision to invade see Melvyn Leffler, *Confronting Saddam Hussein: George W. Bush and the Invasion of Iraq* (New York and Oxford: Oxford University Press, 2023).

6 Herf and Markovits, "Letter to the Editor about John Mearsheimer and Stephen Walt on 'the Israel Lobby.'"

7 On the assertion that there is an "intersectional" connection between racism in the United States and the policies of the government of Israel see Angela Y. Davis, *Freedom Is A Constant Struggle: Ferguson, Palestine, and the Foundations of a Movement* (Chicago, IL: Haymarket Books, 2016), 42–47. For a critique of the use of the concept "intersectionality" in this context see Karin Stögner, "Antisemitism and Intersectional Feminism: Strange Alliances," in Armin Lange, Kerstin Mayerhofer, Dina Porat, and Lawrence H. Schiffman, eds., *Confronting Antisemitism in Media, the Legal, and Political Worlds, Volume 5* (Berlin: De Gruyter, 2021), 69–87; and "New Challenges in Feminism: Intersectionality, Critical Theory, and Anti-Zionism," in Alvin H. Rosenfeld, ed., *Anti-Zionism and Antisemitism: The Dynamics of Delegitimation* (Bloomington: Indiana University Press, 2019), 84–111. On the apartheid comparison and the discussion in South Africa, see Milton Shain, "The Roots of Anti-Zionism in South Africa and the Delegitimization of Israel," in Alvin H. Rosenfeld, ed., *Anti-Zionism and Antisemitism: The Dynamics of Delegitimation* (Bloomington: Indiana University Press, 2019), 397–413.

8 On this see Jeffrey Herf, *Israel's Moment: International Support for and Opposition to Establishing the Jewish State, 1945–1949* (New York and Cambridge: Cambridge University Press, 2022); and my "Israel is Antiracist, Anti-Colonialist, and Anti-Fascist (and was from the Start)," SAPIR, "Israel at 75" (Spring 2023): https://sapirjournal.org/israel-at-75/2023/04/israel-is-antiracist-anti-colonialist-anti-fascist-and-was-from-the-start/.

9 "Declaration and Programme of Action of the World Conference Against Racism, Racial Discrimination, Xenophobia and Related Intolerance," August 31–September 7, 2001, Durban, South Africa: https://www.ohchr.org/sites/default/files/Documents/Publications/Durban_text_en.pdf.

10 David Hirsh, *Contemporary Left Antisemitism* (London and New York: Routledge, 2018), 11–12.

11 Jeffrey Herf and Sonya Michel, "Open Letter to a University President," reprinted in Nelson and Brahm, *The Case Against Academic Boycotts of Israel*, 447–453; also in *The Chronicle of Higher Education*, blog (December 16, 2013): http://chronicle.com/blogs/conversation/2013/12/16/speak-truth-to-folly-boycott-the-american-studies-association/.

12 Ibid., 452–453.

13 Wallace Loh and Mary Ann Rankin, "Statement of the University of Maryland President and Provost Opposing the Boycott of Israeli Academic Institutions" (December 21, 2013): https://www.jewishvirtuallibrary.org/university-statements-rejecting-bds. The original link to the University of Maryland website is here but is now a dead link: http://www.president.umd.edu/statements/campus_message2013_12_22.cfm.

14 Cited in Jeffrey Herf, "A Pro-Hamas Left Emerges," *The American Interest* (August 26, 2014): http://www.the-american-interest.com/articles/2014/08/26/a-pro-hamas-left-emerges/. The link to the HAW statement calling for an end to American support for Israel is "dead."

15 Jeffrey Herf, "A Pro-Hamas Left Emerges," *The American Interest* (August 26, 2014): http://www.the-american-interest.com/articles/2014/08/26/a-pro-hamas-left-emerges/.

16 Ibid.

17 Jeffrey Herf, "Historians Reject Anti-Israel Resolutions," *The American Interest* (January 19, 2015): http://www.the-american-interest.com/2015/01/19/historians-reject-anti-israel-resolutions/; "How BDS Failed in the American Historical Association" (January 26, 2015): http://blogs.timesofisrael.com/how-bds-failed-in-the-american-historical-association/. On the defeat of a similar resolution in 2016 see "Yet Again: The American Historical Association Rejects a Resolution Denouncing Israel," *History News Network* (January 15, 2016): http://historynewsnetwork.org/article/161729; and *Times of Israel* (January 13, 2016): http://blogs.timesofisrael.com/yet-again-the-american-historical-association-rejects-a-resolution-denouncing-israel-3/.

18 Jeffrey Herf, "A Pro-Hamas Left Emerges," *The American Interest* (August 26, 2014): http://www.the-american-interest.com/articles/2014/08/26/a-pro-hamas-left-emerges/.

19 "Middle East Studies Association Members Vote to Ratify BDS Resolution" (March 23, 2022): https://mesana.org/news/2022/03/23/middle-east-scholars-vote-to-endorse-bds. The vote was 768 to 167. On the evolution over many years of MESA to an anti-Zionist and anti-Israeli consensus, see Martin Kramer, *Ivory Towers on Sand: The Failure of Middle Eastern Studies in America* (Washington, DC: Washington Institute for Near East Policy, 2001); and on some of its results see his *The War on Error: Israel, Islam, and the Middle East*, (New Brunswick, NJ, and London: Transaction Publishers, 2016).

20 Author's conversations with Israeli colleagues, 2010–2019.

21 The website of the ASMEA is here: https://www.asmeascholars.org/.

22 "What Is Antisemitism," IHRA: https://www.holocaustremembrance.com/resources/working-definitions-charters/working-definition-antisemitism. For a history of see: https://en.wikipedia.org/wiki/International_Holocaust_Remembrance_Alliance.

23 Jeffrey Herf, "IHRA and JDA: Examining Definitions of Antisemitism in 2021," *Fathom Journal* (April 2021): https://fathomjournal.org/ihra-and-jda-examining-definitions-of-antisemitism-in-2021/.

24 On the history of the late 1940s see Jeffrey Herf, *Israel's Moment: International Support for and Opposition to Establishing the Jewish State, 1945–1949* (New York and Cambridge: Cambridge University Press, 2022); and my "Israel is Antiracist, Anti-Colonialist, and Anti-Fascist (and was from the Start)," SAPIR, "Israel at 75" (Spring 2023): https://sapirjournal.org/israel-at-75/2023/04/israel-is-antiracist-anti-colonialist-anti-fascist-and-was-from-the-start/.

16

CONCLUSION

The Era of Simultaneity of Antisemitism's Three Faces

The distinctive and unique feature of our current period in the longer history of antisemitism is not that it persists. Antisemitism is too deeply embedded in the centuries-old Christian and Islamic antagonism to Judaism and in the modern secular incarnations anti-capitalist sentiments of the left to fade into insignificance. In the Christian churches, reckoning with the anti-Jewish traditions has been significant since the Holocaust, while such reckoning in Islam, overall, is lacking. It remains a latent presence in these two monotheistic successors to Judaism, and thus in the Western tradition as well. Rather, the unprecedented and unique aspect of recent decades consists in *the simultaneity of the three faces of antisemitism*. Throughout the history of modern antisemitism, there have been times when one or two of the three faces examined in the preceding pages have been predominant. Nazism and the Islamism it supported coexisted before and during World War II and the Holocaust. Islamist antisemitism persisted into the late 1940s and offered antisemitic arguments to justify the Arab and Palestinian Arab decision to wage war against the Zionist project and reject the United Nations Partition Resolution of 1947. Now, however, all three forms of antisemitism—right, left, and Islamist—are factors in world politics.

The polarization of politics, intellectual life, and scholarship has meant that this *simultaneity* is too rarely addressed. Instead, observers focus on one or at most two of the sources of antisemitism but less frequently all three at once. I have compiled this collection of essays to draw attention to these varieties of antisemitism and thereby foster recognition of their simultaneous presence in our political life in recent years. Despite their very distinct cultural and political starting points, the three forms of antisemitism often arrive at remarkably similar conclusions about Jews and about Zionism and

DOI: 10.4324/9781003449669-18

Israel. Therefore, intentionally, or not, they reinforce and amplify the energy and breadth of antisemitism. While fervent support for Islamic antisemitism is infrequent in the secular intellectual and academic world, equally rare is the willingness to openly criticize antisemitism when it comes from that quarter. A focus on antisemitism that only examines Nazism and the Holocaust, or far-right extremism in recent years, is not up to the challenge of our times. In contrast to the antisemitism of the far right, it is the leftist and Islamic faces of antisemitism that in the name of anti-Zionism and even "human rights" have achieved a certain cultural respectability and institutional anchor in the universities and cultural institutions.

The essays in this volume offer arguments and evidence about antisemitism that emerged mostly in Europe, and then in the Middle East and in world politics, from the 1920s to the 1970s. The ideas that circulate on the right, left, and among Islamists in the first decades of the twenty-first century have their origins in that half-century of totalitarianism and hatred of Judaism, Jews, and then the Jewish state, Israel. As Nazism was at the core of the explosion of Jew-hatred in Europe's twentieth century, it is understandable that historians of modern German history both during and since Nazi Germany and the Holocaust have played a leading role in examining the Nazi past as well as leftist and Islamist variations since. This historical perspective reminds us that the antisemitism of recent decades that has taken Israel as its target was not new. Its origins lay in the fateful half-century, set in motion to be sure by the Nazis and then by their collaboration with Islamists, and then continued during the Cold War by the Soviet Union, the Soviet bloc, and the global radical left. It was then that "the Jewish question" became "the Israel question." What is "new" is that all three faces of antisemitism have simultaneously become significant political factors.

From the perspective of the histories of Nazism and Communism, Europe's twentieth century was the short one defined by the defeat of Nazism in 1945 and the democratic revolutions of 1989–1991 that brought the Communist regimes in Eastern Europe and then the Soviet Union to an end. From the perspective of the history of antisemitism, however, that aspect of the twentieth century persists into the twenty-first. In that sense, the twentieth century has proven to be long, not short; indeed, it is not over.

The defeat of Nazi Germany and then the revelations of its crimes ended Nazi antisemitism as a major factor in world politics. From 1945 to the first decades of the twenty-first century, the antisemitism of the far right, expressed mostly in various forms of Holocaust denial, emained limited to the political fringes in the Western democracies. Nazism and the Holocaust stood as the ultimate evil of modern history, and the antisemitism associated with it fell into disrepute.

But antisemitism's roots in Western culture have proven too deep for it to disappear following the Holocaust. After the brief but consequential era of

Soviet support for Zionism that lasted only from 1947 to 1949, the Soviet Union, Soviet bloc, and Communist parties turned against Israel and did so with arguments that drew on conspiratorial exaggerations of Zionist power and distortions of the history of Israel's foundation. The Communist states and parties in the Cold War built an ideological bridge that recast the old antisemitic traditions as compatible with a redefined leftist anti-fascism and anti-imperialism. After the Six-Day War of 1967, this type of leftist attack on Israel spread to the generation coming of age in the 1960s both in the Western democracies, the Communist bloc countries, and nationalist intellectuals in the global south. It regularly crossed the line from criticism of Israel's policies to false comparisons of the Jewish state to Nazi Germany, apartheid in South Africa and, most famously, to the United Nations resolutions of 1975 and many others that followed, which blamed Israel exclusively for the absence of a compromise settlement of the conflict with the Palestinians. Some of these arguments echoed criticism of government policies voiced in Israel's parliament and press but others denied the legitimacy of the Jewish state and found a home in the universities and in left-leaning journalism. Following the Arab defeat of in the Six-Day War of 1967 and then the Iranian revolution of 1979 that brought the Islamic Republic into existence, Islamist antisemitism became a larger factor in Arab and Muslim-majority societies. In the last decades of the Cold War, leftist anti-Zionism now coexisted with a revived Islamic antisemitism, evident in the Hamas Covenant of 1988, threats by Iran and its proxy Hezbollah to destroy the state of Israel. The attack of September 11, 2001, those that followed on Jews in Israel and in Europe demonstrated that Islamist Jew-hatred had become the most important form of antisemitism in world politics. Within academia, the arguments of "What is old, and what is new about the terrorism of Islamic fundamentalism," Paul Berman's *Terror and Liberalism*, and Matthias Küntzel's *Islamism, Nazism and the Roots of 9/11*—all of which urged liberals to recognize and criticize the reactionary and totalitarian nature Islamist ideology—met with significant resistance.[1] Few exceptions, academics, and political leaders did not focus public attention on the connection between Islamism and antisemitism for fear that doing so would foster "Islamophobia," that is, antagonism to Muslims in general, and/or due to a conceptual reluctance to acknowledge that reactionary ideologies could come from the countries in "the global south."[2]

Islamic antisemitism is an ideology of the extreme right, a fact obscured by the fog of anti-Western and anti-imperialist rhetoric that is also used. Along with blatant Jew-hatred, its inherent misogyny, threats to homosexuals, celebration of terror, and religious fanaticism have thus stood in the way of Islamist antisemitism finding support within Western academia. Yet, with the use of the term "Islamophobia," Islamists have succeeded in avoiding the sharp criticism in liberal quarters that their reactionary ideology deserves.

Conversely, however, because it lacked those politically incorrect attributes, secular leftist antagonism to the state of Israel of the sort discussed in this work has found academic respectability. Initially, it was the redefinition of anti-fascism in the Soviet bloc in the 1950s that created the possibility for an antisemitism that came with a progressive pedigree. Then the assertion that Zionism was a form of racism, and that therefore anti-Zionism was a form of antiracism, not antisemitism, proved crucial. It fostered antisemitism which, for the first time in the history of that hatred, insisted that it was nothing of the sort and that to accuse it of antisemitism was a form of Zionist propaganda or, more recently, "white privilege" or simply white racism.

In the past two decades, the antisemitism of the far right, which for many years remained on the fringes of Western politics, has made inroads into the political mainstream via the idea of "the great replacement" according to which Jews have been the power behind waves of immigration of peoples of color who will replace and outnumber whites in Europe, the United States, Canada, and Australia. It is the central antisemitic conspiracy theory of the far right around the world. This familiar right-wing Jew-hatred was evident in the attack in Charlottesville in 2017, in the murder of eleven Jews at the Tree of Life Synagogue in Pittsburgh in 2018, and among the right-wing extremists who attacked the U.S. Capitol on January 6, 2021. Trump's comment that there were "good people on both sides" in Charlottesville created connections between the fringe and the mainstream that many of us saw developing in the spring of 2016.

The simultaneous presence of antisemitism's three faces means that each, willingly or not, reinforces the other two by adding to the general climate of antagonism to Jews around the world and to the state of Israel. The simultaneity creates a synergy among right, left, and Islamist faces of antisemitism. It is welcome that scholars, especially in Europe, Israel, and the United States, including scholars of a young generation, have responded with a burst of scholarship about antisemitism's three faces. The results of their work are evident in the preceding chapters.

Work on the history of Nazism and the Holocaust will rightly continue to preoccupy historians of antisemitism. Holocaust denial and sheer ignorance about basic facts persist. However, in 2023, scholarship on the Holocaust and the antisemitism of the far right is essential but not sufficient. Right-wing political parties in the democracies and authoritarian states wage culture wars that flirt with antisemitic conspiracy theories. The danger there is obvious. Yet, to be successful, the fight against antisemitism today must clearly describe and criticize forms that come from the left and the Islamists as well. That effort needs to be intensified within the academy and in our intellectual life. As the three faces of antisemitism persist, so should the efforts of scholars to understand, and fight against them.

Notes

1 Paul Berman, *Terror and Liberalism* (New York: Knopf, 2003); Matthias Küntzel, *Jihad und Judenhass: Über die neuen antijüdischen Krieg* (Freiburg: ca ira Verlag, 2002); and the English edition, *Jihad and Jew-Hatred: Islamism, Nazism, and the Roots of 9/11*, trans. Colin Meade (New York: Telos Press, 2007).
2 Two important exceptions were Bassam Tibi, *Islamism and Islam* (New Haven, CT: Yale University Press, 2012); and Küntzel, *Jihad and Jew-Hatred*.

SELECTED BIBLIOGRAPHY

I list here writings that have been important in writing this book, or that, in recent decades have figured prominently in the now extensive and growing international scholarly discussion of varieties of antisemitism.

Academic Engagement Network. *Academic Freedom, Freedom of Expression, and the BDS Challenge: A Guide and Resource Book for Faculty* (United States: Academic Engagement Network, 2017).

———— *Academic Engagement Network. Antisemitism, Jewish Identity, and Freedom of Expression on Campus: A Guide and Resource Book for Faculty & University Leaders* (Academic Engagement Network: 2022): https://academicengagement. org/2022-guide/.

Ajami, Fouad. *The Arab Predicament: Arab Political Thought and Practice Since 1967* (New York and Cambridge, 1981).

————. *The Dream Palace of the Arabs: A Generation's Odyssey* (New York: Vintage Books, [1998] 1999).

————. *In This Arab Time: The Pursuit of Deliverance* (Stanford, CA: Hoover Institution Press, 2014).

Amery, Jean. *Werke, Band 7: Aufsätze zur Politik und Geschichte* (Stuttgart: Klett-Cotta, 2005).

————. *Essays on Antisemitism, Anti-Zionism, and the Left*. ed. Marlene Gallner. trans. Lars Fischer (Bloomington: Indiana University Press, 2022).

Bauer, Yehuda. *Rethinking the Holocaust* (New Haven, CT: Yale University Press, 2002).

Bendersky, Joseph W. *The Jewish Threat: Anti-Semitic Politics of the U.S. Army* (New York: Basic Books, 2000).

Bensoussan, Georges. *Juifs en Pays Arabes: Le grand déracinement, 1850–1975* (Paris: Edition Tallandier, 2012).

————. ed. "Les Juifs d'Orient face au nazisme et à la Shoah (1930–1945)." In Georges Bensoussan, ed., *Revue D'Histoire de la Shoah* 205 (October 2016) (Paris: Fondation pour la memoire de la Shoah/Centre de documentation juive contemporaine, 2016).

Berman, Paul. *Terror and Liberalism* (New York: W.W. Norton, 2003).

——. *The Flight of the Intellectuals* (Brooklyn, NY: Melville Press, 2010).

Birnbaum, Pierre. "The French Radical Right: From Anti-Semitic Zionism to Anti-Semitic Anti-Zionism." In Jeffrey Herf, ed., *Anti-Semitism and Anti-Zionism in Historical Perspective: Convergence and Divergence* (London and New York: Routledge, 2007).

Bracher, Karl. *The German Dictatorship* (New York: Praeger, 1970).

——. *Zeitgeschichtliche Kontroversen: Um Faschismus, Totalitarismus, Demokratie* (Munich: Piper Verlag, 1976).

——. "The Role of Hitler: Perspectives of Interpretation." In Walter Laqueur, ed., *Fascism: A Reader's Guide* (Berkeley: University of California Press, 1976): 211–225.

Breitman, Richard. *The Architect of Genocide: Himmler and the Final Solution* (New York: Knopf, 1991).

Breitman, Richard and Norman Goda. *Hitler's Shadow: Nazi War Criminals, U.S. Intelligence, and the Cold War* (Create Space Independent Publishing Platform: United States, 2014).

Brent, Jonathan. *Stalin's Last Crime: The Plot Against Jewish Doctors, 1948–1953* (New York: Harper, 2004).

Broder, Henryk M. *Der ewige Antisemit: Über Sinn und Funktion eines beständigen Gefühls*. 2nd ed. (Berlin: Berliner Taschenbuch Verlag, 2006).

——. *Vergesst Auschwitz! Der deutsche Erinnerungswahn und die Endlösung der Israel-Frage* (Munich: Albrecht Knaus Verlag, 2012).

Browning, Christopher with contributions by Jürgen Matthäus. *The Origins of the Final Solution. The Evolution of Nazi Jewish Policy, September 1939–March 1942* (Lincoln, NB: University of Nebraska Press, and Jerusalem: Yad Vashem, 2004).

Chaouat, Bruno. "Antisemitism Redux: On Literary and Theoretical Perversions." In Alvin H. Rosenfeld, ed., *Resurgent Antisemitism: Global* Perspectives (Bloomington: Indiana University Press, 2013): 118–139.

Chatterley, Catherine. *Disenchantment: The Meaning of Western Civilization after Auschwitz* (Syracuse: Syracuse University Press, 2011).

——. "The Antisemitic Imagination." In Charles Asher Small, ed., *Global Antisemitism: A Crisis of Modernity. Volume I: Conceptual Approaches* (Leiden: Brill, 2013): 79–84.

——. "Leaving the Post-Holocaust Period: The Effects of Anti-Israeli Attitudes on Perceptions of the Holocaust." In Alvin H. Rosenfeld., ed. *Anti-Zionism and Antisemitism: The Dynamics of Delegitimization—Studies in Antisemitism* (Bloomington: Indiana University Press, 2019): 158–174.

Dawidowicz, Lucy. *The Historians and the Holocaust* (Cambridge, MA: Harvard University Press, 1981).

Engelstein, Laura. *The Resistable Rise of Antisemitism: Exemplary Cases from Russia, Ukraine, and Poland* (Waltham, MA: Brandeis University Press, 2020).

Erickson, Robert and Susannah Heschel, eds. *Betrayal: The German Churches and the Holocaust* (Minneapolis, MN: Fortress Press, 1999).

Evans, Richard J. *Lying About Hitler* (New York: Basic Books, 2002).

——. *The Hitler's Conspiracies* (New York and London: Oxford University Press, and Allen Lane, 2020).

Fine, Robert, and Philip Spencer. *Antisemitism and the Left: On the Return of the Jewish Question* (Manchester: Manchester University Press, 2017).

Fredrickson, George. *Racism: A Short History* (Princeton, NJ: Princeton University Press, 2002).

Friedlander, Saul. *Nazi Germany and the Jews, Volume I: The Years of Persecution, 1933–1939* (New York: Harper, 1998).

———. *Nazi Germany and the Jews, 1939–1945: The Years of Extermination* (New York: 2008).

Furet, Francois. *The Passing of an Illusion: The Idea of Communism in the Twentieth Century.* trans. Deborah Furet (Chicago, IL: University of Chicago Press, 1999).

———. *"Israel" in Un Itinéraire Intellectuel: L'historien journaliste de France-Observateur au Nouvel Observateur (1958–1997)* (Paris: Calmann-Lévy, 1999), 451–504.

Gallner, Marlene. "Like a Cloud Contains a Storm: Jean Améry's Critique of Anti-Zionism," *Fathom Journal* (August, 2016): https://fathomjournal.org/like-a-cloud-contains-a-storm-jean-amerys-critique-of-anti-zionism/.

Gensicke, Klaus. *The Mufti of Jerusalem and the Nazis: The Berlin Years.* trans. Alexander Fraser Gunn (London and Portland, OR: Vallentine Mitchell, 2011).

Geras, Norman, et al., *The Euston Manifesto* (London: 2006): https://eustonmanifesto.org/the-euston-manifesto/

Goda, Norman, ed. *Envoy to the Promised Land: The Diaries and Papers of James G. McDonald, 1948–1951* (Bloomington: Indiana University Press, 2017).

———. *The Holocaust: Europe, the World, and the Jews, 1918–1945.* 2nd ed. (New York and London: Routledge, 2022).

Grigat, Stephan, "Die Sehnsucht nach Freiheit und die Vernichtungsdrohungen gegen Israel." In Stephan Grigat and Simone Dinah Hartmann, eds., *Iran im Weltsystem: Bündnisse des Regimes und Perspektiven der Freiheitsbewegung.* (Innsbruck and Vienna: Studien Verlag, 2010): 12–20.

———. *Die Einsamkeit Israels: Zionismus, die israelische Linke und die iranische Bedrohung* (Hamburg: Konkret, 2014).

———. "Antisemitic Anti-Zionism: Muslim Brotherhood, Iran, and Hezbollah." In Armin Lange, Kerstin Mayerhofer, Dina Porat, and Lawrence H. Schiffman, eds. *Confronting Antisemitism in Media, the Legal, and Political Worlds: An End to Antisemitism! Volume 5* (Berlin: De Gruyter, 2021): 149–172.

———. ed., *Kritik der Antisemitismus in der Gegenwart: Erscheinungsformen – Theorien – Bekämpfung* (Baden-Baden: Nomos Verlag, 2023).

Grigat, Stephan and Simone Dinah Hartmann eds. *Der Iran: Analyse einer islamischen Diktatur und ihrer europäischen Förderer* (Innsbruck and Vienna: Studien Verlag, 2008).

———. *Iran im Weltsystem: Bündnisse des Regimes und Perspektiven der Freiheitsbewegung* (Innsbruck and Vienna: Studien Verlag, 2010).

Habermas, Jürgen, Saul Friedlander, Norbert Frei, and Sybille Steinbacher. *Ein Verbrechen ohne Namen: Anmerkungen zum neuen Streit über den Holocaust* (Munich: C.H. Beck Verlag, 2022).

Hakakian, Roya. *Assassins of the Turquoise Palace* (New York: Grove Press, 2011).

Hannebrink, Paul. *A Specter Haunting Europe: The Myth of Judeo-Bolshevism* (Cambridge, MA: Harvard University Press, 2018).

Harrison, Bernard. *Blaming the Jews: Politics and Delusion* (Bloomington: Indiana University Press, 2020).

Hartmann, Christian, Thomas Vordermayer, Othmar Plöckinger and Roman Töppel, eds. *Hitler, Mein Kampf: Eine kritische Edition* (Munich-Berlin: Institut für Zeitgeschichte, 2016).

Herf, Jeffrey. "The 'Holocaust' Reception in West Germany: Left, Right and Center," *New German Critique* 19 (Winter, 1980): 30–52.

———. "The Engineer as Ideologue: Reactionary Modernists in Weimar and Nazi Germany." *Journal of Contemporary History.* 19 (1984): 631–648.

———. *Reactionary Modernism: Technology, Culture and Politics in Weimar and the Third Reich* (New York and Cambridge, UK: Cambridge University Press, 1984).

———. "Multiple Restorations: German Political Traditions and the Interpretation of Nazism, 1945–1946." *Central European History.* 26, 1 (1993): 21–55.

———. "Der Geheimprozeß." *Die Zeit.* (October 7, 1994), overseas edition (October 14, 1994), 7–8.

———. "East German Communists and the Jewish Question: The Case of Paul Merker." *Journal of Contemporary History.* 29, 4 (October 1994): 627–662.

———. "Dokumentation: Antisemitismus in der SED: Geheime Dokumente zum Fall Paul Merker aus SED- und MfS-Archiven." *Vierteljahrshefte für Zeitgeschichte.* 42, 4 (October 1994): 1–32.

———. *Divided Memory: The Nazi Past in the Two Germanys* (Cambridge, MA: Harvard University Press, 1997).

———. "The Historian as Provocateur: George Mosse's Accomplishment and Legacy." *Yad Vashem Studies.* 29 (2001): 7–26.

———. "The "Jewish War": Goebbels and the Antisemitic Campaigns of the Nazi Propaganda Ministry." *Holocaust and Genocide Studies.* 19, 1 (Spring 2005): 51–80.

———. The Jewish Enemy: Nazi Propaganda During World War II and the Holocaust. (Cambridge, MA: Harvard University Press, 2006).

———. "Convergence: The Classic Case Nazi Germany, Anti-Semitism and Anti-Zionism during World War II." In Jeffrey Herf, ed., *Anti-Semitism and Anti-Zionism in Historical Perspective: Convergence and Divergence* (New York and London: Routledge, 2007): 50–70.

———. "A Comparative Perspective on Antisemitism, Radical Antisemitism in the Holocaust and American White Racism." *The Journal of Genocide Research.* 9, 4 (December 2007): 575–600.

———. "Nazi Germany's Propaganda Aimed at Arabs and Muslims During World War II and the Holocaust: Old Themes, New Archival Findings." *Central European History.* 42, 4, (December 2009): 709–736.

———. *Nazi Propaganda for the Arab World* (New Haven, CT: Yale University Press, 2009).

———. "Hitlers Dschihad: NS-Rundfunkpropaganda für Nordafrika und den Nahen Osten." *Vierteljahrshefte fuer Zeitgeschichte.* 58, 2 (2010): 259–286.

———. "A Blood Libel for Our Time: Günter Grass's, What Must be Said." *German Studies Review.* 36, 2 (May 2013): 384–388.

———. "'The War and the Jews': Nazi Propaganda in the Second World War." In Jörg Echternkamp, ed., *Germany and the Second World War: Volume IX/II, German Wartime Society 1939–1945: Exploitation, Interpretations, Exclusion* (Oxford: Oxford University Press, 2014): 163–204.

———. "At War with Israel: East Germany's Key Role in Soviet Policy in the Middle East." *Journal of Cold War Studies.* 16, 3 (Summer 2014): 129–163.

———. "Haj Amin el-Husseini, the Nazis and the Holocaust: The Origins, the Nature and Aftereffects of Collaboration." *Jewish Political Studies Review.* 26, 3/4 (Fall 2014): 13–37.

———. Undeclared Wars with Israel: East Germany and the West German Far Left, 1967–1989. (New York and Cambridge: Cambridge University Press, 2016).

———. "The Anti-Zionist Bridge: The East German Communist Contribution to Antisemitism's Revival After the Holocaust." *Antisemitism Studies*. 23, 1 (Spring 2017): 130–156.

———. "Correspondence." *The Jewish Quarterly*. 245 (August 2021): 101–103.

———. Israel's Moment: International Support for and Opposition to Establishing the Jewish State, 1945–1949 (New York and Cambridge: Cambridge University Press, 2022).

Herzinger, Richard. Endzeit-Propheten, oder, Die Offensive der Antiwestler: Fundamentalismus, Antiamerikanismus und neue Rechte (Hamburg: Rowohlt Verlag, 1995).

———. *Hold These Truths*. Website: https://herzinger.org/ueber-diese-seite.

Heschel, Susannah. *The Aryan Jesus: Christian Theologians and the Bible in Nazi Germany* (Princeton, NJ: Princeton University Press, 2010).

Hirsh, David. *Contemporary Left Antisemitism* (London: Routledge/Taylor and Francis, 2018).

Igounet, Valerie. *Histoire due négationisme en France* (Paris: Seuil, 2000).

———. *Robert Faurisson: portrait d'un négationniste* (Paris: Denoél, 2012).

International Holocaust Remembrance Alliance. "Definition of Antisemitism." (May 26, 2016): https://www.holocaustremembrance.com/resources/working-definitions-charters/working-definition-antisemitism.

Jacobs, Jack. *The Frankfurt School, Jewish Lives, and Antisemitism* (New York: Cambridge University Press, 2015).

Jander, Martin, Enrico Heitzer, Anetta Kahane and Patrice G. Poutros, eds. *After Auschwitz: The Difficult Legacies of the GDR* (New York and Oxford: Berghahn Books, 2021).

Jikeli, Günther. "Antisemitic Acts and Attitudes in Contemporary France. The Effects on French Jews." *Antisemitism Studies*. 2, 2 (Fall 2018): 297–320.

———. ed. *The Return of Religious Antisemitism* (Basel: MDPI Books, 2021).

———. "Attitudes of Syrian and Iraqi Refugees in Germany toward Jews." In Armin Lange, Kerstin Mayerhofer, Dixna Porat, and Lawrence H. Schiffmann, eds., *Confronting Antisemitism in Modern Media, the Legal and Political Worlds* (Berlin: De Gruyter: 2021): 239–268.

Johnson, Alan. "Antisemitism in the Guise of Anti-Nazism: Holocaust Inversion in the United Kingdom during Operation Protective Edge." In Alvin H. Rosenfeld., ed., *Anti-Zionism and Antisemitism: The Dynamics of Delegitimization—Studies in Antisemitism* (Bloomington: Indiana University Press, 2019): 175–199.

Julius, Anthony. *Trials of the Diaspora: A History of Antisemitism in England* (New York and Oxford: Oxford University Press, 2010).

Julius, Lynn. *Uprooted: How 3000 Years of Jewish Civilization in the Arab World Vanished Overnight* (London: Vallentine Mitchell, 2018).

Kahane, Anetta, Heike Radvan, and Anetta Leo. *Das hat's bei uns nicht gegeben! Antisemitismus in der DDR: Das Buch zur Ausstellung der Amadeu Antonio Stiftung* (Berlin: Amadeo Antonio Stiftung, 2010).

Katz, Steven, T., ed. *Cambridge Companion to Antisemitism* (New York and Cambridge: Cambridge University Press, 2022).

Klaff, Lesley, "Fraser v University and College Union: Anti-Zionism, Antisemitism, and Racializing Discourse." In Alvin H. Rosenfeld., ed. *Anti-Zionism and Antisemitism: The Dynamics of Delegitimization—Studies in Antisemitism* (Bloomington: Indiana University Press, 2019): 200–220.

Kloke, *Israel und die deutsche Linke: Zur Geschichte eines schwierigen Verhältnisses.* 2nd ed. (Frankfurt/Main: HAAG + HERCHEN, and Deutsch-Israelischen Arbeitskreises für Frieden im Nahen Osten, 1994).

Kramer, Martin. *Ivory Towers on Sand: The Failure of Middle Eastern Studies in America* (Washington, DC: Washington Institute for Near East Policy, 2001).

———. *The War on Error: Israel, Islam, and the Middle East* (New Brunswick, NJ, and London: Transaction Publishers, 2016).

Kraushaar, Wolfgang. *Die Bombe im Jüdischen Gemeindhaus* (Hamburg: Hamburger Edition, 2005).

———. ed. *Die RAF und der linke Terrorismus.* 2 vols (Hamburg: Hamburger Edition, 2006).

———. "Wann endlich begint bei Euch der Kampf gegen die heilige Kuh Israel?" In *München 1970: Über die antisemitischen Wurzeln des deutschen Terrorismus* (Hamburg: Rowohlt Verlag, 2013).

Küntzel, Matthias. *Jihad and Jew-Hatred: Nazism, Islamism and the Roots of 9/11* (New York: Telos Press, 2007).

———. *Islamischer Anti-Semitismus und Deutsche Politik: "Heimliches Einverständnis"?* (Berlin: LIT Verlag, 2007).

———. *Deutschland, Iran und die Bombe: Eine Entgegnung—Auch auf Günter Grass* (Berlin: LIT Verlag, 2012).

———. *Germany and Iran: From the Aryan Axis to the Nuclear Threshold*, trans. Colin Meade (New York: Telos Press, 2014).

———. *Nazis und der Nahe Osten: Wie der Islamische Antisemitismus Entstand* (Berlin and Leipzig: Hentrich & Hentrich, 2019).

———. "Die Besonderheit des Antisemitismus Erkennen. Ansprache der Preisträger." In *Verleihung des Theodor Lessing Preises 2022 an Dr. Matthias Küntzel. Dokumentation der Festreden* (Arbeitsgemeinschaft Hannover Deutsch-Israelische Gesellschaft, 2022): 51–57.

———. *Nazis, Islamic Antisemitism, and the Middle East: The 1948 Arab War against Israel and the Aftershocks of WW II* (London: Routledge, 2023).

———. Website with essays. In German: http://www.matthiaskuentzel.de/contents/. In English: http://www.matthiaskuentzel.de/contents/kategorie/english/?lang=en.

Küntzel, Matthias, Klaus Thörner und Andere. *Goldhagen und die Deutsche Linke* (Berlin: Elefanten Press, 1997).

Landes, Richard. *Can "The Whole World" Be Wrong?: Lethal Journalism, Antisemitism, and Global Jihad* (New York: Academic Press, 2022).

Laqueur, Walter, *The Changing Face of Antisemitism: From Ancient Times to the Present* (New York: Oxford University Press, 2006).

Lewis, Bernard. *Semites and Anti-Semites: An Inquiry into Conflict and Prejudice* (New York and London: W.W. Norton, [1986] 1999).

Linfield, Susie. *The Lions' Den: Zionism and the Left from Hannah Arendt to Noam Chomsky* (New Haven, CT: Yale University Press, 2019).

Lipstadt, Deborah E. *Denying the Holocaust: The Growing Assault on Truth and Memory* (New York: Plume, 1994).

———. *Antisemitism: Here and Now* (New York: Schocken, 2019).

Litvak, Meir, and Esther Webman, *From Empathy to Denial: Arab Responses to the Holocaust* (London: Hurst and Company, 2009).

Mallmann, Klaus-Michael, and Martin Cüppers. *Nazi Palestine: The Plans for the Extermination of the Jews of Palestine.* trans. Krista Smith (New York: Enigma Press, 2010).

Markovits, Andrei. *Uncouth Nation: Why Europe Dislikes America* (Princeton, NJ: Princeton University Press, 2007).

———— and Jeffrey Herf, "Letter to the Editor about John Mearsheimer and Stephen Walt on 'the Israel Lobby.'" *London Review of Books.* 28, 7 (April 6, 2006): https://www.lrb.co.uk/the-paper/v28/n07/letters.

————. "An Inseparable Tandem of European Identity? Anti-Americanism and Anti-Semitism in the Short and Long Run." In Jeffrey Herf, ed., *Anti-Semitism and Anti-Zionism in Historical Perspective: Convergence and Divergence* (London and New York: Routledge, 2007), 71–91.

MEMRI, the Middle East Media, and Research Institute (https://www.memri.org/archives). See its "Lantos Archive on Antisemitism and Holocaust Denial." https://www.memri.org/subjects/antisemitism-documentation-project.

Meuschel, Sigrid. *Legitimation und Parteiherrschaft in der DDR* (Frankfurt/Main: Suhrkamp Verlag, 1992).

Morris, Benny. *1948: A History of the First Arab-Israeli War* (New Haven, CT: Yale University Press, 2008).

Mosse, George, *The Crisis of German Ideology: Intellectual Origins of the Third Reich* (New York: Grosset and Dunlap, 1964; reprint (Madison: University of Wisconsin Press, 2021).

Muller, Jerry Z. *The Other God that Failed: Hans Freyer and the Deradicalization of German Conservatism* (Princeton, NJ: Princeton University Press, 1987).

————. *The Mind and the Market: Capitalism in Modern European Thought* (New York: Knopf, 2002).

————. *Capitalism and the Jews* (Princeton, NJ: Princeton University Press, 2010).

Muravchik, Joshua. *Making David into Goliath: How the World Turned Against Israel* (New York: Encounter, 2014).

Murawiec, Laurent. *The Mind of Jihad* (New York: Cambridge University Press, 2008).

Nelson, Cary, *Israel Denial: Anti-Zionism, Anti-Semitism and The Faculty Campaign Against the Jewish State* (Bloomington, IN: Indiana University Press, and Academic Engagement Network, 2019).

Nelson, Cary, and Gabriel Noah Brahm, eds., *The Case Against Academic Boycotts of Israel.* (Detroit, MI: Wayne State University Press, 2015).

Nirenberg, David. *Anti-Judaism: The Western Tradition* (New York: W.W. Norton, 2013).

Norwood, Stephen H. *Antisemitism and the American Far Left* (New York: Cambridge University Press, 2013).

Patterson, David. *A Genealogy of Evil: Anti-Semitism from Nazism to Islamic Jihad* (New York and Cambridge: Cambridge University Press, 2011).

Perry, Marvin and Frederick M. Schweitzer, eds. *Antisemitic Myths: A Historical and Contemporary Anthology* (Bloomington: Indiana University Press, 2008).

Pipes, Daniel. *Conspiracy: How the Paranoid Style Flourishes and Where It Comes From* (New York: Touchstone/Simon and Schuster, 1999).

Poliakov, Leon, *The History of Antisemitism, Volume I: From the Time of Christ to the Court Jews,* trans. Richard Howard (Philadelphia: University of Pennsylvania Press, 2003).

———. *The History of Antisemitism: Volume II: From Mohammed to the Marranos*, trans. Natalie Gerardi (Philadelphia: University of Pennsylvania Press, 2003).

———. *The History of Antisemitism: Volume III: From Voltaire to Wagner*, trans. Miriam Kochan (Philadelphia: University of Pennsylvania Press, 2003).

———. *The History of Antisemitism: Volume IV: Suicidal Europe, 1870–1933*, trans. George Klin (Philadelphia: University of Pennsylvania Press, 2003).

Porat, Dina. "Holocaust Denial and the Image of the Jew, or: They Boycott Auschwitz as an Israeli Product." In Alvin H. Rosenfeld, ed., *Insurgent Antisemitism: Global Perspectives* (Bloomington: Indiana University Press, 2013): 467–481.

———. "Anti-Zionism as Antisemitism," In Steven T. Katz, ed., *The Cambridge Companion to Antisemitism* (New York and Cambridge: Cambridge University Press, 2022): 448–464.

Probst, Christopher J. *Demonizing the Jews. Luther and the Protestant Church in Nazi Germany.* (Bloomington: Indiana University Press, 2012).

Rabinbach, Anson, *Staging the Third Reich: Essays in Cultural and Intellectual History* (New York: Routledge, 2020).

Rabinbach, Anson and Sander L. Gilman, eds. *The Third Reich Sourcebook* (Berkeley and Los Angeles: University of California Press, 2013).

Rensman, Lars, *The Politics of Unreason: The Frankfurt School and the Origins of Modern Antisemitism* (Albany, NY: SUNY Press, 2017).

Rosenfeld, Alvin H. *Anti-Zionism and Antisemitism: The Dynamics of Delegitmation.* (Bloomigton: Indiana University Press, 2019).

Rubin, Barry, and Wolfgang G. Schwanitz. *Nazis, Islamists and the Making of the Modern Middle East* (New Haven, CT: Yale University Press, 2014).

Salzborn, Samuel. *The Modern State and Its Enemies: Democracy, Nationalism and Antisemitism* (London: Anthem Press, 2020).

———. *Globaler Antisemitismus. Eine Spurensuche in den Abgründen der Moderne.* 3rd ed. (Weinheim, Germany: Juventa Verlag, 2022).

Schwartz, Adi, and Einat Wilf. *The War of Return. How Western Indulgence of the Palestinian Dream Has Obstructed the Path to Peace* (New York: All Points Books/ Martin's Press, 2020).

Schwarz-Friesel, Monika and Jehuda Reinharz. *Inside the Antisemitic Mind: The Language of Jew-Hatred in Contemporary Germany* (Waltham, MA: Brandeis University Press, 2017).

Seymour, David. "'New Europe,' Holocaust Memory and Antisemitism." In Charles Asher Small, ed., *Global Antisemitism: A Crisis of Modernity. Volume I. Conceptual Approaches.* (New York: Institute for the Study of Global Antisemitism and Policy, 2013): 21–29.

———. "Continuity and Discontinuity: From Antisemitism to Antizionism and the Reconfiguration of the Jewish Question." *Journal of Contemporary Antisemitism.* 2, 2 (2019): 11–24.

Sinkoff, Nancy, *From Left to Right: Lucy S. Dawidowicz: New York Intellectuals, and the Politics of Jewish History* (Detroit: Wayne State University Press, 2020).

Small, Charles Asher, ed. *Global Antisemitism: A Crisis of Modernity. Volume 1: Conceptual Approaches. Volume II. The Intellectual Environment. Volume III. Antisemitism in Comparative Perspective. Volume IV. Islamism and the Arab World. Volume V. Reflections* (New York: Institute for the Study of Global Antisemitism and Policy; CreateSpace Independent Publishing Platform, [2013] 2014).

Steigmann-Gall, Richard. *The Holy Reich: Nazi Conceptions of Christianity, 1919–1945* (New York and Cambridge: Cambridge University Press, 2014).

Stögner, Karin. *Antisemitismus und Sexismus: Historisch-gesellschaftliche Konstellationen* (Baden-Baden: Nomos Verlagsgesellschaft, 2014).

———. "New Challenges in Feminism: Intersectionality, Critical Theory, and Anti-Zionism." In Alvin H. Rosenfeld, ed., *Anti-Zionism and Antisemitism: The Dynamics of Delegitimation* (Bloomington: Indiana University Press, 2019): 84–111.

———. "Antisemitism and Intersectional Feminism: Strange Alliances." In Armin Lange, Kerstin Mayerhofer, Dina Porat, and Lawrence H. Schiffman, eds. *Confronting Antisemitism in Media, the Legal, and Political Worlds: An End to Antisemitism! Volume 5* (Berlin: De Gruyter, 2021): 69–87.

——— and Nicholas Bechter, Lesley Klaff, and Philip Spencer, eds. *Contemporary Antisemitism and Racism in the Shadow of the Holocaust*. Special issue of *Journal for the Study of Antisemitism* (Boston, MA: Academic Studies Press, 2021).

Stola, Dariusz. "Anti-Zionism as a Multi-Purpose Policy Instrument: The Anti-Zionist Campaign in Poland, 1967–1968." *Journal of Israeli History*. 25, 1 (March 2006): 175–201.

Tabarovsky, Izabella, "Mahmoud Abbas's Dissertation" (January 18, 2023), *The Tablet Magazine*. https://www.tabletmag.com/sections/arts-letters/articles/mahmoud-abbas-soviet-dissertation.

Taguieff, Pierre-Andre. *L'antisémitisme* (Paris: Que Sais-Je: 2015).

———. *Le grand Remplacement ou la politique du mythe: Généalogie d'une representation polémique* (Paris: L'Observatoire, 2022).

Tibi, Bassam. *Islamism and Islam* (New Haven, CT: Yale University Press, 2012).

Trigano, ed., *La fin du judaisme en terres d'Islam* (Paris: Denöel, 2009).

Volkov. "Readjusting Cultural Codes: Reflections on Anti-Semitism and Anti-Zionism." In Jeffrey Herf, ed., *Anti-Semitism and Anti-Zionism in Historical Perspective: Convergence and Divergence* (London and New York: Routledge, 2007): 38–49.

Vukadinovic, Vojin Sasa, ed., *Freiheit ist Keine Metapher: Antisemitismus, Migration, Rassismus, Religionskritik* (Berlin: Querverlag. 2018).

Wald, "The New Replacement Theory: Anti-Zionism, Antisemitism, and the Denial of History." In Alvin H. Rosenfeld, ed., *Anti-Zionism and Antisemitism: The Dynamics of Delegitimation* (Bloomington: Indiana University Press, 2019): 3–29.

Webman, Esther and Meir Litvak. *From Empathy to Denial: Arab Responses to the Holocaust* (London: Hurst and Company, 2009).

———. "New Islamic Antisemitism, Mid-19th to the 21st Century." In Steven T. Katz, ed., *Cambridge Companion to Antisemitism* (New York and Cambridge: Cambridge University Press, 2022): 430–447.

Whitman, James Q. *Hitler's American Model: The United States and the Making of Nazi Race Law* (Princeton, NJ and Oxford: Princeton University Press, 2017).

Wiese, Christian. *Years of Persecution, Years of Extermination: Saul Friedlander and the Future of Holocaust Studies* (New York: Continuum, 2010).

Weitzman, Mark, Robert J. Williams, and James Wald, *The Routledge History of Antisemitism* (New York and London: Routledge, 2024).

Wistrich, Robert S. *Antisemitism: The Longest Hatred* (New York: Schocken, 1994).

———. *A Lethal Obsession: Antisemitism from Antiquity to the Global Jihad* (New York: Random House, 2010).

———. *From Ambivalence to Betrayal: The Left, the Jews, and Israel* (Lincoln, NB, and London: University of Nebraska Press for the Vidal Sassoon International Center for the Study of Antisemitism, The Hebrew University of Jerusalem, 2012).

———. "Antisemitism and Holocaust Inversion." In Anthony McElligott and Jeffrey Herf, eds., *Antisemitism Before and Since the Holocaust* (London: Palgrave/Macmillan, 2017): 37–49.

Wolin, Richard. *Heidegger in Ruins: Between Philosophy and Ideology* (New Haven, CT: Yale University Press, 2023).

Yakira, Elhanan, *Post-Holocaust, Post-Zionism: Three Essays on Denial, Forgetting and the Delegitimation of Israel* (New York and Cambridge: Cambridge University Press, 2009).

Jeffrey Herf. Essays on Contemporary History and Politics.

Herf, Jeffrey. "Foreword to Mathias Küntzel." In *Jihad and Jew-Hatred: Islamism, Nazism and the Roots of 9/11.* Trans. Colin Meade (New York: Telos Press, 2007): vii–xv.

———. *"Wo sind die Antifaschisten?"* [Where are the anti-fascists?]. *Die Welt.* (December 2, 2007): https://www.welt.de/wams_print/article1421000/Wo-sind-die-Antifaschisten.html.

———. "What Does Coming to Terms with the Past Mean in the Berlin Republic in 2007," *Telos* (February 4, 2008): https://www.telospress.com/what-does-coming-to-terms-with-the-pastmean-in-the-berlin-republic-in-2007/; and *Dissent/Democratiya* (Spring 2008): https://www.dissentmagazine.org/democratiya_article/what-does-coming-to-terms-with-the-past-mean-in-the-berlin-republic-in-2007.

———. "Das Schweigen der Antifaschisten. Ein Geleitwort." In *Der Iran: Analyse einer islamischen Diktatur und ihrer europäischen Förderer* (Innsbruck and Vienna: Studien Verlag, 2008): 9–11.

———. "What Is Old and What Is New in the Terrorism of Islamic Fundamentalism." *Partisan Review.* 69, 1 (Winter 2002): 25–32; also in Murray Baumgarten, Peter Kenez, and Bruce Thompson, eds. *Varieties of Antisemitism: History, Ideology, Discourse* (Newark: University of Delaware Press, 2009): 370–376.

———. "Fresh Air in Central Europe." *The New Republic online* (August 25, 2011): http://www.tnr.com/blog/foreign-policy/77228/fresh-air-in-central-europe.

———. "Ideological Exceptionalism: Taking Iran's Antisemitism Seriously." *The American Interest* (June 2, 2014): https://www.the-american-interest.com/2014/06/02/taking-irans-anti-semitism-seriously/.

———. "Why They Fight: Hamas' Too Little-Known Fascist Charter." *The American Interest* (August 1, 2014): http://www.the-american-interest.com/articles/2014/08/01/why-they-fight-hamas-too-little-known-fascist-charter/.

———. "A Pro-Hamas Left Emerges." *The American Interest* (August 26, 2014): http://www.the-american-interest.com/articles/2014/08/26/a-pro-hamas-left-emerges/.

———. "The Iran Deal and Antisemitism" (April 6, 2015). http://blogs.timesofisrael.com/the-iran-deal-and-anti-semitism/.

———. "Historians Reject Anti-Israel Resolutions." *The American Interest* (January 19, 2015): http://www.the-american-interest.com/2015/01/19/historians-reject-anti-israel-resolutions/.

———. "How BDS Failed in the American Historical Association" (January 26, 2015): http://blogs.timesofisrael.com/how-bds-failed-in-the-american-historical-association/.

———. "Yet Again: The American Historical Association Rejects a Resolution Denouncing Israel." *History News Network* (January 15, 2016): http://historynews-network.org/article/161729. (First published in *Times of Israel* (January 13, 2016):

http://blogs.timesofisrael.com/yet-again-the-american-historical-association-rejects-a-resolution-denouncing-israel-3/).

———. "Is Donald Trump a Fascist," March 7, 2016, in *The American Interest*: https://www.the-american-interest.com/2016/03/07/is-donald-trump-a-fascist/.

———. "Elements of Conspiracy." *The American Interest* (October 31, 2016): http://www.the-american-interest.com/2016/10/31/elements-of-conspiracy/.

———. "1967: The Global Left and the Six Day War." *Fathom Journal* (Spring 2017): https://fathomjournal.org/1967-and-the-global-left-the-case-of-the-east-german-regime-and-the-west-german-radicals/.

———. "Lessons from German History after Charlottesville." *History News Network.* (September 17, 2017): https://historynewsnetwork.org/article/166864.

———. "Trump Doesn't Understand How Antisemitism Works: Neither Do Most Americans." *Washington Post.* (October 27, 2018): https://www.washingtonpost.com/outlook/2018/10/28/trump-doesnt-understand-how-anti-semitism-works-neither-do-most-americans/?utm_term=.e512d3887a0d.

———. "Die drei Gesichter des Antisemitismus." *Frankfurter Allgemeine Zeitung* (March 26, 2020).

———. "The 2020 National Elections: An American Reckoning." *Israel Journal of Foreign Affairs* (September 10, 2020), 169–182: https://www.tandfonline.com/doi/abs/10.1080/23739770.2020.1810405.

———. "Trump's Refusal to Acknowledge Defeat Mirrors the Lie that Fueled the Nazi Rise." *Washington Post* (November 23, 2020): https://www.washingtonpost.com/outlook/2020/11/23/trumps-refusal-acknowledge-defeat-mirrors-lie-that-fueled-nazi-rise/.

———. "The January 6th Assault on Congress and the Fate of the GOP's Faustian Bargain with Trump: Notes from German History." *History News Network*, January 31, 2021: https://historynewsnetwork.org/article/178983.

———. "IHRA and JDA: Examining Definitions of Antisemitism in 2021." *Fathom Journal* (April 2021): https://fathomjournal.org/ihra-and-jda-examining-definitions-of-antisemitism-in-2021/.

———. "Fascism with a Religious Face. Hamas at War with Israel. Forever." *American Purpose* (May 26, 2021): https://www.tandfonline.com/doi/abs/10.1080/23739770.2020.1846108.

———. "Laudatio." In *Verleihung des Theodor Lessing Preises 2022 an Dr. Matthias Küntzel. Dokumentation der Festreden.* June 14, 2022 (Arbeitsgemeinschaft Hannover: Deutsch-Israelische Gesellschaft, 2022): 21–44.

———. "Nazi Antisemitism and Islamist Hate." *The Tablet Magazine* (July 6, 2022): https://www.tabletmag.com/sections/history/articls/the-nazi-roots-of-islamist-hate.

———. "Heidegger's Downfall: Review of Richard Wolin's *Heidegger in Ruins*." *Quillette* (February 22, 2023): https://quillette.com/2023/02/22/heideggers-downfall/.

———. "Israel Is Antiracist, Anti-Colonialist, Anti-Fascist (and Was from the Start)." *SAPIR* 9 (Spring 2023): 96–103: https://sapirjournal.org/israel-at-75/2023/04/israel-is-antiracist-anti-colonialist-anti-fascist-and-was-from-the-start/.

——— and Andrei Markovits, "Letter to the Editor about John Mearsheimer and Stephen Walt on 'the Israel Lobby.'" *London Review of Books.* 28, 7 (April 6, 2006): https://www.lrb.co.uk/the-paper/v28/n07/letters.

——— and Sonya Michel, "Open Letter to a University President." In Cary Nelson and Gabriel Noah Brahm, eds., *The Case Against Academic Boycotts of Israel* (Detroit: MLA Members for Scholars' Rights, and Wayne State University Press. 2015): 447–453.

Journals that Address Varieties of Antisemitism

Antisemitism Studies: https://iupress.org/journals/antisemitismstudies/
Fathom Journal: https://fathomjournal.org/
Holocaust and Genocide Studies: https://academic.oup.com/hgs
Journal of Contemporary Antisemitism: https://www.jcajournal.com/
Journal of Israeli History: https://www.tandfonline.com/journals/fjih20
Journal of the Middle East and Africa: https://www.asmeascholars.org/journal-of-the-middle-east-and-africa
K. Jews, Europe, the XXIst Century: https://k-larevue.com/en/
Leo Baeck Yearbook: https://academic.oup.com/leobaeck
Middle East Forum: https://www.meforum.org/
SAPIR: A Quarterly Journal for a Thriving Jewish Future: https://sapirjournal.org/
The Jewish Quarterly: https://jewishquarterly.com/
The Tablet Magazine: https://www.tabletmag.com/
Yad Vashem Studies: https://www.yadvashem.org/research/about/studies.html

Some Organizations that address varieties of antisemitism

Academic Engagement Network: https://academicengagement.org/
Amadeo Antonio Stiftung, Berlin: https://www.amadeu-antonio-stiftung.de/en/
Anti-Defamation League (ADL): https://www.adl.org/
ASMEA, Association for the Study of the Middle East and Africa: https://www.asmeascholars.org/
Canadian Institute for the Study of Antisemitism (CISA): https://canisa.org/index.html
Centrum für Antisemitismus- und Rassimusforschung, (CARS) Aachen, Germany: (Center for Antisemitism and Racism Studies): https://katho-nrw.de/forschung-und-transfer/forschungsinstitute/centrum-fuer-antisemitismus-und-rassismusstudien-cars
Deutsche-Israelische Gesellschaft: https://www.deutsch-israelische-gesellschaft.de/
Institute for the Study of Contemporary Antisemitism, Indiana University: https://isca.indiana.edu/index.html
Institute for the Study of Global Antisemitism and Policy: https://isgap.org/
International Holocaust Remembrance Alliance: https://www.holocaustremembrance.com/
London Centre for the Study of Contemporary Antisemitism: Challenging the Intellectual Underpinnings of Antisemitism in Public Life: https://londonantisemitism.com/
Mideast Freedom Forum Berlin: https://www.mideastfreedomforum.org/
Middle East Forum: https://www.meforum.org/
NGO Monitor: https://www.ngo-monitor.org/key-issues/ngos-and-antisemitism/about/
Scholars for Peace in the Middle East: https://spme.org/
Vidal Sassoon International Center for the Study of Antisemitism, Hebrew University, Jerusalem: https://sicsa.huji.ac.il/
Zentrum für Antisemitismusforschung, Technische Universität, Berlin (Center for Research on Antisemitism, Technical University, Berlin): https://www.tu.berlin/asf/ueber-uns

INDEX

Note: Page numbers followed by "n" denote endnotes.

Made in United States
Orlando, FL
11 December 2023

40699903R10157